CHARLES DICKENS

CHARLES DICKENS

1812-1870

UNA POPE-HENNESSY

THE REPRINT SOCIETY
LONDON

FIRST PUBLISHED 1945
THIS EDITION FIRST PUBLISHED BY THE REPRINT SOCIETY LTD
BY ARRANGEMENT WITH CHATTO & WINDUS
1947

PRINTED IN GREAT BRITAIN BY
R. & R. CLARK, LIMITED, EDINBURGH

CHARLES DICKENS, AGED 27
by Daniel Maclise, R.A.

" Here we have the real identical man Dickens "
W. M. THACKERAY

TO
RICHARD

Acknowledgements

I OWE a deep debt of gratitude to the late Mr. Walter Dexter, editor of *The Dickensian* and prime authority on every aspect and detail of the life of Charles Dickens. He lent me books, he showed me unpublished letters, and, more valuable than any other form of help, discussed with me the problems that inevitably arose in dealing with the novelist's relations with his family and his contemporaries. All my questions were replied to unequivocally and with patience. It is a source of great regret to me that he is not alive to read the book he saw in typescript.

My warm thanks are due to Mr. William Maxwell of R. & R. Clark, Ltd., Edinburgh, for lending me for four years a copy of *The Letters of Charles Dickens* (edited by Walter Dexter for the Nonesuch Press). It is a book I could neither buy nor borrow from a library, and as my work is for the most part based on these *Letters* it will be understood how vital and important was this loan.

In these days of austerity it would be waste of paper and labour to print the very long list of books I have read or consulted. I must, however, mention the comprehensive bibliography included in *Charles Dickens*, by William Dibelius (1916), as being extremely helpful, and add that I have made use of Mr. Ellis Gummer's book, *Dickens's Works in Germany* (1940) with appreciation. Fresh light is thrown on Dickens's family life in *Mr. and Mrs. Dickens*, by Walter Dexter (1935), and in *Dickens and Daughter* (a record of conversations with Mrs. Perugini), by Gladys Storey (1939).

For help over photographs I wish to thank Sir Eric Maclagan and Mr. Carl Winter of the Victoria and Albert Museum; Mr. A. Hind of the British Museum; Dr. Wittkower of the Warburg Institute; and Lord Glenconner. I must also express my gratitude to the Earl of Lytton for showing me over Knebworth, the cradle of the Guild of Literature and Art. Special thanks go to my kind friend Mr. C. F. Bell for reading through both typescript and proofs, and to my son, John Pope-Hennessy, for constructive criticism.

U. P.-H.

Ladbroke Grove, 1945

List of Contents

List of Illustrations

INTRODUCTION

No Life of Charles Dickens has been written since his collected letters were published by the Nonesuch Press in 1938.[1] These letters not only provide new biographical material, but throw light on the difficult temperament of a writer who said of himself that his inventive faculty must be allowed to master his whole existence. Owing to his unusual psychological make-up Charles Dickens has been the subject of several mutually contradictory appreciations. One biographer has seen in him a satirist and a woman-hater, another a man living his life in a trauma, another an exemplar of applied Christianity, another a neurotic and highly disagreeable sentimentalist, another a social reformer with a tendency towards Marxian views, while to the commonalty the mere name of Dickens conjures up the cosy fireside, the joys of home, glowing hearts and Christmas largess.

Dickens was an adept in what he called laying his hand upon the time, and in doing this became the recognised exponent of the English character to Victorian England, and not to Victorian England only, but to the world. He revealed the masses to the classes in one country and the people of all lands understood what he had to say. In trite and truthful words Bagehot summed up the universality of his appeal:

> The penetrating power of this remarkable genius among all classes at home is not inferior to its diffusive energy abroad. The phrase 'household book' has, when applied to the works of Mr. Dickens, a peculiar propriety. There is no contemporary English writer whose works are read so generally through the whole house, who can give pleasure to the servant as well as to the mistress, to the children as well as to the master.

Dickens was a purely instinctive writer and the creator of the democratic novel. He was the first novelist to give the

[1] *The Letters of Charles Dickens*, edited by Walter Dexter. Nonesuch Press. 3 vols. 1938.

common people of Europe the sentiment of a contagious democratic fraternity. *Cor ad cor loquitur*, for it is heart alone that can speak to heart.

The first and greatest book on Charles Dickens was written seventy years ago.[1] John Forster, its author, apologised for making the letters he had received from his friend, 'letters of unexampled candour and truthfulness', the basis of his narrative, but it turned out to be an excellent method of presentation. The book is readable and as interesting as its prototype, *The Life and Works of Goethe*, by George Lewes, another masterpiece of Victorian biography. The value of Forster's record is in no way diminished by the German criticism that it is not so much a biography as an analytical collection of letters and memoranda, nor is it invalidated by the fact that he eliminated certain people and certain episodes from his story with the aim of presenting a Dickens so consistently great and good as to compel the homage of posterity. Despite its planned limitations, the book remains and must remain the indispensable monument to friendship and genius that it was constructed to be.

Until his own marriage in 1856 Forster, for twenty years, had been Dickens's close companion and the recipient of his confidences. After that date a comparative estrangement developed between them, and as the friendship dwindled in intensity, Forster's account of Dickens flags both in intimacy and accuracy. He says himself that for the last years he had to draw on *The Uncommercial Traveller* for detailed information. The *Letters* printed by the Nonesuch Press (between eight and nine thousand in number) supplement the material provided for us by Forster. They reveal Dickens's motive for speech and action, throw light on the composition of his books and show the great emotional strain under which many of them were written. They also dispel the illusion that their author was a merely insular humorist and prove that the handicap of a defective education did not prevent his becoming a continentally-minded man. He liked and understood

[1] *The Life of Charles Dickens*, by John Forster. 3 vols. 1872-4.

foreigners, learnt to talk French and Italian fluently and felt
as much at home in France and Italy as he did in England.
When he died Genoese newspapers carried the headline *Il
nostro Carlo Dickens è morto.*

Conscious of possessing great reserves of power, Dickens
was so responsive to stimulus from without and to inspiration from within that he surprised people by his capacity for
adaptation. His spontaneity was amazing, he was for ever
bursting out in new directions and it is doubtful whether anyone of his own day really took the measure of his personality.
He was something of an enigma to his contemporaries and he
remains something of an enigma to us. It does not make him
less of one to know how widespread was his influence abroad,
how Tolstoi condemned parliamentary government on the
strength of his books and how Moltke and his staff officers
based their appreciations of the English character on *Pickwick*
and *Little Dorrit.*

Pervasive in influence, Dickens is embedded deep in our
national mind. We cannot ignore him even if we would,
and, liking or disliking him, we have to admit that he is one
of the great pivotal authors of England. Nothing has ever
been quite the same for English folk since Dickens published
his novels, for he faced the stupefying platitude of anonymous
human fates and gave them value, humour and incident.
More than this, his letters and his speeches make it clear that
in Dickens we have to reckon with a seer as well as a very great
novelist. No one of his day understood the condition of
England better or saw more plainly how the dead weight of
conservatism for its own sake tended not to preserve, but to
stifle the essential genius of our people. As we read of his
lifelong crusade against illiteracy, vile industrial conditions
and slumdom, of his contempt for the misuse by rich men of
parliamentary opportunities of procrastination, we see how
inevitable it was that in the end he should appeal to the people
to educate themselves for self-government by means of the
Mechanics' Institutes, Polytechnics and Athenaeums that they
through their own thrift and intelligence had brought into

being. By the classes he was regarded, with few exceptions, as an entertainer, by the masses as a social reformer. To a class-ridden country he gave the watchword, 'Men must get together in good citizenship'; to a class-conscious community he preached class fusion as the best corrective to the confusion of class warfare.

Other great writers, Victor Hugo for example, have found themselves instinctively in opposition to the society of their day and for one reason or another have been thrown out from the country of their birth. Dickens, in spite of his fights for humanity and justice, alienated no one among his compatriots, earned the worship of countless thousands of readers and was taken to all hearts. The people of England responded to the fiery radiation of a soul which in some mysterious way expressed their being in a manner they recognised as their very own. Such an achievement is as inexplicable as it is unique.

Chapter 1

THE FAMILY BACKGROUND

A man, a personal ascendency, is the only great phenomenon.
R. W. EMERSON

IN *Bleak House* it is laid down as 'a melancholy truth' that 'even great men have their poor relations'. To be a great man and to have none but poor relations was the lot of Charles Dickens, who lived in a day when a family background, in so far as it connoted a station in society, was apt to tether a boy for life. Though neither poverty nor lowliness of birth can any longer be viewed as social fixatives, they must still be reckoned with in sizing up the influences that go to the conditioning of personality. In the case of Charles Dickens they were of basic significance, for his horror of patronage and distrust of the aristocratic system masquerading as representative government in the England of his day was probably as much due to the fact that his father had been brought up in the servants' quarters of that typical source of place and power—a political country house—as that he himself had a hard and lonely fight to win a niche in the temple of privilege.

His grandfather, William Dickens, began life as a footman, and after marrying Lady Blandford's housemaid, Elizabeth Ball,[1] became steward at Crewe Hall, the seat of John Crewe, M.P. for Chester. This couple had two sons, William and John, and in the year of John's birth (1785) William Dickens died. For thirty-five years his widow remained on at the Hall as housekeeper. When pensioned in 1820, she settled in lodgings in Oxford Street, and there, as in the 'room' at Crewe Hall, this vivacious little woman spun stories for the children who visited her. Among these children was her grandson, Charles, who was to keep her memory for ever green in the wise and kindly figure who moves through the pages of *Bleak*

[1] See Register, St. George's, Hanover Square.

House as Mrs. Rouncewell, housekeeper to Lady Dedlock at Chesney Wold.

The Crewes interested themselves in Mrs. Dickens's boys, saw to their education, placed William in the world, and obtained for John, through their friend Mr. Canning, a clerkship in the Navy Pay Office. This was an advantageous start in life, as it raised the young man to what would now be called a post in the Civil Service and assured him of £70 a year. Just about the time John Dickens took up his job (1805) another young man, Thomas Culliford Barrow, was nominated to a clerkship in the same office through the interest of his father, Charles Barrow, a senior supervisor in the department. The two young men became friends, John Dickens was introduced to Thomas Barrow's family and in due course fell in love with his sister, Elizabeth, whom he married in 1809 at St. Mary-le-Strand. One gets the impression that the Barrows did not care much about the alliance and it may be supposed that as members, however humble, of the bureaucracy running England, they considered themselves a cut above the housekeeper's son. Anyway when Charles Dickens many years later announced to this maternal uncle his own engagement, he expressed regret that family loyalty prevented him from bringing his young bride to a house in which his father was not received. In later years he was to condemn 'the accursèd gentility' and 'subserviousness' that had eaten the heart out of the body politic of England, by which he meant its social structure in his day. Had the shoe not pinched his own foot in his tender years he might not, so early, have been made aware how badly it fitted the England into which he was born.

We will now look at the other side of the genealogical picture and see whether the Barrows had reason to be proud of their station. Possibly their relationship to Sir John Barrow,[1] second secretary of the Admiralty from 1804 to 1845,

[1] It has been suggested that Mrs. Micawber's references to her 'influential relations' and their ignoring of repeated requests may have originated in Mrs. Dickens's appeals to Sir John Barrow.

may have invested them with a sense of importance, but this must to some extent have been weakened by the conduct of Charles Barrow, John Dickens's father-in-law, who, at the time of his marriage, was 'Chief Conductor of Money in Town', a responsible appointment carrying with it a salary of £350 a year. Part of Mr. Barrow's work was to dispatch money under armed guard to the out-ports, Plymouth, Portsmouth, Sheerness and Chatham, which money he obtained by means of imprest bills for £900 each. These bills were granted upon an account signed by himself as Chief Conductor and endorsed by the Paymaster to the Navy Board. Some two years after his daughter's marriage, Mr. Barrow made up his account in the usual way and handed it to the Paymaster who, as usual, endorsed it and forwarded it to the Navy Board. It was a horrifying surprise for Mr. Barrow when, instead of the cash indented for, a Writ of Extent arrived with the official explanation that, as the Chief Conductor was suspected of having money in hand, an inquiry into previous accounts had been carried out with the result that a debit balance, to the tune of nearly four thousand pounds, was found to exist against him. Further investigation showed that as Mr. Barrow since 1803 had on every application for an imprest bill stated a false balance, the deficiency was even larger than was at first calculated. Mr. Barrow at once resigned his appointment and in extenuation pleaded ten children and ill-health. When criminal proceedings were instituted against him he left England.[1] Though it was a shaming business to his family it does not seem to have affected their careers adversely. His third son, John Henry, was already a barrister of Gray's Inn and law-reporter for the *Times*, and Thomas, his eldest son, clerk in the Prize Branch of the Navy Pay Office, was allowed to qualify for the considerable pension of £710 a year. His second son, Edward, married to Janet Ross the miniaturist,

[1] For details of the Barrow inquest see Admiralty Navy Pay Office correspondence. Public Record Office. Quoted in *Dickens and Daughter* by Miss Gladys Storey.

may not have made good as we find Charles Dickens ruefully paying a £57 debt for him in 1838.   One daughter, Mary, was married to a naval lieutenant, Allen, and the other, Elizabeth, with whom we are directly concerned, to the navy pay clerk, John Dickens.   These facts, though not of any intrinsic interest, give atmosphere and perspective to the family background and show that it comprised a social position from which it was possible to slip down.   We can find no excuse in this ancestral record for the failure of Charles Dickens's father to keep his own head above water or submerge his children in a sea of poverty.   His circumstances were not so very good, but they were not so bad as inevitably to bring him to destitution or his family to neglect.   The clue to his misfortune must have lain in his own habits or character.

John Dickens had married on £200 a year and had taken his wife to live at Landport.[1]   A daughter, Fanny, was born in 1810 and a son, Charles, in 1812.   Both were christened at St. Mary's, Portsea.   No foursquare account of John Dickens exists.   He is alluded to by a woman friend of the family as 'an old buck' who dressed well and was always fingering the large bunch of seals attached to his watch.   Charles sometimes spoke of him with an admiring affection he never extended to his mother, and at other times groaned at the financial handicap imposed on him by his father's irresponsible running-up of bills.   He seems to have been a jovial opportunist without money sense, who borrowed from anyone foolish enough to make him cash advances.   Unlike little Nell's grandfather in *The Old Curiosity Shop*, he does not seem to have been a gambler though he indulged a taste for expensive wines.   The debt that landed him in the Marshalsea in 1834 for the second time was incurred to a wine merchant, but what the nature of the debt was that caused his first arrest in 1824 is not revealed.   There was never a time in young Charles's life when he did not hear of money difficulties, never a time when he could believe his feet were planted on a rock,

[1] 387 Commercial Road, Portsmouth, once Mile End Terrace.

and the memory of the shifting sands through which he as a child had stumbled made him desperately anxious in later years to secure that solid foothold which a steady income alone can ensure.

Naval pay clerks had no fixed residence and were liable to be pushed about the country at short notice. In 1814 John Dickens was transferred to Somerset House and lodged himself and family at 10 Norfolk Street, near the Middlesex Hospital. In 1817 he was shifted to Chatham. Their house was 11 Ordnance Terrace [1] on the border-line between Chatham and Rochester, where (according to the Rate Book) he lived till Lady Day 1821. Mrs. Allen, Mrs. Dickens's widowed sister, lived with them and shared expenses. Her Commander husband had been drowned at Rio, but by 1821 she had engaged herself to marry Surgeon Lamert of the Chatham Hospital who is supposed to be Dr. Slammer in *Pickwick*. When she re-married, the John Dickens family, father, mother and five children, moved for the remainder of the assignment to Chatham (1822–3) into a cheaper house, 18 St. Mary's Place, The Brook, where James Lamert, Mrs. Allen's stepson, boarded with them. *A Child's Dream of a Star* is said to be a reminiscence of childhood at St. Mary's Place.

No one can hope to reconstruct the family circumstances precisely, nor indeed would it be interesting to do so, but it is something of a clue to know that when Charles was eight years old his father was earning £350 a year, more than the equivalent of £700 a year to-day, and that when they first got to Chatham, he with his sister Fanny attended a day school. Their nurse, Mary Weller, described Charles as 'a terrible boy to read . . . his custom was to sit with his book in his left hand, holding his wrist with his right, and constantly moving it up and down and at the same time sucking his tongue'.[2] In spite of chronic shortness of cash John Dickens managed to acquire

[1] Now No. 2. Harriet Ellen (1819) and Frederick William (1820) born here.
[2] *Childhood and Youth of Charles Dickens*, by R. Langton.

a collection of cheaply-produced novels including *Roderick Random*, *Peregrine Pickle*, *Humphrey Clinker*, *Tom Jones*, *The Vicar of Wakefield*, *Robinson Crusoe*, *The Arabian Nights*, *The Tales of the Genii* and *Don Quixote*. It was Smollett's translation of *Gil Blas* that introduced Charles to the greatest of the picaresque stories. In one of the many true passages in *David Copperfield* he speaks of the company of this 'glorious host'. 'They kept alive my fancy and my hope of something beyond that place and time', and he could console himself in trouble by impersonating from out this host his favourite characters. '. . . I have been Tom Jones for a week together, I have sustained my own idea of Roderick Random for a month at a stretch.' When he thought of these books in later years, the picture always came into his mind 'of a summer evening, the boys at play in the churchyard and I sitting on my bed reading as if for life'. And he was reading for life. Read and re-read by this alert, sensitive boy, these books opened up for him a limitless world of adventure and romance.

One of Charles Dickens's happiest recollections was of trips down the Medway to Sheerness on the Navy Pay Office yacht *Chatham*, a high-sterned, cutter-rigged craft pierced with circular ports, dating from the time of the Commonwealth, a sluggish boat except in a stiff breeze. In view of the part it was to play in *Great Expectations*, the convict hulk, 'roofed like a Noah's Ark', that lay off the dockyard must also be mentioned. Another early memory was that of a visit to the theatre in London to see the great clown Grimaldi, whose *Memoirs* he was as an adult to edit. Yet another was the 'Lines' review of the 43rd and 52nd Light Infantry described in *Pickwick*. But the best memory of all was that of his schooling with William Giles, son of the Baptist minister, William Giles, of Providence Chapel on The Brook. Young Giles's school was made up of his own brothers and sisters and the children of officers and naval employees, and he established it in a largish house on the corner of Rhode Street and Best Street adjoining Clover Lane. Giles, who had been at Oxford and was an 'accomplished scholar', recognised

Charles's unusual aptitudes and did his best to train the boy's mind and taste, pointing out in particular how pure and flowing was Goldsmith's English. When he parted with his pupil in 1823, he gave him a set of *The Bee* (a miniature periodical of eight weeks' life edited and written by Oliver Goldsmith[1]) as a keepsake. *The Bee* was a Saturday miscellany, containing 'a select collection of essays on the most interesting and entertaining subjects'. There were three, four, or five essays in a number with titles such as 'Remarks on Theatres', 'Travellers' Letters', 'Charles XII', 'Dress', 'M. Maupertuis', 'Happiness dependent on Constitution', 'Use of Language', 'A City Nightpiece'. It must have been his great enjoyment of *The Bee* that gave Dickens his enduring passion for the miscellany with which he experimented at different periods of his life under the title of *Master Humphrey's Clock*, *Household Words* and *All the Year Round*. *The Bee*, he used to say, always called up in his mind the past and made him wonder whether he had himself 'ever fledged any little bees whose humming had been heard abroad'.

In the winter of 1822–3 John Dickens was transferred to Somerset House again, still at the same salary, and before moving he arranged with Mr. Giles that Charles should continue being educated at his school. The young pedagogue, of twenty-four, was delighted to be left in charge of so unusually bright and eager a learner. Living at Chatham, the boy naturally came to know every cranny of Rochester. It was the first place he wrote about in the opening chapters of *Pickwick*: it was the last place he wrote about in *Edwin Drood*. And in his last will and testament he directed that his body should be laid near Rochester.

John Dickens and his family moved to London by coach, sending their heavy goods by water, and settled themselves at 16 Bayham Street,[2] Camden Town, on the outer fringe of the

[1] October 6–November 24, 1759.
[2] Apart from basement, garret and outhouse, a four-roomed house. Probably the home of the Micawbers and the Cratchits.

city, close to the arboured tea-gardens at Chalk Farm. Most writers on Dickens describe it as a squalid neighbourhood, but no railway building had as yet scarred the district and country roads linked the newly-built blocks of little town houses. James Lamert, who was awaiting a commission in the army, moved with the Dickens family to London as did a sharp little maid from Chatham Workhouse—the 'Marchioness' of *The Old Curiosity Shop*. Fanny, the eldest girl, turned out to be musical and somehow, through the family friend Tomkisson, a piano-maker of 77 Dean Street, Soho, obtained a nomination[1] as 'a pupilage-boarder' to the Royal Academy of Music where she spent four happy years and won distinctions.

John Dickens arranged for his son to leave Mr. Giles's Academy in the spring of 1823, 'the end of the winter term'. Charles was put into the stage-coach Commodore, and never forgot during all the years of his life the smell of the damp straw in which he was packed, 'like game, carriage paid'. 'There was no other inside passenger, and I consumed my sandwiches in solitude and dreariness, and it rained hard all the way, and I thought life sloppier than I expected to find it.' It was a painful shock to the lad to find on arriving in Bayham Street that he was expected to do house-work, clean boots and brush clothes; he had counted on going to school again, but the family seemed to have no idea of paying any more school fees. Boy-like and insatiably curious, he set out to examine the adjacent streets and soon knew every corner of the three little towns of Camden, Kentish and Somers as well as every path leading to Chalcot and Chalk farms. The whole neighbourhood appears and reappears in his books. Bob Cratchit lived in Camden Town, so did Jemima Evans: Traddles lodged there with Micawber: the Toodles family lived in Staggs's Garden, 'Camberling' Town: Heyling in *Pickwick* ran down his victim in Little College Street, Camden Town, 'a desolate place surrounded by fields and ditches'.

Often the boy went further afield, getting James Lamert, or

[1] April 23, 1823.

anyone else available, to pilot him to Seven Dials, a locality that fascinated him on account of its name, its wickedness and its squalor. He liked, too, going to see his godfather, Christopher Huffam, at Limehouse Hole.[1] Huffam was an oar- and block-maker and 'Rigger to His Majesty's Navy'.[2] He had come to the notice of the Regent for fitting out a privateer against the French, and was said to have been offered an honour for this service. Charles also explored the nearer region of Soho, where his mother's eldest brother, Thomas Barrow, lodged over Manson's, the bookshop in Gerrard Street. To this sick uncle the boy became a 'little companion and nurse'. Through this association he found material for subsequent *Sketches*, notably his uncle's barber, a very old man who talked of Napoleon's campaigns, and he also depicted, on the pattern of Gil Blas' housekeeper, the deaf old woman who waited on Mr. Barrow. Miscellaneous reading, too, came his way, as Mrs. Manson, widow of the bookseller, let him see the *Tatler* and *Spectator*, and lent him Miss Porter's *Scottish Chiefs*, George Colman's *Broad Grins* and Holbein's *Dance of Death*.

The happiness he derived from these contacts was dimmed by the poverty at home. At Michaelmas 1823 Mrs. Dickens, who had the rather scrambling notion of making money by running a small school for the children of parents living in the Indies, rented number 4 Gower Street, North, in her own name with money said to have been guaranteed by Christopher Huffam.[3] Partly furnishing the house and fixing a brass plate upon the door with the words 'Mrs. Dickens's Establishment', she caused handbills to be printed for distribution in the neighbourhood. Charles and the other children were called on to push them into letter-boxes. None of them drew custom and no pupil appeared. Her son was to crystallise the venture in 'Mrs. Micawber's Boarding Establishment for Young Ladies'.

---

[1] *Our Mutual Friend* has scenes in Limehouse.

[2] Cuttle, Peggotty and the seafaring characters are said to have had their origin in Huffam.

[3] Michaelmas 1823 to Lady Day 1824 at £50 per annum.

Things went so badly that even the well-fingered library of fiction had to be taken down from the chiffonier to be sold to a bookseller in the Hampstead Road. Possessions other than books went to the pawn-shop where Charles was pleased to find that the pawnbroker's assistant liked to listen to him conjugating Latin verbs and declining his *musa* and *dominus*. One day when things were looking hopeless and arrest for debt unavoidable, James Lamert turned up with an offer of employment for Charles. James, having given up his prospective commission to a younger brother, had gone into partnership with his cousin George Lamert who was running Warren's Blacking Factory at Hungerford Stairs near Charing Cross. When he said he could give Charles six or seven shillings a week, Mrs. Dickens jumped at the offer, and even John Dickens, dearly as he wished his son to be educated, felt the circumstances to be so desperate that acceptance was necessary. This blow fell on Charles's twelfth birthday, February 7, 1824. So many children were in harness in those days that James Lamert may have thought he was doing the boy a kindness as he promised him instruction and a 'station', but to the boy, knowing himself to be 'of good ability, quick, eager, delicate', it was a shattering blow to be cast away at such an age with all early hopes of learning and distinction crushed. He describes himself as sunk in 'a deep sense of abandonment'. The worst pang of all was that his parents seemed pleased to have him off their hands. With despair in his heart he realised that they frankly welcomed his being entered to servitude. He says himself that they could not have appeared more satisfied had he had a 'distinguished career at a grammar-school' and had qualified to go to Cambridge.

In the fragment of autobiography he dredged out of himself before deciding to sublimate his experience in *David Copperfield* he says:

The blacking warehouse was the last house on the left-hand side of the way at old Hungerford Stairs. It was a crazy, tumble-down old house, abutting of course, on the river and literally over-run with rats. Its wainscotted rooms and its rotten floors and stair-case, and the old grey rats swarming down in the cellars, and the sound of their squeaking and scuffling coming up the stairs at all times, and the dirt and decay of the place rise up visibly before me.

As day succeeded day, never to be redeemed, the boy had the sensation of being utterly neglected and without hope:

My whole nature was so penetrated with the grief and humiliation of such considerations, that even now, famous and caressed and happy, I often forget in my dreams that I have a dear wife and children; even that I am a man; and wander desolately back to that time of my life.

A fortnight after poor Charles had become a wage-drudge the long-expected blow fell and John Dickens, at the suit of James Karr, was arrested for a £40 debt and incarcerated at the Marshalsea.[1] His entire property was sworn at £10 and Charles had to go before an appraiser, 'near the Obelisk', to have the clothes on his back and the silver watch in his pocket valued. Mrs. Dickens in her hand-to-mouth fashion still tried to carry on by pawning brooches and spoons, but eventually gave up the struggle and, gathering up her brood of young children, at Lady Day she also moved into the Marshalsea. The maid who accompanied her found a lodging near the gates and the family confessed to each other that they felt more comfortable and unmolestable there than they ever had at home.

Charles, being already employed at Warren's Blacking Factory, was not included in the Marshalsea party but lodged by his mother's arrangement in Little College Street, Camden Town, with a Mrs. Roylance, to become famous as Mrs. Pipchin in *Dombey and Son*. At the factory he received a shilling a day on which to support himself. The weekly

[1] Copy of register at Record Office. Admitted Friday, February 20, 1824; discharged May 28, 1824. See Facsimile *Dickensian*, 1932, p. 227.

pittance did not go far.   When he had no money for food he
'took a turn in Covent Garden and stared at the pineapples'.
His work was simple; it consisted of tying bottles up neatly
and sticking labels on to them, a task at which he soon became
expeditious.   To begin with, the boy walked daily from
Camden Town to the Strand and back at night.   On Sundays
he would call at the Royal Academy of Music for his sister
Fanny and take her to spend the day at the Marshalsea which
lay beyond St. George's Church, Southwark.   Camden
Town, however, soon proved so distant and so unbearably
lonely that he got his father's consent to move to Lant Street,
on the south side of the river, the street 'near Guy's and
handy for me' in which he was to lodge Bob Sawyer.   Charles
occupied a back attic looking on to 'the pleasant prospect of a
timber-yard' and found the situation 'a Paradise'.   The landlord of his lodging had a quiet wife and a lame son.   They
were all very good to him and they live on as the Garland
family in *The Old Curiosity Shop*.   He now breakfasted and
supped at the Marshalsea and in the evenings explored the
creeks and jetties by the river, discovering all sorts of water-
side secrets.   Sometimes he went to a shabby public-house,
the Fox-under-the-Hill, and on the bench there would eat his
sandwiches and watch its patrons, the coal-heavers, dance.
At the outside he could not have slept in Lant Street for more
than six or seven weeks, but into these weeks was packed a
gamut of experience.

Another boy, Robert Browning (just Charles's age), was
also living south of the Thames at this time, imbibing a
different set of experiences in a garden in Camberwell.   In
this garden was an old laburnum tree, the haunt of nightin-
gales, and Robert, as he listened to their song, was imbued
with a positive conviction that in these birds were reincarnated
the spirits of two great poets, Keats and Shelley, who had
settled in leafy Camberwell to sing to the only person in all
suburbia who would understand their song.   Yet another
boy (six months older than Charles), an Anglo-Indian boy,
William Makepeace Thackeray, was living north of the river

in Chiswick in the house known in *Vanity Fair* as Miss Pinkerton's Academy. Both these boys had incomparably better starts in life's race than Charles Dickens, but in the long run he was to out-distance them.

One of the odd facts of the Marshalsea situation is that all the time that John Dickens and family were incarcerated there, they were in receipt of over £6 a week income, but made no effort to clear themselves of debt. 'They had no want of bodily comforts', and being tucked safely away from creditors they felt free from care, and were not anxious to be released. Outside agencies, however, were at work to return them to normal life.

When Mrs. William Dickens, John Dickens's mother, died in April 1824, her elder son arranged that the funeral service should take place at St. George's Church where she had been married. During retirement she had lived quietly in London on the interest of her savings and the pension granted by the family she had served. On her death £500 of the £750 invested savings went to William and the remainder to John, who had from time to time extracted gifts of money from her. William at once paid £40 into court for James Karr and thus effected his brother's discharge from the Marshalsea.

After an absence of three months, John Dickens resumed work at the Navy Pay Office despite the fact that he had from the Marshalsea respectfully solicited the Hon. William Huskisson to recommend him for a superannuation grant on the grounds of ill-health.[1] The family, like homing pigeons, returned to Camden Town, this time to Little College Street. Charles still went daily to the factory, now transferred to Chandos Street, but was suddenly withdrawn when his father had 'words' with James Lamert. Mrs. Dickens did her best to patch the quarrel and get James to take the boy back. 'I never afterwards forgot, I never shall forget, I never can forget that my mother was warm for my being sent back', records

[1] He enclosed a medical certificate stating that he had a chronic affection of the urinary organs.

Charles. His father would have none of it, nor hear of his return, and set out to find his son a school. By June 1824 the whole family had transferred from Little College Street to 29 (later 13) Johnson Street, Somers Town, a small house in an even poorer locality rented in the name of Mrs. Dickens.[1]

In due course the case of Mr. John Dickens passed from the hands of the Treasurer of the Navy to those of Mr. Croker, Secretary to the Admiralty, who had to lay it before the Commissioners and the First Lord, Viscount Melville. Mr. Croker was informed by Mr. Huskisson[2] that John Dickens having taken advantage of the Insolvent Debtors Act, could not continue to be employed in the Navy Pay Office. In consideration of his twenty years of service and six children he would, however, on compassionate grounds, be granted 'a retired allowance' of £145 a year.

Bracing himself to meet the fall in income, John Dickens at once applied to his brother-in-law, J. H. Barrow, editor of the *Mirror of Parliament*, for work as a political reporter. He had already dabbled in journalism at Chatham, but his proficiency in shorthand is such a surprising development that one wonders whether he may not have practised it in prison. However it came about, stout, active, anecdotic John Dickens, aged forty, by January 1825 was an established parliamentary reporter for the *British Press*, a newspaper with which S. C. Hall was connected.[3] This enabled him to continue paying fees at 'the very superior school' to which he had entered Charles six months previously. The dear boy had had a bad educational break of a year, but now he could study as much as he pleased. S. C. Hall, who saw him at this time, said he was 'a handsome lad gleaning intelligence in the byeways of the metropolis'. A new life now dawned for Charles Dickens. His youth hitherto had been characterised by sharp suffering and bitter disappointment. The crumbling of his private world had made such terrible inroads into his sensibility that he buried all remembrance of it fathoms deep

---

[1] Tenant from July 1824 to July 1827.   [2] December 1, 1824.
[3] *Memories of S. C. Hall*, p. 456.

in his subconsciousness. His own children were grown up before he could summon the resolution needed to disinter and face up to his own childhood. Delving into a past which he had never disclosed even to his wife, he twenty-five years later drew from it material for the romanticised autobiography which is the distinguishing and touching feature of *David Copperfield*.

Mr. Jones's Classical and Commercial Academy, otherwise Wellington House, was situated at the corner of Granby Street, Hampstead Road. The subjects taught there were Latin, mathematics, history and the hornpipe. For at least two years Charles attended the classes there as a day-boy, and it is probable that he worked there for nine months more.[1] He described the school later on for *Household Words*,[2] dwelling specially on the pets kept by the boys, who contrived 'to drill their white mice much better than the master trained the boys'. They were very strong in theatricals and mounted small stage-sets for themselves. A school-fellow, Owen Thomas, remembered him as a healthy-looking boy with a general air of smartness, but with nothing to indicate that he would ever 'become a literary celebrity'.

Though there is nothing remarkable to record about the years at school, they did enable Charles to recover and improve on the teaching given him by Mr. Giles at Chatham. Education was almost entirely classical in those days and we can form a good notion of what the boy studied by glancing at the curriculum of Salem House in *David Copperfield*. The gap in his schooling that prevented him from competing with boys who had had no break in their education did not hinder him from picking up a great deal of information which he at once put to operative use.

When John Dickens was asked by a prospective employer where his son Charles had been educated he replied, 'Why, indeed sir, (ha! ha!) he may be said to have educated himself!' The high value of that form of education is to be found in the

---

[1] June 1824 to June 1826 and probably stayed on till April 1827.
[2] October 11, 1851.

quality of observation embodied in the thousands of pages of Charles Dickens's novels. No other education could possibly have formed the intellectual background to his interpretation of the very peculiar England of which he knew the under-side, and we may be thankful that his knowledge of the upper-side was so long deferred as to enable him thoroughly to understand the point of view of the disinherited.

While Charles was still at school his father's elder brother, William, died suddenly at the age of forty-three, leaving his whole estate of £1300 to be shared, after his wife's demise, equally between his nephews and nieces. The prospect of some day becoming owners of capital rejoiced the hearts of Charles and his sister Fanny, who realised only too clearly by this time that they could not look to their father for a living.

Chapter 2

CLERK AND REPORTER

These years, the usefullest of my life.
CHARLES DICKENS

ON leaving school just before Easter 1827 Charles Dickens became office-boy to Charles Molloy, solicitor, of 6 Symonds Inn.[1] He could only have been there for six or seven weeks, but it was long enough for him to display his peculiar fearlessness and his even more peculiar faculty of incorporating the people with whom he came in daily contact into the texture of his life. A fellow clerk, Thomas Mitton, became his 'dear Tom' and first business agent: he even managed to make use of his employer as legal adviser. Remarkable in. Charles Dickens is a kind of octopus quality of absorbing into himself human material of every variety, good, bad, and indifferent. To begin with it was an instinctive technique and was developed by degrees into a method which served him very well in writing his novels, and is proof, if proof were needed, of the quiddity of his genius.

By May in this year John Dickens had managed, through his wife's aunt, Mrs. Charlton, who kept a boarding house at 16 Berners Street, to obtain for Charles a clerkship in the firm of Ellis and Blackmore, solicitors, of 1 Raymond Buildings, Gray's Inn. Edward Blackmore, one of the partners, lodged with Mrs. Charlton, whose son, Thomas, was a reporter in Doctors' Commons. Charles worked for Ellis and Blackmore till November 1828, and was paid after the first month 15s. a week. He lived with his parents at 17 The Polygon, Somers Town, a place of tenuous literary affiliations in so far as Mary Wollstonecraft had died there thirty years earlier in giving birth to the daughter who was to marry Shelley.[2] In

---

[1] Later of 4 New Square, Lincoln's Inn.
[2] December 30, 1816. Cassell's *Old and New London*. Dickens housed Skimpole in The Polygon.

his off-time Charles learnt shorthand, possibly from his father, possibly from his uncle, John Henry Barrow.   What he calls 'the intensity' of his nature prevented him from doing things by halves and eighteen months of persistent application to 'Mr. Gurney's Half-guinea Brachygraphy' gave him confidence to hand in his notice to Ellis and Blackmore in order to join his cousin, Thomas Charlton, as a reporter in the Consistory Court of Doctors' Commons.   It was his intention eventually to follow his father to the gallery of the House of Commons, but as he was still very young he had to make do for the time being with legal reporting, which gave him opportunity to gain speed, self-reliance and experience.   In partnership therefore with Thomas Charlton he rented a box in Doctors' Commons where, to begin with, he sat waiting for custom.   He also shared in the expense of a room or transcribing office[1] where the longhand copies of his notes could be made.

As he went about he absorbed varied impressions which composed themselves into pictures in his mind.   Doctors' Commons with its many courts and its aloof, robed personnel of doctors and proctors struck him strangely, for it had so little relation with the tide of life that flowed down Ludgate Hill to the Strand.   He was later to describe its ways in a 'Sketch', and make play with its activities in *David Copperfield*.   'What is a proctor?' David asks Steerforth and is told,

He is a sort of monkish attorney . . . a functionary whose existence, in the natural course of things would have terminated about two hundred years ago.   I can tell you best what he is by telling you what Doctors' Commons is. It's a little out-of-the-way place, where they administer what is called ecclesiastical law and play all kinds of tricks with obsolete old monsters of Acts of Parliament. . . . It's a place that has an ancient monopoly in suits about people's wills and people's marriages and disputes among ships and boats.

[1] 5 Bell Yard, Paul's Chain.

Doctors' Commons[1] lay on the south side of St. Paul's and was approached by a street called 'Paul's Chain'. Paul's Chain led to an archway which gave on to 'a quiet shady courtyard paved with stone', and frowned upon by old red brick houses. One of its doors, a green-baize one studded with brass nails, admitted visitors to the Court of Doctors' Commons, all the other doors were painted in white letters with the names of learned civilians. Here the noise of the city was muffled and seemed to melt as if by magic into a softened distance. Attached to Doctors' Commons were various sinecure appointments in the gift of the Lord Chancellor. The poet James Thomson had held one of them, the Secretaryship for Briefs. In these ghostly precincts Dickens became familiar with the many types of legal gentlemen that thread the pages of his novels—Vholes, Heep, Dodson and Fogg, Sampson Brass, Spenlow, Jorkins, Tulkinghorn and the rest. As a body of men they were probably more real to him than the men of other educated professions—such as medicine or the church. Doctors and clergy when they have to be called in to fill up a chink in a narrative are never more than lay figures.

The term Doctors' Commons covered an agglomeration of 'courts' using the same premises and the same officials. There was the Court of Arches, the provincial court of the Archbishop of Canterbury, whose Dean was President of Doctors' Commons: and there was the Consistory Court, the diocesan court of the Bishop of London, in which Dickens chose to work. There was the Prerogative Court dealing with testamentary matters in the dioceses: the Prerogative Office in which wills were registered and filed, and then the Admiralty Court which occasioned David Copperfield's protest to Steerforth that there could be no affinity between ecclesiastical and nautical matters and the explanation that there was no affinity, but that all courts were managed and all cases decided by the same set of people.

[1] Doctors' Commons abolished as such in 1857 when its jurisdiction was taken over by the new Probate Court. The land on which it stood was then sold.

You go there one day and find them blundering through the nautical terms in Young's Dictionary and you go there another day and find the judge going through evidence respecting a clergyman who has misbehaved himself.

The unfavourable impression made on Charles Dickens's mind by wandering in and out of courts of law was imparted by him years after to Mr. Frederick Pollock:[1]

I have that high opinion of the law of England generally, which one is likely to derive from the impression that it puts all the honest men under the diabolical hoofs of all the scoundrels.

The cases Charles Dickens was called on to report were heard and argued in a large room resembling a dissenters' chapel. In *David Copperfield* he describes this place in a manner that presents a lively visual image:

The upper part of this room was fenced off from the rest; and there on the two sides of a raised platform of the horse-shoe form, sitting on easy old-fashioned dining-room chairs, were sundry gentlemen in red gowns and grey wigs, whom I found to be the Doctors. Blinking over a little desk like a pulpit desk, in the curve of the horse-shoe, was an old gentleman, whom if I had seen him in an aviary I should certainly have taken for an owl, but who I learned was the presiding judge. In the space within the horse-shoe about the level of the floor, were sundry other gentle-men . . . dressed . . . in black gowns with white fur upon them sitting at a long green table.

We may in this connection remind ourselves that Charles Dickens was not alone in his opinion of the anachronistic character of the Law Courts of his day for at the very same time Mr. Macaulay, the nominee of the East India Company in the House of Commons, was charging Parliament with failing to keep in order the machinery of justice and of winking at the tangle of procedures kept up for the good of the lawyers.

[1] May 2, 1870.

'Look,' he said, 'at that series of penal statutes the most bloody and the most inefficient in the world, at the puerile fictions which make every declaration and every plea unintelligible both to the plaintiff and the defendant, at the chaos of precedents, and *the bottomless pit of Chancery*. . . . Place the people and the Government side by side and you will see barbarism belongs to the Government, civilisation to the people.'

The legal profession, distinguished by its 'costiveness', was in no way, Macaulay alleged, controlled by Parliament, the reverse in fact being true. In his opinion one great reform remained to be satisfied—a rational system of private law.

It was into a strange, crabbed, dusty world that Charles Dickens had entered himself and in the beginning he had leisure to observe it in all its convolutions, for patrons were few and custom 'wearily uncertain'. If not called on by the proctors to report, he occupied himself in reading or learning parts in plays. Conscious that he had a great deal of leeway to make up both educationally and culturally, he secured (on the day after he was eighteen) a reader's ticket for the British Museum[1] and there set himself to make good some of the gaps in his accomplishment. He was extremely thorough in anything he undertook, and once it was discovered by clients how reliable and rapid was the young clerk's reporting, commissions poured in and in middle life he would sometimes say that the two years spent in Doctors' Commons were 'the usefullest of my life'.

The home background although still set in lodging-houses was at this time pleasant enough, for his sister Fanny and her musical friends clustered round the piano of an evening. Charles sang and so did John Hullah and J. P. Harley, ex-pupils at the College of Music. Henry Austin, an artist, and Henry Kolle, a calico-printer with a voice, formed part of the circle. Between them they produced the Covent Garden

[1] February 8, 1830. Vouched for by Mrs. Charlton of 16 Berners Street.

success of some years earlier, *Clari, the Maid of Milan*,[1] with its popular song 'Home, Sweet Home'.

For a time Charles, partly from love of the stage and partly with the idea of becoming, if other trades failed, a professional actor, spent all his spare evenings at the theatre, 'always studying the bills first, always seeing the best plays', and following Charles Mathews in all his impersonations. Prescribing for himself 'a kind of Hamiltonian system' for learning parts he memorised a good number, took lessons from the actor Robert Keeley, and practised at home before a mirror how to enter a room, how to sit down on a chair, how to bow. He went so far as to apply for an audition to Mathews and to approach the comedian George Bartley, manager of Covent Garden. Owing to 'disfiguring illness', in other words a swollen face, he could not keep his appointment with these gentlemen and before he could ask for another, success as a political journalist had made a theatrical career out of the question. The training for the stage was not wasted, nothing ever was wasted in Dickens's life; he managed to make good use of every experience, and the self-assurance acquired in this way stood him in good stead when making his debut in the salon of Lady Blessington and in the Holland House circle.

Henry Kolle, the young man with the voice, idolised Charles and insisted, when he engaged himself to Anne, daughter of George Beadnell, a bank manager in the city,[2] on taking him to the Beadnell home in Lombard Street. This was probably the first family circle to which Dickens had been introduced and he enjoyed it, even taking a fancy to Mrs. Beadnell, who treated him almost as a servant and addressed him as 'Mr. Dickin'. Anne turned out to be a lute-player and one of three musical sisters, the youngest of whom, Maria, was a harpist. Extremely pretty, Maria asked nothing better than to flirt with the good-looking, charming boy produced by Kolle. No one in the family could regard him as a

---

[1] See *Sketches by 'Boz'* for skit on rehearsals.
[2] Of Smith, Payne, Smith.

possible suitor, he was just a penniless reporter who could laugh and sing; but negligible and innocuous as he appeared to the prosperous Beadnells, he fell head and ears in love with their daughter. For Maria's album[1] Charles constructed an acrostic of the thirteen letters of her name, and just adored her 'every minute, day and night' since the first moment he saw her. His friend, Henry Austin, also adored Maria, and painted her and her little brother George in *gouache* as Dido and Ascanius. He did a tinted drawing of her, too, for Charles as 'The Milkmaid', depicting her under a tree with dangling sun-bonnet and bucket at her side. As go-between for letters, Kolle became party to the development of a clandestine romance. One assumes there must have been the encouragement of a secret engagement for, for Maria's sweet sake, Dickens slaved to raise himself from the rut of family circumstance. He worked harder than ever in Doctors' Commons, he read harder than ever in the British Museum, and was lifted by his passion for Maria out of black memories of suffering and humiliation. By this stiff struggle against poverty and obscurity he laid the foundation of his future success.

Maria played with his devotion and extracted all the fun there was to be got out of the situation, little knowing that one day she and her pet, 'Daphne', immortalised as 'Dora' and 'Jip', would wring the hearts of thousands. The game went on for some two years, but after Henry Kolle's marriage to Anne, at which Charles was best man, the Beadnell parents whisked their youngest daughter off to 'a finishing establishment' in Paris. For Charles, out of sight was not out of memory; Maria still 'pervaded every corner and crevice' of his mind and this love affair went as deep as his blacking factory experience in shaping his attitude to life. When Maria spurned his suit, he told her roundly that 'whatever of fancy, romance, passion, aspiration and determination belong to me I never have separated and never shall separate from that hard-hearted little woman—you'. Again he wrote:

[1] Maria's album is preserved in the Huntington Library (U.S.A.).

I can claim for myself and *feel* that I deserve the merit of having ever throughout our intercourse acted fairly, intelligently and honourably, under kindness and encouragement one day and a cold change of conduct the next. . . . I have ever acted without reserve. . . . I have never loved and I never can love any human creature breathing but yourself.

When he could no longer stand her ridicule, he returned her presents and set his teeth, determining 'to ride on, rough-shod if need be, smooth-shod if that will do, but ride on'.

In the pages of *David Copperfield* the story of Charles's love for Maria lives for ever. Twenty years on, Lady Olliffe asked the famous Mr. Dickens when he was dining with her in Paris whether it was really true that he used to love Maria Beadnell so very, very, very much. And Mr. Dickens replied that there was no woman in the world and very few men who could ever imagine how much. He paused and then said reflectively, 'When we were falling off each other I came from the House of Commons many a night at two or three o'clock in the morning only to wander past the place she was asleep in.'

When years later Maria dined as a married woman with Mr. and Mrs. Charles Dickens at Tavistock House she was fat and middle-aged, and her host saw fit to turn her into Flora Finching of *Little Dorrit*. But even the realisation that she was stupid, commonplace and had never cared, did not kill within him the image he had once made of her because his original perception was stored like a sun-picture in his mind.

Charles celebrated his twentieth birthday with a quadrille party. His always nomadic parents were at the time living in furnished lodgings at 70 Margaret Street.[1] Tom Beard of the Gallery came to the feast and congratulated his friend, who had at last, owing to the expenditure of his 'celestial or diabolical energy', qualified as 'a first-class parliamentary re-

[1] 10 Norfolk Street, Fitzroy Square, over a grocer's shop, 1831; 70 Margaret Street, February 1832; 13 Fitzroy Street, July 1832; 18 Bentinck Street, over an upholsterer's shop, June 1838.

porter' and was to join him in the House of Commons almost immediately. Most cheerfully Charles reconciled himself to forgoing plays, announcing to a friend that he would now have no certain night at his disposal. To have qualified for the Gallery at twenty was a minor triumph, but could anyone have guessed that it could be a way of catching up with those unknown competitors in life's race, Robert Browning and William Makepiece Thackeray? Most people, it may be assumed, would at this time have backed both these promising young men against an unknown journalist. Prosperous Robert Browning with *Pauline* written and *Paracelsus* planned, and Thackeray, a student at the Middle Temple, with a good working knowledge of French and German to his credit and a *Wanderjahr* behind him. What had young Mr. Dickens to show against such achievements?

Joining the staff of the *True Sun* (a sevenpenny evening paper owned by Murdo Young and edited by Laman Blanchard) on the first day of its publication, March 5, 1832, Charles Dickens got to the House of Commons just in time to take down the last speeches made during the Committee stage of the Reform Bill.

Chapter 3

THE GALLERY

I wallow in words. Britannia, that unfortunate female, is always before me like a trussed fowl: skewered through and through with office pins and bound hand and foot with red tape. I am sufficiently behind the scenes to know the worth of political life. I am quite an Infidel about it and shall never be converted. 'DAVID COPPERFIELD'

IT has been well said that the Reform debates may be reckoned as the first term in the education of most Englishmen in politics. So eager was the man in the street to read the speeches in full that every morning paper engaged at least ten reporters, at a cost of something like £3000 a year, to satisfy this craving. A sevenpenny newspaper taken twenty miles out of London was readily snapped up for a shilling. The thirst for political information was really a new thing, so new that up till this time no official effort had been made to meet the demand, no formal permission given to reporters either to note down or to publish debates, no facilities such as seats or tables provided for their use. This keen intelligent group of men were in the House, as it were, on sufferance, for many legislators, including of course the Duke of Wellington, steadily refused to admit that the people of England had any right, through the medium of the press, to know what was said in Parliament.

The Committee stage of the Reform Bill ended a few days after Dickens had begun regular work in the Gallery. Passing its third reading on March 23, it was sent up to the Lords on March 26 and read there for the second time on April 9 when it was carried by nine votes. Lord Grey then moved the adjournment of the debate and fixed May 10 for further consideration of the Bill. This interval was wasted on the Lords, who in May 1832 put up as sharp an opposition as they had done in October 1831. Lord Grey at once tendered his resignation, which was accepted by the King. As neither Lord Lyndhurst nor the Duke of Wellington were able to form an administration and Sir Robert Peel refused to make himself responsible for an anti-reform cabinet, the King had to recall Lord Grey and consent to grant the measures necessary for pushing the Bill through, even if it involved the creation of peers. What Macaulay termed 'our glorious ten days' was now breathlessly experienced by the members of both Houses and by the pressmen of the Gallery. When the Bill finally became law it set bells ringing and flags flying throughout the country.

Charles Dickens was neither excited nor impressed by the enthusiasm of those who supported reform or the anger of those who opposed it. One might be inclined to put this down to ignorance of politics and parliamentary history if he had not left behind him the skit on the 'Howsa Kummauns' in which the lovely odalisque, 'Reefawm', is shown as an illusory phantom of delight. Instinctively he realised that the Bill had changed nothing for the great bulk of the working classes, though it certainly had made the State a partnership between two great powers instead of the monopoly of one. As Dickens began so he ended. After four years' work in the Gallery, involving as it did an intensive political and administrative education, he wholeheartedly condemned and despised the activities that went on in what he was apt to designate 'the great dustheap of Westminster'.

During the first session of the reformed parliament Charles Dickens looked down from his Gallery on an assembly that appeared, and in fact was, a little older than the average in the unreformed parliament. Its members worked harder than their predecessors and, in token of earnestness, met at noon and seldom rose before midnight. A Tory Speaker presided in a House in which the Whigs outnumbered the Tories by nearly three to one. Among the new faces he observed was that of William Cobbett of the *Two-penny Postbag*, the first journalist to sit in the House of Commons. Cobbett took his seat on the Treasury bench, and when gently squeezed from there sat down next to Sir Robert Peel on the front Opposition bench, to the amusement of his colleagues up above. The leaders of the old parliament were leaders of the new, beginning with Lord Grey as Prime Minister and continuing with the veterans of the Reform debates, Lord Althorp, Lord John Russell and Mr. Stanley, whose brilliant, nimble powers of dialectic had supplied and were still to supply the vigour lacking in his colleagues. Dickens got to know the look of many famous people as they filed from lobby to chamber. Among them were Macaulay, Gladstone, Grote, Edward Bulwer, James Silk Buckingham as well as O'Connell and Grattan. If personalities make a good House of Commons this should have been a specially remarkable one.

Dickens was kept hard at work, for it fell to him to report three important measures, the Peace Preservation Bill (Ireland), the Abolition of Slavery (British Colonies) and a measure for the administration of British India by which the East India Company was turned by charter into a trustee for the Crown. Having resigned from the *True Sun* in the autumn of 1832, he reported all these debates for a kind of Hansard, specialising in exact transcription, called the *Mirror of Parliament*.[1] The *Mirror* was produced at 3 Abingdon Street and was both owned and edited by his uncle, John Henry Barrow.[2] Charles, it seems, had now earned favour with his mother's family, for we find one uncle offering him a job and the wife of another uncle painting his miniature. It was at last recognised that this young nephew was someone to be encouraged, even to be proud of. John Henry Barrow, author of *The Battle of Talavera*, an epic poem, of the type made fashionable by Scott and Southey, was well up in Indian affairs and still on the staff of the *Times*, in connection with which he had earned a great reputation at the time of the

[1] Superseded October 1841.
[2] J. H. Barrow, member of Gray's Inn, 1823. Third son of Charles Barrow. Died Stoke Newington, March 30, 1858 (it is said in poverty).

Queen's Trial. The grey paper covers of his *Mirror of Parliament*, in shape and size like a blue book, contain very well printed reports. They are verbally accurate and carefully punctuated with 'No! No!' 'Slight laughter' and so on. All this in spite of the prohibition which still in form existed against the publishing of debates. As reward for his conscientious work on the *Mirror* Charles was often invited to accompany his uncle at week-ends to his house at Norwood, a house that was to figure as the home of Mr. Spenlow in *David Copperfield*.

Sixteen years later we find Charles Dickens writing to Tom Beard from his fine house in Devonshire Terrace, 'John Henry Barrow dines here next Sunday at half-past five for a quarter to six. Will you come and meet the little man?'[1] Could the tables of patronage be more completely turned? A testimonial to Barrow, which incidentally reflects credit on his nephew, was spoken by Gladstone in the House of Commons in 1877. He said, 'At the time of the Reform Bill an attempt was made by a gentleman of the name of Barrow to produce verbatim reports of the debates in that House. . . . Barrow's work was done in the highest degree of perfection.'[2]

In February 1833 Dickens was reporting speeches on the Bill for the Suppression of Disturbances in Ireland and curiously enough by so doing was brought into direct contact with the Chief Secretary himself, Mr. Stanley. This Coercion Bill had been drafted in Mr. Stanley's office in Dublin and was approved by Lord Grey. It embodied the usual features proper to such measures, including the replacing of trials by jury by courts-martial. In fact it was the application to Leinster peasants of the dragooning of the Scottish lowlands under Charles II and of the Cevennes under Louis XV, a more severe measure than any passed by Tories. It is a tribute both to O'Connell's eloquence and to Dickens's sensibility that when taking down a speech describing a scene

[1] 20. II. L.   [2] *Daily News*, April 21, 1877.

at an Irish anti-tithe riot the reporter had to abandon his pencil
and weep.   When moving the second reading of the Bill Mr.
Stanley spoke at great length.   *Mirror* reporters, working
for three-quarters of an hour each, were on the job, and Charles
Dickens who reported the first part of the speech also reported
the last part.   When it appeared in print Mr. Stanley found all
except the beginning and the end full of mistakes; he therefore
requested the editor of the *Mirror* to send across the reporter
of the first and last sections to take down the whole speech as
it was to be printed for circulation in Ireland.   Barrow instructed John Dickens to fetch Charles up from the country
whither he had gone for a rest, and dispatched the lad to
Carlton House Terrace.   Shown into a room the tables of
which were covered with newspapers, young Mr. Dickens
awaited the minister who had summoned him.   Mr. Stanley
walked in and eyeing him suspiciously said, 'I beg pardon,
but I had hoped to see the gentleman who had reported part
of my speech.'   'I am that gentleman,' said Dickens, redden-
ing.   'Oh indeed,' responded Mr. Stanley, looking down to
conceal a half smile.   Sir James Graham coming in at this
moment, Mr. Stanley began to walk up and down the room
declaiming his speech.   Sir James followed his words with
the newspaper version and occasionally intervened.   The
ordeal over, Mr. Stanley wrote a highly complimentary note
to Barrow thanking him for sending so smart a stenographer,
while in the hall his private secretary, Richard Earle, praised
Dickens to his face.   This encouraged him to write to Earle
explaining that as he was entirely unemployed during the
recess he would be thankful to be recommended as shorthand
writer to a Commission or Board.   First and last things
sometimes meet.   When dining, as a famous man, with Mr.
Gladstone many years later, Dickens found himself in the
very room in which he had taken down Mr. Stanley's speech.
The scene flashed back and he spoke to his host about the
incident, whereupon Lord Derby who was present told his
version of the story.   Another witness to Dickens's excellence as a reporter is William Harness, who says that when

Joseph Hume in 1834 complained that his speeches on the
Repeal of the Corn Laws were not faithfully reported in
the *Times*, the editor of the *Mirror* put his young nephew
on to him and the dissatisfied member very soon called
'Peccavi'.[1]

As soon as Mr. Stanley had seen the Coercion Bill become
law he ceased to be Irish Secretary and went to the Colonial
Office, where he at once framed a Bill for the Abolition of
Slavery in the British Colonies, a measure certain of success
in the reformed House.   It was Dickens's duty to record the
debates on this measure which include the maiden speech of
Mr. Gladstone, the young hope of the Conservative party,
whose (family) fortunes were partially derived from Demerara
and who was forced to his feet when Lord Howick during the
course of the discussion accused the administrator of the family
estates of being a 'murderer of slaves'.   He also reported
Bulwer, whose rhetorical speech about keeping faith with the
negro went down so well with the House that O'Connell
tore his speech-notes in half, saying, 'There is nothing to add,
the House must divide!'   During the same session (1833)
Dickens was on duty in the Gallery for the India Act debates
in which Silk Buckingham and Macaulay played so large a
part.   Macaulay, who had been brought up by his father (at
one time Governor of Sierra Leone) to respect coloured
people, was all for the equality of races and warm-hearted for
the employment of natives in official positions.   When the
Governing Corporation of India was forced to abandon its
commercial monopolies and trading activities and was limited
to administration and patronage, Macaulay was appointed to
the Supreme Council of India and went out to work under
that ardent reformer, Lord William Bentinck, the first
Governor-General under the new Constitution.   Reformers
differ from improvers in being guided by faith and imagination to the discernment of things possible.   Discernment and
hope were needed then in full measure if the customs of the
dwellers in India (even with regard to Lord William's special

[1] L'Estrange, *Life of W. Harness*, p. 169.

bugbears suttee and thuggee) were to be in any degree modified.

It is important in assessing Dickens's career to stress the character of the education he absorbed while working in the Gallery. There is too great a tendency among biographers to regard him in a parochial way as a man only acquainted with English middle and lower class life, who, owing to circumstances, was shut out from the affairs of the great world until the great world, discovering him in his amazingly successful books, took him up and made him into an idol. Of course we see in reading his novels that he was always emotionalising his personal experience and dealing with examples of private suffering in a way that the humblest understood, but this did not mean that he himself was not fully alive to wider social issues. Always anxious that the people, so uninterested in their own interests, should be made aware that they were quite needlessly living a disinherited life, he addressed himself to the common folk and the generality of the humble. Never after his experience in the House of Commons would he have thought it worth while to appeal to legislators as such. Conscious of the power within him of stirring men to laughter or tears, he knew that if he could move them enough they must themselves seek to remedy their condition. The manner in which he worked on society was almost stealthy; it was as if he felt that it would invalidate the magic in his books, if it ever became generally known that he was a philanthropist at heart working for the abolition of slums, the founding of Ragged Schools and the reclaiming of girls from the streets. These activities for years remained a secret between himself and Miss Burdett Coutts. Some native instinct made him wise and caused him to realise that his real magic was vested in the wand, Romance, with which he could stir men powerfully to achieve their own salvation.

Impressed by his nephew's ability and by the testimonials to his efficiency furnished by Mr. Stanley and Mr. Hume, John

Henry Barrow spoke to his friend Payne Collier, then in charge of parliamentary reporting on the *Morning Chronicle*,[1] about the young man's future. He called him 'an extremely clever youth' and said he would have liked, had there been a vacancy, to get him on to the staff of the *Times*. Was it possible for Payne Collier to introduce him to the new stock-broker proprietor of the *Morning Chronicle*, Mr. John East-hope? Payne Collier at once asked where the nephew had been educated and what his record was, for it was more than his place was worth to recommend an unknown person to an employer so irascible and so disagreeable to employees as to be nicknamed 'Blasthope'. The reply he received to his question being ambiguous, he said he must see the candidate himself. Barrow arranged for them to meet at dinner at his house at Norwood. Charles disarmed criticism by chattering merrily and, after a good deal of pressure, singing two comic songs. Payne Collier was charmed with the young man and readily wrote out an introduction to the editor of the *Chronicle*, John Black, who had been commissioned by the new proprietor to look for a staff good enough to compete with the *Times*. Black had already engaged Eyre Crowe as Paris correspondent and George Hogarth as theatrical and musical critic. Thackeray had offered himself as sub-editor, but was not wanted, as Payne Collier and Charles Mackay, both of whom had greater experience, were preferred before him and later on he was engaged by the *Times*. Tom Beard, one of Black's parliamentary reporters, vouched for his friend, Charles Dickens, as 'the fastest and most accurate man in the Gallery'. This chit in the end got him the job. He was engaged at five guineas a week, a salary which (unlike that of the *Mirror*) was to be paid session or no session. With this team the *Morning Chronicle* after one year became, according to Charles Mackay, the commercial and literary rival of the *Times*.[2]

[1] The *Morning Chronicle* was established (1769) twenty years before the *Times*. It had declined in circulation and Easthope bought it for £17,000 to turn into a Liberal paper.

[2] C. Mackay, *Through the Long Day*, 1887.

The *Morning Chronicle* had its office at 332 Strand and John
Black his private residence above it.   The account of Pott
and Slurk, the Eatanswill editors in *Pickwick*, may be taken as
Edward Sterling rolling out thunder from Printing House
Square and Black discharging answering bolts from the
Strand.[1]   This was in accordance with the Dickens method.
In the opening chapter of *Pickwick* a quarrel between the
founder of the Club and a member called Blotton is recorded.
This was undoubtedly suggested by a famous House of
Commons scene in which Brougham and Canning were the
chief figures.[2]   Brougham had described Canning's accession
to a divided cabinet as an incredible specimen of monstrous
trickery for the sake of obtaining office.   Canning at once
interrupted with the words 'That is false!'   The two political
rivals were about to be committed to the Serjeant-at-Arms
when Sir Robert Wilson suggested the explanation that
Brougham's offensive words were applied to Canning not in
his personal, but in his official character.   Thirteen years
later, when *Pickwick* was at the height of its renown, Fonblanque, referring to the adroitness with which the disturbance had been quelled, commented, 'In fact Brougham and
Canning only called each other liars in the Pickwickian sense,
just as in the story Blotton said he had merely considered Mr.
Pickwick a humbug in the Pickwickian sense'.

We get a further side-light on Dickens at this time from
James Grant of the *Morning Advertiser*.   He says that of the
eighty or ninety men in the Gallery young Dickens not only
occupied the highest rank for rapidity and accuracy of transcription but that 'a more talented reporter never sat in the
Gallery'.   The 'faithful stenographer' as they called him was
described as 'exceedingly reserved in manners, courteous, but
personally intimate only with Thomas Beard also reporting
for the *Morning Chronicle*'.   As soon as Dickens began drawing his salary from the *Chronicle*,[3] Payne Collier noted a
remarkable smartening-up of his appearance which made him

[1] T. H. S. Escott, *Masters of Journalism*, p. 160.   [2] April 17, 1823.
[3] August 1834.

wonder whether his uncle might not have been underpaying him. The young fellow was now to be seen wearing a new hat and a handsome blue cloak with black velvet facings 'which he threw over his shoulders *à l'Espagnole*'.

For the *Chronicle* Dickens was called on to report the debates on the Poor Law Bill with its hundred and more clauses on guardians, parishes and paupers. It was a racking but deeply interesting spell of duty, a duty by execution of which he may be said to have qualified himself forcefully to attack the conditions created by the new legislation. Critics reviewing *Oliver Twist* thought it impertinent for a young new author to write in this vein, for how could so young a novelist possibly know what he was talking about? But then few, if any, critics of that day realised in what school 'Boz' had graduated.

As the House of Commons was burnt out in October 1834 Dickens had the experience of reporting both in the old Chamber and in the House of Lords where the Commons were accommodated after the fire. He says he wore out his knees by writing on them in the old House and wore out his feet in the temporary House by standing to write in 'a preposterous pen where we used to be huddled together like so many sheep kept in waiting say—until the wool-sack might need restuffing'.

To Dickens the attitude of the House towards commonsense reforms was perfectly epitomised in the origin of the fire that had destroyed it. Had there been no mania for preserving outworn customs there would have been no fire. It pleased him to tell the story of how in ages past a savage method of keeping accounts, Crusoe-wise on notched sticks, was introduced into the Court of Exchequer. These notched sticks were treated by officials as pillars of the Constitution and it was ordained that Exchequer accounts should always be kept on splints of elm-wood called 'tallies'. In the reign of George III some revolutionary spirit suggested that the tallies should be replaced by accounts kept in pen and ink on paper. A long wrangle ensued ending in the abolition of tallies in 1826. Eight years later someone noticed an accumulation of splints, some of them worm-eaten and perished, and suggested that they should be disposed of. Instead of being given to the poor as firewood, an order went forth that they were to be destroyed 'privately and confidentially'. Crammed into a stove in the House of Lords, they set fire to the panelling and the panelling to the House itself. At the height of the blaze a stickler for etiquette and precedent presented himself in the shape of Joseph Hume who watched the Guards coming in to fight the flames and addressed their commanding officer thus: 'There ought to be ten pioneers to each regiment. I see only eight. How is this, Lord Hill?' Bulwer writing to Lady Blessington next day said, 'Only think of burning down the two Houses! I am so delighted we shall now be able to breathe, I hope![1] And the moral drawn by Dickens from the occurrence was that 'all obstinate adherence to rubbish which the time has long outlived is certain to have in the soul of it more or less what is pernicious and destructive and will one day set fire to something or other'.

Rarely did Dickens comment on anything he had seen in the House, but a short post-fire account by him of what the place looked like appears in a *Sketch*. He tells of the little stair leading to the 'first gallery ever allocated to reporters' from which a fair view of the House could be obtained. As the eyes accustomed themselves to the misty atmosphere and the glare of the gas chandeliers, and the ears attuned themselves to the confused sound of voices, it might be possible to distinguish the words of the speaker 'to whom nobody listens'. He describes the body of the House and the side galleries full of members, some with legs on backs of seats, some with them stretched full length, all laughing, coughing, oh-ing, groaning, questioning, in short presenting to an onlooker 'a conglomeration of noise and confusion to be met with in no other place in existence not even excepting Smith-

[1] Earl of Lytton, *Life of Edward Bulwer Lytton*, vol. ii. p. 461.

field on a market-day or a cock-pit in its glory'. 'Talk of mobs!' said William Hazlitt after his year's experience as a reporter for the *Morning Chronicle*. 'See how few who have distinguished themselves in the House of Commons have ever done anything else.' To Carlyle the sight of members 'sitting in their hats and talking to one another' during speeches was almost as provoking as it was to Dickens. How was it possible to believe, much less to think, that in the Commons was rooted the strength of England and not its weakness?

Such allusions as Dickens makes in his novels to Parliament and its members are not complimentary. In the *Sketches* we meet Cornelius Brook Dingwall, M.P., solemn and portentous, drawing up a Bill for the better observance of Easter Monday. In *Pickwick* the account of the Eatanswill election leaves us with the impression that parliamentary government is deep-rooted in stupidity, chicanery and corruption. In *Nicholas Nickleby* we make acquaintance with Gregsbury, M.P., a mere windbag, and in *Dombey and Son* with Warming Pan Adams who is keeping a place warm for a minor. In *Hard Times* we meet Gradgrind, M.P., and in *Our Mutual Friend* Boots and Brewer. Then in *Bleak House* we are taken to Chesney Wold and shown how governments are formed by Lord Boodle with his followers Coodle, Doodle and Foodle, or by an opposition under the Right Honourable William Buffy with his retinue of Cuffy, Duffy and Fuffy. No other leaders are so much as mentioned. Either the Boodles or the Buffys act the play, Administration, and the stage is always reserved for these great performers who from time to time address audiences known as 'the People' and evoke shouts, choruses and general applause. Nothing favourable to the House or its members was ever said or suggested in any of the Dickens novels.

Between sessions Dickens was sent to report speeches by political leaders all over the country. For instance, in September 1834 he and Tom Beard were ordered to Edinburgh to cover the banquet given to Lord Grey on his retirement from office. The young men went by sea to Leith and it delighted Dickens to see a bagman on the boat reading *The Bloomsbury Christening* with chuckles of laughter. Nat Willis was also in Edinburgh on a similar errand and noted 'Lord Grey's statesman-like head, as it bowed industriously from the platform' and the expression on Lord Brougham's ugliest and shrewdest of human faces'. To the American it was an amusing occasion.

The *Morning Chronicle* of Wednesday, September 17, printed a bright half column from 'Our own correspondent', describing Edinburgh in festal mood:

> The Earl of Durham is here and the Lord Chancellor arrived at three o'clock this afternoon. . . . I obtained a view of the temporary banqueting hall (the Grey Pavilion as it is called) this morning. It is erecting in the High School grounds on Calton Hill and . . . capable of dining 1500 individuals. The room is square with seven entrances: it has no ventilation. . . . Earl Grey staying with Sir John Dalrymple at Oxenford will receive a deputation en route at Dalkeith.

The correspondent goes on to tell of the arrival at Dalkeith of four carriages and four escorted by bands, of the stage opposite the church where Earl Grey received addresses, of Edinburgh crowds and a progress to the Waterloo Hotel where the Guilds met the statesman to make him a freeman of the city.

Dickens waited inside the Grey Pavilion 'which with chandeliers borrowed from the Theatre Royal, armorial designs, gilt laurels and crimson pillars' had been made to look quite gay. Earl Grey, due to arrive at five-thirty, did not come till six. At five-thirty people began to consume the food on the tables. Owing to the absence of the Duke of Hamilton, Lord Rosebery took the chair and Dickens, pencil poised, set himself to report what the big-wigs had to say.

And who among the distinguished guests gathered in the Grey Pavilion that evening could have guessed that an insignificant young reporter, at that moment on duty, would in seven years' time be going through the identical experience of Lord Grey in being made a freeman of the city of Edinburgh?

The *Times* by its new system of 'extraordinary expresses', costing £290 a journey, was able to print, by delaying for four hours the publication of the paper, a full report of the speeches on Wednesday, September 17. The *Morning Chronicle* printed the speeches on the day following, and the *Times* of September 19 jeered at the editor for labelling his report 'By Express'. This was a lesson Dickens did not forget and from henceforth we shall find him too making use of 'extraordinary expresses'.

In October Dickens took lodgings in Cecil Street, Strand, so as to be near his newspaper office, and shortly afterwards moved to 15 Buckingham Street in the same neighbourhood. These lodgings were so unsatisfactory that he began to consider taking unfurnished rooms and setting up house for himself. Rooms, however, were by no means his only worry at this time, as we may gather from his letters to Henry Kolle in which he alludes to his father's borrowing habits as 'the damnable shadow' cast over his life. The shadow at this time was lengthening. To Tom Mitton he wrote, 'my father went out yesterday accompanied by Alfred to endeavour to get some money as Burr refused to wait beyond last evening. He sent the boy [Alfred] home to say he had been unsuccessful and has not made his appearance all night or forwarded a message of any kind.'[1] Next day the news of John Dickens's arrest by 'Shaw and Maxwell the quondam wine people' reached him, and a much-harassed Charles had to rush off to Sloman's sponging-house before taking his turn of duty for the *Morning Chronicle*. In *Pickwick* we shall find a description of this half-way house to prison. Cash had to be found at once to provide 'the Governor' with his keep, so Tom Mitton was asked to advance £5 against the 'money order from my French employer' which he encloses.[2] As 'it

[1] 33. I. N.L.   [2] 34. I. N.L.

had to be assumed that John Dickens would not rejoin his family for some time', a domestic council was called whereat it was decided that the family must for the time being disperse. The best arrangement Charles could make at the moment was to rent cheap lodgings for his mother, sister and the other children and take Frederick under his own wing in the unfurnished rooms he was renting at Furnival's Inn. Manfully and cheerfully he shouldered these heavy responsibilities, telling Beard that his salary was 'completely mortgaged for weeks to come' and adding, 'I am determined to see everything in as bright a light as possible'.

This was the first step on the long road of family commitments, commitments which in the end were to be his spiritual undoing. Just because he was open-hearted as well as openhanded and seemed able to deal with difficulties of the kind easily, it became the custom in his own family, and later on in his wife's family, to expect him to find money and appointments for as spineless a set of people as ever bread-winner was saddled with. He was too capable, prompt and generous in the beginning not to fall victim to his own ability in the end. To this theme we shall have to recur.

Thus it came about that for the first time since he had taken to earning his living Charles was short of cash and had to camp sans curtains or crockery in the 'three-pair-back' at 13 Furnival's Inn. The 'flare' or house-warming he had meant to give his friends was for the time being postponed. In a letter of January 1835 a bleak statement lets the curtain down on John Dickens: 'I have just returned from accompanying father to Coldbath Fields'.

Shortly after this melancholy outing Charles was ordered to cover the Chelmsford election. It was a joy to get out of London for the time being and his spirits rose as he drove himself to Braintree in a gig,

> tooling in and out of the banners, drums, conservative emblems, horsemen, go-carts, with which every little green was filled as the processions were waiting for Sir John Tyrell and Baring. Every time the horse heard a drum he

bounced into the hedge on the left side of the road and every time I got him out of that he bounded into the hedge on the right side . . . with the trifling exception of breaking my whip, I flatter myself I did the whole thing in something like style.[1]

A wet week-end at the Black Boy Hotel exhausted his good temper and turned Chelmsford into 'the dullest and most stupid spot on the face of the earth'.

> I can't get an *Athenaeum* or *Literary Gazette*—no not even a penny magazine and here I am on a wet Sunday looking out of a d——d large bow window at the rain as it falls into the puddles opposite: wondering when it will be dinner-time and cursing my folly in having put no books into my portmanteau. The only book I have seen here is one that lies upon the sofa. It is entitled 'Field Exercises and Evolution of the Army by Sir Henry Towers'. I have read it through so often that I am sure I could drill a hundred recruits from memory. There is not even anything to look at in the place except two immense prisons, large enough to hold all the inhabitants of the county—whom they can have been built for I can't imagine.[2]

Quotations from letters often cause one to deplore the fact that Dickens never kept a diary and never described the houses he was entertained in nor his meetings with famous people.

Twice during the year 1835 Dickens went reporting into the west country, once in May and once in November, each time to take down the speeches of Lord John Russell. In May, on accepting the office of Home Secretary in Lord Melbourne's government, Lord John had to offer himself for re-election in South Devon. The *Chronicle* men, Dickens and Tom Beard, set out in tearing spirits and worked in rain that lasted through the short campaign. In the castle yard at Exeter Lord John made an open-air speech which Dickens took down at full speed while friends held a pocket-handkerchief over his notebook to keep it dry 'after the manner of a

[1] 39. I. N.L.   [2] 40. I. N.L.

state canopy in an ecclesiastical procession'. By dint of
bribing the post-boys 'tremendously', he got his report to
London in time for the *Chronicle* to print before the *Times*,
and as his account was longer and more accurate than that
of any other London paper it gave great satisfaction. John
Black, clapping him on the shoulder, told him the whole affair
was a complete and signal success. The triumphant reporter
said the rain had made him deaf and had given him rheu-
matism, that Lord John had been defeated, but that all the
same he had enjoyed the excitement immensely.

Lord John Russell being the Government candidate at a
by-election in Stroud in November 1835, Dickens and Beard
took the road to the west country again and kept their sub-
editor, Thomas Fraser, informed what their scheme for transmission was. They had arranged for 'a Horse Express from
Marlborough to London to go the whole distance at the rate
of thirteen miles an hour for six guineas'. If they are as
fortunate in 'laying chaise horses' from Bristol to Marlborough
the packet should reach town by seven. He and Beard are
'working together sharply' and were expecting to sit up all
night.

> As all papers have arranged to leave Bristol the moment
> Russell is down . . . one of us will go to Marlborough in the
> chaise with one *Herald* man and the other remain at Bristol
> with the other *Herald* man to conclude the account for the
> next day. The *Times* has ordered a chaise and four for the
> whole distance, so there is every prospect of beating them
> hollow.[1]

And the result was that the *Chronicle* could print three and a
half columns of the speech the following morning and this
was noted by the *Spectator* as 'a feat'. The occasion coped
with was a dinner to Lord John Russell on November 10.
In another letter (ante-dated by Forster by six months)
written from the Bush Inn, Bristol, he stated that a full
account of the Bath dinner of November 17 should reach the
office two days later.

[1] 50. I. N.L.

In the last week of May 1836 he was sent to report O'Connell's speech at Ipswich. There he stayed at the Suffolk Hotel and the whole episode is said to be incorporated in Eatanswill, but then the same is said of other political episodes in which he took part.

The wear and tear of these gallopades caused Dickens to indent for broken hats, broken luggage, and damage to clothes from wax candles guttering during transcription *en route*. He always found his employers 'great gentlemen' in meeting his claims. Whenever he arrived in London after a reporting tour he would be welcomed by an admiring editor in 'the broadest of Scotch accents from the broadest of hearts'. He would say 'Dear old Black, my first out and out appreciator. . . . It was John Black that flung the slipper after me!'

If Dickens can be said to have had a favourite political hero it would be Lord John, for by dint of reporting his speeches both inside and outside the House he had conceived a great respect for him. For one thing he was a consistent advocate of educational reform and always struck Dickens as speaking on this subject with intelligence and conviction. Somewhere they met and talked and a kind of friendship was engendered which later on ripened into mutual confidence. One night, years later, Dickens dined with Lord John and aired his views about the Lord's Day Observance Act, 'giving them a little truth about Sunday that was like bringing a Sebastopol battery among the polite company'. Dickens's views on Sunday observance had always been continental and by now he was convinced that the type of religion to which the poor English had been obliged to sacrifice theatre-going and much innocent enjoyment must be to say the least of it defective. Meyerbeer, another guest, burst out, 'Ah mon ami illustre! que c'est noble de vous entendre parler d'haute voix morale à la table d'un ministre!'

In December 1835, while watching a by-election at Kettering, Dickens wrote to John Macrone,[1] 'If you could see the beastly swine who wallow in the public-houses down here under the denomination of Conservatives, you would renounce your creed for ever'. In their convivial moments the people of the place seemed to him 'perfect savages'.

> If a foreigner were brought here on a first visit to an English town, to form his estimate of the national character, I am quite satisfied he would return forthwith to France, and never set foot in England again. The remark will apply in greater or less degree to all agricultural places during the pendency of an election, but beastly as the electors usually are, these men are superlative blackguards. Would you believe that a large body of horsemen mounted and armed, who galloped on a defenceless crowd yesterday, striking about them in all directions and protecting a man who cocked a loaded pistol, were led by clergymen and magistrates?[1]

Escaping the mob for an hour or two, he walked up the Boughton avenue to inspect the house and pacify his temper.

The opening by Lord Melbourne of the Licensed Victuallers' School in Kennington was reported by Dickens about a month before he accepted the *Pickwick* contract which brought the end of journalistic work in its wake. In June 1836 we find him writing to Macrone: 'I am tired to death to-night, though I have been in bed all day. Melbourne *v.* Norton has played the devil with me.' The reporting of this sensational trial was his last job for the *Morning Chronicle*. It took place in the Court of Common Pleas at Westminster on June 22 (now a lawn to the west of Westminster Hall where the statue of Cromwell stands) and was tried before Lord Chief Justice Tindal. Captain Norton, who brought the action for criminal conversation against Lord Melbourne, the Prime Minister, had as counsel Sir William Follett,[2] and Lord Melbourne's defence was conducted by the Attorney-General, Sir John Campbell. Dickens's great friend, Serjeant Talfourd, was in court, having been retained in support of the

---

[1] *Mr. and Mrs. Charles Dickens*, p. 44.
[2] Solicitor-General in the Peel administration of 1835.

defendant's counsel. Mrs. Norton made a tensely observed entry on the arm of Samuel Rogers.

The court was packed with men and women of fashion some of whom had given five or ten guineas for a seat. It was believed that compromising letters would be read and the lives of the great exposed in all their deceit and littleness. It turned out to be a disgusting case based not on Lord Melbourne's correspondence, but on the evidence of servants. Lady Blessington's comment to Countess Guiccioli is to the point: 'Nothing can be more calculated to strike at the root of morals than the vile system in England of bringing forward discharged servants, often of bad character, to give evidence against their mistresses'.[1] Stories were told of Mrs. Norton painting and powdering herself up to receive her lover's visits at the house with two entrances, one in Birdcage Walk and the other in Prince's Court, of Lord Melbourne's afternoon calls lasting from three to six, of his visits to her bedroom, of her disarray, of her visits to him in South Street. No other evidence was brought by the plaintiff, and when in cross-examination the witnesses called were shown to be themselves of low moral character the case crumbled. Sir William Follett asked his client whether he had ever escorted his wife to Lord Melbourne's door, and when Captain Norton admitted that he had done so, Follett told him it was the end of the action. No witnesses were called for the defence, and the jury without leaving the court at 11.50 P.M. declared Lord Melbourne acquitted of the charges brought against him. The verdict was received by the House of Commons that night with acclamation. The nauseous and trivial evidence dragged out by the plaintiff's counsel sickens us as no doubt it sickened Dickens, but Lord Melbourne had to submit to indecent allegations implying proof of sexual intercourse, evidence such as no newspaper ought to have published then and no newspaper would dream of publishing now even were a judge to-day to allow such questions in open court. Lord Melbourne, who had been Home Secretary in 1833, was

[1] *Letters of Marguerite Blessington*, vol. ii. p. 235.

Prime Minister by 1836 and therefore excellent quarry for a blackmailer, and it seems clear that Captain Norton expected to be bought off with hush money.[1]

Just after the trial Dickens wrote to a friend:

> I see a decent prospect of the House being up at last, and I devoutly hope ere next Session I may make some arrangements which will render its sittings a matter of indifference to me—as the story-books say—for ever after.

The 'arrangements' adumbrated in this letter matured, and in July he was in a position to abandon journalism and shake the dust of Westminster off his shoes. In taking to reporting as a means of keeping himself, Dickens had chosen a job that brought him in touch with a great variety of human beings. The legal types he found sympathetic, but the political or parliamentary types were never congenial. He had spent five years in and out of law offices and law courts, and four years in and out of the House of Commons and up and down the country reporting elections. He made no use of this political experience. The octopus-quality so observable where a legal *entourage* was concerned appeared to desert him, negatived, it would seem, by the make-believe atmosphere of politics. To him political life was a sham—to be escaped from as soon as might be. Dickens told Mrs. J. T. Fields, wife of the Boston publisher, that never since he left the House of Commons as a reporter had he entered it again, and that his hatred of the falseness of the talk and his horror of the bombastic eloquence he had been obliged to record made it impossible for him ever to go there to listen to another speech.

The father of one of his colleagues on the *Morning Chronicle*, William Hazlitt, had also served his turn as a reporter in the House of Commons. He too had been repelled by the somnambulism of the proceedings, and has left these words on record:

> It may appear at first sight that here are a number of persons got together, picked out from the whole nation

---

[1] T. Raikes, *Journal*, vol. ii. p. 387; *Times*, June 25, 1836.

who can speak at all times upon all subjects . . . but the fact is they only repeat the same things over and over on the same subjects. . . . Read over the old debates, they are *mutatis mutandis* as those of yesterday. . . . You serve an apprenticeship to a want of originality, to a suspension of thought and feeling.   You are in a go-cart of prejudices, in a regularly constructed machine of pretexts and precedents . . . there is a House of Commons jargon that must be used by everyone . . . you are hemmed in, stifled, pinioned, pressed to death. . . . Talk of mobs!   Is there any body of people that has this character in a more consummate degree than the House of Commons?[1]

Dickens gave expression to what he really felt about the House of Commons in that strange skit *The Thousand and One Humbugs*, written in early life and tinkered at, brought up to date and published when Palmerston became Prime Minister. Modelled on the *Arabian Nights*, this burlesque shows a Sultan, 'Taxedtaurus' (Fleeced Bull), who has been married scores of times and who in so doing has raised to the dignity of 'Howsa Kummauns' (or Peerless Chatterer) a great variety of beautiful women.   The result of their promotion was uniformly unfortunate for the Sultan.   All proved unfaithful, talkative, idle, extravagant, inefficient and boastful.   And so it came about that a 'Howsa Kummauns' very rarely died a natural death, she was generally cut short in some violent manner.   The youngest and fairest of all the Peerless Chatterers was the lovely 'Reefawm' (Light of Reason). 'Taxedtaurus' had looked to her to recompense him for all his many disappointments, but she turned out quite as unreliable as her predecessors.   The poor Sultan fell into a profound melancholy and wailed, 'Every Howsa Kummauns has deceived me.   Every Howsa Kummauns is a Humbug.   I must slay the present Howsa Kummauns as I have slain so many others.'   His grief so overpowered him that he fainted away. At this juncture the glib vizier, 'Parmarstoon' (or Twirling Weathercock) tried to console him by introducing to the

[1] *Hazlitt's Selected Essays*, p. 551.

harem his lovely daughter 'Hansardadade'. Preceded by 'Mistaspeeka', the black mute, chief of the Seraglio, she entered the presence, and taking a one-stringed lute sang a lengthy song in prose. Its purport was, 'I am the recorder of brilliant eloquence, I am the chronicler of patriotism, I am the pride of sages, and the joy of nations. The continued salvation of the country is owing to what I preserve and without it there would be no business done.

> Sweet are the voices of the crow and chough
> And Persia never, never, never can have words enough.'

At the conclusion of this delightful strain, the Sultan and the whole divan were so faint with rapture that they remained in a comatose state for seven hours.

Dickens in telling *The Story of the Talkative Barber* pokes fun at all the stock performances he had witnessed from the Gallery. The barber dances the dance of 'Mistapit', sings the song of 'Mistafoks' and jokes the joke of 'Jomillah'. He even proceeds to improvise impertinent verse:

> When Britteen first at Heaven's command
> Arose from out the azure main
> This was the charter of the land
> And guardian angels sang this strain:
> Singing, as first Lord was a wallerking the Office-garding around
> No end of born barbers he picked up and found,
> Says he I will load them with silvier and gold,
> For the country's a donkey, and as such is sold.

A significant light is thrown on Dickens by this burlesque, which shows that he deliberately preferred to make war on what he conceived as shams by appealing to the Englishman's sense of humour rather than to his judgment and deliberative faculties. And the shrewd Americans, apprehending this, were the first to hail him as a reformer who had done more in his short life to better the condition of the downtrodden than the whole of the House of Commons put together.

It is evident from his letters as well as from this skit that Dickens was totally unimpressed by the accomplishments of

the Reform Ministry which claimed as its 'chief glory' the
Poor Law, the Poor Law with its simple invention of hiding
up poverty and its magic formula 'No out-door relief'. How
long, he wondered, would the helpless people of England put
up with the barmecidal feast set before them? In all the
hundreds of columns transcribed for the *Mirror* and the
Chronicle, on Canada, the West Indies, the Game Laws, Hill
Coolies, the Irish Question, Dogcarts and the rest, was there
any mention of the condition-of-England question? It was
plain to him that Parliament, so far as England was concerned,
had for decades undertaken the adjustment of one thing and
one alone, itself and its own interests, leaving domestic
interests to rub along as best they could. It was high time
that the do-nothing-for-the-people routine should be ended,
for to carry the eighteenth century over into the nineteenth
must sooner or later provoke a revolution.

At the time Dickens left the Gallery he had not met Carlyle
who had arrived at similar conclusions by quite different
paths. Carlyle had welcomed the Reform Bill till he found
it in no way affected the existing form of society with its
extremes of poverty and wealth. Prosperity only made the
rich richer and the poor poorer. The 'huge damp putrid
mass' remained rotting and would continue to rot if men had
to depend on an extended suffrage to clean it up. There was
a right way and a wrong way to do things, and it was absurd
to suppose that the right way of organising a people could be
ascertained by a majority of votes any more than could the
cultivation of the soil, the maintenance of public health or the
promotion of public education.

De Quincey draws a distinction between the literature of
Knowledge and the literature of Power. The function of the
first is to teach; the function of the second is to move. The
first appeals to the intellect and the second to the heart and the
emotions, and from this point of view it is not the understanding, but the understanding heart that matters. It is not
so much the subject in itself that affects us as the treatment of
it, the charging of it with humanly generated electricity. No

better illustration of this contention can be brought forward than that of Mrs. Trollope's novel on the factory child, *Michael Armstrong*. Informative, didactic, derived from official reports and intended to influence opinion, it neither interested nor moved anyone, whereas the story of the parish boy, Oliver Twist, not only moved every reader, but left on their minds an indelible impression. As Dickens's friend Gilbert à Beckett said, 'There is something feminine about Dickens that leads him to the core of the heart of the situation in hand'.

If it were not for the literature of Power, justice, for example, might remain an ideal whereas in a book it may germinate into vitalising activity. The commonest novel, by moving in alliance with human fears and hopes, with human instincts of right and wrong, sustains and quickens those affections, and working by deep agencies rescues them from torpor. Dim in origin, these emotions welled up like hidden springs in Dickens and influenced his whole being as may the forgotten incidents of childhood.

Chapter 4

THE UNDERTOW

The muffled majesty of authorship.
HENRY JAMES

IN the professions it is always possible to change roles: a soldier may become a company promoter or a lawyer a politician, but in the deeper vocational life that calls for the emission of power duality is abolished, for an artist is inwardly compelled to be true to himself and his purpose whatever it may be. Charles Dickens had chosen by profession to become a shorthand expert and worked so hard in the process that he soon topped the list of political reporters, giving his colleagues the impression that his whole mind was set on excelling them. This is the measure of his tremendous will, a will that seems to have operated in retarding his vocational instincts and forcing his attention to external achievement. For a man whose tendency was to emotionalise all experience it must have been a struggle to turn himself into the perfect, passionless recorder of other men's utterances and to win commendation for accuracy and speed.

After working for over a year in the Gallery, Charles Dickens began to set things down, as they struck him, in a very simple, handy, even ordinary way. Like many of the people who possess in a strong degree the story-telling faculty, his work showed a relish for the commoner stuff of human nature. He called these jottings 'Sketches'. They were to begin with snapshots of actual people and actual occurrences, and then were given the humorous twist which became their leading characteristic. Amusing to write, they made him forget the drudgery of perpetual shorthand. Many young authors have had their first work rejected, so it was without any particular feeling of optimism that he pushed one of his 'Sketches' anonymously into the letter-box of the *Monthly*

Magazine in Johnson's Court, Fleet Street.

The *Monthly Magazine* or *British Register* had just changed owners, having been bought for £300 by a Captain Holland from South America. Only one number had appeared under the new editorship so its files were unlikely to be cluttered up with old manuscripts. On his way to the House late one afternoon Dickens stepped into Chapman and Hall's double-fronted shop, 186 Strand, and spent half a crown on the December number to find that it contained his 'Sketch', *A Dinner in Poplar Walk*. Too excited and upset to feel pleasure in the discovery, he wrote asking for Mrs. Kolle's verdict, 'I am so dreadfully nervous that my hand shakes to such an extent as to prevent my writing a word legibly'. With tears in his eyes he walked into Westminster Hall to master his emotion before going into the Gallery. The undertow had made itself felt powerfully for the first time, the undertow that was to surge up and sweep away his avocational life. Hugging his secret from all but the Kolles, he quickly followed up his first success by pushing six other 'Sketches' into the same letter-box, content to be for the time being unpaid and unrecognised. He soon made acquaintance with Captain Holland and found that it was an understood thing among writers that contributions to his magazine were never at this time paid for. The editor had made it clear to aspirants for fame that as he was fresh from the Bolivar campaigns in South America, and had no financial reserves, he could only serve youthful authors by giving them a chance to see themselves in print. If they liked to avail themselves of the publicity he offered, it might advantage them as well as the public at large. The authors chose to write for him and Captain Holland soon managed to build up a reputation for the magazine and was able in the autumn of 1835 to sell it at a profit.

Dickens soon became confident that he could write what people wanted to read, but it was not till August 1834 that he ventured to set up a second personality and sign himself 'Boz', a nickname derived from his young adenoidal brother,

Augustus, who answered in the family to the name of Moses and called himself 'Boses'. When he let John Black and George Hogarth into his secret, they at once offered to place some 'Sketches' in the *Morning Chronicle*, and on September 26, 1834, the first of four London *Street Sketches* was printed in their paper. These articles were widely read and attracted the notice of editors on the look-out for new writers. Albany Fonblanque of the *Examiner* liked them and so did S. C. Hall of the *New Monthly*. Best of all, William Jerdan of the *Literary Gazette* approved of them and at this time a laudatory notice in the *Literary Gazette* would sell an edition of any book. It stood alone (1820–40) as the arbiter of fame, literary and artistic, till the *Athenaeum* under Dilke rose and killed it.

At last Charles Dickens could savour the kind of approval his whole being craved for, recognition as an author, which was something very different in quality from the kudos attaching to professional reporting. He now undertook any job of work that might help him to get known in the sphere he meant to make his own, writing dramatic critiques for plays at the Adelphi and Olympic Theatres, and correcting the proofs of *Journies through France and Italy*[1] to oblige Macrone. Universally obliging and untiring, he did not at first ask for payment for his *Street Sketches* in the *Morning Chronicle*, but earned merit from his employers by throwing them in for his five-guinea wage as a reporter. Having, however, created a demand for his work he could, when the *Evening Chronicle*[2] was launched under the editorship of George Hogarth, offer as one of its regular features *Sketches of London* and thus extract from the management another two guineas a week. Some twenty *Sketches* dealing with London were published in this way. He also, as a sideline, contributed twelve *Scenes and Characters* to *Bell's Life in London* under the hush-hush name of Tibbs. No one but Robert Smith Surtees was doing quite this sort of work and there can

[1] By William Thomson, uncle of Mrs. George Hogarth.
[2] January 31, 1835.

be no doubt that Dickens profited greatly from reading Mr. Jorrocks's adventures at Ramsgate, Herne Bay and other places, which had been coming out in the *New Sporting Magazine* for three years. They were technically far in advance of anything he could at the time accomplish. Surtees, however, though he wrote well within the compass of the un-educated reader, was never a serious competitor with his younger contemporary, partly owing to the fact that his medium of publication circulated exclusively in clubs and country house, partly because his preoccupation with field sports appealed particularly to the richer sections of society, and partly because he left London to live in the north of England in 1834. For these reasons, if for no others, the more vulgar and universal publicity of the *Sketches* was denied to his *Jaunts and Jollities*.

In the Gallery it soon leaked out that the star reporter, Charles Dickens, was really 'Boz' of the *Sketches*, and presently authors began to take notice of this new recruit to their ranks. Harrison Ainsworth, who had read his articles as they came out, was the first professional writer to invite him to his house as a fellow author. Ainsworth was seven years older than Dickens and in a miniature, feline way very handsome; women called him the Antinous of literature. He had come to London from Manchester in 1824 to finish his legal education at the Inner Temple. In London he got to know John Ebers, publisher, and manager of Covent Garden, married Fanny Ebers in 1826 and began business as a publisher himself. Having brought out a book for Mrs. Norton and a cookery manual by Ude, he gave the job up and sat down at The Elms, Kilburn, to write *Rookwood*. By the time Dickens got to know him he was separated from his wife and with his little girls was living with a Mrs. le Touchet and her sister at Kensal Lodge, near the scattered village of Willesden. Mrs. le Touchet, a hunting woman from Cheshire, used to quiz the Cockney horsemen who visited Ainsworth. Dickens, to avoid her critical eye, would mount and dismount out of sight. After the sensational success won by *Rookwood* the Lodge became a literary rallying-point with many writers flocking to its pleasant Sunday afternoon parties. Ainsworth's publisher was Macrone, a Manxman, with business premises at 3 St. James's Square. He and Dickens met one day at the Lodge and took a great fancy to each other. As they walked towards London together it pleased Dickens to find that Macrone, too, was bound for Furnival's Inn. Almost at once we find him volunteering to help Macrone with proofs and being told in return that his *Sketches* were 'capital value' and ought to be gathered into a volume. It was also suggested that George Cruikshank, with whom they had been talking at Kensal Lodge, should illustrate the *Sketches*. This was a highly complimentary suggestion, for this fine draughtsman and cartoonist had made a great name for himself and was twenty years older than Dickens. Co-operation with such a distinguished man would certainly insure the commercial success of the *Sketches*.

John Macrone, whose publishing career was almost as ephemeral as Captain Holland's, was a sociable young man of a certain charm who borrowed money from his fiancée, Sophie Sala, to promote his business, then threw her over and married somebody else. At the time Dickens made his acquaintance he was handling a book by the American author Nat Willis, an amusing fellow commissioned by the *New York Mirror* to report on Europe. Willis, who had reached England on June 1, 1834, had at once begun to pay court to the women writers. Jane Porter liked him and Mary Russell Mitford said he was 'more like one of the best of our Peers' sons than a rough republican'. It is no wonder that he made this silky impression as in character he was something between a d'Orsay and an Oscar Wilde. To J. G. Lockhart, for whom a 'society reporter was little better than a spy', he was a bugbear. Lockhart vented his spleen on Willis in the *Quarterly* by citing him as 'an example of a man creeping into your home and before your claret is dry upon his lips describing table-talk and guests for an American paper'. In

MR BOZ   MR TINTO   M^r MAC.   Mr PROUT.

Dickens, Thackeray, Maclise, and Mahony conferring together at Macrone's publishing office in St. James's Square. A sketch made by Thackeray in 1837

spite of J. G.'s strictures Willis was made welcome by the
ladies of the greater country houses of England and Scotland,
and petted to such an extent that, though always maintaining
his native American shrewdness, he became even more
dandified and conceited than when he arrived. Macrone
hobnobbed a good deal with him when he was bringing out
his 'Letters' and one day offered to take him to see his new
friend 'Boz', who was the author of some rather clever
pictures of London life published from time to time in the
Morning or *Evening Chronicle*.

It is from Nat Willis that we get a really unaffected vignette
of Charles Dickens at this time. Some Dickensians have
tried to demolish the story and to pretend Willis never saw
him, because it seems they do not think the account reflects
credit on their hero. They are the same critics who deny the
validity of Dickens's liaison with Ellen Ternan, being themselves unable to reconcile it with their preconception of his
character. Almost as soon as Dickens had settled into his
three-pair-back at Furnival's Inn,[1] he received a visit from the
American *littérateur*, who described 'the young paragraphist'
for the benefit of his fellow countrymen. He told how
Macrone had driven him from St. James's Square to Holborn
and had pulled up at the entrance of some buildings used for
lawyer's chambers, not far from the door of the Bull and
Mouth Inn. This area is that now covered by the Prudential
insurance offices, a vast pseudo-Gothic structure of red brick
wherein, under the vaulting on the left of the gateway, a small
bust of Dickens cowers.

In Dickens's day it presented a façade of pale brick broken
by stucco pilasters and cornice built round three sides of a
courtyard, the whole being known as Furnival's Inn. After
following Macrone up a long flight of stairs, Willis found
himself ushered into 'an uncarpeted and bleak-looking room
with a deal table, two or three chairs and a few books, a small
boy and Mr. Dickens for the contents'. This 'three-pair-
back' was indeed a contrast to his own luxurious apartment

[1] January 1835.

in New York, which was graced at all seasons by singing
birds and hothouse flowers.   Quickly this observer glanced
around, noting that even the journalist's clothes betrayed his
poverty.   As they entered he was changing rapidly from a
ragged office coat to a blue surtout and stood 'collarless and
buttoned up before them', overpowered, as Willis assumed,
by the honour of his publisher's visit.   It was, as he said
afterwards, the strongest instance he had seen of 'English
obsequiousness to employers'.   This interpretation of
Dickens's obvious embarrassment was of course nonsense.
Dickens was never socially embarrassed.   Macrone, however,
had broken in on him at a bad moment, the moment at which
he had handed over all the cash he could raise to his father
at Sloman's sponging-house, the moment in which he had
resolved to adopt his young brother Frederick, postpone his
furnishing, and give up all idea of a house-warming.

As Nat Willis seated himself on one of the two chairs in the
room he said to himself, 'My good fellow, if your were in
America with that fine face and your ready quill you would
have no need to be condescended to by a publisher'.   Though
neither Macrone nor Willis knew just why Dickens's room
was so comfortless and his manner so constrained, they would
have been even more mystified if they could have had a pre-
view of this same young man in seven years' time installed in
a luxury suite in the Tremont Hotel at Boston with all the
distinguished folk of America competing to pay him homage.

Presently at Macrone's instigation Dickens began to
assemble his *Sketches* and discuss their publication in volume
form.   He will write as many more as are required to make a
good volume, he can describe anything Macrone thinks ought
to be described.   He has visited the House of Correction at
Coldbath Fields and has begged Black 'to get old Alderman
Wood' to take him to Newgate. . . . 'I have long projected
sketching its interior and I think it would sell extremely well.'
He has memoranda by him for 'The Cook's Shop', 'Bedlam',
'The Prisoner's Van', 'The Streets—Noon and Night',

'Banking Houses', 'Covent Garden', 'Hospitals' and 'Lodging
Houses'.   He thanks Macrone for his belief that he will write
a successful book and approves his choice of Cruikshank as
illustrator.   He is still working hard at reporting, as we may
see from a note written November 7, 1835, in which he says
that he cannot keep his appointment with Cruikshank as he is
off to Bristol.   He is shivering with cold and writing by
candlelight, the kettle will not boil, it is foggy, there are no
cabs on the stand, he must shoulder his portmanteau and be
off to catch the coach.

On his return he found that though George Hogarth had
completed his proof-correcting for him, Cruikshank had not
yet delivered the illustrations.   Cruikshank was altogether
too dilatory, he told Macrone, and must be prodded: the list
of illustrations and frontispieces should be sent to him with
all possible dispatch.   There seems to have been a scramble
in getting the book out, but it was not altogether Cruikshank's fault.   Dickens found *The Visit to Newgate* 'a very
difficult subject'; he could not work himself up to the requisite
pitch about it, and it was not till November 20 that he got
it off to the printer.   In December we find him going over
Coldbath Fields again in order to put vigour into *The House
of Correction*.   Comparing it with *Newgate* he observed, 'the
treadmill will not interest men like the gallows'.   Macrone
praised his melodramatic sketch *The Black Veil*, so did Ainsworth, and so did another publisher, and this appreciation went
to fortify the young author's belief in his creative faculty.
Private interests were constantly impinged on by reporting
assignments from the *Chronicle*.   In December he was sent
to Hatfield to cover a fire, and writing thence to Catharine
Hogarth from the Salisbury Arms, says, 'Here I am waiting
until the remains of the Marchioness of Salisbury are dug from
the ruins of her ancestor's castle.   I went over the place this
morning and shall "flare" briefly in the *Chronicle* to-morrow.'

To Furnival's Inn soon after Christmas 1835 came a partner
of the newly-formed publishing firm of Chapman and Hall.

It seemed to 'Boz' like the visit of an angel, for in young Mr. Hall he recognised the man who had two years earlier sold him the copy of the *Monthly Magazine* containing his first printed story. The unforgettable moment in which he knew himself, first, last and all the time, an author, came surging back. Mr. Hall explained that he had come on the recommendation of Charles Whitehead, editor of their Library of Fiction, to ask for more work on the lines already contributed by Mr. Dickens to this series, notably *The Tuggs's at Ramsgate* and *A Little Talk about Spring*. Mr. Dickens's heart bounded in his breast and was only quietened by the nature of the proposals made to him. The new series were to be continuous in character. Mr. Hall's firm could assure this continuity by providing illustrations of a sporting character which it would be Mr. Dickens's task to link together. Sport? Mr. Dickens jibbed at the word, he knew nothing of sport and anyway could only write on subjects chosen by himself. Mr. Hall was persuasive; his firm had already published a little book, the *Squib Annual*, with plates by Seymour, and Seymour would like to do 'something superior on the same line' to illustrate the mishaps and adventures of a band of amateur sportsmen who had formed themselves into a Nimrod Club. It was not an engaging vista to Mr. Dickens, only the money offered, £14 a month plus additional payment on sales, made him so much as consider it, but 'the emolument was too tempting to resist' and we shall presently see the reason for his decision.

About the same time James Grant, newly made editor of the *Monthly Magazine*, wrote to ask the price of contributions by Mr. Dickens. The author replied that he was pledged to Chapman and Hall for a monthly serial, but would write 'Sketches' for him at eight guineas a sheet. This was a moderate charge as Grant knew well, since for similar work he was himself getting ten guineas a sheet from Captain Marryat of the *Metropolitan Magazine*, and twenty guineas a sheet from the *Penny Cyclopaedia*. Moderate as the fee demanded was, the proprietors, rather to Grant's annoyance, refused to sanction the outlay. He thought it extremely short-sighted of them.

As the time for launching his first book drew near Dickens began to worry about publicity. How soon can he count on Macrone for sending first advertisements to the *Chronicle?* 'I can hardly begin to puff it till then.' But when it actually comes to drafting a notice of the *Sketches*, it turned itself into a modest little paragraph, for, like every other artist invited to praise his own work, he shied off doing it, pleading, 'I really *cannot* do tremendous puffing of myself'. Two days later we find him condoling with 'poor Macrone' on the death of his baby, and a week later again trying to get Cruikshank to hand in his last illustration. The book appeared on Dickens's twenty-fourth birthday: its full title was *Sketches by Boz. Illustrative of Every Day Life and Every Day People.*[1]

The reviews caused the author's heart to flutter. George Hogarth, who had corrected the proofs, likened his style to that of Washington Irving 'in his happiest hours', and said that the most remarkable sketch in the volume, *The Visit to Newgate*, was reminiscent of Victor Hugo's *Dernier Jour d'un Condamné*, thus in a skilful way setting Dickens in the gallery of great contemporaries. The *Literary Gazette* praised the book, so did the *Satirist* and the *Athenaeum*. John Forster reviewed it in the *Examiner*, and the *Sun, Sunday Times* and *Sunday Herald* noticed it favourably. It was particularly gratifying to the author that the *Morning Post* should commend it under 'Literature'.

A copy was sent to Lord Stanley, who had been one of the first to recognise how unusual were Dickens's capacity and intelligence. Reminding him of the report he had taken down from his own mouth on the Irish Disturbances Bill, the author humbly placed the *Sketches* at his feet, begging him to accept the volume as a mark of admiration. Thomas Noon Talfourd also received a copy of the book.

Dickens had first met Serjeant Talfourd when he was law reporter for the *Times* and in 1835 had watched him take his

[1] 2 vols. duodecimo at one guinea. February 1836.

seat as member for his native town of Reading. He was extremely lucky to have his friendship, for everyone of the date testifies to Talfourd's charm, sincerity and generosity and to his desire to do right before God and man. He had a special weakness for writers and therefore took Charles Dickens under his wing socially, introducing him both to Lady Blessington and Lady Holland, and engineering his early election to the Athenaeum. Talfourd's clerk used to say that half his time was employed in preventing the Serjeant from giving away the hat off his head or the watch from his pocket. Author of *The Memorials of Lamb*, he made a hobby of playwriting. Miss Mitford, who thought his talk 'dazzling', one day took Byron's friend, William Harness, to listen to it. The clergyman was amused by the talk but even more amused to find that Mr. and Mrs. Talfourd's devotion to cats was such that they sat at dinner each with a cat on their knees.

Everyone with any literary pretentions wrote plays at this time just as in Scott's day everyone wrote ballads, and Talfourd had *Ion* and *The Athenian Captive* (of which he was very vain) to his credit. Bulwer had written *Richelieu*, Browning *Strafford*, Miss Mitford *Rienzi* and *Otto of Wittelsbach*. Macready, to whom most of these dramas were submitted, used to groan at the time he was forced to spend on 'the unprofitable labour' of reading them. An entry in his diary in May 1835 complains of being 'reduced to despair' by three acts of a play by his dear friend, Agnes Strickland. Even when he did light on something actable he had to doctor it into acting shape. This process was not popular with authors. *Ion* was one of the plays made over in this way. Miss Mitford tells that she was staying with the Talfourds for the first night at Drury Lane. It happened to follow a fiftynight run of her own *Rienzi*. To Talfourd's annoyance *Ion* got a bad notice in the *Times*, and when his guest tried to console him by saying that if the same strictures had been made upon *Rienzi* she would not have minded, he exclaimed testily, 'Your *Rienzi* indeed! I daresay not. That is very different.' *Ion* in the end turned out a box office success and Miss Mitford, who could on occasion be as tart as Macready, says that it quite turned Talfourd's head and indeed he gloated over it for the rest of his life. One summer evening at Broadstairs years later Dickens and Rogers were talking together and Dickens remarked, 'We shall have Talfourd here to-night.' Rogers asked, 'Why? Is he here?' to which Dickens replied, '*Ion* is to be acted at Margate and he is never absent from any of its representations.'

We shall meet Talfourd at book dinners and over the copyright bill, but to clinch the impression that he was a good friend to Charles Dickens in early days it may be well here to quote Dickens's words spoken at the time of his death in 1854:

> The hand that lays this poor flower on his grave was a mere boy's when he first clasped it—newly come from the work in which he himself had begun life—and little used to the plough it has followed since—obscure enough with much to correct and learn. Each of its successive tasks through many intervening years has been cheered by his warmest interest and the friendship then begun ripened to maturity in the passage of time.

Another man who turns up in Dickens's life at this time is Edward Marjoribanks, a partner in Coutts's about whose relationship with Dickens little has been recorded except that it was to him that Dickens applied for letters of credit to the United States. Marjoribanks, however, proved a very important factor in Dickens's life, for it was he who invited the young author to dinner late in 1835[1] to meet Miss Angela Burdett, so soon to be known to the world as Miss Burdett Coutts, the great heiress.

Angela was the fifth daughter of Sir Francis Burdett, member for Westminster, a girl who had been brought up in the society of Rogers, Moore and Disraeli at home, and abroad had studied under foreign masters and had met

[1] *Letters of Charles Dickens to Baroness Burdett Coutts*, p. 29.

leaders of advanced opinion on the continent. Eager to learn
and eager to meet rising authors and philanthropists, she
never till the end of her long life considered her education
completed. Of his first meeting with Miss Burdett Dickens
wrote, 'It must have been on a Friday, for I was born on a
Friday and never began a book or began anything of interest
to me or done anything of importance to me, but it was on a
Friday'. Angela Burdett, a demure slip of a girl with deep-
set eyes, was twenty-one at the time she met Charles Dickens,
and he was twenty-three; they took to each other at once.
In a flash there was established between them a profound
and faithful friendship that manifested itself in a life-long
correspondence. Dickens's understanding of her and her at
first romantic idealisation of him may have contributed to her
decision not to marry till she was an old woman. Though
no touch of sentiment has been allowed to seep into the
selection of letters published, there is evidence that for many
years she relied on him for advice in personal matters and for
guidance in the direction of her often original and immense
benefactions. With Charles Dickens she planned to reclaim
slums, to rescue girls from a life of shame, to educate children,
and to humanise the lives of those degraded by grinding
poverty. In Angela Burdett Charles Dickens recognised a
heart aflame with indignation against existing social conditions. As a natural humanitarian she found in Dickens her
complementary self and a genius who, though she had no
inkling of it, had in his own soul experienced the searing fate
of the social outcast.

CHARLES DICKENS, AGED 25
by Samuel Laurence

CATHARINE HOGARTH BEFORE
HER MARRIAGE
by Daniel Maclise, R.A.

CATHARINE DICKENS SIX
YEARS LATER
by Daniel Maclise, R.A.

Chapter 5

MARRIAGE AND OTHER MATTERS

Life is all a variorum.
ROBERT BURNS

To try and understand how a sensitive human being comes to respond to the promptings of a mercurial and complex nature is in itself intensely interesting. Charles Dickens, almost over-eager to lead a completely adult life, marry, and set up a family, being cast adrift by his first love, fell easily into the company of a circle of sisters, the daughters of George Hogarth, with whom he came in daily contact on the *Chronicle*. Only one of the Miss Hogarths was old enough to be marriageable and to her he paid his court. Three of these young ladies were as alike as chestnuts; they were small, sweet, and pretty in a general rather characterless way. So unindividualised were they that when Dickens came to feel he could love every one of them in turn, one is not at all surprised. On becoming engaged to Catharine Hogarth, or 'Kate' as he called her, he ordered as betrothal gift a miniature of himself by Rose Drummond [1] and, in order to see as much as possible of his future wife's relations, took rooms at Selwood Place close to 18 York Place, Fulham Road, where the Hogarths had their home, and startled them all by appearing, dressed as a sailor, outside their window dancing a hornpipe with immense gusto, an accomplishment acquired at Wellington House. George Hogarth was an Edinburgh man, a Writer to the Signet, who had what, even by Victorian standards, would be called 'a long family' comprising fourteen children. Mrs. Hogarth and the elder girls spoke with a Scotch accent. During a discussion on Eve in the Garden of Eden his daughter Catharine is reported to have said, 'Eh,

[1] Rose Drummond, said to be the original for Miss La Creevy in *Nicholas Nickleby*.

mon, it would be nae temptation to me to gae rinning about a gairden stark naked ating green apples.'

Catharine has been described by a woman friend as pretty, plump and fresh-coloured with 'the large heavy-lidded blue eyes so much admired by men'. A slightly *retroussé* nose, good forehead, red rosebud mouth and receding chin completed a physiognomy which was animated from time to time by a sweet smile. Daniel Maclise, who was in love with her as a girl, painted a charming portrait before marriage and made two pictures of her as a married woman at the ages of twenty-six and thirty years.

Quiet, silent and unenterprising, Catharine had dull friends, and as she never developed the social gift of discriminating between one person and another essential to intelligent intercourse, she was incapable later on of playing her part as celebrity's wife. None of these things seemed to matter at the time she married, though in the long run her inadequacy in these respects became a kind of grievance. Charles was not unduly worried by her persistently low spirits, for the warm welcome extended to him by the entire family more than made up for any coolness on her part at this time. It seems improbable that she was ever really in love, for there is no sign in her of the *élan* proper to young persons in that state. Early in the engagement, which lasted for about a year, the lover wrote, after spending an evening in her company:

My dear Catherine,

It is with the greatest pain that I sit down before I go to bed to-night, to say one word which can bear the appearance of unkindness or reproach; But I owe a duty to myself as well as to you, and as I am wild enough to think that an engagement of even three weeks might pass without any such display as you have favoured me with twice already, I am the more strongly induced to discharge it.

The sudden and uncalled for coldness with which you treated me before I left last night surprised and deeply hurt me—surprised because I could not have believed that such sullen and inflexible obstinacy could exist in the breast of any girl in whose heart love had found a place; and hurt me because I feel for you far more than I have ever professed, and feel a slight from you more than I can tell.[1]

Kate must often have suffered from depression for we find him writing, 'I hope you will not get low again' and 'you are in better spirits than yesterday I hope?' Charles had spirits enough for two, but it was uphill work making this lethargic, unimaginative girl understand just how hard he was working and how anxious he was to make their future secure. 'You know that my composition is peculiar . . . and that I never can write till I have got my steam up or . . . until I have become so excited with my subject that I cannot leave off.' His 'dearest Mouse' and 'dearest Life' is exacting and seems incapable of understanding the claims of his profession. One night he writes that he must stay at home, he has not produced sufficient copy to justify him in going out. 'If the representations I have so often made to you, be not sufficient to keep you in good humour . . . why then my dear you must be out of humour, and there is no help for it.' These words, written three weeks before the marriage day, show that Kate had learnt nothing during their long engagement.

Charles had formed for himself an ideal picture of home, of a fireside presided over by a kind and gentle wife, and he thanks God for the many opportunities he will have in the future of showing Kate how unjustly she had judged him, and of convincing her that his pursuits and labours were not selfish and that her advancement and happiness was the mainspring of them all. When Kate complained of her health he almost snapped, 'I hope your cold is better and that you have no other complaint bodily or mental'. Surely it should have been proof of devotion enough that her lover should sit with her daily when she took the scarlet fever though he fully believed he could not escape catching it from her, but it was little to her credit that she should have let him run so grave a risk. In writing of Dickens some authors have accounted

[1] W. Dexter, *Mr. and Mrs. Charles Dickens*, p. 1.

for the final break in the marriage by saying that he married in haste, but, as his letters show, he did not marry in haste. He married after a most deliberate and long-drawn courtship.

As soon as his earnings warranted it, Charles Dickens applied for a special marriage licence which, as every reader of *Pickwick* knows, was to be obtained from the Vicar-General's office in Doctors' Commons. It consisted of a highly flattering address on parchment from the Archbishop of Canterbury to his 'trusty and well-beloved Charles Huffam Dickens and Catharine Hogarth' enabling them to be married at any time or place without banns. Lord Byron in his day had made use of a similar licence in order to avoid a fashionable wedding. The ceremony was fixed for Easter at the vast new parish church of St. Luke, Chelsea. The bridegroom had asked Macrone to be his best man, but this was disallowed by the ladies as he was not a bachelor. In the end Tom Beard took his place. A faintly literary flavour might have been imparted to the occasion had they been married by the rector, Mr. Kingsley (father of Charles), but it was the curate who made them man and wife.

Two days beforehand Dickens wrote to his uncle Thomas Barrow informing him that 'the great success of his new book' (*Sketches by Boz*) enables him 'to settle at an earlier period' than he had anticipated and that his 'marriage to Miss Hogarth, daughter of the author of the celebrated work on music and intimate friend of Sir Walter Scott', had been fixed 'for midday Saturday the 2nd of April'. We note that the cultural aspect of the connection is stressed as if it must impress his uncle favourably. He would, of course, have liked to introduce his wife to his uncle, but how could he 'married or single visit a relation's house from which his father is excluded'? He continues:

> I should be more happy than I could possibly express if you would place it in my power to know you once again on those terms of intimacy and friendship I so sincerely desire, I hope you will not misunderstand my meaning. I do not ask you—I should conceive that I lowered and

disgraced myself if I did—to alter your determination.   I
might think that time might have softened the determined
animosity. . . . I do not presume to arraign your decision.
Nothing that has occurred to me in my life has given me
greater pain than thus denying myself the society of yourself and aunt.[1]

This letter serves to show that John Dickens was still on the
Barrow black list.   It is possible that he had borrowed money
from them and had never repaid the loan.

The first number of *Pickwick* was published on March 31
and by the evening of April 2 Charles and Kate had arrived
at the little slatted house in Chalk near his dream city of
Rochester.   The honeymoon lasted a week, and Dickens,
who did not care about the country for its own sake and had
never had a complete holiday before, was restless.   He did
his best to amuse Kate by turning a 'Sketch' into a play and
devising a burletta, but he was glad to get back to Furnival's
Inn, glad to begin work on the second number of *Pickwick*
and eager to see how Robert Seymour's illustrations were
turning out.   Tom Beard showed him some of the reviews
of the first number: they were neither flattering nor encouraging, in spite of the fact that the *Pickwick Papers* were in every
way an advance on the *Sketches*.   Confidence in wielding
words and characters now enabled their author to produce
effects of extraordinary richness and variety.   He is sure of
his power of differentiation and is not afraid of handling at
the same time several people of a kind and in the shortest time
individualising them.   Take Mrs. Bardell, for example, and
her two cronies sitting down to a cosy evening over 'pettitoes
and toasted cheese', or Bob Sawyer entertaining his student
friends in Lant Street, scenes that go easily.   Dickens has become a master of men and can get their common comfort and
their fun down on to paper, portraying the kind of enjoyment
and humour that will warm the cockles of all hearts.   Not,
however, till the introduction of Sam Weller in the fifth
number (August 1836) did the circulation leap visibly.   With

[1] 68.   I.   N.L.

Sam Weller, the Sancho Panza to Mr. Pickwick's Quixote, England took these *Papers* to her heart for ever. So far Dickens had not become obviously conscious of a mission. This creeps into the texture of the narrative with the Fleet and the deplorable conditions obtaining there. Indeed the whole book takes on a purposeful character after he had experienced a great personal sorrow. As a presentation of the day-to-day life of his age *Pickwick* is perhaps Dickens's greatest achievement.

Robert Seymour's design for *The Stroller's Tale*, 'The Dying Clown', was not to Dickens's liking, so writing a very polite letter he asked him to make another and to bring it completed to Furnival's Inn the following Sunday. He will invite Chapman and Hall to meet him, and together, over a glass of grog, they can discuss further illustrations. Seymour turned up as requested: the publishers did not. Seymour had not met Dickens previously and now found himself shaking hands with Mrs. Dickens and a young brother of his host. As an established illustrator, with *Figaro in London*, *Humorous Sketches* and the *Book of Christmas* to his credit, he was inclined to stand on his dignity and think that he was being treated in an offhand way by a cocky young fellow who was presuming to teach him his business. Dickens tried to be amiable, but his visitor would insist on pointing out that if there were to be no sporting scenes in *Pickwick* a younger and more adaptable artist would perhaps suit Mr. Dickens better. Seymour was but twelve years the senior of the two but spoke as if the disparity in years was considerable. Vainly did Dickens try to conciliate him; Seymour would have none of it, cut the interview short and left. Two days later Frederick, newspaper in hand, rapped at his brother's door to say that Mr. Seymour had been found shot in his Islington garden. It came out later that Seymour, after working at a new design for *The Stroller's Tale*, had committed suicide. Naturally Dickens was shocked by the occurrence, but it was not the kind of tragedy that moved him deeply and he was too busy finding someone to take Seymour's place to worry over it.

John Jackson, wood engraver working for Chapman and Hall, recommended Robert Buss who had 'never had an etching needle in his hand', but his designs for the third number of *Pickwick* did not please at all. He could neither cope with the philandering of Mr. Tupman nor the cricket-match at Dingley Dell. Cruikshank then recommended John Leech, but he was considered too young, and when Thackeray recommended himself with sample drawings by Mr. Michael Angelo Titmarsh tucked under his arm, he also was turned down as unsuitable. In the end Hablot Browne, aged twenty, was produced by Jackson. Dickens took an immediate fancy to him, he became 'Phiz' of the fourth number and was to prove a most congenial partner for 'Boz'.

Work for the *Morning Chronicle* had still to be coped with. A Bill for the stricter observance of Sunday (sponsored by Sir Andrew Agnew) was reported at this time by Dickens. Edward Bulwer spoke most strongly against the bill, arguing that there was no warrant for Sabbatarianism in Scripture—and that it was anti-Christian and anti-social. Dickens, very much concerned, and fearful lest the Bill pass into law,[1] wrote a pamphlet, *Sunday under Three Heads*, signing it Timothy Sparks.[2] He dedicated it to the Bishop of London who had expatiated on the vicious addiction of the lower classes of society to Sunday excursions, thus showing himself like all the members of both Houses completely out of touch with common life. 'That your lordship could ever have contemplated Sunday recreations with so much horror if you had been at all acquainted with the wants and necessities of the people who indulge in them I cannot imagine possible.' Sunday, he went on to say, has been for many workers a happy day, a day to look forward to. What was wrong with numerous boats standing at river piers to take people out to excursions? Why should they not go off early with their picnic-baskets to Kent and Greenwich, Shooters Hill and Twickenham? What was wrong with opening a few coffee

---

[1] Rejected on third reading by 32 votes.
[2] Chapman and Hall, June 1836.

and food stalls to enable them to fill those baskets? Junketings of the sort in no way interfered with the Sunday observances indulged in by the well-to-do. He has himself watched
carriages with footmen rattle up before the porticoes of St.
Martin, St. George and St. Marylebone: he has seen 'the
powdered minions glide along the aisles and place the prayer-
books in the right pews'. He has waited for the carriages'
return to pick up their smart owners, has observed the
carriage steps being pushed up, the carriage doors shut, and
above all studied the complacent faces of the worshippers
who drive away congratulating themselves on the excellent
example they have set to the lower orders.

Look at this Bill, he says, and see how far the fanatics are
prepared to go. It proposes penalties for keeping shops
open, for travelling on steamboats, attending public meetings
and hiring carriages. It is an egregious specimen of legislative folly. Dickens had always been in favour of opening
museums and galleries and of playing cricket on Sunday
afternoons, for what point could there be in making the only
holiday of the week miserable?

Now that he had definitely made up his mind to give up the
Gallery and live by his pen Charles Dickens accepted almost
anything offered to him in the way of work, including a June
contract from Macrone for a novel at £200 to be ready in six
months. In August, when the *Carlton Chronicle* requested
him to supply a fortnightly 'Sketch' (mentioning, as befitted
the Carlton Club, liberal terms), he agreed to do so, telling
Macrone that the circulation of the *Carlton Chronicle* though
small was 'all among the nobs' and the nobs were the people
who bought books. At this moment, too, he was negotiating
with Thomas Tegg, the well-known Cheapside publisher, for
a child's Christmas book to be called *Solomon Bell: the Raree
Showman*. For this he was to be paid £100. It never
appeared; possibly he had to cancel it when he signed his
agreement with Bentley to edit a new magazine. On July 25
Dickens in a postscript to a letter to Macrone wrote PICK-

WICK TRIUMPHANT. The triumph was so striking that his publishers raised his monthly pay.

Kate Dickens had been brought up in a musical *milieu* and Dickens, through his sister Fanny, who was now on the stage, already knew a good many singers and actors. We have seen him employing his short honeymoon in working for the theatre to amuse Kate, and the result was *The Strange Gentleman*, a stage version of his story *The Great Winglebury Duel*. This farce was followed up by a burletta, *The Village Coquettes*, for which John Hullah supplied the music. The family collaborated in trying music and libretto out on Saturday evening, July 23, at Furnival's Inn 'before a few confidential friends literary and musical'. Macrone was bidden by Dickens in a civil note:

> I intend reading my opera and trying the music next Saturday evening at 7 o'clock. Mrs. Dickens desires me to say that if you will with Mrs. Macrone join the friends who wish to hear it she will be most happy to see you.[1]

The little audience demonstrated its approval and at the end of the first act Macrone offered to purchase the copyright. Dickens half accepted, but on second thoughts wrote:

> Mr. Hullah and I have come to the determination of publishing the books of the songs ourselves. Being required only for distribution in the theatre, they do not require a bookseller's aid.[2]

Publication of the libretto was left open for the time being: the music, however, was disposed of to Cramers for 'a good round sum'.

Mr. and Mrs. Dickens rented a furnished house, Elm Lodge, Petersham, for August 1836. There they had the happiness of being visited by Braham of the newly-built St. James's play-house, 'the most splendid theatre in Europe'. He brought with him his stage-manager Harley; both were enthusiastic about the operetta. Harley wrote, 'It's a sure

[1] 74. I. N.L.   [2] 76. I. N.L.

D 2

card: nothing wrong there. Bet you ten pounds it runs fifty
nights'. While at Petersham they were flattered at being
approached by Richard Bentley, the Savile Row publisher.
Bentley offered 'Boz' £500 for the 'entire copyright' of a
novel of undetermined title and subject without any time limit
for delivery. The author jumped at this offer and signed a
contract[1] promising to supply a second novel on the same
terms as the first, just as if his engagement to Macrone of
two months earlier had entirely slipped his mind. Richard
Bentley was on the alert for new writers, for he had recently
dissolved partnership with Henry Colburn, who was setting
up a rival establishment in Great Marlborough Street and
drawing away some of his authors. Jealousy almost amount-
ing to enmity existed between the two men. When Bentley
announced that he was about to produce a comic miscellany,
or rather a magazine of which humour was to be the leading
characteristic, Colburn immediately countered by scheming
to produce a similar monthly with Theodore Hook, editor of
The Joker's Magazine, in control. Hook, who was always
in financial straits, accepted the post and an advance of salary,
but when Colburn changed his mind about launching a new
magazine, he told Hook he must work out the advance he
had received on the *New Monthly*, an arrangement that disgusted S. C. Hall since it relegated him to the position of sub-
editor. Hall resigned and Hook became editor. Eventually
the *New Monthly* was sold to Harrison Ainsworth. Bentley
meanwhile was completing his plans for *The Wits' Miscellany*,
but who to make editor was the puzzle. George Hogarth
put forward the name of his son-in-law, 'young Dickens', and
young Dickens was appointed.[2] Owing to the threat of Colburn's competition the name *Wits' Miscellany* was changed
to *Bentley's Miscellany*, whereupon Barham of *Ingoldsby
Legends* fame exclaimed, 'But why go to the other extreme?'

When Mr. and Mrs. Dickens took up residence again at
Furnival's Inn they invited Mary Hogarth, a pretty child of

---

[1] August 22, 1836.
[2] Editorship offered November 4, 1836. First issue January 2, 1837.

sixteen, to live with them in their tiny apartment. Kate stayed at home a good deal for she was expecting a baby at Christmas, so Mary went about everywhere with Charles. One day he took her to Macrone's office in St. James's Square which was furnished with busts of 'distinguished men' (including one of Macrone himself and one of John Sadleir, M.P., reputed to have been the model for Mr. Merdle in *Little Dorrit*). These busts had been presented to him by John Strang, the wine-merchant author, who had cultivated his taste by travel in France and Italy. Angus Fletcher, the maker of some of them, was often in the office. Dickens annexed Fletcher at once as a friend and called him 'Kindheart'. All the people with whom Charles brought Mary in contact took a fancy to the girl whose coy appearance covered a keen sense of fun. At New Year 1837 John Strang wrote to Macrone:

> Our acquaintance 'Boz' seems also not to be sleeping. His name appears to irradiate three publishers lists. How does his pretty little sister-in-law get on? She is a sweet interesting creature. I wonder some two-legged monster does not carry her off. It might save many a yonker losing his night's rest.

In looking back on this halcyon autumn Dickens described the way he sat at home working over the fire 'among merry banterings' and basking in 'a sympathy more precious than the applause of the whole world'. How often he felt like trilling 'Home sweet home' as he walked about the streets!

While *The Strange Gentleman* and later on *The Village Coquettes* were in rehearsal, Dickens had to spend a good deal of time in the theatre wrestling with rather absurd difficulties such as the objection of the two Miss Smiths, who were singing in the operetta, to the immodesty of some of the lines.

> A winter's night has its delight,
> Well-warmed to bed they go:
> A winter's day we're blithe and gay
> Snipe-shooting in the snow

was something they really could not bring themselves to voice.

> If the young ladies are specially horrified at the bare notion of anyone going to bed, I have no objection to substitute for the objectionable line, 'Well-warmed to bed they go', 'Around old stories go' [wrote Dickens to John Hullah]. But you may respectfully signify to Cramers that I will see them d——d before I make any further alterations . . . you will see that we ought not to emasculate the very spirit of the song to suit boarding schools.[1]

Madame Sala made such a success of the part of Julia Dobbs and *The Strange Gentleman* ran for so long that the production of *The Village Coquettes* had to be postponed till December 6. The reviews were none too kind. Forster, who was as yet unacquainted with Dickens, was depreciatory in the *Examiner*, and the *Sunday Times*, *Weekly Dispatch* and *Satirist*, 'all', as Dickens put it, 'blow their little trumpets against unhappy me'. It was suggested that the plays would 'blast his reputations as a periodical writer'. Both plays, however, got good notices in the *Carlton Chronicle*; it is just possible that Dickens wrote them himself. Another burletta by 'Boz' was staged at the St. James's Theatre in March 1837, in which Madame Sala and J. P. Harley played. Its name was *Is She his Wife?* and it may have some bearing on the tastes and bickerings of Mr. and Mrs. Charles Dickens themselves, since Mr. Lovetown hates the country with its blooming hedges, feathered songsters and such like, while adoring area railings, dustman's bells and pavements. Mrs. Lovetown loves flowers, country walks and the song of birds and is distressed that her husband should yawn with ennui if taken out of London. The play had but a short run but its copyright was sold to Braham for £100. Dickens lived to be ashamed of his early dramatic experiments as we learn from Frederick Locker Lampson, who once asked him at Gad's Hill whether he possessed a copy of *The Village Coquettes*. 'No,' he retorted; 'if I knew it was in my house and if I could not get rid of it in any other way, I would burn the wing of the house where it was.'

During the autumn Dickens made a second contract with Bentley. He was getting £20 a month for editing the *Miscellany* and now was to receive an extra £2 for the sixteen pages of original matter he was to provide for each number. The agreement ran for twelve months and was renewable by Bentley for three years. The copyright was to be Bentley's absolutely. To 'Boz' this, for-the-time-being, satisfactory arrangement secured for him nearly £500 a year which, added to some £300 a year for *Pickwick*, gave him a feeling of security. In view of the eventual estrangement of Bentley and Dickens it is not uninteresting to note that at this time Bentley thought so well of his new editor as to insist on putting him up for the Garrick Club. And indeed the publisher had every reason to be pleased with his choice.

Bentley's Miscellany was from the first a success. At the end of six months its editor could announce that he was 'inundated' with orders and that all looked well for the future. The contributors, most of whom were friends of Bentley, were Father Prout, Samuel Lover, Theodore Hook, C. Whitehead, Fenimore Cooper, Dr. Maginn, Captain Medwin, Morier the author of *Hajji Baba*, William Jerdan and George Hogarth. It can have required but slight editing and was in every sense of the word easy money both for promoters and contributors. Except for the Dickens serials and *Handy Andy*, little has been found worth reprinting. In the original opening of *Oliver Twist* the workhouse in which he was born was situated in Mudfog; this was deleted later. Dickens had begun *The Public Life of Tulrumble*, its Mayor, in the second number of the magazine and evidently at one moment meant to link Oliver with Mudfog. He also wrote two stray chapters, one on '*Pantomimes*' in which he guys the opening of parliament and the other on '*Lions*' in which he cuts some heavy jokes about literary celebrities at parties.

At last Dickens with over £65 a month assured income felt

himself justified in giving notice to the *Morning Chronicle*, terminating his engagement as a parliamentary reporter. Mr. Easthope, the proprietor, extremely annoyed to receive it, was disposed to suggest that his employee was behaving unfairly, for had he not been paid in advance to supply weekly *Sketches*? Nettled, Dickens replied, 'I shall return the six guineas with the utmost pleasure', and then went on to say how on many occasions at a sacrifice of health, rest and personal comfort, he has done what was always before considered impossible and what in all probability will never be accomplished again. He had been selected for difficult, harassing duty—travelling at a few hours' notice hundreds of miles in the depth of winter—leaving hot and crowded rooms to write, the night through, in a close, damp chaise—tearing along and copying the most important speeches under every possible circumstance of disadvantage and difficulty. He has eclipsed other papers again and again, other papers with double the means, there is not another newspaper office in London where these services have not been watched and appreciated. 'Instead of an appreciatory farewell letter he gets a reminder that he has been overpaid by six guineas!'[1]

Resentment over the behaviour of an employer he had served with all his might, made Dickens feel he had been treated like a servant, and a dishonest servant at that. It confirmed him in his belief that the rich were heartless and had an inveterate tendency to exploit those in their power. Life certainly taught one lessons. Again he set his teeth and determined to ride on. One day he might be able to pay Easthope back in his own coin.

He had no time to waste on recrimination, for the *Pickwick* instalments had to be produced to time. To Chapman and Hall they seemed of unequal merit, and in reply to their complaint that the papers were getting a little tedious Dickens replied:

> You may rest assured that the disease has reached its height and that it will now take a more favourable turn. I

only entreat you to recollect two things—first that I have
many occupations; and secondly that spirits are not to be
forced up to *Pickwick* level every day. Although, thank
God, I have as few worldly cares as most people, you would
scarcely believe how often I sit down to begin a number and
feeling unequal to the task, do what is far better than
writing under such circumstances—get up and wait till I
am. . . . If I were to live one hundred years and wrote three
novels in each I should never be so proud of any of them as
I am of *Pickwick* feeling as I do that it has made its own way
and hoping as I must own I do hope, that long after my
hand is withered as the pens it held, *Pickwick* will be found
on many a dusty shelf with many a better work.[1]

Charles now had domestic affairs as well as serial instalments to worry over. A Christmas baby was expected,
and what a first baby means to a young couple has to be
experienced to be believed. In the rather cramped chambers
of Furnival's Inn a son was born on Twelfth Night 1837.
When the mothers of both parents settled in to preside over
the birth, Dickens and Mary were obliged to fend for themselves. The ejectment made Charles realise how necessary
it was to find a house to live in where upheavals of the kind
would not be a regular feature of family life. After all he and
Kate might reasonably expect to have a number of children,
and a home ought to be a refuge in all domestic crises whether
of joy or sorrow as well as an inviolable workshop for the
breadwinner. With his sister-in-law Charles went house-
hunting and, before getting rid of the Furnival's Inn chambers,
took over the lease of a twelve-roomed house in Doughty
Street, just north of Gray's Inn, a no-thoroughfare with gates
and a liveried watchman at either end in which Sydney Smith
had lived when chaplain at the Foundling Hospital hard by.
In great spirits Mr. and Mrs. Dickens, the baby and Mary
Hogarth moved into this place in April 1837. Mary helped
Kate with the baby, and Charles's brother Frederick, aged
sixteen, who was too young to live by himself, was also

included in the household. Mary seemed to grow more lovable and happy every day and certainly showed no symptom of delicacy. The little family was thoroughly satisfied and rejoiced at the space and convenience of its new home.[1]

Charles settled down seriously to work: he was, as we know, writing *Pickwick* and *Oliver Twist* fortnight and fortnight about. The mornings he spent in strict solitude in his study overlooking the tiny back garden: in the afternoons he went for long walks or, when money became more plentiful, hired a horse and rode to Epping Forest, Highgate or Richmond. Many people came and went, including Macready who had by this time become a close friend. It is from Macready's diary that we see how life went on in Doughty Street. One day he went there to meet Cattermole, Browne ('Phiz') and Forster and then they all went on to see the House of Correction in Coldbath Fields. What were they planning in that scene of punishment and why did they go straight from there to Newgate? In Newgate they saw a man with long heavy moustaches reading quietly. Macready gave a start and exclaimed, 'Good God! there's Wainewright the poisoner!' Another man was pointed out to them who was just about to be hanged for rape. These sights did not affect the high spirits of the party, who returned to Doughty Street for a jolly dinner at which Harley, Hogarth and Maclise's brother-in-law, Banks, joined them.

One of the visitors at Doughty Street that summer was young George Lewes, 'a miniature Mirabeau' to George Eliot, and 'Ape' Lewes to Carlyle. Dickens had asked him to call as he was pleased with what he had written about *Pickwick*. It damped Lewes's enthusiasm a little to be set down in a small study with bookshelves containing nothing but three-volume novels and books of travel, all obvious presentation copies. There were no treasures from the bookstall, no pick-ups of any kind. As he observed later, 'I did not expect to find a bookworm nor even a student in the marvellous 'Boz', but nevertheless the collection of books was

[1] Leased for three years April 3, 1837.

a shock.' Presently Dickens burst into the room in great spirits and Lewes confessed himself 'more impressed with Dickens's fulness of life and energy than with any sense of distinction'.

There was nothing Dickens enjoyed more than dispensing hospitality unless it was taking his 'petticoats' to the theatre. One evening some seven or eight weeks after the move to Doughty Street, they all came home in tearing spirits from the play. Mary's laugh rippled as she tripped upstairs. Bed-room doors were closed, candles blown out, when suddenly Dickens heard a strange choking cry from Mary's room. Running in he found her struggling for breath; Kate joined him and Frederick was sent for a doctor. Charles held Mary up in his arms, but neither the doctor nor any one of them could save the precious life. It was unbelievable and un-bearable to Charles that this angel should be deprived of breath. In an agony he took the ring from her hand and slipped it on his little finger where it remained till his death. The shock to Kate brought on a miscarriage and a happy united family was reduced to mourn the extinguishment of life and hope. It fell to Charles to arrange the 'last dreadful ceremony' in the new cemetery at Kensal Green and to write for little Mary Scott Hogarth (named for Sir Walter) a gentle epitaph.

> Young, beautiful, and good, God in His mercy numbered her among his angels at the early age of seventeen.

After the funeral Charles left a note with Ainsworth begging him to arrange for a rose tree to be planted on that early grave, and then carried Kate off 'to the country', to Collins's Farm, North End. He could write no *Pickwick* that month and no *Oliver Twist*, and *Bentley's Miscellany* carried the following notice:

> Since the appearance of the last number of this work the editor has to mourn the sudden death of a very dear young relative to whom he was most affectionately attached and

. whose society has been for a long time the chief solace of
his labours.

Collins's Farm, the home of Linnell and the haunt of Blake,
still stands.   To Dickens a country bolt-hole, to us a
strangely secluded, touching relic of the fifteenth century
existing as if by a miracle amidst a garrotting crowd of villa-
residences.   In form it is substantially the same as it was five
hundred years ago and the grey match-boarded walls are well
screened from passing eyes.   A rickety-looking lean-to (a
kind of verandah) runs along the front of the house and a
huge cherry tree has become incorporated in the angle of the
building.   Why one should get the sense of great nearness
to Dickens in this place is a mystery; but in walking through
the narrow door and up the narrow stair to the slanting rooms
above he springs to life, as does the pursuing grief from which
he fled to this refuge.[1]   Here in the rickety lean-to he sat
with Forster and Maclise and talked and talked of Mary.

Never did Charles lose the sense of grief caused by Mary's
death.   In all the descriptions of all the deaths in his novels
we get reminders of his suffering, in Little Nell, in Paul
Dombey, in Rose Maylie, whom at the last moment he
spared, for how could he let Rose die in May when humbler
things were glad and gay?   May was no time for death;
graves were for the cheerless winter, shrouds for the old and
the shrunken.   Writing with infinite tenderness he said:

> We need be careful how we deal with those about us,
> when every death carries to some small circle of survivors
> thoughts of so much omitted and so little done, of so many
> things forgotten and so many more which might have been
> repaired.

Hablot Browne helped them through the sad days and persuaded them to venture on the continent.   They were away
under a fortnight, but there was time to pilot them to Calais

[1] The fact that this remarkable relic has been preserved at all is due to the
foresight of a distinguished architect who preserved it and some of its land
from development.

and arrange for a post-coach to take them to Ghent, Brussels and Antwerp. In Brussels Browne took them to see his friend, Charles Lever, at that time appointed physician to the British Legation, but with no licence to practise among Belgians. This continental trip was a revelation. Charles now knew that he enjoyed meeting foreigners and the plunge into foreign parts woke in him the longing to repeat the experience, a longing that was to lead him later on to live abroad for months together.

By the time he returned home he had, as it were, assimilated Mary's death into his subconsciousness where it lay germinating and enriching his imaginative life. Superficially he was able to enjoy himself again, as a vist to Broadstairs proves. Broadstairs was a favourite playground for the theatrical profession. The Macready and Sala families went there for summer bathing and Dickens's great friends, the Smithsons, had arranged to move there during the hot weather of 1837. Charles and Kate dined with them in London on returning from abroad, and at the dinner was present a certain 'Eleanor P.' (whom we get to know later as Mrs. Christian), the first of the many young women over whom Dickens cast a spell. She was fascinated by 'the power of his eyes'; they looked to her warm grey in repose, and they seemed to light up with a luminous depth of hue as she watched him. When her eyes were 'released by his eyes', she began to see him as a whole. His get-up she did not like; why should he wear so wide a collar and lapel to his surtout? why should it be thrown back to give effect to a vast expanse of white waistcoat? Then his drab trousers and his drab boots with their black patent toe-caps were dreadful, and the flowing locks that emphasised his poetic air were surely an affectation? Why did he let other guests do the talking and sit apparently abstracted and with a rapt preoccupied look? Why did he make no effort to be amusing? When 'Eleanor P.' got to know this preoccupied look better, she knew it meant that he was taking things in 'most comprehensively'.

Smithson was a partner of Tom Mitton and one of Dickens's earliest friends. Mrs. Smithson was the sister of T. J. Thompson, another early friend whom we shall meet on several interesting occasions. Broadstairs that summer was packed with people. The John Dickens', their married daughters and Frederick, were there. When 'Eleanor P.' arrived to stay with the Smithsons she met them all: John Dickens a cork-like optimist, and jolly Mrs. John Dickens who entered heartily into any amusement going. Charles, like one or two other members of the family, spoke as if their tongues were too large for their mouths; Charles's speech in especial had a certain thickness in it. It intrigued this young woman, though it did not surprise her, to find that both the Dickens parents stood a little in awe of their eldest son, his moods being to them so unaccountable. The weather was fine and everyone basked on the sands and played absurd games like 'Animal, Vegetable and Mineral'. Kate Dickens would perpetrate terrible puns with an expression of innocence and deprecation. Charles would assume disgust, she would pout and he would giggle and altogether they behaved like lovers. But this did not prevent him from flirting hard with 'Eleanor P.'

The Tivoli Gardens at Broadstairs were a kind of miniature Vauxhall where people listened to concerts and danced in the evenings. Eleanor would dance in quadrilles there, but 'Boz' stood out, afraid of being recognised. One evening he was watching 'a young Morleena Kenwigs' capering about, when a man, who had been following him, took his stand beside him. Lifting his hat Charles said, 'Are you a native of this place, sir?' 'No, no sir, I am not,' replied the stranger. 'I beg your pardon, I fancied I could detect broad stares upon your face.' So much for his professed horror of puns!

Sheer high spirits inspired Charles to many pranks. Impulsive, erratic Angus Fletcher had joined the party and played the fool as well as any man. On the pier one evening they railed off a space with long benches in which to dance a private quadrille. They called it 'the family pew'. Dickens loved dancing there in the dusk as he escaped recognition by gaping holiday makers. For music he blew upon the comb to Fletcher's whistling and this was all the melody they had. After dancing they would stroll to the end of the pier to watch the tide flooding in. One evening Charles, seemingly bedevilled, flung his arm round 'Eleanor P.'s' waist and whirled her down the inclined plane of the jetty towards a tall upright pole fixed at the extreme end. To this pole he clung with his disengaged arm, declaiming theatrically that he would hold her till the wild waves drowned them both. Eleanor struggled; he held her fast saying, 'Let your mind dwell on the column in the *Times* wherein will be vividly described the fate of the lovely E. P. drowned by D. in a fit of dementia. Don't struggle, poor little bird! You are powerless in the claw of such a kite as this, child!' The water plashed round their knees. 'My dress! my best dress! my only silk dress!' screamed Eleanor. 'Dress,' shouted her captor, 'talk not to me of dress when we already stand on the brink of the great mystery. Am I not immolating a brand new pair of patent leathers still unpaid for? Perish such low-born thoughts! In this hour of abandonment to the voice of destiny, shall we be held back by the puerilities of silken raiment? Shall leather or prunella (whatever that may be) stop the bolt of Fate?'[1]

At length Eleanor managed to free herself and, leaving a watery track behind her, stumbled up the incline in a dress soaked well above the knees. Mrs. Smithson in a displeased voice told her to run home and change. She was both shocked and surprised at her guest's hysterical behaviour.

To Pegwell Bay the same party drove one day in two landaus. Charles had bought a sheaf of ballads from a pedlar and insisted on shouting them all the way there, to the great amusement of the people they passed on the road. On another sunny day they went sailing in a hired boat, and Dickens kept the crew in fits of laughter by roaring 'A reef in your taff-rail! Sheepshank your mizzen! Brail up your

[1] *Temple Bar*, LXXXII.

capstan bar!' In the evenings they sometimes acted charades. For Pompadour (pompadore) Dickens, in a wide brimmed hat pinned up at the side with a long feather, played Louis XV majestically. At one concert they attended, a gentleman sang 'By the sad sea waves', finishing on a high note with an embellishing turn. 'What does that mean?' asked 'Eleanor P.' Dickens flashed back with, 'That's quite the rule in music, as well as in accordance with proverbial philosophy. When things are at their worst they always take a turn.' One day he was discussing *Childe Harold* and took exception to 'Dazzled and drunk with beauty, The heart reels in its fulness' as too suggestive of the beverage (gin and water) which sometimes inspired the poet's high flights. The friend to whom he spoke defended the verses, whereupon Dickens tossed back his hair shouting, 'Stand back, I am suddenly seized with the divine afflatus! Don't disturb me till I have given birth to my inspired conceptions.' Seizing a pencil, he stalked to the window and wrote on the white paint of the shutter:

Lines to E. P., after Byron

O maiden of the amber-dropping hair
May I Byronically thy praises utter?
Drunk with thy beauty, tell me, may I dare
To sing thy paeans borne upon a shutter?

Dickens had an odd trick of sucking his thumbs when thinking, and of worrying at a lock of hair with his left hand. As the result of her experiences and of watching him when he was staring with lustreless eyes at the sea and recognising no one, 'Eleanor P.' became 'horribly' afraid of him. One day she told him this. 'Why, there is nothing to be afraid of about *me*,' he protested. 'Isn't there?' she retorted. 'You look like a forest lion with a shaggy mane on the prowl,

He roared so loud and looked so wondrous grim
His very shadow dare not follow him.'

Dickens laughed. 'What? do you play shadow to my lion? Nay then, as Bottom the Weaver says,

I will aggravate my voice so that I will roar you as gently as any sucking dove.'

Never again was 'Eleanor P.' to see him in this hilarious, care-free mood. When they met in London a year or two later he had changed and seemed both preoccupied and self-important.

During the autumn of 1837 Dickens worked hard at *Oliver Twist* and edited the *Memoirs of Grimaldi*; at least he wrote the preface and dictated the book to his father from the narrative compiled by Egerton Wilks. It seemed to him great twaddle, but his father enjoyed the work and Cruik-shank's illustrations were satisfactory. The commission brought with it the useful fee of £300.

One of the serious interests of the spring of 1837 had been Serjeant Talfourd's Copyright Bill the provisions of which he had talked over in detail with Dickens. Its aim was to safe-guard the rights of an author in his own work for sixty years. As things stood books could hardly be classed as property in the real sense of the word, as all rights expired at death and during life there was no protection against piracy. The classic example of hardship was Scott, whose bankruptcy might have been averted had the French and American publishers given him a share in the profits they amassed by the sale of his books. But it must be admitted that the firms of Galignani in Paris and Cary in Philadelphia behaved no worse in this respect than the less reputable publishers of London. Even Dickens, when he brought an action against a firm for pirating *A Christmas Carol*, though technically he won his case, had to pay such heavy costs that he determined never to hunt pirates again. Talfourd's Bill was thrown out in October 1837 and in the same month Dickens received a letter from an American publisher[1] offering him a small bonus from the profits derived by them from sales of his works. He refused it, possibly because Talfourd thought it better that he should take his stand with other authors in demanding as a

[1] October 26, 1837.

right what was now being offered as a gratuity. While declining to accept any money present for *Pickwick*, he stated that he would be willing to enter into an arrangement with Messrs. Cary to transmit early proofs of *Oliver Twist* and *Barnaby Rudge* should the firm consider it desirable.

Dickens dedicated *Pickwick* to Serjeant Talfourd in recognition of his services to authors and wrote:

> If I had not long enjoyed the happiness of your private friendship, I should still have dedicated this work to you, as a slight and most inadequate acknowledgment of the inestimable services you are rendering the literature of your country, and of the lasting benefits you will confer upon the authors of this and succeeding generations by securing to them and their descendants a permanent interest in the copyright of their works. . . . Accept the dedication of this book, my dear sir, as a mark of my warmest regard and esteem, as a memorial for the most gratifying friendship I have ever contracted, of some of the pleasantest hours I have ever spent, and as a token of my fervent admiration of every fine quality of your head and heart.

It was a handsome testimonial, but no more than Serjeant Talfourd merited. Copyright was a cause Dickens had very much at heart and we shall see that his outspokenness in America on this subject roused the greatest personal animosity against him and made a comparative failure of what should have been a triumphal tour.

Chapter 6

JOHN FORSTER

What a thing friendship is, world without end!
ROBERT BROWNING

WHEN Charles Dickens first met the man who was to be his close friend and eventual biographer, John Forster, his reputation was already considerable. We may, in reading Forster's *Life of Dickens*, get the impression that the author acted as *compère* to his hero though this was not in fact the relationship, since by the time the two young men of twenty-five met, Dickens had already published the *Sketches*, an operetta, a play, was writing monthly instalments of *Pickwick*, was booked to write two novels for Bentley, and had been appointed editor of a new Miscellany. All of which goes to show that he was not in need of any man's patronage.

Two months younger than Dickens, John Forster had the manner of a mature business man. Son of a northern cattle-dealer, he did brilliantly at Newcastle Grammar School and was fired by a passion for literature as real as Talfourd's. In coming to London in 1830 he had attached himself to S. C. Hall, editor of the *New Monthly Magazine*, with whom he dined weekly. Later on he dropped Hall, who said of him, 'I found him a friend when he needed me, but not a friend when I needed him'.

Forster began his literary career as theatrical critic on the *True Sun* and in this way got to know Sheridan Knowles, Barry Cornwall, W. J. Fox, Edward Bulwer, Maclise and Macready. He then became colleague on the *Examiner* of the brilliant Albany Fonblanque whom he eventually succeeded as editor. It was while working for the *Examiner* that he received a 'My dear Sir' letter from Charles Dickens accompanied by the book of *The Village Coquettes* just published by Bentley. A few days later they met face to face under

Harrison Ainsworth's roof. In a way it is odd that they
had not come across each other earlier, as it was Forster's
hobby to get to know every scribbler in London. Macready
used to say that Forster was sycophantic in his approach to
the literary figures of his day, but Macready picked holes in
most people and was unfair to a man who did his best to be of
service to authors and tirelessly pushed the books he admired.
The first critic, except W. J. Fox of the *Monthly Repository*,
to appreciate Browning's quality, he, in 1836, was already
badgering Ainsworth to get *Sordello* published and Macready
to produce *Strafford*. Landor, Carlyle and Tennyson came
to hold Forster in high regard and he was to prove a useful
friend to all of them. His unadvertised finger was in many a
literary pie and it was reward enough for him if his manipula-
tions turned to the advantage of the author concerned. He is
best known to posterity as Dickens's Boswell.

It is through John Forster's biography that we get to know
Dickens; in fact till the Nonesuch *Letters* were published, it
was the only way we could get to know him except by reading
his books and some expurgated letters edited by members of
the family.

Everyone of the day testifies to Forster's unflagging interest
in writers. He was helpful to Lady Blessington over manuscripts and so kind to L. E. L. over her poems that men
assumed he must be going to marry her. Bluff in manner,
he was rather apt to talk people down even at their own tables,
but it was generally agreed that by nature he was 'a block of
gold', which possibly means that he was without the alloy of
self-interest and was thoroughly dependable. Rosina Bulwer
hated him and said his manner was a bad understudy of
Macready's. In her novel *Cheveley* she caricatured him as
Fuz-Buz, 'a very ugly noseless likeness of a great tragedian
whom he tried to imitate even to his handwriting . . . a sort
of lick-dust to Mr. Fonnoir (Fonblanque) and to Mr. Anybody and everybody else to whom he could gain access.[1] It
was he who did the theatrical plasterings in the "Investigator"

[1] p. 115.

. . he being a perfect Boreas at a puff.' Other less cruel
observers, including Espinasse, confirm Forster's habit of
imitating Macready and tell how he would stride into a room
with his hand on his heart and a stock phrase on his lips such
as 'It is with infinite regret', or 'Believe me I feel it sensibly'.
Sturdily built, with fresh complexion, dark hair and what
was called a 'stentorian' voice, he made a rather bullying
impression on most people. In drawings by Cruikshank,
Browne and others one sees John Forster as a stocky man
tightly buttoned up in a short frock-coat, twiddling a monocle
in one hand and looking as if he were sitting in judgment on
the follies of his friends. Dickens, who was supposed to stand
a little in awe of him, used to call him 'the Lincolnian mamm-
moth', and Douglas Jerrold, picking up a pencil stump, said
it was like Forster, 'short, thick and full of lead'. When
Our Mutual Friend came out, some people recognised a
portrait of Forster in Podsnap, 'the Mr. Podsnap who was
well-to-do and stood very high in Mr. Podsnap's opinion'.
Mrs. Lynn Linton, usually uncharitable about authors, said
he was 'pompous, cynical and jealous', and snapped at the
chance when his *Life of Landor* came out of reviewing it
venomously. On the other hand Lady Blessington told
Landor that he was 'a noble-minded man'. Carlyle, though
at first put off by his manner, came to feel affectionately towards him and, copying Rosina Bulwer, nicknamed him
'Fuz'. 'Fuz' was for ever quarrelling with those he most
admired and imperilling their relations. Dickens was no
exception and their friendship was on several occasions on the
edge of rupture. In August 1840 for example Macready
records a dinner at Devonshire Terrace at which 'a most painful' scene occurred. Forster embarked on 'one of his headlong streams of talk (which he thinks argument) and waxed
warm. . . . His sharp observations led to personal retorts with
Dickens.' Forster was so tactless and overbearing that his
host flew into a violent passion and told his guest he would be
glad if he would leave the house. Mrs. Dickens ran out of
the dining-room in tears and for some angry moments it

looked as if an association valuable to them both was about to
be destroyed. James Payn tells us that many people, including himself, could not understand Dickens's feeling for
Forster. 'I have rarely seen them together without witness-
ing some sparring between them, sometimes without the
gloves.' Forster would pay compliments to the Inimitable
in a patronising way which Dickens would acknowledge in
the drollest manner. In 1847 the friendship again was on the
verge of collapse. Forster dining with Macready spoke as if
it were almost at an end, but somehow things righted themselves and intercourse persisted, which may be a tribute to
something rare in the quality of Forster. Dickens used to
say rather plaintively, 'I don't quarrel with my other friends'.

Forster never cared at all about Ainsworth and mentions his
name but five times in his *Life of Dickens* and these are incidental, unavoidable allusions. Possibly Forster was jealous
of the part Ainsworth had played in introducing 'Boz' to his
first publisher and first illustrator. Ainsworth to him was a
very boring third party 'who shared with us incessantly for
three years in the companionship begun at his house'. 'Boz',
'Fuz' and Ainsworth used to ride together and sometimes
spend week-ends in each other's company, but we are left in
no doubt that Forster would far rather have been alone with
Dickens.

The possessiveness of Forster manifested itself in rather
tiresome ways. He treated Mrs. Dickens as a cypher and
took no pains to ingratiate himself with her. Not only did he
seem suspicious of all Dickens's friends and anxious to be his
one and only confidant, but he tried to exercise proprietary,
almost patent, rights over his latest literary discovery.
Dickens, who was not at this time very business-like, was
tremendously impressed by Forster's competence and at once
fell to discussing with him the business side of authorship.
In the intoxication of initial success, one can explain it by no
rational process, Dickens had signed contracts with three publishers, Macrone, Bentley and Chapman and Hall. He was
beginning to be worried by what he had done and was only

too thankful to unburden his mind to so sympathetic and experienced a person. As he talked to Forster in rather an aggrieved way about the boggle he was in, Forster realised that it was all of his own contriving and that the over-eager author wanted rescuing from himself quite as much as from the over-eager publishers! What was bothering Dickens most was a novel he had promised to Macrone which was already long overdue. Why had he promised it? He didn't quite know now, but he had been grateful at the time and only too glad to accept the £200 offered. He had committed himself in writing, perhaps Forster should see a copy of the letter he had sent to John Macrone. He had actually signed his name to the following undertaking:

I shall have great pleasure in accepting from you the sum of £200 for the first edition of a work of Fiction (in three volumes of the usual type) to be written by me and to be entitled *Gabriel Vardon, the Locksmith of London*, of which not more than 1000 copies are to be printed. I also agree to your printing an extra number of copies, if it should appear desirable; on condition that the profits therefrom, all expenses being first deducted, be divided between us. I also understand that the before-mentioned £200 are to be paid by you on delivery of the entire manuscript on or before the 30th day of November next, or as soon after as I can possibly complete it by your acceptances at such dates as may be acceptable to both of us.[1]

Was it possible to annul this obligation? he asked earnestly. Forster thought not, contracts were binding in law, but he would first like to hear how he stood with regard to publishers generally, so Dickens proceeded to give an account of commitments which were both numerous and conflicting. In the first place, he had sold the original series of *Sketches by Boz* to Macrone for £150 and had just handed in another series for which he had received £150 on account.[2] In the second

---

[1] 71-2. I. N.L.
[2] In a letter to Mitton (1839) he states that he got £400 in all for these books.

place, as he had just explained to Forster, he had agreed to write a novel for the same publisher; this was only partly written and overdue. In the third place, he had contracted to supply Chapman and Hall with a monthly *Sketch* at fourteen pounds a number to be published under the title of the *Pickwick Papers*: this he was in process of fulfilling. In the fourth place, he had signed an agreement with Bentley[1] to supply one novel for £500 and a second on the same terms. In the fifth place, he had accepted the post of editor of *Bentley's Miscellany*[2] which involved supplying sixteen pages of original matter for each issue, and over this Bentley was inclined to be shabby, deducting half-pages and counting up lines. Was it possible for any human being working day and night to fulfil these undertakings? 'Why,' as he protested, 'Sir Walter Scott himself could not have coped with them!' Something would have to be scrapped; what should it be? Forster listened carefully, but did not at once give his opinion. Dickens went on talking. No one could have any idea how worried he was or how it destroyed his pleasure in his success to see in the second series of *Sketches*, published a few days earlier, an announcement of *Gabriel Vardon*, 'a new novel by Boz to be issued in three volumes'. Hurriedly he had stopped further advertisements from appearing in *Bentley's Miscellany* and in the monthly number of *Pickwick*. He was so scared that he had asked Thomas Hansard, the printer of the second series of *Sketches*, whether there was any loophole of escape. Hansard, who was probably at this time financing Macrone, had said 'No', and told him plainly that having agreed to furnish a novel for £200 he must do his best to fulfil his contract. Macready had expressed the same opinion. As a last resort he had then approached Macrone direct and begged him to let him off his bargain. But no move of his could dispel the nightmare.

The case of 'Boz' was decidedly more complicated than anything Forster had hitherto tackled for any protégé. It required a great deal of consideration before he could see his

---

[1] August 22, 1836.   [2] November 4, 1836.

way to intervene with effect. Meanwhile, he assured his new client that he would take over all his proof-correcting as this would give him more time for writing. Finding Forster too deliberative for his now frantic mood, Dickens fell back on his old friend Tom Mitton. Mitton was shrewd, Mitton knew the legal ropes and Mitton had a real desire to help him. Neither Dickens nor Mitton knew something that we know which may have stiffened the attitude of both Macrone and Hansard, and that is that a trusted friend was behaving in an unfriendly way. At least this is how one may interpret a letter from the legally trained Ainsworth to Macrone which seems to show greater loyalty to his publisher than to a fellow author:

I write in strictest confidence and I trust to your honour as a gentleman not to quote me, or to shew this letter. I now write I say to advise you to place the matter between Mr. Dickens and yourself immediately in legal hands. Your reply to him ought simply to have been—My dear Dickens, In reply to your note I beg to state that *I shall hold you to your agreement*. Nothing more. . . . I hope you have agreements both for the 'Sketches' and the 'Novel'. I fear the latter does not fix any time for its appearance. But get legal advice at once, and I pray of you to write no more hasty letters in which you commit yourself more than you imagine. Mr. Dickens clearly has no right to destroy his agreement, but this information will be much better conveyed to him by a solicitor.[1]

It may be presumed that Macrone, acting on Ainsworth's advice, informed Dickens that he held him to his agreement. Maddened by the shackles he had wound round himself, Dickens, without consulting anyone, rushed off to Thomas Hansard saying he would waive all claim for ever on the *Sketches* for the return of the *Gabriel Vardon* contract. Mitton then stepped in to regularise matters and regained for Dickens possession of the agreement.

The return of the novel-contract pacified the excited author

[1] January 2, 1837.

for the moment, but he soon worked himself up over a new scare. Friends told him that Macrone was 'making thousands' out of the *Sketches* he had so impatiently surrendered. That was irritating enough, but his binder told him something worse, that Macrone, who had watched the sensational rise in sales of *Pickwick*[1] in its green paper covers, was about to issue all the *Sketches* got up in green covers to look precisely like *Pickwick*. Dickens was so positive that this manœuvre would not only damage his own character with Chapman and Hall, but prejudice the sales of *Pickwick*, that he entreated John Forster to try and dissuade Macrone from carrying out his plan. Forster agreed to do what he could. Macrone, however, flatly refused to meet 'Boz' in the matter, saying that the copyright was his and that he could do what he liked with his own. Forster, at the muzzle of this legal pistol, then asked what he would take for the copyright and he rapped out, 'Not a penny less than £2000'. When reporting to Dickens Forster advised him to let the matter rest, but Dickens in a state bordering on hysteria flew round to Chapman and Hall and urged them to come to terms with Macrone forthwith. The publishers were sympathetic, went into the matter at once and advised Dickens, to his great relief, that 'even at this large price of £2000, we might, besides retaining the copyright, reasonably hope for a good profit on the outlay'. They would buy the copyright for the sum named and themselves issue the *Sketches* in parts. Dickens, of course, would have to stand security for their purchase, but this was easy to arrange; they would just retain the profits from *Pickwick* for five years, and at the end of that period the author might share in them. Furthermore they bound him down to write a similar book in twenty monthly instalments at £150 a month, the copyright of which would belong to Chapman and Hall for five years and then revert to the author. By this arrangement Dickens was assured of a regular income wherewith to support a family and he was not obliged to forfeit the ultimate benefit of the copyright.

---

[1] 400 copies of first, and 40,000 of fifteenth number sold.

Hardly was the business settled between Macrone and Chapman and Hall than Macrone died suddenly—leaving his wife in very poor circumstances. Dickens, full of regrets, edited *The Pic-Nic Papers* for the benefit of the widow, contributing thereto *The Lamplighter's Story*. As a result £300 were handed to Mrs. Macrone.

The real trouble between Dickens and his publishers was that the market price of his work was rising so fast as to make a contract of a year or even six months earlier appear a swindle. The agreements were certainly not swindles at the time they were made; they were inelastic cash-down contracts, and it drove Dickens nearly mad to think that he was the only person not to profit by the rapidly increasing popularity of his books. In 1835 he was glad to take £200 for a novel. Two months after agreeing with Bentley to let him have the *Barnaby Rudge* copyright for three years for £700, he got paid £3000 by Chapman and Hall for five years' copyright of *Nicholas Nickleby*.

Dickens had no peace of mind or joy in his work because he was so worryingly conscious that his books were 'enriching everyone connected with them' except himself. And this was literally true. The *Sketches* had enriched Macrone, *Pickwick* was enriching Chapman and Hall, and now *Oliver Twist* in the *Miscellany* was enriching Bentley, and all the while the creator of this great body of original work, the maker of their profits, was being paid what he considered a most inadequate share of those profits.[1] Must publishers, he wondered, always drink their wine out of authors' skulls?

Let us look for a moment at Dickens's relations in 1836–7 with Bentley, the publisher he was so soon to refer to as 'the Brigand of Burlington Street'. Bentley was his friend when he published *The Village Coquettes*: Bentley was still his friend when, after reading the first five numbers of the *Pickwick Papers*, he decided to back his opinion of their excellence by offering the young author £500 for a novel with no time fixed for delivering the manuscript. Dickens had been so

[1] See footnote 1 on following page.

E

pleased at the time that he promised him a second novel on
the same terms[2] and Bentley was so pleased with 'Boz' that he
put him up for the Garrick Club. Bentley was still a friend
when he offered Dickens the editorship of his new *Wits'
Miscellany*,[3] and dined him and his contributors, Moore,
Lever, Barham, Ainsworth and Marryat, in the cosy 'red
room' in New Burlington Street: still a friend when three
months later he raised his pay by giving him a direct interest
in sales. This concession, though it was almost forced on
him by the immense vogue of *Oliver Twist*, was thought at
the time to be generous. It would have paid Bentley to be a
great deal more generous. If he had not been purblind and
mean of soul, the partnership would not have collapsed. As
things were, Charles resigned editorship of the *Miscellany* at
the ninth number and was only induced to oblige Mr. Bentley
further by another rise in salary and an increase of £200 on the
second of the contracted novels. The friendship seemed to
be warming up again when Bentley asked Dickens to edit the
Memoirs of Grimaldi for which he offered an advance of £300
and half profits on sales. Though the *Miscellany* prospered
exceedingly one is conscious that some disturbing influence

[1] SUMMARY OF INCOME NOVEMBER 1837–JUNE 1841
Extracted from an account book by permission of the late
Mr. Walter Dexter

From	To	Receipts			Expenditure			Balance in Bank		
		£	s.	d.	£	s.	d.	£	s.	d.
Nov. 20, 1837	Dec. 31, 1837	559	10	0	257	18	8	301	11	4
Jan. 1, 1838	June 24, 1838	1297	4	0	1453	8	6	145	6	10
June 25 ,,	Dec. 31, ,,	1271	5	0	1318	13	4	97	18	6
Jan. 1, 1839	June 24, 1839	1915	5	0	1920	9	11	92	13	7
June 25 ,,	Dec. 31, ,,	2244	8	0	1759	14	1	577	7	6
Jan. 1, 1840	June 24, 1840	700	0	0	1304	9	6	27	2	0
June 25 ,,	Dec. 31 ,,	1765	0	0	1510	9	6	227	8	6
Jan. 1, 1841	June 24, 1841	1435	6	7	1626	3	8	36	11	5
June 25 ,,	Oct. 28 ,,	948	1	7	940	11	7	44	1	5

[2] August 22, 1836.   [3] November 4, 1836.

was at work, for the more it prospered the more Dickens moped. His suppressed resentment against his employer finally took shape as a real grievance.[1] He had talked to Kate, he had talked to Forster, he had talked to Macready: all sympathised with him and told him he was badly used. Why should he not demand a show-down? Why should he not challenge Bentley to produce the accounts of the *Miscellany*? If it was doing as well as he believed it to be doing, there could be no possible excuse for pinching over half-pages and other irritating economies. It was at this point that Forster took charge of the situation, and we know that in the opinion of Chapman and Hall he was 'a remarkable intermediary' occupying a unique position between patron and literary agent. A letter written to Bentley at this time, which is not in Dickens's style though signed by him, seems proof of his well-timed intervention.

Forster had evidently advised Dickens not to give way to disgust and bad temper, but to go on with the *Miscellany*. If it could be arranged, the serial *Oliver Twist* should be followed by the half-written book *Gabriel Vardon*, now re-named *Barnaby Rudge*. In other words, if Bentley could be persuaded to forgo *Barnaby Rudge* as a novel and allow it to appear as a serial in the *Miscellany*, it would simplify Dickens's problem of production. He would draft a letter for Dickens to send. The author was in a fairly strong position, for the *Memoirs of Grimaldi*, alluded to in this document, had just been completed.

The letter ran as follows:

> I have been recently thinking a great deal about *Barnaby Rudge*. Grimaldi has occupied so much of the short interval I had between the completion of *Pickwick* and the commencement of the new work, that I see it will be wholly impossible for me to produce it by the time I had hoped, with justice to myself or profit to you. What I wish you to consider is this: would it not be far more to your interest as well as within the scope of my ability, if *Barnaby Rudge*

[1] See Moore's *Diary*, vii. 244.

began in the *Miscellany* immediately on the conclusion of *Oliver Twist* and were continued there for some time, and then published in three volumes? Take these simple facts into consideration. If the *Miscellany* is to keep its ground, it must have some continuous tale from me when *Oliver* stops. If I sat down to *Barnaby Rudge* writing a little of it when I could, it would be clearly impossible for me to begin a new series of papers in the *Miscellany*. The conduct of three different stories at the same time, and the production of a large portion of each every month would have been beyond Scott himself. Whereas having *Barnaby* for the *Miscellany* we could at once supply the gap which the cessation of *Oliver* must create, and you would have all the advantage of that prestige in favour of the work which is certain to enhance the value of *Oliver Twist* considerably. Just think of this at your leisure. I am really anxious to do the best I can for you as well as for myself and in this case the pecuniary advantage must be all on your side.[1]

The answer to this letter is not available, but we do know that John Forster was able to arrange with Bentley that *Barnaby Rudge* should be serialised in the *Miscellany* on the conclusion of *Oliver Twist* in April 1839.

John Forster probably thought he had settled things up in a very satisfactory way, but there was always Dickens's temperament to be reckoned with. Having once begun to dislike and distrust Bentley, Dickens went on disliking and distrusting him. No mere contract could allay his resentment. The relationship was just intolerable to him and no matter at what cost he must end it. Bentley was 'a nefarious rascal who expected to publish serials for his own benefit and authors to acquiesce in toiling to make him rich'. One cannot help suspecting that Ainsworth, of whom Dickens was seeing a great deal, may have been working behind the scenes to promote friction. He had written an odd letter, as we have seen, to Macrone over *Gabriel Vardon*, and is said to have written similar letters to Bentley over *Barnaby Rudge*.

[1] 159. I. N.L.

Although Ainsworth professed sympathy with Dickens in his woes it may have had the effect of aggravating him still further, and we must not forget that in his dealings with Bentley Ainsworth was angling for the reversion of the editorship of the *Miscellany*.

A day came when Dickens had to tell Forster that he simply could not force himself to work for Bentley any longer.

> The immense profits *Oliver* has realised to its publisher and is still realising: the paltry, wretched miserable sum it brought to me . . . the consciousness that I have still the slavery and drudgery of another work on the same journeyman terms;—that I am struggling in old toils and wasting my energies in the very height and freshness of my fame, and the best part of my life, to fill the pockets of others, while for those nearest and dearest to me I can realise but little more than a genteel subsistence . . . I do most solemnly declare that morally before God and man I hold myself released. . . . This net that has been wound about me, so chafes me, so exasperates and irritates my mind, that to break it at whatever cost is my constant impulse.[1]

He took the plunge and relinquished the *Miscellany*. To Talfourd he wrote, 'You will be glad to hear I have burst the Bentleian bonds'.

In the last number he edited, that of February 1839, he inserted a 'farewell to a child two years and two months old'. Everyone, including Dickens, now seemed pacified, but by April, soon after he had handed the editorship of the *Miscellany* over to Ainsworth, 'Boz' had become feverishly anxious to get altogether 'out of the clutches of Bentley'. Appealing once again to Chapman and Hall to rescue him, he, with Forster's help, persuaded them to buy all rights in *Oliver Twist* for £2250 with the annulment of the *Barnaby Rudge* contract thrown in. At last his affairs were being straightened out: he had now eliminated two of his publishers and had Chapman and Hall alone to reckon with.

[1] 196. I. N.L.

Chapter 7

SCHOOLS AND FACTORIES

*To leave one's hand upon the time, with one tender touch for
the mass of the toiling people that nothing could obliterate,
would be to lift oneself above the dust of all the Doges.*
CHARLES DICKENS

A BEING so capable of lightning adjustment to circumstances calling out height or depth of feeling is a puzzling
person to write about, for what is true at one moment becomes untrue the next. As anguish over the death of Mary
alternates with bubbling jubilation over the sweeping success
of *Pickwick*, one stands back astonished at both the depth and
the elasticity of temperament displayed. The same man who
could sit immobile in his study in front of Mary's picture
mourning as if he could not be comforted, would a few hours
later preside over a book-banquet or dance delightedly at a
party. Kate Dickens's friends thought she 'bore sweetly'
with her husband's romantic adoration of Mary, but she, like
ourselves, must have been aware that every experience in turn
was absolute and intoxicated him more or less. His temperament cannot be accounted for; it is only possible to state how
it operated. Kate Dickens, in fact, was not much concerned
by his changes of mood; she was indolent by nature and disposed in any case to let things take their course and not attempt
to control them.

Increasing fame now obliged Dickens to provide portraits
for the press, so during the autumn of 1837 he gave sittings in
Doughty Street to George Cruikshank who was touchy and
would not let him see callers while he was doing his work.
He also sat to his friend and admirer Samuel Laurence and
arranged that he should also paint Kate, insisting on a business
contract 'as if we were strangers. This being so I shall
consign her to you as often as you think proper.' To the
subject of portraits we shall return presently.

Baby Charles, now almost a year old, was christened in December 1837 at 'New Pancridge' church at the east end of Euston Square, a building modelled on the Erechtheum. In its tomb-like, almost windowless interior did Miss Burdett Coutts promise, on the infant's behalf, to renounce the world, the flesh and the devil. At the evening christening party Edward Chapman, the William Halls, the S. C. Halls and the relations drank to the health of the first-born, who went through his ordeal fractiously. Measles supervening two days later, entertaining in Doughty Street ceased for a short while, and Dickens immersed himself in *Oliver Twist*. After Christmas he got down to work on *Sketches of Young Gentlemen*,[1] a windfall contract for £125 that did not oblige him to reveal his identity. Mr. and Mrs. Chirrup, *The Nice Little Couple*, in this series are taken from Mr. and Mrs. William Hall, and their bachelor friend from Hall's partner, Edward Chapman. A letter to Ainsworth of this date shows just how much work had to be got out of the way before Charles could permit himself to go for a short holiday. Inviting his friend to dinner he wrote:

> Little Hall and his wife and big partner are going to dine here on Saturday next at half-past five. . . . The illustrious George [Cruikshank] and his stout lady are coming too so that the anti-Bores will be triumphant and keep the Bores in due subjection. . . . My month's work has been dreadful, *Grimaldi*, the anonymous book for C. and H., *Oliver* and the *Miscellany*. They are all done thank God! and I start on my pilgrimage to the cheap schools of Yorkshire (a mighty secret of course) next Monday morning.[2]

The journey to Yorkshire was being made (in company with the illustrator, Hablot Browne), to gather material for *Nicholas Nickleby*. The 'cheap schools', as Dickens called them, had been on his mind for some time. They advertised regularly in the London papers as teaching Latin, Greek, French, Mathematics and Navigation. Why they clustered

[1] Chapman and Hall, 1838. Followed by *Sketches of Young Couples*, 1840.
[2] 154. I. N.L.

in Yorkshire is not known, but there were four of these schools in Bowes alone as the burial records show, one at Barnard Castle, and another at Startforth near by. To visit them without awakening suspicion the investigator travelled under an assumed name, taking with him a formal letter from C. Smithson, 'a London attorney', to R. Barnes, 'a Yorkshire attorney', at Barnard Castle. The letter, a plausible one, explained that he was acting for a widowed friend who wanted to place her boys at school in the neighbourhood. In good faith Barnes provided two introductions to local schoolmasters and then, repenting him of his action, walked across to the King's Head to tell the stranger that these schools were sad places for mothers to send orphan boys to. 'It really would be better', he said, 'to let them run errands, hold horses, or fling themselves in any way upon the mercy of the world than consign them to such dens.' The stranger, who had been gazing out on the market-place from the coffee-room window, had noted with interest that a clockmaker's shop with the name 'Master Humphrey' stood across the way. When he had listened to Mr. Barnes's kindly warnings, he stepped over to see Master Humphrey and hear what he had to say about local schools. What a good name for a clockmaker, to be sure: like many other half-conscious observations it sank into his memory to bob up again one day in the title of a book.

Introduction in hand Dickens went to Bowes Academy, kept by a Mr. Shaw who advertised regularly in the *Times* and had a London agent. One of the features of his curriculum was 'no vacations', which in practice meant that it was only boys unwanted by parents and guardians who were put in his charge. This gave the master unlimited power, for no boy could tell during the holidays what life at school was like, nor could he, since letters were read, appeal to any outsider for help. Though Dickens protested that he had no particular school in mind, his readers assumed that Squeers of Dotheboys Hall was taken from Shaw of Bowes Academy, a man who had had a case brought against him six years earlier for gross neglect and starvation of boys entrusted to his care. The verdict having gone against him, he had been forced to be more circumspect in his ways.

To the atmosphere of Bowes Academy Dickens reacted as if stung, it put him in a fever to get down to work; so hurrying back to London he began on February 6 to write *Nicholas Nickleby*. By February 9 the first number was complete, and at this book and at *Oliver Twist* he slaved, turn and turn about, for the next eight months. All Dickens's novels came out serially in 20 parts, and were, with three exceptions, roughly the same length, averaging 350,000 words apiece. If he had but one book on the stocks, his method of working was to write hard for a fortnight, then knock off and do something different. In this way he prevented himself from becoming stale and was always eager to get down to the story again. When he was writing two serials at the same time he played one off against the other and had no leisure at all.

By the end of October 1838 he was so tired from overwork that he did not attend even to private correspondence: letters would lie for a month unopened on his desk. As soon as *Oliver Twist* was off his hands, he felt he must escape from his study, so taking seats on the Leamington coach he set off again with Hablot Browne to sight-see in Warwickshire. Having just joined the Shakespeare Society run by Payne Collier, he made a point of acquainting himself with Stratford-on-Avon. He also went to Kenilworth, with which place he was so charmed that he told Kate they really must get lodgings there for their next summer outing. Warwick Castle, 'an ancient building lately restored and possessing no very great attraction beyond a fine view and some beautiful pictures', did not interest him at all. Deep down in him, however, something else was being registered that only came to the surface eight years later when Mrs. Skewton, her daughter Edith, Major Bagstock and Mr. Dombey made the same tour. Dickens certainly took no notes at the time; it does not seem that he ever took notes of what he saw at any time, but in this instance we can observe his mind doing its peculiar work of transmuting what seem to be on the surface commonplace impressions into a distillation of an exquisitely humorous character. The subconscious mind had selected its material strictly, taking the party to Kenilworth and Warwick, but not to Stratford. It was on Warwick that it had fixed itself to our great benefit.

'The Castle is charming,' said Mrs. Skewton, 'associations of the Middle Ages and all that—which is so truly exquisite. Don't you dote upon the Middle Ages, Mr. Carker?'

'Very much indeed,' said Mr. Carker.

'Those darling bygone times, Mr. Carker, with their delicious fortresses and their dear old dungeons and their delightful places of torture and their romantic vengeances and their picturesque assaults and sieges and everything that makes life truly charming. How dreadfully we have degenerated.'

'Yes, we have fallen off deplorably,' said Mr. Carker.

'We have no faith left positively,' said Mrs. Skewton. . . . 'We have no faith in the dear old Barons, who were the most delightful creatures, or in the dear old priests, who were the most warlike of men—or even in the days of that inestimable Queen Bess, upon the wall there, which were so extremely golden. Dear creature! she was all heart and that charming father of hers; I hope you dote on Harry the eighth?'

'I admire him very much,' said Carker.

'So bluff,' cried Mrs. Skewton, 'wasn't he? so burly. So truly English. Such a picture, too, he makes, with his dear little peepy eyes, and his benevolent chin!'

After this digression we must follow Dickens to north Wales which he reached by way of Birmingham and Shrewsbury, travelling through 'miles of cinder paths and blazing furnaces and steam engines—a mass of dirt and misery'. And these glimpses of an industrial world will, as we shall presently see, reappear in *The Old Curiosity Shop* in a sudden transfer of little Nell and her grandfather to a setting of the kind.

At Manchester Dickens met John Forster who brought with him some letters of introduction from Harrison Ainsworth. One of them was addressed to James Crossley, who was informed that Dickens's object in coming north was to see the interior of a cotton mill. Dining with Mr. Gilbert Winter, Dickens met Mr. Crossley and the brothers Grant who worked in Cheeryble House, Canon Street, and were to be perpetuated as 'the Cheeryble brothers' in *Nicholas Nickleby*. The visitors spent three days in Manchester and found time to go to Cheadle Hall to see Ainsworth's three little girls who were at a boarding school there. Dickens made one of them a present of an inscribed copy of Agnes Strickland's *Juvenile Scrapbook*, while Forster and Browne provided books for the other two.

Rather surprisingly—but then one is constantly surprised by the number and variety of Dickens's contacts—we find him writing to Edward FitzGerald about his visit to the cotton mills:

I went to Manchester [he writes] and saw the *worst* cotton mill and then I saw the *best*. *Ex uno disce omnes*. There was no great difference between them. I was obliged to come back suddenly on some matters connected with the publication of *Oliver Twist*. . . . On the eleventh of next month I am going down again only for three days, and then into the enemy's camp and the very headquarters of the Factory System advocates. I fear I shall have very little opportunity of looking about me, but I shall be most happy to avail myself of any introduction from Lord Ashley which in the course of an hour or so would enable me to make any fresh observations. . . . So far as seeing goes, I have seen enough for my purpose, and what I have seen has astonished and disgusted me beyond all measure. I mean to strike the heaviest blow in my power for those unfortunate creatures, but whether I shall do so in *Nickleby* or wait some other opportunity I have not yet determined.[1]

This letter reveals what is nowhere else indicated, that Dickens had been turning over in his mind the idea of writing a novel to back Lord Ashley's campaign to alleviate the lot of

[1] *Life of 7th Earl of Shaftesbury*, by E. Hodder, vol. i. p. 227.

children in factories.   Once he had inspected the cotton mills he found himself so disgusted and so angered at the horrors he had witnessed that he did not find it possible to sit down and write about them in the half-sentimental, half-humorous way that alone got under the skin of his readers.   A third visit to Manchester in company with Ainsworth (in January 1839 to attend a public dinner to both authors) had no more fruitful results though he spent two whole days sightseeing.   Perfectly aware that his power did not lie in being either didactic or minatory, he had to give way to his immediate reactions of fury and despair at the 'keeping down of thousands and thousands of God's images', and for the time being had to leave the subject alone.   When he did recur to the exploitation of human beings under the industrial system he wrote a different kind of book, *Hard Times*, different because by then he was strongly under the influence of Carlyle.

From the time of his visits to the cotton mills Dickens began with increasing seriousness, partly at Miss Coutts's request and partly on his own account, to study social conditions in London.   He read, for example, Dr. Southwood Smith's report (drawn up by order of the Poor Law Authorities) on the housing of the poor in Whitechapel and Bethnal Green.   Nothing more disgusting in the way of human habitations could be imagined than the houses he described as responsible for the abnormal death rate from typhus.   Dr. Southwood Smith's report had so impressed the Home Secretary, Lord Normanby, that he had decided to make a personal inspection of the hideous conditions disclosed. Lord Ashley followed suit and then Charles Dickens, who reported to Miss Coutts with results observable later on, when the first model dwellings were erected at her charge in Bethnal Green.

In many ways Dr. Southwood Smith, whose acquaintance Dickens now made, was a very important reformer, a reformer, howbeit, who has never received the credit due to him as the originator and tireless advocate of the first Public Health Act of 1848.   Of angelic appearance, he faced horrors with the

courage of a martyr. He was the disciple and friend of
Jeremy Bentham and it was to him that Bentham (owing to the
difficulty of obtaining corpses for medical students to dissect)
had bequeathed his own body with instructions that Smith
must himself deliver a lecture on it in the Webb School of
Anatomy. Dr. Smith carried out this behest, but it was
observed by students present that his face was as blenched as
that of the corpse. The clothed skeleton of Bentham with a
face made up in wax sat with broad-brimmed hat covering
long white hair, in a mahogany case in his house, and everyone who dined with the doctor had to face this *memento mori*.
Dickens used to dine with him and learnt to love and respect
his selfless host. Presently we shall find him helping Dr.
Southwood Smith to establish the first private-patient nursing
home in England.

As always in Dickens's life, light interludes succeeded
serious experiences and some of these lighter interludes were
generated by his growing popularity. Theatrical producers
were beginning to see money in dramatising his novels, and
one named Sterling seized upon the story of *Nicholas Nickleby*
when it was but one-third written, gave it a plot and ending
of his own, and produced it with Yates at the Adelphi.
Dickens protested vehemently, but, after seeing what they
had made of the Mantalinis, he felt obliged to withdraw his
objection and say that it was 'beyond all praise and admirably
done in every respect'. An unauthorised version of *Oliver
Twist* at the Surrey, however, upset him terribly. Forster,
who was with him, said that after glancing at the production
for a few moments he lay down on the floor of the box and
never rose from it till the drop scene fell.

The Old Curiosity Shop was adapted for the Adelphi in
1840, and as Yates was now a friend of Dickens, the author
attended rehearsals and 'made a great many improvements'.
Even so he could not brace himself to be present on the first
night, and Kate, escorted by Frederick, went to the theatre
without him. He said to Tom Mitton, 'The thing may be
better than I expect, but I have no faith in it at all'.

Chapter 8

LONDON SALONS

I have heard . . . that the sense of being well-dressed gives
a feeling of inward tranquility which religion is powerless
to bestow.   R. W. EMERSON

LIKE Mrs. Boffin in *Our Mutual Friend*, Charles Dickens was
'a highflyer at fashion'. He had always been fond of
clothes and by this time was the proud owner of many bright
waistcoats, coloured neckcloths and jewelled pins and rings.
Both he and Ainsworth modelled themselves upon Count
d'Orsay, in so far as two little men could venture to imitate a
man of six feet four, and very natty do they appear in the
sketches of Alfred Croquis. Dickens, however, was lured
from the straight and narrow path of good taste by his admiration for Disraeli's dress and his own love of the stage. It was
irresistible to him to combine the role of personable young
man with that of famous person, indeed in practice one could
be made to set off the other. Before he became a public
figure he had short hair and his Aunt Janet's miniature shows
a severe young face poised on the top of a very high stock.
An engraving adapted from this miniature was used in the
Court Journal to illustrate an article on 'the genius of Boz, the
portrayer of the true and the natural'. It was a little out of
date, but Laman Blanchard, the editor, could find nothing else
to insert, though actually by this time Cruikshank had included several likenesses of 'Boz' in his illustrations for the
Sketches showing a dark-haired youth buying a coach ticket,
or in 'Public Dinners' as an usher leading a procession of
children to a feast,[1] as well as in a drawing labelled 'Sir Lionel
Flamstead and his Friends'[2] in which the likeness of Ainsworth

[1] In company with Chapman and Hall.
[2] Etched by Cruikshank for Macrone but not used by him. See *Ainsworth's Magazine*, 1840.

also appears. Cruikshank introduced himself in an easy-to-be-recognised way into all of these scenes.

In a more serious pencil sketch made of Dickens in his study in Doughty Street, Cruikshank shows us an elegant figure in slim-waisted frock-coat, tightly fitting trousers strapped over pointed boots, voluminous satin cravat and curled locks producing a finnicky dandified effect. Samuel Laurence drew Dickens about the same time in chalk, and a few months later made a painting of him in water-colour. Laurence, who saw him less effeminate-looking than Cruikshank, depicted his subject with determined jaw, firm countenance and uncurled bobbed hair. It is probably the best portrait ever done of him and gives, as it were, the eternal qualities resident in the man who could set his teeth and write stories that almost eviscerated him in the telling. Laurence at least realised that though Dickens had risen very fast, it had been entirely by his own exertions—in other words, by the exercise of terrific will-power.

There must have been something very striking and attractive about Dickens's appearance at this time. Not only did women fall before him, but Leigh Hunt said, 'What a face to meet in a drawing room! It has the life and soul in it of fifty human beings!' And it must have been his personal distinction and adaptability as much as his genius that opened to him the doors of the more particular houses of Mayfair and St. James's, but, however it came about, at twenty-six Mr. Dickens had the to him great satisfaction of being recognisably distinguished, the kind of young man that every artist wanted to paint and every hostess to see in their salons. Of course he was socially inexperienced, but his aplomb was such that neither the exotic atmosphere generated by Count d'Orsay nor the asperities of Lady Holland could now disturb the assurance of a celebrity most of whose spare time had hitherto been spent in furnished lodgings and a three-pair suite in Holborn.

One should bear in mind that all the people of the world he was now so confidently entering had had natural advantages that he had never enjoyed. They had come from country houses well furnished with libraries and 'marbles': they had travelled in Italy: they knew Paris: they could read French and Italian: they were well grounded in the classics: they had a nodding acquaintance with the great pictures, statues and buildings of Europe. Monckton Milnes had travelled in Greece and Landor had lived in Italy, but Dickens, except as a child, had lived nowhere except in London. Nothing he saw in the way of objects meant anything to him; he would not at this time have recognised the Apollo Belvedere or the Venus de Milo. He had done some reading in past years at the British Museum to post himself in history, law and politics, but, judged by public school and university standards, he was still under-educated. He now applied himself with extraordinary success to another kind of self-instruction, that of contacts with the then leaders of literary and political society. How unpredictable it was that a few years later he would be talking Italian easily with Genoese friends and conversing in fluent French with Émile de Girardin and George Sand!

Dickens was very sharp, of course, at picking up hints, especially in the matter of social behaviour. One can imagine how on the alert he must have been when first admitted to the house of Mr. Rogers, whose windows looked into the Green Park at its most pleasant point. With the exception of a few visits to Sir Francis Burdett's house, it was the first cultivated *milieu* to which he gained access. If he thought a young guest worth while Mr. Rogers was quick at the uptake, so as soon as Sir Francis Burdett presented 'Boz', the foundation of a friendship was laid which we see reflected in the glowing dedication of *The Old Curiosity Shop*, wherein Mr. Rogers is depicted as 'one of the few men whom Riches and Honours have not spoiled and who have preserved in High Places active Sympathy with the Poorest and the Humblest of their kind'. Mr. Rogers was always extremely nice to Mrs. Dickens which some of the people who took Dickens up were not; in fact he was one of the very few

literary people she liked or trusted or to whom she signed
herself 'Yours very affectionately'.

More significant, in a manner of speaking, was 22 St.
James's Place than Gore House or Holland House, because it
was a revelation to Charles Dickens, brought up as he had
been, to see what a member of the elastic middle class could
achieve in the way of distinction of living. Sydney Smith
used to say that Sam 'hived very comfortably' and most
Americans were impressed by the hospitality meted out by
the banker-poet. Washington Irving spoke of his 'classic
little mansion', and Bancroft described it to Emerson as 'a
Pantheon in miniature'.

Though Rogers kept but very few servants, he entertained
everybody of note and said he did it on £2000 a year. Owing
to his purchase of pictures from the Orleans Gallery and to
their being hung against a background of crimson damask,
his rather small rooms made an opulent, half-suffocating impression which the gold frames, silver wall-sconces and red
brocade-upholstered furniture enhanced. The rooms were
far too dark for Sydney Smith's taste as there was no light
except that thrown on to the pictures by candles. But grand
as were his surroundings, Mr. Rogers was very unalarming in
himself, being so small of stature and so small of voice and so
anxious always to bring the best out in people. The pictures
Mr. Dickens was not capable of appreciating, though he soon
learnt to recognise the Raphael Madonna, the two Titians on
which their owner doted, and the little St. George of which he
was so proud because he believed it to be the work of that
rarest of masters, Giorgione. It was easier for an author,
even a not very well-read author, to admire the well-bound
books arranged in bookcases painted by Stothard with scenes
from Boccaccio, Chaucer and Shakespeare, as well as to
appreciate the fine workmanship of the Flaxman mantelpieces
and the claw-footed mahogany tables 'carved by a journeyman
of the name of Chantrey working for 5/- a day'. The rooms
were strikingly characteristic of the taste of a man who had
made the grand tour, written verse and worshipped literature.

Not the least considered of his treasures was a cast of Pope's face taken after death by Roubillac, and Milton's receipt for *Paradise Lost* which hung framed upon a door.

Taking note of habits and manners as well as objects, Dickens especially liked the way Mr. Rogers entertained children and grown-ups on Twelfth Night with his skilful conjuring tricks. He also admired his easy conversational breakfasts of eight people and longed to emulate them. But the breakfasts could not be copied at Doughty Street because he was neither an old bachelor like Mr. Rogers nor a young bachelor like his imitator Richard Monckton Milnes. He could, however, reproduce the delightful Twelfth Night entertainments, and as soon as he had a suitable house of his own we find him doing so with great enjoyment.

Mr. Rogers invited ladies to his breakfasts, but they had to qualify either by intelligence or position for inclusion in this select coterie. Mrs. Charles Dickens never breakfasted with Mr. Rogers. That they were fond of each other is clear from the letters she wrote to him when abroad, but she was just not conversable. Let us look at a guest's account of a breakfast in order to see what kind of conversation was expected of the company round the table. On this occasion Mr. Rogers was entertaining Mrs. Norton, Lady Blessington, Mr. Macaulay and Dr. Mackay, and as host indicated that 'rhyming' was to be the topic for discussion.[1] Mrs. Norton spoke of *Hudibras* and laughed at Butler's 'desperate ingenuity'. Why his lines,

> Pulpit, drum, ecclesiastic,
> Was beat with fist instead of a stick,

were really comparable to those comic lines of Lord Byron,

> But—Oh! ye lords of ladies intellectual,
> Inform us truly, have they not hen-peck'd you all?

'But they are *meant* to be comic lines!' objected Macaulay, adding that he certainly preferred what he called 'real rhyming', whereupon Lady Blessington remarked how poor

[1] Ch. Mackay, *Through the Long Day.*

we were in rhymes. Could anyone tell her whether there
were rhymes to music, silver, orange, noble, herald? Much
English verse struck her as hurdy-gurdy like. Someone
then raised the subject of assonance in ballads. Macaulay
said blank verse was not satisfactory to the English ear unless,
as was so often the case with Shakespeare and Milton, it was
decasyllabic. Mrs. Norton chipped in with, 'Narrative verse
palls in any case; why, look at *The Lay of the Last Minstrel*
and *The Lady of the Lake*'.

Mr. Macaulay turning to his host asked, 'Can I have a
Piers Plowman, Mr. Rogers?' When it was handed to him
he read,

> In a somer seson whan soft was the sonne
> I shope me in shroudes as I a shepe were,

and then jumped to

> Patriarchs and Prophets and Preachers of God's Wordes,

saying how pleasing to him was the sound of alliteration.
'Tedious to a modern ear like mine', commented Lady
Blessington, but Mrs. Norton stopped her by spouting,

> Rushed into the *f*ield and *f*oremost *f*ighting *f*ell.

They then discussed *The Ingoldsby Legends* about which
opinion was sharply divided, and then the hexameter for
which all expressed dislike, though Macaulay intoned lines
from *The Vision of Judgement* to show what an effect Southey
got with the metre:

> ... Toll, toll, through the silence of evening;
> 'Tis a deep dull sound that is heavy and mournful at all times,
> For it tells of mortality always.

Mr. Rogers was so upset by this passage—he was seventy-five
and hated to be reminded of death—that Mrs. Norton tried
to cheer him by bringing forward *Chevy Chase* and Lady
Blessington *The Nut-Brown Maid* as fine *happy* ballads. The
ladies managed to put their host in good humour again and

they parted in a spirit of enjoyment, for they were all versifiers. It was to this kind of company and conversation that Dickens now chose to adapt himself.

It would seem that Charles Dickens was introduced to Count d'Orsay by Serjeant Talfourd in 1836 and that his first appearance in the Gore House salon of Lady Blessington was at the house-warming in May of the same year. Walter Savage Landor, an old and dear friend from Italian days, had come up to stay for the occasion and she was ransacking the town to secure for him pleasant company nightly, and a sight of the new lions. 'I wish to procure for him as much enjoyment as I can', she wrote when inviting Talfourd to meet him. He must not fail her whatever happened and he must bring a young writer with him. And in Talfourd's company Dickens went to his first great party, drove through the carriage gates and walked through doors flung wide by powdered footmen in green and gold—on through the hall to the library, a long room with a fireplace at either end and columns supporting the ceiling. He was gifted, as Taine was to discover later, with the camera's eye and nothing escaped him. He saw the ivory-coloured bookshelves with their glass inlay, the white-and-gold furniture, the apple-green damask, the green carpet at his feet, and last of all his hostess beaming a welcome on him. As the author of a widely-read book on Lord Byron, Lady Blessington was regarded as a friend by editors and contributors to magazines. She was, as it were, of their confraternity, for she worked steadily producing a book a year from 1833 on. She also edited the *Keepsake* and various *Books of Beauty*. Few women, excepting Miss Landon, Mrs. S. C. Hall, Lady Emmeline Stuart-Wortley, Countess Guiccioli and her own sisters Lady Canterbury and the Countess de Saint Marsault, ever set foot in her house, for her relations with Count d'Orsay, her stepson-in-law, were considered unconventional. Nat Willis got his first glimpse of this most attractive woman sitting reading half-buried in a *fauteuil* of yellow satin

in 'a room of rather crowded sumptuousness'. Hall[1] had
come to know her very well when he was persuading her to
set down her conversations with Lord Byron for the *New
Monthly* which he, at the time, was editing.   Mrs. S. C. Hall
liked her for her good heart and said there was 'nothing
artificial about her, nothing fussy or self-distrustful', and that
though conscious of power she was 'utterly without pre-
tension'.   To her there seemed an admirable fitness in all
Lady Blessington did and a deep-seated good intent in both
her words and actions.   Every man took to her, including
the Duke of Wellington, who was amused to be greeted by
her talking crow with, 'Up, Guards and at 'em!', and Disraeli
paid her the extravagant compliment of saying her pen must
have been plucked from the pinion of the bird of paradise.
Her evenings in Seamore Place had been famous for five years,
and her receptions at Gore House, to which abode she moved
in 1836, were to be even more famous.

Most of the well-known men in London were to be met in
her rooms.   In reading the diaries of the day, in which the
names of Disraeli, the brothers Bulwer, Captain Marryat,
Albany Fonblanque, Barry Cornwall, Sir Martin Shee, Lords
Durham, Abinger, Strangford, Lyndhurst appear, we see how
wide was her circle.   Nat Willis had once spent an exciting
evening watching Disraeli (not at that time in the House),
'lividly pale, eye black as Erebus, ringlets falling over left
cheek', sitting in the window looking out over the Park, 'his
gold-flowered waistcoat reflecting the rays of the setting sun',
a contrast indeed with ill-dressed Lord Durham who 'would
never have passed for a lord at all in America'.   To Nat
Willis Count d'Orsay appeared 'very splendid and very in-
definable'.

The Count was one of the sights of London as he drove
from his little house in Curzon Street to Hyde Park.   To
his smart, hooded cabriolet was harnessed a seventeen-hand
horse, and behind, clinging to the straps, bounced a tiny tiger.
The reins were handled in white kid gloves and Dickens,

[1] *Memories of S. C. Hall*, p. 403.

who watched him carefully from the pavement, noted with
admiring approval that his wristbands were turned back over
his coat cuffs, a fashion he was not slow to imitate, nor the
Bostonians to observe and comment on.   The equipage of
the Countess of Blessington, glistening with varnish and
emblazoned with heraldic devices, was also to be seen daily in
the Park.   Its green hammercloth edged with white, its silver-
wigged coachman, its tall footmen, cane-carrying, powder-
headed and silk-stockinged, formed the stately setting to the
still beautiful woman who acknowledged the bows of the
innumerable men who saluted her.

For young Mr. Dickens the Blessington-d'Orsay parties
were most polishing for they acquainted him with the ways of
the *beau monde*.   They were not alarming as were the parties
at Holland House for no one quizzed him under Lady
Blessington's roof.   The talk was not like the talk at Mr.
Rogers's because it was not directed, but allowed to flow
freely.   Mr. Disraeli, who when worked up talked 'like a
racehorse approaching a winning post', one evening described
Beckford's *Italy* and went on to tell of its author's fantastical
life at Bath where he was said to own two houses joined by a
covered bridge, his servants living on one side and he and his
companion, a Spanish dwarf, 'who believes himself a duke
and is treated as such', on the other.   Then he told of a high
tower lined with books and of a grave below the pavement in
which he was arranging a double sepulchre for himself and the
dwarf.   Victor Hugo and his newest books also came in for
discussion, champagne flowed, and all the while d'Orsay kept
the conversation alive by a running fire of witty parentheses
in French and English.   Usually silent and often aloof, in a
corner of the saloon sat Prince Louis Napoleon, the future
Emperor of the French.

One never ceases to wish that Dickens had kept a diary in
which he recorded his first impressions of well-known people
and houses, but his mind did not work like that: it was too
busy registering and transforming a different set of impressions and describing a different and irreconcilable set of

people.   No matter how much he enjoyed his evenings with d'Orsay or Rogers, they did not make him wish to write down anything about them.   Whatever the secret processes of absorption that went to the making of his books and the stimulation of his creative powers, they were automatically selective and independent of his conscious will.   As to keeping an engagement book methodically he could not do it, as it depressed him too deeply to record the dying days.   Therefore we have no description from him of Sydney Smith, no Carlylean vignette of those piercing hazel eyes, that massive Roman nose, the shrewdness and fun that lent life to every gathering he attended.   Nor have we any picture from his pen of the Misses Berry or of Lord and Lady Holland.

The Holland House circle differed from that of Gore House in being more political and diplomatic in composition than literary.   The discussions that took place there were also more serious in tone, and it was a feather in the cap of a mere writer (without birth to recommend him or make him *salonfähig*) to be invited there.   In another way the company was not different, for it was as masculine in character as that of Gore House.   Many ladies of the day refused to know Lady Holland since she had once violated their code and still remained outside the pale of society.   This embargo was imposed even in Dickens's day, as we realise only too clearly in reading a letter written by Sydney Smith to Lord Denman in 1841.   Sydney Smith was one of Lady Holland's dearest and most intimate friends and yet he could write to a prospective dinner guest as follows:

> Mrs. Sydney and I have made a blunder. . . . Lady Holland dines with us on the 17th.   Does Lady Denman know Lady Holland, and if not will that deprive us of the pleasure of Lady Denman's company?   Lady Holland sinned early in life, with Methuselah and Enoch, but still she is out of the pale of the regular ladies, and the case ought to have been put.[1]

A letter like this from one *habitué* of Holland House to

[1] *Thomas, First Lord Denman*, by Sir Joseph Arnould, vol. ii. p. 150.

another recreates for us the stuffiness and rigidity of early Victorian society better and more exactly than any description, for it is a slice from life as it was being lived at the moment.

Lady Holland in her turn would not know Lady Blessington, and their two circles, though intersecting frequently, never coalesced. It was two years after his introduction to Gore House that Dickens made his bow at Holland House. Serjeant Talfourd, whom Lady Holland liked very much, had waited for a favourable opportunity to present his young friend. Lady Holland asked 'dear Bulwer' whether Talfourd's protégé was presentable, and on receiving an affirmative reply invited queer little 'Boz' to visit her. For the date she named he had an engagement he could not throw over, so was obliged to wait for another summons. That moment came when she began to read *Nicholas Nickleby*. When finally he could make his bow, Lady Holland found him 'modest and well-behaved', and Lord Holland said he was 'very unobtrusive, yet not shy, intelligent in countenance and altogether prepossessing'.

Carlyle described Lady Holland as 'a proud old dame' in the habit of being obeyed and entertained, and used to say that her face when he caught it in profile had something of the falcon character, if a falcon's bill were straight. Macaulay thought there was a good deal of Queen Elizabeth about her. Till Dickens got used to her ways he could not defend himself against her acute questioning and found himself forced against his will to disclose to her the plot of *Nicholas Nickleby*, of which the first numbers only had appeared. To steel oneself against such persistent and ruthless probings was an art in itself, for, as Talleyrand used to say, 'Lady Holland is all assertion'.

Soon after his first venture into this exclusive circle, Dickens was annoyed to find that Bentley had inserted into the September number of the *Miscellany* a gossipy article on Holland House entertaining. Writing off at once to Lady Holland, he said:

I saw yesterday for the first time that in this month's number there is some impromptu of Sydney Smith's purporting to have been written at your table some years ago which Bentley, I assume, obtained gratis from some well-informed babbler and printed accordingly.

To clear himself of indiscretion, he here reveals that though his name appears as that of editor of *Bentley's Miscellany* he had 'little to do with the business part of the publication', and therefore had no previous knowledge of the list of contents. He wishes her to understand that he entertains so great an abhorrence of printed recollections of private conversations and so great a detestation of the impertinence and vulgarity which makes them public that he must assure her that the production in question has never been authorised by him.[1]

A born dictator, Lady Holland kept control of the guests invited to her table both as to quality and conversation. Lord Holland, incurably good-natured, would, if not checked, have invited almost anybody to dinner, but she always had the general level in view and not the particular kindness, and a bore was to be feared like death. She did not hesitate to stem a monopolistic talker and would squeeze sixteen people into a table laid for nine and not mind that no elbow could be raised. She levied tribute of game, venison and cheeses from guests capable of paying it, as well as foreign delicacies from ambassadorial houses. She could be coldly offensive to those for whom she took a dislike and also so frigidly polite as to paralyse the neophyte. Writers inclined to be vain might be told off like poor Rogers with, 'Your poetry is bad enough so pray be sparing of your prose', and she liked Rogers! Macaulay she would pull up remorselessly. Having cut short one of his discourses and switched the conversation on to the Christian Fathers, Macaulay showed himself too fluent about St. Chrysostom and St. Athanasius, so once more she tried to floor him with, 'Pray, Macaulay, what was the origin of the doll? When were dolls first mentioned in history?' Macaulay, neither floored nor out of temper, at once began to

[1] September 1838. *The Dickensian*, 1936, pp. 33-41.

tell the company about the Roman doll.   Guests were sometimes ordered about like servants and few resented it.   No
one but Sydney Smith, however, on being told peremptorily
to ring the bell, would obey promptly and then inquire
should he dust the room?[1]

Somehow Dickens managed to get through the preliminary
ordeal of Holland House entertaining with calm and credit,
and when he dined there Lord Holland's sister wrote that she
liked everything about him except the intolerable dandyism of
his dress.   'His countenance' she thought 'beautiful, because
blended with his intelligence there is such an expression of
goodness.'   Somehow this nondescript young man managed
to touch the heart of Lady Holland, and we see from his letters
to her after Lord Holland's death that he seemed to understand her and give her the kind of friendship she required.
The letters are cosy, straightforward and confidential.

Almost as soon as Holland House had set the seal of its
approval on Dickens the Misses Berry got on his track.
They really must have the remarkable young author of
Nicholas Nickleby to their parties.   From Richmond, where
they were living for the hot months, they called on Mr. and
Mrs. Dickens, who were summering once again at Petersham.
Mrs. Dickens was in no condition to dine out, and Mr.
Dickens excused himself on the plea that he 'had not finished
the month's instalment of his new book'.   This did not
satisfy the eager Berrys, who got Sydney Smith to write
again on their behalf.   His letter, written from 'The Hole'
(33 Charles Street, Berkeley Square), is so characteristic of the
man that it is irresistible to quote his actual words:

> Nobody more, and more justly talked of than yourself.
> The Miss Berrys now at Richmond live only to become
> acquainted with you and have commissioned me to request
> you to dine with them on Friday 29th [June] or Monday
> July 1st to meet a Canon of St. Pauls, the Rector of Combe
> Florey, and the Vicar of Halberton, all equally well known
> to you; to say nothing of other and better people.   The

---

[1] *The Greville Memoirs*, vol. i. pp. 367-8.

Miss Berrys and Lady Charlotte Lindsay have not the smallest objection to be put into a Number, but on the contrary would be proud of the distinction; and Lady Charlotte, in particular, you may marry to Newman Noggs. Pray come, it is as much as my place is worth to send them a refusal.—SYDNEY SMITH.

And to the Misses Berry Dickens went, though he tells us nothing about it; indeed, had it not been for Sydney Smith we should not even know that these delightful ladies had craved his acquaintanceship.

One of the hall-marks of success in the society in which Dickens now moved, as of right, was election to the Athenaeum Club, for which Serjeant Talfourd had proposed him in May 1838, getting Serjeant Storks to second him. He became a member the following month, being brought in as one of forty persons eminent in literature, art and science. Among the forty were Grote and Charles Darwin, Macready and the grandson of his grandmother's employer, Richard Monckton Milnes. One sees from looking at the dates when Dickens's contemporaries were admitted to membership what a compliment it was to 'Boz' that he should be made free of the Athenaeum at the age of twenty-six. Macready had been turned down three years earlier. Robert Browning with *Paracelsus* and *Strafford* to his credit was not elected till 1862. Thackeray was not admitted till 1851 and John Forster with five volumes of historical biographies to his pen was not chosen till 1852. The Athenaeum not only gave the younger men elected to it a certain cachet, but also the opportunity for meeting almost everyone of note. The Club had been Croker's idea, for by his day the meeting-places of the wits—coffee-houses and taverns—had gone out and it had become desirable to have a common meeting-ground not so much for wits as for men of achievement. Sir Walter Scott, Samuel Rogers, Sir Thomas Lawrence, Sir Francis Chantrey and Lord Spencer were on the original committee and proceeded solemnly to choose the first members from the lists of the Society of Antiquaries, the Royal College of Surgeons, and from the judges' and bishops' benches. It was decided that the Club premises must be noble in themselves and distinguished in decoration, and the result was that a palace was erected in Waterloo Place capped by a classical frieze of Bath stone carved by John Henning. The sum of £500 was allocated to a library, which eventually housed Captain Basil Hall's collection of publications on the United States of America, the Civil War tracts of Gibbon, and, in another century, was to receive the Warren Vernon books on Dante. A certain cachet was given to the note-paper by a Minerva seal cut by Sir Francis Chantrey to the design of Sir Thomas Lawrence. Intended to be a centre of culture, the Club, owing to its non-political character, could open its doors to foreigners of heterodox views. It also threw wide its portals on the occasions of the Coronation and Royal Wedding. Eleven hundred and thirty ladies and children sat there in a stand to see the Queen go by to her marriage, and among them was Mrs. Charles Dickens.

The social success that came so swiftly and easily to Charles Dickens carried with it implications that affected marital adjustments in so far as it tended to create a gulf between his amusements and those of his wife, since in the Holland-Berry-Blessington world Mrs. Dickens never gained a foothold. Rosina Bulwer, who loathed men's clubs, said in *Cheveley* that lexicographers should in future define the word 'home' as 'a pen in which to keep women and children'. Mrs. Dickens would certainly have endorsed this recommendation.

Chapter 9

BOOK-BANQUETS AND FRIENDS

The friendship of some men is quite Briarean.
DOUGLAS JERROLD

CONFIDENCE in himself was one of Charles Dickens's leading characteristics and it never failed him no matter how adverse the circumstances he had to face. Neither worry over social conditions, quarrels with publishers nor fluctuations in income deterred him from his decision to live his life on a grand scale. He had no doubt whatever that once his affairs had been put into Forster's competent hands he could make all the money he needed. Feckless relations were still a drain upon his resources and threatened to become a menace to his good name; indeed the ingenious dodges contrived by his father to obtain advances from Chapman and Hall on the strength of his son's success, and the fact that he from time to time parted with autographs or sheets of manuscript for cash, tended to make his presence in London an embarrassment. Now Charles, as we know, was not a man to shirk family responsibilities, and in talking over his dilemma with Forster it became clear to him that he must establish his parents and brothers in a home of their own sufficiently far away from London to shield him from new annoyances. As there could be no financial peace while they were on his doorstep, he took steps to shift them to the country. Acting swiftly as was his wont, he hurried down to Exeter, pitching on this district because he had known it well in reporting days and carried in his mind pictures of pleasant cottages and gardens on the Plymouth road. At Alphington he rented a six-roomed house and garden for £20 a year, arranged for it to be papered 'snowy-clean' immediately, ordered in coal and wood and bought seventy pounds' worth of carpets, furniture,

glass and crockery, all to be delivered within two days.   He
had left London on a Monday (March 4), had arranged for his
mother to join him in an hotel at Exeter on the Thursday, and
for his father, brothers, and Dash the dog to arrive on the
Saturday so that he himself could be back at work on the
Monday.   Speed and secrecy were essential to the success of
the scheme, as John Dickens was liable to re-arrest by any one
of the tradesmen to whom he owed money, and the only
chance his son would have of compounding his debts was, as
Forster agreed, for the debtor to be *non est inventus*. Forster
advanced the pocket-money and Tom Beard played the part
assigned to him of buying the coach-tickets and seeing the
travellers off.   Both parents seemed to fall in amiably with
the arrangements made, though John Dickens was heard
wondering what on earth he would do with himself in the
country.   Mrs. Dickens reached Exeter on the appointed day
and was taken to see the cottage on the Friday: it was a
contrast to the shabby lodgings in which she had camped for
so many years.   When his father turned up in good spirits
with the rest of the family, Charles began to think he had
'settled the governor for life', and went back to London happy
in this belief, but at the end of March his troubles began again
with an 'unsatisfactory' letter from Mrs. Dickens.   By June
both parents were writing 'sneering, hateful letters' and
Charles groaned to Forster over his mother's behaviour, 'I
do swear I am sick at heart with both her and father too.'
By July, however, they appeared to him to have settled down
into a kind of contentment, and he was able to report after a
visit that 'the dolls' house was perfect and beautifully kept'.
Seven years later, Charles was to recall his father to London
to take up a post on the *Daily News* of which he was editor-
designate.   In the intervening years it is evident that John
Dickens did not stay put at Alphington, for we hear of him
at Greenwich, the Isle of Man and other places, and as
scheming to take his boys to Paris to complete their education.
He was every bit as buoyant as Mr. Micawber.

We shall have reason to remember the Alphington episode

when we come to the parting between Dickens and his wife. The same rather ruthless speed is noticeable in the execution of the later sentence as is observable in the earlier, and with both arrangements Forster had a good deal to do.

Having disposed for the time being of his parents, Dickens resumed his personal life again, attending at the end of March a dinner to Macready on his retirement from management of Covent Garden. One of the guests, Mrs. Cowden Clarke, the compiler of a well-known Shakespeare concordance, was struck by the 'superlatively handsome face' of the young writer as he stood to speak. His 'magnificent lustrous eyes', his rich 'wavy locks of hair', his 'perpetually discursive glances' which seemed to miss nothing. What a picture he made, never had she seen anyone who interested her more! And to crown all he spoke with real feeling and understanding of the stage, with intelligence of the experimental and instructive seasons they had all enjoyed under Macready's management, of the living playwrights whose works he had presented—Bulwer, Mitford, Browning, Talfourd—and of the manner he had produced the dramas of Shakespeare. And it passed through her mind that nothing could have been more impressive than the performance of *Henry V* for which Stanfield had painted the scenery and Bulwer, Forster and Dickens himself had supervised the mounting. The young man's ringing speech brought tears to the eyes of the guest they had assembled to honour.

The Shakespeare Society dinner over which Charles Dickens presided a few months later did not go quite so smoothly. Present were Talfourd, the two Landseers, Forster, Maclise, Macready, Frank Stone, Jerrold, Thackeray, Stanfield, Cattermole, Proctor, Blanchard, Charles Knight and many more. Charles Knight records that Forster addressed the assembled company very pompously in his Macready manner and that some young men sitting at the table began to laugh, crack nuts and jingle glasses loudly. Forster, irritated by the din, spoke sharply to his interrupters. The noises got worse, the chairman tried to restore order, did not succeed, abandoned the chair, and this was the end not only of the dinner but of the Society.

At the end of April the Doughty Street household repaired to Petersham for four months, Charles taking with him quite a variety of books—translations from French and German novels, Swift's Works, a volume of English Essays and Leigh Hunt's *Indicator*. He was playing with the idea of a new magazine to be written, compiled and edited by himself, and talked ceaselessly about the project. Experience with *Bentley's Miscellany* disposed him to believe that there was a good deal of money to be made in a threepenny weekly that would appeal to a poorer class of people than a shilling monthly could attract. He seems at this time to have been haunted by visions of lonely people sitting by desolate hearths all of whom might be comforted if the right word were said. If he could create an intimate and personal magazine he might be the man to say that word, for no one understood better than he that it is the unexpected human touch that makes the whole world kin and sometimes kind. If *Master Humphrey's Clock*[1] when it finally took shape did not for long carry out its mission of 'addressing friends from the chimney-corner', it was because the public showed no interest in the sentiments of Master Humphrey and his deaf old friend and could only be lured to purchase the magazine by the promise that each number would contain part of a straightforward serial by 'Boz'.

At Petersham Dickens still worked on *Nicholas Nickleby* which had been running for a year and had six months to go before completion. Its sales surpassed those of the *Pickwick* serial, and *Pickwick* in volume form was selling briskly. As there was nothing to follow them up with except the partially written *Barnaby Rudge*, Dickens felt that it was time he made a move to get his future straightened out. It seemed to him odd that Chapman and Hall had not approached him with some 'handsome retaining offer'; could it be that they were

[1] April 4, 1840.

CHARLES DICKENS, AGED 30
by Francis Alexander

" Very like the original " GEORGE PUTNAM

READING TO FRIENDS 1844
by Daniel Maclise, R.A.

"In the grave attention of Carlyle, the eager interest of Stanfield and Maclise, the keen look of poor Laman Blanchard, Fox's rapt solemnity, Jerrold's skyward gaze, the characteristic points of the scene are sufficiently rendered."   JOHN FORSTER waiting for him to take the initiative? With Forster to back him he felt in a stronger position vis-à-vis of publishers than ever before; perhaps Forster could find out for him how matters stood. Obligingly Forster interviewed Chapman and Hall and was able to report them ready to consider any scheme put forward by Mr. Dickens. This induced Dickens to set down on paper the ideas he had been turning over in his head.

> I should be willing [he wrote] to commence on the thirty-first of March, 1840, a new publication consisting entirely of original matter, of which one number price threepence, should be published every week. . . . The best general idea of the plan of the work might be given perhaps by reference to *The Tatler*, *The Spectator* and Goldsmith's *Bee*; but it would be far more popular both in the subjects of which it treats and its mode of treating them.[1]

He went on to expound his plan of contents. It would include amusing essays, stories, satirical papers on the administration of justice, conversations on historic London between Gog and Magog, and a club of originals to carry on in the Pickwickian way. Nebulous as his plans were on the literary side, they were definite enough on the financial side. He demanded to be paid fifty pounds weekly and would undertake no risk of any kind. Profits must be shared on a fifty-fifty basis, and the periodical to be named *Master Humphrey's Clock* must be continued for twelve months certain. To these rather onerous conditions Chapman and Hall agreed.

For September the Dickens family moved from Petersham to Broadstairs, and as it happened 'Eleanor P.', now Mrs. Christian, was spending the end of a long honeymoon there. One night they all met in the Tivoli Gardens where 'Eleanor P.' watched Dickens dancing with Georgina Hogarth. It was extremely pleasant by the sea. Sam Rogers was living at the Albion and Harley and his sister in lodgings close by. 'We enjoy this place amazingly', wrote Dickens to Forster, in spite of the fact that Kate was preoccupied with the thoughts

---

[1] 213. I. N.L.

of an October baby—and Charles himself with the planning of the *Nicholas Nickleby* banquet. Both baby and book were to be dedicated to Macready. During this summer they discussed leaving their home in Doughty Street for a house nearer to an open space. Macready frequently praised Clarence Terrace overlooking the Regent's Park which, compared with other districts of London, was in his opinion a health resort. Why should not Dickens have a look at his former house in Kent Terrace which was vacant? Dickens did so and favoured it until he fell in love with a bow-fronted house, 1 Devonshire Terrace, almost next to the imposing portico of St. Marylebone. Here indeed was a residence of 'great promise and undeniable situation' with a private garden shielded by a high wall. He secured a twelve-year lease of it at once and took John Chapman, 'a genius in houses', over it to make suggestions about water-closets to be carried out forthwith. Doughty Street had been rather meagrely fitted out with chattels from Furnival's Inn and second-hand furniture picked up piece by piece with Mary. These things would do no more than furnish the top floor of the new house. Mr. and Mrs. Dickens now had recourse to the big firms in the Tottenham Court Road where they placed orders for complete suites for reception rooms and bedrooms. White window-blinds and festooned curtains were installed and thick pile carpets laid. Doors of deal were replaced by doors of mahogany and wooden mantels by carved marble chimney-pieces. In all this one sees the taste of Forster who was sumptuous-minded and always acted in accordance with his adage 'The best is good enough for me'. Forster himself lived under painted ceilings in Lincoln's Inn Fields in the fine rooms described in *Bleak House* as inhabited by Mr. Tulkinghorn. Later on, after his marriage to the widow of Henry Colburn, his setting in Palace Gate Gardens became almost princely.

Baby Kate Macready made her appearance in October and in the same month the *Nicholas Nickleby* dinner took place.

Nicholas Nickleby was the second of the novels to be honoured in this way, the completion of *Oliver Twist*, six months earlier, having passed without notice of the kind. It is interesting to scrutinise the list of guests at these periodical book-banquets for they are valuable pointers in a biography. Dickens was what would now be called a good mixer and had no desire for solitude as such, since he was neither a thinker nor a reader.

1 Devonshire Terrace, by Daniel Maclise, 1839

Except when engaged in the violently creative effort of planning or writing a book, when he was inaccessible to everyone, he liked to have people about. Convivial, sentimental and easily moved to tears and laughter, his path through life bloomed in a series of happy attachments few of which shrivelled under the touch of time or circumstance. It is evident that his power of attraction was immense. Anthony Trollope confirms this when he says:

Of the general charm of his manner I despair of giving any idea to those who have not seen or known him. He warmed the social atmosphere, wherever he appeared, with

that summer glow which seemed to attend him.   His laugh
was brimful of enjoyment.

Dickens's earlier friendships are for the most part en-
shrined in the lists of guests attending the book-dinners.   The
first of these, given to celebrate the completion of *Pickwick*,
had taken place on November 18, 1837, when the diners were
Harrison Ainsworth, William Jerdan, Thomas Hill[1] (book
collector), Samuel Lover,[2] Chapman, Hall, Maclise, Macready,
John Forster and of course the guest of honour, Serjeant
Talfourd.   They met at the Prince of Wales's Hotel in
Leicester Street and, just as Talfourd was about to give the
health of the chairman, Charles Dickens, the head waiter, to
everyone's delight, carried in a snowy temple of sugar under
which stood a miniature Mr. Pickwick, a complimentary confection made by the landlord himself.   When Chapman and
Hall presented 'Boz' with a bonus cheque and a set of 'apostle'
ladles embodying characters in *Pickwick*, there was great
laughter and applause.

At the *Nicholas Nickleby* dinner held at the Albion, Ald-
gate, the new names are those of Clarkson Stanfield, Hablot
Browne, David Wilkie, George Cattermole, Thomas Beard,
Bradbury, Evans and J. P. Harley.   Again Chapman and
Hall proved themselves worthy of the occasion, for, following
the fine tradition of Constable in commissioning Raeburn to
paint Walter Scott, they had commissioned Maclise to paint
Dickens, and this portrait was displayed in the room in which
the dinner took place.   An engraving from it was used as
frontispiece for *Nicholas Nickleby* in volume form.   The
picture was later presented to Mrs. Dickens.   Macready in
his speech acknowledged the honour done to him by the
dedication, and recently knighted David Wilkie, painter in
ordinary to the Queen, lauded 'the reality of Dickens's
genius' and said rather breathlessly that 'there had been
nothing like him issuing his novels part by part, since Richard-

---

[1] The Hull of Hook's *Gilbert Gurney*.
[2] Miniaturist and composer of songs. Best remembered for *Handy Andy*.

son had issued his novels volume by volume', and how in both cases people talked about the characters as if they were next-door neighbours or friends and how 'as many letters were written to the author of *Nickleby* to implore him not to kill poor Smike as had been sent by young ladies to the author of *Clarissa* to save Lovelace's soul alive'.

Many of the book-guests we get to know well as in company with Dickens we travel along the road of a life marked by prandial milestones. Macready, twenty years older than Dickens, we meet again and again. Their first encounter had taken place at Covent Garden in June 1837. Forster had, as it were casually, thrown open a green-room door saying 'Here is Boz!' *Othello* was in rehearsal at the time and Macready was worrying over the King's health. Was William IV going to die? Would he have to cancel his first night? What an absurdity that the natural ailment of an old and ungifted man should be the cause of such perplexity and annoyance! Macready rambled on, airing his republican views, kings were no use, and lords were blots on humanity. He did not mind bending the knee to Voltaire, for he was a man of taste and virtue and 'in every way superior to the gold-besotted prurient people for whom nonsensical entertainments like *Semiramide* had to be devised'. The visitors had struck Macready on a bad day, but, in spite of his display of petulance, Dickens took to him at once and found in him a very faithful friend. In a sense they had a common background or grievance, for Macready's father too had been committed to prison for debt and his son had had to go straight to the boards from Rugby instead of to the University as planned. Macready's diary shows him to have been very sensitive to opinion and very easily depressed. His temper was difficult and he took for his motto the saying of Seneca, *Inveniat viam aut faciat* (Find a way or make one). In spite of his temperament he never quarrelled with Dickens and remained, in bad days and good, one of his closest confidants.

Another lifelong friendship had come into being when Kate's friend Daniel Maclise entered the family circle.

Dickens describes this young Irish artist as a wayward, delightful fellow 'golden throughout', a man who 'could have been as good a writer as he was a painter'. As Alfred Croquis of *Fraser's Magazine* he was very well known in literary circles, for he had made pen sketches of all the writers from Lady Morgan to L. E. L. and from Sir Walter Scott to Thomas Campbell. He spent a good deal of time with the Dickenses at Twickenham in 1838 and again at Petersham in 1839 when he was making studies for the Nickelby portrait. As a sitter Charles Dickens was difficult to please and insisted that Maclise should scrap all his first sketches, but the morning came when he could write 'Maclise has made another face of me which all people say is astonishing'.

William Jerdan, editor of the *Literary Gazette*, had been one of the first to recognise the merits of Sam Weller when he made his bow in the fifth number of *Pickwick*. Seizing his pen he begged the author 'to develop the character to the uttermost'. A 'genial alliance' ensued and Jerdan, who liked helping young writers, seems to have exercised his good offices in helping to persuade Bentley to relinquish all claims to *Barnaby Rudge*. Jerdan was a standing dish at the 'Boz' banquets.

Not all the early friends, howbeit, were bidden to the book-dinners. Leigh Hunt, for example, was only invited to birthday parties at the Dickenses' home, on which occasions he proved himself a charming converser and a lovable companion. When presenting Leigh Hunt with his novels in 1838 their author wrote:

> You are an old stager in works, but a young one in faith —faith in all beautiful and excellent things. If you can only find it in that green heart of yours to tell me one of these days that you have met, in wading through the accompanying trifles, with anything that felt like a vibration of the old chord you have touched so often and sounded so well you will confer the truest gratification on your faithful friend.[1]

[1] 170-71. I. N.L.

Douglas Jerrold's name does not appear in the first dinner lists though Dickens had got to know him as early as 1835 when he was living at Brompton as a temporary invalid. Seven years older than Dickens, he had been midshipman, actor and playwright and is best remembered to-day for *Black-eyed Susan* (1829) and *Mrs. Caudle's Curtain Lectures* (1846). It was Jerrold who made one of his former ship-mates known to Dickens—Clarkson Stanfield. Stanfield, like Macready, was twenty years older than 'Boz', but this proved no barrier and as 'Stanny' he became a dearly loved friend. Stanfield was called by his contemporaries the English Vandervelde, and, when Dickens first knew him, was employed as a scene-painter at Drury Lane. He designed a few illustrations for the 'Boz' novels, but only enters seriously into the pattern of Dickens's life as limner of stage sets for the theatrical performances at Tavistock House,—*The Lighthouse* and *The Frozen Deep*. He turns up both at the *Nickleby* and *Chuzzlewit* dinners and to the latter brought his friend the 'eccentric Turner'. In after years *Little Dorrit* was to be dedicated to him.

Another artist friend was George Cattermole, a relation by marriage living at Clapham, who did many of the illustrations for *Master Humphrey's Clock* and *The Old Curiosity Shop*. Forster did not like him much, but admits he had fun enough for a dozen humorists though lacking in balance and steadi-ness.

Hablot Browne was also at the *Nickleby* dinner. He had got to know Dickens well while working at the drawings for *Pickwick* and *Sunday Under Three Heads*. A much feebler artist than Cruikshank, his employer found him amenable and willing to accept suggestions and even orders. Of a retiring nature and dreading company, he had refused to appear at the *Pickwick* dinner though he plucked up courage for the *Nickleby* feast and attended all subsequent celebrations until 1859, when *A Tale of Two Cities* was published and he ceased to work for Dickens.

Thackeray was not invited to any of the earlier book-dinners. As we have seen, these young men had met for a moment in 1835 when Mr. Michael Angelo Titmarsh had called at Furnival's Inn to offer to illustrate *Pickwick*, but they did not meet again till both dined with Ainsworth in 1838. Thackeray, unlike Dickens, was a long time finding out what he could do best, and this was chiefly because he had never had to fight for a living. Maybe that his close association with Dickens in the summer of 1838 at Twickenham had an influence on his decision to become a novelist. At the time he was contributing *The Yellowplush Papers* to *Fraser's Magazine* and also working for the *Times*. *Vanity Fair*, which established his fame, was not published till ten years later and his name first appears as a guest at the *Copperfield* dinner of 1849. Was it the success of *Vanity Fair* or admiration for Dickens's work that led to his presence on this occasion? The break in relations which was one of the literary scandals of 1858 inclines one to assume it was the former, since when true sympathy of personality was the foundation, we find Dickens in friendship faithful to the end.

Chapter 10

THE QUEEN, CARLYLE AND POLITICS

Royalty is a Government in which the attention of the nation is on one person doing interesting actions. A Republic is a Government in which that attention is divided between many, who are all doing uninteresting actions. Accordingly so long as the human heart is strong and the human reason weak Royalty will be strong because it appeals to diffused feelings. WALTER BAGEHOT

FOR many simple British citizens the chief event of 1840 was the girl-Queen's wedding. It appealed to every home-lover and brought royalty for the first time for many generations within reach of all hearts. Embosomed in the warm tide of popular sentiment Charles Dickens went about lamenting his hopeless passion for the princess and envying Daniel Maclise, who was almost as it were inside the idyll, since the bride, with whom he was so great a favourite, had requested him to paint secret pictures for her to give to Prince Albert on his birthday and like occasions. Dickens wrote to T. J. Thompson:

Maclise and I are raving with love for the queen . . . we sallied down to Windsor, prowled about the Castle, saw the corridor, and their private rooms, nay the very bed-chamber lighted up with such a ruddy, homely, brilliant glow bespeaking so much bliss and happiness that I lay down in the mud at the top of the Long Walk and refused all comfort. . . . We drove home in a post-chaise and now we wear marriage medals next our hearts.[1]

For days and days he could settle to nothing, work went by the board, and to Kate's annoyance he wandered about the house singing,

My heart is at Windsor
My heart is not here,
My heart is at Windsor
A-following my dear.

[1] 248. I. N.L.

F 2

Running off to the Athenaeum, he cracked jokes with Monck-ton Milnes about what he called 'the national anthem of Seven Dials', which ran like this,

> So let 'em say whate'er they may
> Or do whate'er they can,
> Prince Halbert he will always be
> My own dear Fancy Man,

and asked his friend whether he too had not heard it sung in the streets?   To Forster Dickens spoke of razors, of throwing himself into the Serpentine or Regent's Canal, professed to loathe his family, detest his house, and be irritated by his wife. He told T. J. Thompson as executor of his will that there was a little bequest having reference to Her:

I have heard on the Lord Chamberlain's authority, that she reads my books, and is very fond of them.   I think she will be sorry when I am gone.   I should wish to be embalmed and to be kept (if practicable) on the top of the triumphal arch[1] at Buckingham Palace when she is in town and on the north-east turrets of the Round Tower when she is at Windsor.[2]

To the puzzled Landor he wrote:

Society is unhinged by her majesty's marriage and I am sorry to add that I have fallen hopelessly in love with the Queen and wander up and down with vague and dismal thoughts of running away to some uninhabited island with a maid of honour to be entrapped by conspiracy for that purpose. . . .[3]

In spite of these theatrical outbursts, when the actual marriage morning dawned Charles went off docilely with Kate to the stand at the Athenaeum from which they obtained a good view of the wedding procession.   Both craned their necks as Miss Coutts drove by wearing the tiara of Marie Antoinette and other historic jewels.   People round them gossiped about the offers of marriage she had refused from

---

[1] The Marble Arch, then in front of the Palace.
[2] 249. I. N.L.   [3] 247. I. N.L.

every young man of birth in England, as well as from Prince
Louis Napoleon. And who, they asked, would there be for
her to marry in the end? It entered no one's head that she
could remain a spinster for another forty years.

To distract Charles and turn his thoughts from the bride to
his own work Forster now arranged that he should pay a visit
to Landor. He knew Landor would never tolerate mad talk
about the Queen, but would switch the conversation to books
and especially to his favourite *Pickwick*, which he said had
drawn from him 'more tears and more smiles than were
remaining to him for all the rest of the world real or ideal'.
Near the end of the marriage month 'Fuz', 'Boz' and 'Phiz'
set out for 25 St. James's Square, Bath, where lived one of the
most original of English men of letters, an author who displayed apathy, not to say antipathy, to popular success, saying
he would be well content with ten intelligent readers. His
rooms, including the doors, were plastered with Italian pictures, each of which he thought the finest specimen of the
finest master and each of which had its story. It became an
annual habit for 'Fuz' and 'Boz' to go to Bath to dine with
Landor on his birthday. Eliza Lynn (later Mrs. Lynn
Linton) made a fourth on one of these occasions, and with her
usual plain-spokenness recorded that she did not take to
Forster at all; his tiresome manner gave the impression that
he thought he owned both her host and 'Boz'. Dickens
struck her as bright, gay, 'winsome' and altogether charming,
but Forster remained throughout the evening heavy, pompous
and ungenial. Dickens seemed to know instinctively how to
treat his host, first with the respect of a young man for an
older man and then allowing his wit to play about him, bright
and harmless as summer lightning. At this time Eliza Lynn,
in the early twenties, was being treated as a spoilt daughter by
Landor, who, in spite of his sixty-five years, would hire
sedan-chairs to escort her to the Assembly Rooms for balls.
As she adored him, she was watchful of the behaviour of
visitors and reacted sharply to their remarks. The conversation between Dickens and Landor on the first meeting was so

pleasant and so stimulating as to put Landor into a good
temper and make Dickens anxious to begin work again.   A
story he heard at Bath now inspired him with the vision of a
child who for a year and more was to be his constant pre-
occupying companion.   The story of Little Nell, when it
became public, plunged half the world in tears.   It is a story
that George Lewes in that day and Mr. Aldous Huxley in our
own day have condemned for its ineptitude and sentimentality.
The behaviour of the Victorian heart is a study in itself, as
we shall see in discussing *The Old Curiosity Shop*.   For the
moment it may be stated that Nell's odyssey impressed most
of Dickens's contemporaries as a credible and beautiful
achievement.   Almost without exception they wept over it
as uncritically as did its author.

On arriving home Dickens set to work to get *Master
Humphrey's Clock* 'striking by the end of March'.   He took a
deal of trouble over the illustrations, which were not to be
full plate but 'dropped into the text'.   In his instructions for
the clock-case on which his scheme pivoted, he told Cattermole to set it in an old quaint room with antique Elizabethan
furniture.   'In the chimney-corner must stand an extraordinary old clock, the clock belonging to Master H. in
fact.'

The drawing supplied to this order presented a clock of
rococo outline, Dutch dimensions and great holding capacity, the artist having been more intent on producing a
good manuscript cupboard than a clock-case of the Elizabethan period.   Dickens, however, was pleased with it and,
as soon as he had passed the last proofs of the magazine,
rushed off to the country with Kate so as to avoid being in
London on the day the new venture was launched.   The
Clock made a fast start, seventy thousand copies of the first
number being sold.   With the second number, after the
public had discovered that there was no serial by 'Boz' but
a good deal of sermonising, sales fell sharply.   Praise from
critics could not vivify the failure.   It was to no purpose that
Tom Hood lauded its intention and called Dickens 'the cham-

pion of the poor and of worth in low places'; the *Clock* had to have its mainspring changed before becoming popular.

In his leisure hours Dickens was at this time reading a thick pamphlet, *Chartism* by Carlyle. He had not met the sage at this time, but like every man of his day was concerned over the Charter campaign that had been launched shortly after the Queen's Coronation and had arisen out of Lord John Russell's formal declaration in Parliament against further measures of Reform. A group of Liberal members of Parliament at a meeting in Birmingham had drawn up a six-points People's Charter comprising manhood suffrage, annual Parliaments, vote by ballot, abolition of property qualification for election of members to Parliament, payments of members, and the division of the country into equal electoral districts.

Dickens heard that Carlyle saw in this movement an expression of justifiable discontent and found himself in agreement with this view. There was no doubt that government by the upper classes on the principle of letting the under classes alone was as sterile in result as the gospel preached to the workless about being at the mercy of the laws of supply and demand. What, Dickens asked himself, did these laws mean in his own profession? Why, Samuel Johnson earning fivepence a day! or Talfourd fighting a losing battle to safeguard the creations of a writer's brain! *Laissez faire* posturing as freedom was certainly the curse of England.

It had always worried Dickens during his reporting tours to note the apathy displayed by electors and the extent to which the people, in spite of the Reform Bill, were still alienated from their own affairs. He welcomed the People's Charter, for he took it to be a sign that the nation was developing political consciousness. As he read the clauses which 'respectfully' called attention to the existing monopolies of the suffrage, of paper money, of machinery, of land, of the public press, of religion, of the means of travelling and transit, he rejoiced to see these grievances formulated. They might alarm the drawing-rooms of Mayfair, but had they not all arisen from class legislation? and was not class legislation the enemy to be held responsible for the 'accursèd gentility' of English life? This gentility appeared to him as a blight pervading society as a whole and emasculating the natural vigour of the people. The so-called middle class, to which he himself belonged, was not really a class, but only 'the poor fringe on the mantle of the upper class'. It could not be counted on to form a buffer between high and low, for its interests were really identical with those of the governing class, into whose ranks it was slowly and continuously being absorbed.

The year 1840 must be reckoned an important year for Dickens in so far as it brought him under the influence of Carlyle. The first time he clapped eyes on him was at a lecture on 'Great Men' given at Willis's Rooms. Maclise, Macready, Browning, Forster and other friends were also listening, but no one of them imbibed a more definite message than Dickens, who began to feel as if the aspirations of his youth were being precipitated by contact with this powerful brain. From now on he went about with a copy of Carlyle's *French Revolution* in his pocket, reading it over and over again. And we see the outcome in *Bleak House, Hard Times* and *A Tale of Two Cities*.

Carlyle seemed to Dickens to have a deeper understanding than anyone of the inadequacy of the reforms undertaken by Parliament. What was the good of improving the talking apparatus if the acting apparatus was not improved too? Political reform unaccompanied by administrative reform must be a mockery. Carlyle, he found, was all for breaking down what he himself dubbed the Buffy-Boodle system, for did he not hold that the able man should be preferred no matter what his birth? and did he not point out that the 'poor old benighted Catholic Church' had set the world an example in this respect, since by 'a thrice glorious arrangement' she had shown how aptitude should rise and rise to the top of the tree? Right through the dim oppressed strata of society ran the institution of the priesthood like a great mine-shaft opening from the lowest depths towards all heights, towards heaven itself, and inviting noble souls whether neatherds' or butchers' sons to tread the noble path. This was the secret of the health and vitality of the old society, now lungless and wheezing itself to death. In these flights Dickens could not follow Carlyle for he knew nothing about the Catholic Church and in theory despised it, but he was conscious in a quite definite way of the decay of Christian feeling in the economic life of the day and knew this decay to be responsible for much oppression and avoidable misery. This was why he set such store on the spirit of Christmas: it was all he knew of Christianity in action and he preached it with all his might.

On his long night walks in mean streets he often felt suffocated by the conditions he encountered. Could education possibly be the key to the conundrum of poverty, and if it were, how could education make its way in a kingdom wherein children were wage slaves? England, he knew, lay under the stigma of being the worst educated country in Northern Europe, and he also knew, from studying Lord John Russell's figures that out of the 14,000 children in Bethnal Green but 2000 attended any school. So much for the appalling indifference of the Buffy-Boodle gang to the future of England! But then what future except servitude everlasting had a people that could neither read nor write? Day after day with Miss Coutts Dickens discussed these problems as together they drew up schemes for Ragged Schools and slum clearance. He was always very silent about his philanthropic activities which for many years remained a secret between himself and the generous lady in Piccadilly whose benefactions he constantly guided into new channels.

The first face-to-face meeting between Dickens and Carlyle took place under Lord Stanley's roof at what the sage called 'a dinner of lords and lions'. Lord and Lady Holland, Lord Normanby and M. Guizot were among the guests. Carlyle, who had been rather bored than otherwise by Dickens's first books, was in process of succumbing to the sentimental appeal of *The Old Curiosity Shop* and therefore studied the appearance of its author in an interested way. He struck him as a quiet, shrewd little fellow who had sized both himself and others up. A head with 'a loose coil' of hair and a face of extreme mobility were carried by a small compact figure dressed *à la* d'Orsay. Darting eyes, arching eyebrows, mouth—all expressive, went to produce a 'shuttling' effect, which was Carlyle's way of saying that Dickens was perpetually responding to the stimulus of the conversation that surged about him. From Dickens's angle we know nothing about this meeting, for social happenings were never chronicled by him; he had far too much to do in getting the creatures of his imagination down on to paper to have any time to spare for chance encounters even when they proved as significant as did his introduction to Carlyle.

Dickens was a man of his day in one sense and far ahead of his day in another. To begin with, he was a pioneer of the modern classless type to which we are now accustomed, a type with little respect for tradition and which is inclined to view the mechanism of parliamentary government as outworn and obstructionist. Dickens held no second-hand opinions. His judgments, such as they were, sprang from experience and observation, and his four years' service in the House of Commons had made him doubt the seriousness, integrity and even the good-will of the majority of members. It was clear that certain men like Grote, who worked for the extension of the franchise, Lord Ashley, who strove to secure decent conditions of employment for workers, Lord John Russell, who fought for education, stood out from their kind as upright reformers, but he resented seeing their energies and enthusiasm being fretted away in ceaseless and relentless attack by the opponents of social reform. The failure too of these good men to support each other seemed to him another weakness of the parliamentary system. Each man played a lone hand; for example Lord John Russell, in spite of his advocacy of universal education, would not consider extending the franchise,

and eyed social legislation of Lord Ashley's type as a dangerous incline leading to the foundering of the existing social
fabric.

In view of his distrust of parliamentary methods it is a
surprise when in 1841 we find Dickens beginning to consider
putting up for Parliament himself. It may be that Miss
Burdett Coutts, whose plans for rehousing slum-dwellers and
reclaiming children from the streets needed a spokesman, may
have advised him in this matter, or it may be that Serjeant
Talfourd recommended him to seize the opportunity for forwarding social reform offered by a seat in the House of
Commons. It is almost certainly to Talfourd that we must
attribute the final push towards politics. On the fall (in
1841) of Lord Melbourne's government and the initiation of
the Free Trade agitation, Dickens was approached by certain
persons from Reading with the proposal that he should stand
at the forthcoming election as their second candidate. As
Talfourd, the son of a local brewer, was their sitting member
it seems certain that the recommendation must have come
from him.

It would have been superfluous for the author of *Oliver
Twist* and *Nicholas Nickleby* to state his convictions and views
on the Poor Law or on Education. He was well known, for
he had been much spoken of by public men. Sir Francis
Burdett had alluded to him as 'the advocate of the poor', Lord
Ashley had called him 'a public benefactor', to Tom Hood he
was 'the champion of the poor'. In the minds of the electors
of Reading he would represent a young and better England,
the England of the future. In replying to a formal letter
asking for his consent to nomination Dickens wrote[1] that,
though obliged and flattered by their communication and
aspiring to the distinction they invite him to seek, he cannot
afford the expense of a contested election. He was at once
requested to come to Reading for an interview and there it
was revealed to him that though they wanted him as a candidate they did not want him enough to pay any part of his

[1] May 31, 1841, p. 325. I. N.L.

expenses.   Subsequently he wrote with reference to the interview:

> The sum you mention, although small I am aware in the abstract, is greater than I could afford for such a purpose; as the mere sitting in the House and attending to my duties, if I were a Member, would oblige me to make many pecuniary sacrifices, consequent upon the very nature of my pursuits.[1]

The next paragraph reveals that 'the magnates' had suggested that Dickens should apply to be financed by party funds, but this proposal was repugnant to him.   He had no wish to become a party hack.

> The course you suggest did occur to me when I received your first letter, and I have very little doubt indeed that the Government would support me—perhaps to the whole extent.   But I cannot satisfy myself that to enter Parliament under such circumstances, would enable me to pursue that honourable independence without which I could neither preserve my own self-respect nor that of my constituents.   I confess therefore . . . that I cannot bring myself to propound the subject to any member of the Administration whom I know.   I am truly obliged to you nevertheless.[2]

And so the proposal came to nothing, and it is well for the world that it did.   The approach to politics had been a diversion and 'Boz' returned to his proper sphere to discover that an undreamed-of success awaited him therein.   With Little Nell he had captured the ardent heart of America, and surely that was a better thing by far than capturing the votes of Reading electors.

Some time in 1838 Dickens had made friends with Dr. John Elliotson, a distinguished physician, who was losing the confidence of his colleagues at University College Hospital owing to his deep interest in hypnotism.   He had founded a small mesmeric hospital where he had cured tic douloureux

[1] June 10, 1841, *ibid.*   [2] *Ibid.*

and had carried out various minor operations under the anaesthesia induced by magnetic passes. His patients were many and among them was Thackeray, who dedicated *Pendennis* to him out of gratitude for having saved his life. One August evening in 1840 Dickens dined with him to meet the Reverend Chauncey Hare Townshend, a rich young clergyman who had made a habit of travelling about the continent in search of health and who had spent some time in Antwerp studying mesmerism. He had just brought out an account of what he had witnessed, *Facts in Mesmerism*, which he had dedicated to John Elliotson in a preface penned at 'Inspruck' in November 1839. His approach to the subject, as he was not a medical man, was different from that of Elliotson, but they had, he asserted, arrived at the same results, *i.e.* that somnambulism could be induced: that spirit demonstrably dominated matter: that the mind was the only source of power. Elliotson and Townshend had only known each other a few weeks when this dinner took place. Dickens listened spell-bound to the conversation of the experts and made Elliotson promise to instruct him in the art of animal magnetism. To his surprise and pleasure he found he was apt at it; it was quite easy, it seemed, to send people to sleep and even to make them wake up again. No one could have foreseen the curious dilemma in which the possession of this knowledge was a few years later to place him. Though he seems to have refused to be magnetised himself, he frequently practised on Kate and her sister and on other non-resisters. We find him recommending 'Townshend's magnetic boy' to Lady Blessington for a séance at Gore House and warning her not to invite more than eight people, four being really the better number for getting interesting results.

Spiritualism, on the other hand, never attracted him at all though it was all the rage. Mrs. Trollope, whom he did not much like, and who was never invited to Devonshire Terrace, tried to lure him to table-turnings and séances, and Lady Morgan, too, through her famous homoeopathic doctor, Quin, would urge him to grace her evenings, but he remained deaf to their appeals. He did however make certain experiments with one Bührer, the owner of a psychograph said to write at the dictation of the foreign count alleged to materialise in Bührer's rooms. These diversions from the main purpose of Dickens's life could only be indulged in fitfully. As he became more famous the claims of the world became more insistent.

In removing from Bloomsbury and placing themselves in a quarter of London that was fashionable and specialised in dinner-giving, Mr. and Mrs. Charles Dickens indicated their willingness to take and to receive hospitality. Now that they had a good cook, three other maids and a man servant of their own they could and did vie with their neighbours and friends. This still youthful couple, the host of twenty-eight and the hostess of twenty-four, cast their net wide, including Lord Jeffrey, Edwin Landseer, the Carlyles, Mr. Rogers, Canon Sydney Smith, Miss Burdett Coutts, Richard Monckton Milnes and Edward Bulwer in their gatherings. Sydney Smith, whose humour Dickens admired vastly, accepted one of his invitations in the following words:

> If I am invited by any man of greater genius than yourself or by one in whose works I have been more completely interested I will repudiate you and dine with the more splendid phenomenon of the two.[1]

But not everyone was such a wag as the Canon of St. Paul's nor did everyone give such agreeable breakfast parties. The Canon used to say that breakfast parties were always pleasant 'because no one is conceited before one o'clock'. Breakfast in company was with Dickens a very rare indulgence for he never allowed amusement to eat into his working hours and usually shut himself away behind baize doors from early morning till three in the afternoon. After this spell of application he was ready for anything, a long walk, a ride, a potter round auction rooms or any other pastime.

[1] May 14, 1841.

One day on returning from a visit to the Smithsons in Yorkshire Mrs. Christian and T. J. Thompson dropped in for luncheon at Devonshire Terrace. It ruined Dickens's working day to be hauled out of his study to talk to guests and 'Eleanor P.' received rather a rude shock, for her host seemed to have forgotten all their friendly fun at Broadstairs. He was distant in manner and only thawed a little when the raven pecked at her ankles squawking 'Hullo, old gal!' Fred Dickens, who was standing by, announced that he was going to see Courvoisier receive 'a well-deserved hanging'. Charles looked annoyed. 'What!', he said. 'You're never going to be such an idiot! Whence comes this morbid craving to gloat over such a loathsome exhibition?' 'Oh, Thackeray is going,' retorted Fred, 'and I am joining a select circle of reporters.' On this Thompson observed, 'Well, you'll be squeamish for a couple of days afterwards'. 'Have you ever seen a man hanged?' eagerly questioned Fred. 'No, but I've seen a man guillotined', replied Thompson. Then Dickens gave a shudder and exclaimed, 'Ugh! That's a messy business, all gore and sawdust. The inverted rope-dance is cleaner though less impressive. I'd keep away from such a hideous spectacle from principle. I'm not sure that we ought to dispose of even murderers in such barbarous ways.'

'Eleanor P.' was not the only visitor to notice how greatly Dickens had changed in two years. George Lewes too observed that he took himself with new seriousness and was quite the great man.

From some of those who went to Devonshire Terrace we may learn just what it was like to dine with Mr. Dickens. Mrs. Carlyle, often tart in comment and never making allowances, tells us that the dinner she attended was 'served in the new fashion', in other words that the dishes were not placed on the table but were handed round by servants. Though Mrs. Carlyle was not in a position to give dinners herself, she at least knew how Lady Ashburton did things. The poor inexperienced young Dickenses had artificial flowers, *only*, upon the table and such quantities of them! and then 'the profusion of figs, raisins, oranges, och! such overloaded dessert!' At the Ashburton dinner served on the same principle she had noticed 'just four cowslips in china pots, four silver bells containing sweets, and a silver filigree temple', but at the Devonshire Terrace dinner 'the very candles rose out of an artificial rose!'

From Lord Jeffrey we get yet another glimpse. An enthusiastic admirer of the genius of 'Boz', this Scotsman had gone about saying there had been nothing so good as Little Nell since Cordelia and had invited her creator to come and see him. Stepping across from Devonshire Terrace to visit this near neighbour, Dickens found himself charmed exceedingly by the courtesy shown him and by the veteran reader's praise of *The Old Curiosity Shop*. 'Upon my word,' he said to Tom Beard, 'I came out of the house more delighted than if I had been ten thousand pounds richer than when I went in.' The acquaintance grew and we find Lord Jeffrey writing to Lord Cockburn that he was seeing a good deal of Charles Dickens with whom he meant to strike up an eternal and intimate friendship.

> He lives very near to us and I often run over and sit an hour tête-à-tête or take a long walk in the Park with him . . . taken in this way I think him very amiable and agreeable. In mixed company where he is now much sought after he is rather reserved. He has dined here and we with him at rather too sumptuous a dinner for a man with a family and only beginning to be rich.

Pressing the young author to come to Edinburgh later on, Lord Jeffrey assured Dickens of a real Scottish welcome. Kate Dickens was particularly pleased with this invitation. Edinburgh was her birthplace and to her the city of all others where a triumph was worth scoring. As soon as Lord Jeffrey got back home he arranged to take the chair at a banquet in honour of 'Boz', fixing the date for June 25, 1841. In refusing a dinner invitation from Lady Holland for June 19 that year Dickens explained that he was due in Edinburgh for a public dinner and was visiting a friend in Yorkshire beforehand. He thanks her for an introduction to Lord Lauder-dale.

Mr. and Mrs. Dickens arrived at the Royal Hotel, Edin-burgh, on June 22 and there enjoyed their first taste of real celebrity in finding themselves provided with a grand suite of rooms in a hotel besieged by admirers. The terrors of lion-isation were to some extent dispelled for Kate by the kind-heartedness of the people who welcomed them. Miss Allan took her off to renew her acquaintance with the sights while Sir William Allan took charge of her husband. The banquet went off brilliantly though Lord Jeffrey was ill and had to be replaced by 'Christopher North' (John Wilson). Looking down on the guests from the high table, Dickens realised that however warm the 'enthoosymoosy' displayed it did not affect him at all. He felt cool as a cucumber and preened himself on the number of greyheads come to honour his brown flowing locks. In his speech he said that in his books he had tried to 'show forth the soul of goodness in men' of every walk in life,

> The rank is but the guinea stamp,
> The man's the gowd for a' that.

He then referred to *The Old Curiosity Shop* and explained why he had had to kill Little Nell. It was done that he might substitute a garland of fresh flowers for the sculptured horrors that usually disgrace a tomb. He had wanted to fill young minds with better thoughts of death, to soften the grief in older hearts, to console old and young in time of trial. Therefore, in spite of all the letters requesting Nell's reprieve, he had kept to his purpose and Little Nell had died. He then went on to say,

> The distinction you have conferred upon me is one I never hoped for and of which I never dared to dream. I thank you again and again with the energy of a thousand thanks in each one.

Later in the evening he proposed the health of the Chairman and then spoke to the memory of Sir David Wilkie (recently dead and buried at sea off Gibraltar). He had seen a good deal of Wilkie, who had made of humble life a noble thing, who had left memories behind him 'as pure as the blue waves that now roll over him', and who had died in the fulness of fame before age or sickness had dimmed his powers.

No occasion could have given greater satisfaction to speaker or listener, but there was no whisper of the great surprise to be sprung on the guest of honour on the day following when Dickens learnt that the Lord Provost, Council and Magistrates of Edinburgh had voted by acclamation that the freedom of the city should be conferred on him 'in testimony of his distinguished abilities as an author'. In mind Dickens reverted to his experience of seven years earlier when he, a mere reporter, had taken down the speeches made at the banquet to Lord Grey. A further surprise arising from this wonderful visit was another offer of a seat in the House of Commons, this time 'for a Scotch county that's going a-begging'. He turned the offer down at once and notified the same to Forster, writing, 'I have declined to be brought in free gratis and for nothing'.

For the first time Charles Dickens knew what it felt like to perch on a pinnacle of the temple of fame. He was not unduly excited by his elevation: it had in a sense been achieved in his heart's blood. Taking the homage as it came, he remained simple, feeling there was no place like home and thanking God for having given him a quiet spirit and 'a heart that won't hold many people'.

Chapter 11

SAMPLING AMERICA

America, half-brother of the world.

P. J. BAILEY

IN his draft scheme for *Master Humphrey's Clock* Dickens had broached the idea that its editor should travel, and by the summer of 1841 his desire to cut free from the fetters of serial slavery had become 'an imperative necessity'. He had reviewed Lockhart's *Life of Scott* for *The Examiner*, and this had interested him so much that he had gone on to read Scott's *Diary*, much of which he found poignantly applicable to himself. The pathetic account of Sir Walter Scott's journey to Italy made him realise with sudden intensity how important it was to travel in youth and 'plenitude of power' rather than in weakness and senility. America was now the lure, partly because in America he thought he could see which way the world was going and partly because he believed that in a modern and kingless country he would feel thoroughly at home and escape from the snobbery engendered by class rule. How much more akin he was to old-fashioned Europeans than to the citizens of the New World it did not require six months' experience in the United States to bring home to him.

Biographers have thought up other reasons that may have induced him to cross the ocean. Some said that he wanted to meet Washington Irving, some have supposed that he had invested savings in the 'Cairo City and Canal Company' and wished to see the grand city at the junction of the Mississippi and Ohio rivers advertised by its promoters in London with 'flaming lithographs': some that the ecstatic letters he had received from America about Little Nell had made him eager to contact a new public: some that he was the secret emissary of London publishers in the matter of international copyright. Perhaps an operative clue is to be found in the fourteenth number of *Pickwick* where Tony Weller says to Sam Weller, 'Have a passage taken ready for 'Merrika and then let him come back and write a book about the 'Merrikins as'll pay his expenses and more, if he blows 'em up enough.'

Fanny Trollope's book *Domestic Manners of the Americans* had appeared in 1832. Of course Dickens had read it carefully as he had that of Harriet Martineau, *Society in America*. Both works had been disapproved of in the United States as much for the patronising tone of their praise, when they gave any, as for the depreciatory nature of their blame, and both confirmed Dickens in his resolve that 'in going to the New World one must for the time being utterly forget and push out of sight the Old one and bring none of its customs or observances into the comparison'.[1] A resolution easy to make and hard to carry out, though as a man of the people Dickens in his heart of hearts believed himself more qualified than either of these ladies to understand and appreciate democracy in being. He was careful, therefore, to check feminine statements and conclusions against those of a male crony, Captain Marryat, who had spent two years in the United States and on his return had not only published his *Diary in America*, but was willing to discuss his more private impressions in long-drawn conversations.

In considering the American adventure we must bear in mind that there was a love of experiment in Dickens's nature. From time to time it overpowered him and then he would jump out of his setting and start a new break—a house in Paris maybe, a palace in Genoa or a villa by Leman. Mrs. Dickens did not share these impulses, went unwillingly abroad, pined in strange surroundings and in the end suffered the penalties entailed in unadaptability. It was with something like dismay that she watched her husband making the arrangements, literary and financial, that would enable him to carry out his plan of conveying her to America. The house, carriages and staff were let over her head to Sir John Wilson, for a period of six months, and it was arranged that the four

[1] To A. Bell. October 12, 1841.

precious children should be dumped on the Macreadys during her absence. Half hypnotised by her husband's decisions, she still hoped that something, money perhaps, might hold up the proceedings, but even on the subject of money the publishers were amiable and put no obstacles in the way. Rather the reverse, for Chapman and Hall were perfectly willing to wind up *Master Humphrey's Clock* if Mr. Dickens would promise them a new novel in November 1842—a novel on the lines of that best-seller *Nicholas Nickleby*. In the agreement finally come to between author and publisher[1] Dickens was granted a holiday of fourteen months at £150 a month secured against future earnings. Overjoyed at this arrangement, he offered to write a travel-book on America which Chapman and Hall jumped at the idea of publishing.

October 1841 brought a new shock to the little family in that Kate's young brother, aged twenty, died as suddenly as Mary had died four years earlier. All the pain of the old wound revived as Charles, who had always meant to be buried in Mary's grave, now had to abandon the idea though it 'was still strong in him'. Again he cries, 'I don't think there ever was love like that I bear her,' and we are reminded of Léon Bloy's memorable phrase *Plus on est homme de génie, plus on est homme* and of Carlyle's 'Genius gives intensity of spiritual suffering'. It was almost a relief from heart-ache for Dickens to be told at this time by his doctor that he must submit to 'the cutting-out root and branch of a disease caused by working overmuch, which has been gathering for years'. 'I laboured under the complaint called Fistula, the consequence of too much sitting at my desk.'

While recovering from this cruel operation, which of course had to be endured without an anaesthetic, he discussed with John Forster the planning of his journey. Certain preparations would bring certain results. Money was important, clothes were important, letters of introduction were important. Five pounds a day should cover all expenses

[1] Signed September 6, 1841.

while travelling, but a considerable sum must be disbursed on
tailors and dressmakers if Mr. and Mrs. Charles Dickens were
to make their American bow in a distinguished way. Kate,
who never ceased repining at having to put the Atlantic
between herself and her children, wept quietly at intervals,
though the business of trying on pretty frocks, shawls and
bonnets took up all her spare time. Economy was not
allowed to hamper her choice; she must have clothes suitable
for all occasions, even for Embassy balls and dinners at the
White House. We can see in Maclise's charming portraits
of her that she could wear dresses elegantly and that Charles
was right in insisting that she should make herself as attractive
as possible. In order to smooth her path it was arranged that
her competent maid, Anne, should travel with them. Charles
was as kind as he could be, and Maclise seconded him by
making a life-like group of the children which could be set up
in any cabin, bedroom or parlour. This picture, as we shall
see, was to prove a great solace in unhomelike surroundings.

Before leaving London Dickens called on Lady Holland.
As she disliked Americans, she tried to persuade him not to go
to the United States at all, saying, 'Why cannot you go down
to Bristol and see some of the third and fourth class people
there and they'll do just as well?' Lady Blessington, on the
contrary, approved of his plans and wished him godspeed.

One of the most constant factors in Dickens's make-up,
his confidence in himself, was, as we have seen, partially
derived from his theatrical instinct, and it is plain that the
stranger the circumstances the more support and comfort he
found in the right clothes. As a frequenter of Gore House
and a friend of Macready he had learnt from observation how
important it was to look the part one was to play. He was
visiting America in the role of a distinguished author and
therefore must provide himself with fashionably-cut coats,
coloured vests, and the brocade dressing-gowns in which
gentlemen gave interviews to callers before donning their
frock-coats for the street. He must also buy for his adorn-
ment new tie-pins, chains and rings. When preparations

were complete, the travellers were accompanied to Liverpool and seen on to the steamship 'Britannia' by John Forster, who presented his friend with a pocket Shakespeare that proved 'an unspeakable source of delight'. The evening before the ship sailed Dickens found time to write to Lord Brougham (to whom he had already recommended Chapman and Hall as a publishing firm of high integrity for the Society for the Diffusion of Useful Knowledge) telling him that his father-in-law, George Hogarth, may submit a book to the Society and that he has written very admirable works of instruction on Music and History: 'You will remember the name by the great painter's,' and then added, 'The ship weighs anchor at two o'clock'. After a horrible voyage, eclipsing in terror anything that even Kate Dickens had imagined, they reached Halifax and there enjoyed a foretaste of the excitements Dickens's appearance was to evoke in America.

To begin with, the Speaker of the Legislative Assembly came aboard to carry Charles Dickens off to his house, while Mrs. Dickens was driven away in a carriage by the Speaker's wife. It happened to be a great day in Halifax, for it was the first day of the session, and Dickens, to whom the mechanism of Crown Colony Government was entirely unknown, attended the opening ceremony and was astonished to hear 'a mock speech from the throne'. But it was not Lord Falkland or his legislators who really interested the visitor, it was himself and the sensation his appearance created. 'I wish you could have seen the crowds cheering the Inimitable in the streets', he wrote exultingly to John Forster, 'I wish you could have seen the judges, law-officers, bishops and law-makers welcoming the Inimitable, I wish you could have seen the Inimitable shown to a great elbow-chair by the Speaker's throne.' What he called the 'enthoosymoosy' of Nova Scotians was even warmer than that of Scots in Edinburgh, and yet he was pleased to think that he remained cool and self-possessed as ever.

The 'Britannia' steamed into Boston harbour on a Saturday

afternoon in January 1842.   Spectators waiting on the wharf
discerned on the paddle-box beside the captain a little fellow,
a foppish little fellow, in what he afterwards described as
'full-fig'.   The 'full-fig' consisted of a beaver hat, a brown
frock-coat, a vest figured in red, and a voluminous fancy scarf
fastened by two diamond pins linked by a gold chain.   His
looks, though entirely unlike anything to be met with at the
time in Boston, took no one by surprise; people were merely
seeing what they expected to see, for engravings of Maclise's
portrait had been displayed in every shop window.   This
likeness showed an elegant youth seated nonchalantly beside
a writing-table, curled hair over ears, fully puffed cravat-scarf
fastened with the famous diamond pins, frock-coat with deep
collar and revers, and trousers strapped over pointed highly
polished footgear.   It might have been the advertisement for
a mannequin travelling for a firm of fashionable tailors.   The
only surprise to Bostonians was that the renowned 'Boz'
should look so juvenile, that his skin should flush so easily,
that his lustrous eyes should brim with moisture.   Could he
be even more sensitive than his work had suggested?   But if
so, why did he show no shyness in grasping the hands of the
editors who swarmed on to the 'Britannia's' deck as soon as
she docked?

Before leaving London Dickens had agreed to sit for his
portrait to Francis Alexander of Boston.   The painter was
one of the first to welcome the voyagers at the wharf with a
posy for Mrs. Dickens in his hand.   Amiably enough he had
then rushed away to secure rooms at Tremont House (close
to his own studio), to which hotel he conducted them as soon
as Customs formalities were concluded.   Lord Mulgrave, a
young officer in the Coldstream Guards and a fellow passenger, drove with them, and when he saw the letters, invitations and flowers that were awaiting the novelist's arrival, he
urged Dickens to engage a secretary at once to cope with the
offers of hospitality and demands for lectures and interviews.
Alexander, the ever-helpful, produced George Putnam, an
artist, to act in this capacity.   He is discreetly alluded to as

'Mr. Q.' in Forster's biography. Putnam was modest, and obliging, and silent except when he was 'imitating cows and pigs', and began to work at once at the nominal salary of £10 a month and his keep. To his amusement his new employer and Lord Mulgrave reacted from their cramped voyage by running out after dinner. The moon was at the full and the streets snow-covered. They were as exhilarated as school-boys and laughed as they hurried along, with Putnam at their heels to see they did not get lost.

The travellers having landed in Boston on a Saturday were treated to a specially American form of hospitality, an invitation to a pew in church the following morning. Miss Martineau had commented on this charming civility which Mrs. Dickens, like Harriet, was unable to avail herself of, and for the same reason, that her Sunday dress was not yet unpacked. As it was not considered correct that husband and wife should appear separately for the first time in public, Dickens had the fun of wandering about the city incognito with coat collar up while Mrs. Dickens unpacked. He was all unaware that he was enjoying his last moments of care-free leisure.

Francis Alexander (to whom Dickens in four days' time was signing himself yours affectionately) lost no time in making his first sketch of the author and he begged that his friend Henry Dexter should be allowed to model his sitter at the same time as he was painting him. Dickens had no objection; he was well broken in by sitting to Maclise and d'Orsay. Mr. Putnam recounts that at breakfast-time Dexter would be busy working in one corner of the room while Alexander would make sketches in another, though insisting that Dickens must come to his studio, 41 Tremont Road, to pose for the painted portrait. Dexter would watch Dickens with 'the utmost earnestness' and would sometimes dart out with his calipers to measure his nose, forehead or chin. At one time an unsuccessful portrait painter, he had gained fame by executing (1839) a statue for a tomb in Mount Alban's cemetery known as 'The Binney Child'. To make a good bust of Dickens was obviously for him the chance of a lifetime. He succeeded in pleasing Kate, who wrote 'I think it a beautiful likeness'.

On the Monday began the crowds, the cheers, the verses, letters, dinners, assemblies, for a great free people had decided to offer to a young and self-made man a welcome as appreciative as that given to Lafayette twenty years earlier. 'Boz', the Nation's guest, was to be lionised to capacity and handed on from city to city throughout the far-flung states of the Union. At first he was childishly pleased by the enthusiasm, and even at the end of a week was still delighting in the homage offered him—banquets planned in his honour, theatre audiences rising at his entry, and daily levees packed. It was to be roses, roses all the way, or so it seemed at first sight.

If he felt it odd that he should be treated with such grandeur and solemnity he did not show it, for his adaptability enabled him to rise to every occasion. He was waited on by deputations from the Far West, from state authorities, and bodies public and private of every kind. 'It is all heart', wrote Dr. Channing, the great Boston preacher; 'there never was, never will be such a triumph!' To Charles Dickens it was so stimulating as to be almost supernatural. 'I feel in the best aspects of this welcome something of the presence and influence of that spirit which directs my life', he wrote in all sincerity to John Forster before he had found out what long thorns American roses concealed.

It seems to have dawned on him but slowly that it was not so much as a novelist that he was being fêted as a great moral force. He found himself saddled with a reformer's reputation and was expected to live up to it. Daniel Webster made this clear when he announced that Dickens had 'done more to ameliorate the condition of the English poor than all the statesmen that Great Britain had sent into Parliament'. A Boston preacher followed suit and boomed of 'Dickens's tendency to awaken sympathy with our race and change the unfeeling indifference which has prevailed towards the de-

THE DICKENS CHILDREN
by Daniel Maclise, R.A.

In this water-colour the two elder children, Charley and Mamie, are shown drinking the health of their parents. A toy decanter stands on one volume of Strutt's *Antiques of England* while Katie turns the leaves of the other.

" We carry with us a sketch of our darlings by Maclise. It is a great comfort. We unpack it every night, if we be on a journey; and make as much of this little household god as if it were alive."

CHARLES DICKENS TO LADY HOLLAND (22.3.42)

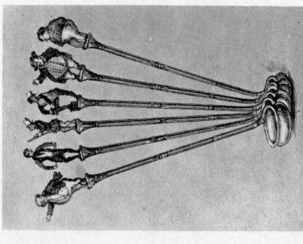

CATHARINE DICKENS, GEORGINA
HOGARTH AND CHARLES DICKENS
by Daniel Maclise, R.A.

SET OF PUNCH LADLES PRESENTED
TO DICKENS BY CHAPMAN AND HALL
Designed by George Cruikshank

pressed multitude into a sorrowful and indignant sensibility to their wrongs and woes'. Americans have a knack of guessing right, and when they welcomed Dickens less as an imaginative writer than as a moral force they made what at the time being was a good shot, for it was only later that he developed to the full his imaginative power. Never had he been publicly welcomed in this way in England and at first it seemed like a lift-up, though it soon proved to be a drag on his spontaneity and enjoyment of life. No one but a missionary bishop or Mary Baker Eddy could have sustained the part assigned to him by the Americans.

In becoming the Nation's guest Charles Dickens was soon forced to realise the utterly binding nature of the new fetters he was expected to assume. Not only must he give up leisure, freedom of talk and opinion, but he must henceforth conform to a pattern portrait. As a moral exemplar borne shoulder-high on public esteem he must at a nod submerge in the warm tide of popular favour, a tide that threatened to be asphyxiating.

A certain discrepancy between the appearance of the missionary and the solemnity of his mission was noted by some of the curious strangers who crowded the daily Dickens levees. No slighter or more effeminate-looking knight could ever have entered the lists on behalf of humanity. In the Alexander portrait, completed within a few days of his landing, we see the same slender figure depicted by Maclise. He is writing at a table and his aquiline nose, mild eyes, parted locks curtaining the ears, all give the effect of girlishness and ingenuosity. Nevertheless he was presented to the American public as a great force, as one who sympathised with the very dregs of the people and touched hearts to ease their condition, as a self-made man who had himself experienced the degradation of poverty, a man whose will-power was as terrific as his industry and whose genius enabled him to get under the skin of all his contemporaries. His genius, his universality had been recognised by parliamentarians in London, by teachers in Russia, by burgesses in Germany and Italy, and yet what was there in his appearance to justify these claims? His first public dinner enabled him to demonstrate that outward appearance was not the most important clue to his personality.

It had been arranged that Mr. Dickens should meet the leading men of Boston at a banquet, the quality of which may be measured by the fact that the tickets were sold at $15 each. Most of the guests were already at the tables when Josiah Quincy with Oliver Wendell Holmes and the distinguished guest appeared in the banqueting chamber. 'God save the Queen' was played and the chairman set the key to the proceedings in his speech of welcome. 'What is Dickens's charm?' he asked, and, answering his own question, stated, 'He is a reformer.' Applause greeted this auspicious opening, and Mr. Quincy went on to say,

> He infuses a moral tone into everything. He is not only a portrayer of public wrongs, but he makes men feel that there is no condition so degraded as not to be visited by gleams of a higher nature.

The fatal germ of complacency had somehow insinuated itself into the company present, which settled itself down comfortably to absorb moral uplift.

Presently a girlish figure rose and, speaking with deep feeling, said: 'You give me no chance of playing at company or holding you at a distance, but flock about me like a host of brothers and make this place like home'. He had received many touching letters from Americans about Little Nell: he was glad to be with friends. The speech pleased all present until he raised the question of international copyright and then immediately and as if by magic he conjured up a host of enemies. He alluded to the fact that his own books had all been reprinted in the United States, most of them in monthly parts, just as soon as they could be ferried over from London. Tens of thousands had been sold at six cents against the twenty-five cents charged in England. 'Of all men living', he said, 'I am the greatest loser by it.' And he was not the only sufferer. Sir Walter Scott had also been a great loser in this matter and had made an appeal through Fenimore Cooper 'to the liberality, perhaps in some sort the justice of American feeling'. It had had no effect. In making his attack on piracy Dickens did not mince matters; he stated it to be 'a plain question of right or wrong, justice or injustice. There *must*', he concluded, 'be an international arrangement in this respect.'

No American speaker at the banquet supported his plea or so much as alluded to copyright. It was bad taste to introduce a controversial subject into a gathering of the kind. Ignoring the painful breach in etiquette, they proceeded to platitudinise on morality and genius and then passed on to formal toasts. The historian Prescott's health was drunk in his absence, the historian Bancroft's in his presence. Mr. Bancroft gave the toast, 'The Memory of Byron, Byron who had so often expressed the wish to visit America'. A letter from Washington Irving was read regretting his enforced absence, and the toast 'Geoffrey Crayon' followed. There were numbers of toasts and numbers of speakers, but no one breathed the word copyright. Mr. Dickens had offended all present by his *gaffe* and caused, as he was to learn from newspaper columns next day, 'huge dissonance where all else was triumphant unison'.

Taken aback at the effect he had produced and feeling for the first time qualms as to his capacity for understanding America, Dickens wrote to Macready:[1]

Loving you . . . I would not condemn you to a year's residence on this side of the Atlantic for any money. Freedom of opinion! Where is it? I see a press more mean and paltry, and silly, and disgraceful than any country I ever knew. If that is its standard, here it is . . . I speak of Bancroft and am advised to be silent . . . he is a black sheep —a Democrat. . . . I speak of Bryant and am entreated to be more careful for the same reason. I speak of inter-

[1] 413. I. N.L.

national copyright and am implored not to ruin myself outright. I speak of Miss Martineau and all parties . . . shower down upon me a perfect cataract of abuse. . . . Americans can't bear to be told of their faults. 'Don't split on that rock, Mr. Dickens, don't write about America, we are so very suspicious.' Freedom of opinion! Macready, if I had been born here and had written my books in this country, producing them with no stamp of approval from any other land, it is my solemn belief that I should have lived and died poor, unnoticed, and a 'black sheep' to boot.

In meeting most of the people of note in Boston, among them Longfellow, Richard Dana, George Bancroft, Dr. Channing, Jared Sparks and Ticknor, Dickens made at least two lifelong friends in Cornelius Felton, professor of Greek at Harvard, and Jonathan Chapman, mayor of the city. Rather unfortunately he did not meet either Hawthorne or Margaret Fuller, both of whom had been absorbed into the Brook Farm circle the previous year. Hawthorne held strong views about the conceit displayed by English travellers in their comments on the American way of life. 'Never', he used to say, 'has an Englishman spared America for courtesy's sake or kindness.' One of the few American books specially praised by Dickens is *Mosses from an Old Manse*, and if he could have met its author he might have been saved disillusionment and at any rate would have been warned that he must not expect an extension of New England in other states of the Union. With Longfellow (who secretly thought Bostonians were making fools of themselves over 'Boz') he struck up a sudden intimacy born of the fact that the poet was just sailing for Europe. At once Dickens made plans for future meetings in London. Longfellow must stay with him, an invitation the American author was only too pleased to accept. Reinforcing his invitation in a letter from New York he said:

Write to me from the continent and tell me when to expect you. We live quietly,—not uncomfortably—and among people I am sure you would like to know as much as they would like to know you. Have no home but mine, see nothing in town on your way to Germany and let me be your London host and cicerone. Is that a bargain?

It was a little surprising to Dickens to find that nearly all the cultivated men of Boston were Unitarians and that Harvard, though undenominational in principle, was staffed by professors of this creed just as in England Oxford and Cambridge Universities were staffed by men of the Church of England. This form of non-miraculous Christianity had established a rather dim association in London in 1825, the same year in which the more prosperous Unitarian Association of America had been founded. As a creed it was in keeping with the movement of an age that was to produce Strauss's *Leben Jesu* and Renan's *Vie de Jésus*, and in Boston it was represented by all that was most cultured and elevated in American life. Dickens was very favourably impressed by the people who called themselves Unitarians and especially with their leading pastor, Dr. Channing. It occurred to him that as he adhered to no formal religion he might do worse than join the London Association at the Essex Street Chapel on his return. He would find no difficulty in accepting his friend W. J. Fox's definition of this faith: 'Belief in God the Father and in the humanity and divine mission of Jesus of Nazareth'. To himself he called it 'the religion that has sympathy for men of every creed and ventures to pass judgment on none'. On getting home from America we shall find him attending the Essex Street meetings, and then renting sittings for himself and family at the chapel in Little Portland Street, the minister of which, Mr. Tagart, was to become a trusted friend.

There was for Dickens an extraordinary relish to be derived not only from the discovery of Unitarianism, but also from meetings with people of achievement, just as for Bostonians there was a rare excitement in entertaining the most talked-of writer in the world. In America the emphasis is always on the man, for Americans are liable to be greatly stimulated by viewing people or listening to people who have actually accomplished something.   Dickens, too, was electrified by his first contacts with distinguished Americans, but even in refined Boston the pace was too fast and the demands made on him too exhausting, as we learn from Mrs. John Motley's letter to her husband written the day 'Boz' left the city:[1]

> Dickens goes to-day, but has promised to return in June. I only had a glimpse of him in the street getting in and out of a carriage when he came to breakfast with Dr. Channing the other morning.   I went to Miss Peabody's where he promised to go; instead of which, however, he went to bed and sent an apology, and disappointed the Paiges too, who had prepared a magnificent dinner for him—half an hour after dinner he sent an apology.... Poor man, he is literally used up ... giving himself up as a spectacle.   He says this second edition, this epitome of London will never do; he must see something besides.

It was only a fortnight since Dickens had stepped ashore and yet already he lay in a state of collapse on a sofa in Tremont House quite unable to face the women who mobbed his movements and even pushed their way into Alexander's studio.   Mrs. Dickens also was quite overcome by the furore her husband had excited and could not speak of it without bursting into tears.   This, to the Americans, strange reaction was accounted for by the ladies gossiping at tea-tables by the suggestion that Mrs. Dickens must be going to have another baby.   One lady, who talked with Kate at a dinner-party given by the W. H. Prescotts, said she seemed highly embarrassed by the situation in which she found herself, being unaccustomed to dwell in the 'fierce light that shone upon every deed and word of the popular idol'.   It was a great satisfaction to her to talk about 'the best shops in Oxford Street and other homely and familiar matters'.   To her

[1] February 5, 1842. *Dickensian*, 1926, p. 271.

fellow guest she showed obvious signs of having been born
and bred her husband's social superior.

On leaving Boston Dickens and his wife went to Worcester
for a week-end, to stay with George Bancroft's sister, who
was married to the Governor of Massachusetts. They then
proceeded to Hartford, where they held formal levees each
morning and shook hands with at least two hundred people a
day. Later in their tour the numbers increased to six and
seven hundred. The presence of Kate, Charles used to say,
afforded him some protection at these impromptu gatherings.
'If I had not a lady with me I should be obliged to leave the
country. But for her they would never leave me alone day
or night.'

One of the American muses of the moment, Mrs. Sigourney, was among those who called on him at Hartford.
Always on the alert for literary lions, she brought with her a
poem written in honour of 'Boz', which she declaimed. The
opening quatrain struck a genial note:

> Welcome! o'er the ocean blue,
> Welcome to the youthful West,
> Ardent hearts and spirits true
> Greet thee as a favoured guest.

A contrast with Mrs. Sigourney were the carmen of Hartford, who gave Dickens great pleasure by presenting themselves in their blue overalls to bid him welcome. It appeared
from their spokesman's speech that they had all read his books
and all perfectly understood them. This was the sort of
compliment that made Dickens very much happier than did
verses like those of Mrs. Sigourney. A boy of twelve who
was watching him on this occasion was struck by his peculiar waistcoat. It was of a 'very vivid colour' and from
its pockets dangled 'a very prodigious watch-chain'. As
Dickens laughed, he tossed the chain up and down in his
hands and then, as he got more excited, twiddled it round his
fingers.

At the Hartford banquet that evening chairman William Hammersley, following Mrs. Sigourney's example, broke into verse:

> I'll sing you a new-made song,
> But from no agéd pate,
> Of a fine young English gentleman
> Whose mind is his estate.

Nothing really ever came amiss to Dickens in the way of formal homage, and when he got up to address his fellow guests it seemed as if he had quietly accepted the uplift cue tendered him by all speakers. Of the home-like quality of his reception he said:

> I have faith and I wish to diffuse faith in the existence—yes, of beautiful things even in those conditions of society which are so degenerate, degraded, and forlorn. . . . I take it that we . . . hold our sympathies, hopes, and energies in trust for the Many not the Few.   That we cannot hold in too strong a light of disgust and contempt all meanness, falsehood, cruelty and oppression.   Above all that nothing is high because it is in a high place and nothing is low because it is in a low one.   [Loud applause].   This is the lesson taught by the great Book of Nature.

So far so good, but he spoiled the effect of these meritorious sentiments on those present by begging leave to whisper the words—international copyright.

> I use them in no sordid sense. . . . I would rather my children coming after me trudged in the mud and knew by the general feeling that their father was beloved and of some use than I would have them ride in their carriages and know by their banker's books he was rich.   But I do not see why one should be obliged to make the choice. . . . A copyright law would have saved Scott great suffering. . . .

The faces along the banqueting - table registered disapproval, but Dickens was not going to spare his auditors. As he wrote home, 'My blood so boiled as I thought of the monstrous injustice that I felt as if I were twelve feet high when I thrust it down their throats'.[1] No one of the speakers who followed him mentioned the odious theme. It was as if the words he had spoken had never been uttered at all.

The public and the press did not follow the example of the dinner guests. Anonymous letters reached him, newspaper reporters battered him as 'no gentleman, but a mercenary scoundrel'. In a vigorously administered snubbing the *Hartford Times* said:

> It happens that we want no advice on this subject and it will be better for Mr. D. if he refrains from introducing the subject hereafter, but it is not pleasant to pursue the subject further at this time.

There is something peculiarly affronting to English people in not being allowed to express opinions freely. We do not object to disagreement, even to contradiction so long as it is expressed in argument and not in condemnatory silence and press abuse. Dickens was now subjected to the same mortifying experience as Harriet Martineau, who had been taken up with warm enthusiasm and then dropped like a stone when her opinions were found to be unacceptable to the *bien pensants* of America. She only had to say once that she considered slavery inconsistent with the law of God to be condemned and cut. After receiving universal homage and enjoying great personal popularity it was humiliating in the extreme to be treated thus, and it caused her to 'revise the over-favourable estimates' made in the earlier part of her tour. With Dickens it was a little different, for he put his foot wrong almost at the start and felt obliged to withdraw from the part he had at first seen himself playing in every great city of the Union. Indeed he was so upset by the effect of his second copyright speech that he had a mind to abandon his tour altogether. As this might have been difficult to explain, he adopted an alternative course of action, that of withdrawing into his shell and refusing to be booked for any public occasion. In the role of private person he at least

[1] 386. I. N.L.

could hold private opinions. Sadly did he write to Macready, 'This is not the Republic I came to see. This is not the Republic of my imagination.'

New Haven was the scene of the next reception and there a *mêlée* instead of a levee took place at the Tontine Hotel. It was midnight before Mr. and Mrs. Dickens could escape to their room, and even then they were serenaded till dawn by choristers from the College. Hardly had they stepped aboard the New York packet next morning than they were again mobbed. Kate, whose face was dreadfully swollen, longed more than ever for the privacy of home and saw with dismay what unfair advantage was being taken by souvenir-hunters pressing up against Charles. Some 'twenty or thirty people were screwing small dabs of fur out of the back of the costly great-coat' bought by her husband in Regent Street just before they left London. Would they also snip pieces from her dress? Was it possible that they might both arrive at their destination in tatters?

Their friend David Colden had begged them to take no steps about getting introductions to people in New York, he himself would see to it that they were 'brought out' properly and not subjected to persecution. When they got to the Carlton Hotel on Broadway, they found that a committee of influential residents had booked accommodation for them and had arranged that they should attend a great ball at the Park Theatre on the following night, Valentine night. This they were told was to be a gala affair with three thousand guests in 'full dress' and a stage transformed into 'a large magnificent chamber of carved and gilded oak with deep gothick windows and lofty fretted ceiling'—an English baronial hall, in short, 'beyond description grand'. Mr. and Mrs. Dickens were conducted to the central box whence a ramp led to the stage. There they were introduced to the Mayor of New York and had to parade round the enormous ballroom to the tune of 'See the conquering hero comes'. Dickens wore a black suit with a gay vest and Mrs. Dickens

'a white-figured Irish tabinet trimmed with mazarine blue
flowers to match her eyes'.   A wreath, also of mazarine blue,
crowned her fair ringlets and a pearl necklace adorned her
neck.   Both were carefully scrutinised as they danced in the
opening cotillon.   The paragraphists said that Mrs. Dickens
though smartly dressed was not smart in manner: she spoke
little and seemed resigned to her position as wife of a lion.
As for the lion, he was 'bright-eyed, intelligent-looking, brisk
in manner, lively in talk, somewhat of a dandy with rings and
things in fine array', and women were particularly interested
in the lion's mane.   The hair seemed to wave naturally at the
parting, but were the corkscrew curls also natural or merely
soap-locks 'fixed' with a lotion?   No matter how closely
they leered, no female could decide.   Had they but seen
Count d'Orsay's sketch, made just before Dickens left
England, its straight and ragged locks would have convinced
them that the much-admired curls had been 'induced'.

Pressmen reported that at Park Theatre 'Boz' looked
'thunderstruck', and wondered whether he was used to such
high society.   He may have felt half dazed with fever and
sore throat; anyway he spent the four days following the ball
in bed.   It was at this rather depressing moment that Washington Irving called at the Carlton Hotel and persuaded the
sick lion and his mate to come and take refuge with him at
Sunnyside, a gabled, creeper-clad villa on the Hudson.   This
lovely interlude of understanding, was remarked on by
Professor Felton, another guest, who spoke of the 'mutual
cordiality' displayed by both authors.

Irving realised, as few Americans did, the importance of
the copyright question, for he had suffered under it himself
when his books were published in London.   Indifferent to
popularity, since he was on the point of leaving America for
the embassy at Madrid, he seized the opportunity presented
by a public dinner at the City Hotel,[1] New York, to give the
toast of 'Charles Dickens, the Nation's guest, coupled with

[1] February 19, 1842.

International Copyright'. 'It is but fair', he observed humorously, 'that those who have laurels for their brows should be permitted to browse on their laurels.'

In responding to this toast Dickens spoke of his great admiration for Washington Irving, who had, after reading *The Old Curiosity Shop*, written him 'a letter so generous, so affectionate, and so manly as to strike a sympathetic chord at once'.

> I answered him and he answered me and so we kept shaking autobiographically as if no ocean rolled between us. . . . Washington Irving! Why, gentlemen, I don't go upstairs to bed two nights out of the seven . . . without taking Washington Irving under my arm and when I don't take him I take his own brother, Oliver Goldsmith. Washington Irving, Knickerbocker, Geoffrey Crayon. Why, where can you go that they have not been there before?

Other speakers followed, one of whom, Cornelius Matthews, inquired by what casuistry does that which is property in one latitude cease to be property when transferred within the limits of another? 'I offer', he said, 'an international copyright as the only honest turnpike between the readers of two great nations.'

The *New York Tribune* supported Dickens nobly in an advance editorial:

> We have heard rumours that Mr. Dickens has ventured to allude in his replies to complimentary addresses to the gross injustice and spoliation to which he and foreign authors are exposed in this country from the absence of an International Copyright. We trust he will not be deterred from speaking the frank round truth. Who shall protest against robbery if those who are robbed may not? Here is a man who writes for a living. Do we look well offering him toasts, compliments and other syllabub while we refuse him naked justice? . . . He has a wife and four children whom his death may possibly leave destitute while publishers, grown rich by his writings, roll by in their carriages.

It was not till fifty years after this article was written[1] that a law regulating international copyright came into operation.

From this time on Dickens seems to have lost something of his zest for experience and something of his native buoyancy of temperament. The vista that had bewitched him in Boston 'of dinners and balls at Philadelphia, Baltimore and Washington and I believe everywhere' had faded. Finding he could do nothing in New York without being mobbed, he sometimes took refuge in a church, but when he did so neighbouring pews filled up with staring faces. In trains, in the street and at parties he found himself smothered and exhausted. To escape 'febrile circumstance' he declined in advance all public entertainments and told Putnam to make no future arrangements of any kind, anywhere. Shocked, melancholy and no longer floating on an ocean of approval, he began to fear that 'the heaviest blow ever dealt to liberty will be dealt by this country', and by liberty he meant not only liberty of thought but liberty of action.

Each one of us forms a mental concept of America and goes there expecting to find this concept operative. Emerging from the toils of a social system heavily weighed down by overhead charges, it was at first a delight to Dickens, as it has been to many others, to find himself in a classless land in which every man had access to the same education and could grow to the height for which his energy and intelligence fitted him. The absence of servile standards and social barriers, the fluidity of society and its interchangeability of parts at the first blush appeared to Dickens to be a realisation of equality, but even equality he found had its snags. Equality to some extent must be a matter of the flat-iron —and where the flat-iron makes itself felt most acutely on the few is in the pressing out of ideas and freedom of opinion.

He had been warned that he would find much to dislike in the United States. Fanny Trollope had told him about the tobacco-chewing and the spitting indulged in by American

[1] 1892.

men of that date. He believed he had discounted these things in advance, but as he cowered 'in the shabby omnibuses called railway-cars' he could not help shuddering at the flashes of saliva that streamed past the windows. Odious to him, too, was the charcoal heating of the trains, and as for the anthracite, burnt in the 'beastly furnaces' of hotels and institutions, it made him faint and gave him a headache 'morning, noon and night'. His spirits sank so low that he could see no fun in anything.

Though depression and a general sense of disillusionment had caused him to decline advance invitations from Philadelphia, and even to stay *perdu* in New York for three days after he was supposed to have left for the Quaker stronghold, the *Public Ledger* of that city got even with him as soon as they heard of his arrival by announcing that Mr. Dickens would be gratified to shake hands with his friends between the hours of 10.30 A.M. and 11.30 A.M. at the United States Hotel on Chestnut Street. As soon as he stepped into the lobby of the hotel, Mr. Dickens was requested by the landlord to name the hour for receiving 'a committee' next morning. The committee, to the author's horror, turned out to be a mob! For two hours poor, angry Mr. Dickens toiled away in a large room shaking hands with everyone, for the landlord had informed him that his refusal to do so would cause a riot. George Putnam who thought the whole business a cruel imposition, stood at his side while introductions were effected, many of them prefixed by the words 'one of the most remarkable men in our country'. 'Good God, Mr. Putnam,' he said, 'they are all so!' This scene is vividly described in *Martin Chuzzlewit*.

There were calmer and pleasanter moments in which he was entertained privately by Carey the bookseller, who was married to a sister of his artist friend, Charles Leslie. Then the editor of *Graham's Magazine*, Edgar Allan Poe, three years older than the English author, left his article on *Barnaby Rudge* and his *Tales of the Grotesque and Arabesque* at the hotel where Mr. Dickens was staying. On calling for an interview he was received by a small, dapper figure in a dressing-gown with purple facings. At first the American poet, a slovenly fellow himself, did not feel too much at ease with the foppish young man who was decked out with cravat pins and chains preparatory to slipping on a frock-coat for the street. They talked of international copyright and of contemporary writers. Poe was anxious to get his stories published in England and this Dickens promised to inquire about, a promise he fulfilled by going to Moxon and other publishers on his return. In the following November he wrote to Poe, 'They have one and all declined the venture'. Dickens did not appear to have realised that *The Fall of the House of Usher* had already appeared anonymously in *Bentley's Miscellany* under Ainsworth's editorship. Even if he had read it and known the name of the author, the morbidity of the theme would not at this time have predisposed him in Poe's favour, though later in his life he might have greatly admired him. The interview between the two authors at the Philadelphia hotel proved sterile and closed coldly. Neither seems to have liked the other much.

Dickens had brought with him from London a letter to Lucretia Mott, the Quaker anti-slavery advocate. She wrote:[1]

Another lion has just arrived in the city—Charles Dickens. Our children have a strong desire to see him. I, too, have liked the benevolent tendency of his writings, though I have read very little in them. I did not expect to seek an interview or invite him here, as he was not quite of our sort. But just now there was left at our door his and . his wife's card with a kind letter from our dear friend E. J. Reed, of London, introducing them and expressing a strong desire that we would make their acquaintance. There is not a woman in London whose draft I would more gladly honour. So now we shall call on them and our daughters are in high glee.

At Baltimore the travellers tried to evade notice by sticking

[1] See Oberholtzer, *Literary History of Philadelphia*.

to the train, but people pressed against the windows and peered at them. Very little fuss was made of Dickens in Washington though he was warmly welcomed in private, and after paying his respects to President Tyler at a levee was entertained by him informally at the White House. Tyler expressed surprise that 'Boz', the famous, should look so young. Dickens says he would like to have returned the compliment, but that the poor fellow looked 'so jaded' that it stuck in his throat 'like Macbeth's Amen'. It gave him a homely feeling to see that the President had a trick of curling his legs under him 'just like Talfourd'. Admitted to the floor of House and Senate as a distinguished visitor, he listened to the speaking, which on the whole struck him as less good than in England. The men seemed to him more remarkable than their orations. But then in America the focus of interest is the man rather than his office or the measure for which he stands. J. Q. Adams, Henry Clay, Calhoun and Quincy were among those he most admired. Daniel Webster, on the other hand, struck him as thoroughly unreal—'a sublime caricature of Lord Burleigh feigning abstraction in the dreadful pressure of affairs of state'. Henry Clay he liked immensely, J. Q. Adams reminded him of Sam Rogers, and Charles Sumner, who had been much in Europe, he found most sympathetic. In his dispatch-case he had brought from New York copies of a petition on international copyright signed by Washington Irving and other American authors. One copy he presented to the House of Representatives and the other, placed in Clay's keeping, was destined for the Senate.

From Washington Dickens and his party visited Richmond and Harrisburg, both seats of State Legislatures. At the Virginian capital he was 'informally' entertained at a *petit souper* where he hobnobbed with ninety of the commission merchants and tobacconists of the city at the Exchange Hotel. They were friendly and assured him that, though they had little time for reading themselves, their wives and daughters liked his books. One man beamingly told him how much he had enjoyed his *Last Days of Pompeii*.   The chairman of the supper party, Mr. Ritchie, owner of the *Richmond Enquirer*, praised Mr. Dickens in stilted fashion for having 'sought the violet in its lowly bed so as to give its perfume to the light of day', adding that their guest of honour had 'seized upon humble points in the human landscape and had lighted them up with the fire of his genius'.   It was true that 'no Washington Irving or William Bryant had appeared in their midst', the forte of the Old Dominion was rather to be found in the masculine productions of her statesmen—her Washington, her Jefferson, her Madison, 'men who had never indulged in imaginative works, in the charms of romance or in the mere beauties of literature'.   With phrases like these did the business men of Richmond, while honouring the success and large sales of Mr. Dickens's novels, pay lip service to the pen-driving profession.

Writing to Lady Holland, Dickens says that she will have heard of the public progress imposed on him, he can't bear it, and has refused everything but an invitation to dine at St. Louis, 'quite next door—2000 miles away'.   He has spoken much of her with Washington Irving, and then continues: 'We hold a levee for all comers.   The Queen and Prince Albert can hardly be more tied, for ours is a perpetual Drawing-room.   Our Crown too is not a Golden one except in opinion.   We have been . . . to Richmond and were going on to Charleston, but the sight of slavery turned us back.' Everywhere they 'found themselves a week behind Lord Morpeth'.[1]

At the Pennsylvanian capital, Harrisburg, 'Boz' was acclaimed by both Houses.   His spirits rose unaccountably; once again he felt himself to be 'the Inimitable', once again he was delighted that members of the legislature should pay him the compliment of following him back to his hotel.   Mixed with this feeling was a certain impatience at the insufferably apish character of the legislatures that honoured him and the men who paid him compliments: he called it 'a feeling of bile'.

[1] March 22, 1842.

Next came a canal voyage to Pittsburg, then a voyage down-river to Cincinnati, the city in which gallant Mrs. Trollope had dwelt so long and which she had described in such detail. Here Mr. and Mrs. Dickens were badly mobbed. By dinner-time they were in a fainting condition. A Cincinnati lady after staring at Mrs. Dickens described her as 'a large woman' with a good deal of colour and a good face. As no one in the city had seen the engraving from Maclise's portrait, no one had any idea in advance how very young Mr. Dickens was going to look or how very smart his clothes and his jewelry were going to be. Porter, the Kentucky giant, called his appearance 'flash, like one of our river gamblers'. It was all very well to call Cincinnati a beautiful city, but meeting its inhabitants was not a beautiful experience, and the poor visitor's face acquired an expression of sadness from 'the constant and unmitigated boring' he endured. A letter written from Cincinnati makes Kate out to be a sort of Tilly Slowboy:

> As we made our way on foot over the broken pavement, Anne measured her length on the ground, but didn't hurt herself. I say nothing of Kate's tumbles—but you recollect her propensity? She falls into, or out of, every coach or boat we enter; scrapes the skin off her legs; brings great sores and swellings on her feet; chips large fragments out of her ankle-bones, and makes herself blue with bruises. She really has, however, since we got over the first trial of being among circumstances so new and fatiguing, made a *most admirable* traveller in every respect. She has never screamed . . . never given way to despondency or fatigue . . . has always accommodated herself well . . . has pleased me very much and proved herself perfectly game.[1]

Somehow Dickens did not go down so well in the west and south as in New England. The people of St. Louis, for instance, were frankly critical. The papers objected to his hair, it did not curl sufficiently; to his dress, it was somewhat too foppish and, contrasted with the black suits worn by the gentry of St. Louis, a little vulgar.

Of course Dickens made a point of visiting 'Cairo', the concession in which he is said to have invested some of his first earnings. It lay at the junction of the Mississippi and Ohio and is described as 'Eden' in *Martin Chuzzlewit*. It was 'a dismal swamp vaunted in England as a mine of Golden Hope and speculated in on the faith of monstrous representations to many people's ruin'.

Before they left for Canada the travellers went with David Colden to stay with the Ticknors at Lebanon Springs. Ticknor did his best to introduce Dickens to the Quaker Settlement. The Quakers would have none of him. It grieved Ticknor to find that they were so insensible to Dickens's widespread merit and so little respecters of persons as to refuse to show him 'any of their mysteries or managements touching men or beasts'. The *Western Star*,[1] a Lebanon paper commenting on Mr. Dickens's visit, stated that he had been travelling 'very quietly' in the West, and that it was 'gratified to observe the total absence of all that parade and sycophancy which characterised his reception in Eastern cities', adding with that self-consciousness which at the time was characteristic of American journalism, 'It will give us a better opinion of ourselves even if Mr. Dickens should not think the better of us for it'.

They looked forward to having a rest in Canada, a rest from jolting stages, corduroy roads, tobacco-chewing, spitting, uncouth manners, and all the other disadvantages that seemed to be inherent in pioneer company. Ears alert to catch the thunder of Niagara, Dickens worked himself up into an extreme state of tension as they got near the frontier, and when not only the thunder was audible, but high clouds of spray visible, he leapt from the carriage and ran down to the water's edge to get ferried without further delay up to the Falls. What transports of joy they both enjoyed at seeing

[1] April 20, 1842.

an English sentinel! Wet through by spray, Charles joined Kate at the hotel facing the Falls on the Canadian side. As soon as he had changed into dry clothes Dickens hurried his wife off to the Horseshoe Falls and helped her clamber down to the basin, for in those days there seems to have been no staging behind the curtain of water. How green, how marvellous it all was! it quite took their breath away. Rather inexplicably it made Charles think of Mary:

> What would I give if the dear girl whose ashes lie in Kensal Green had lived to come so far along with us—but she has been here many times, I doubt not, since her sweet face faded from my earthly sight.

They spent a whole week, to their 'unspeakable delight, without company'. They had the Falls to themselves, rambled about in old clothes, 'played cribbage o' nights' and did just as they pleased. Dickens in high spirits quoted the words of Mr. Brass to express his contentment, 'A still small voice is a-singing comic songs within us and all is happiness and peace'. Documents reached him at Niagara concerning international copyright. 'Organised by Forster, the Greater Writers of England have flung their gauntlets down on top of mine', he said, and at once posted their manifesto to the editor of the *Evening Post* in Boston and, as he did so, all the old indignation once again boiled up within him. It was horrible to think that scoundrelly booksellers should grow rich from publishing books the authors of which did not reap one farthing. Equally horrible was it that blackguardly newspapers, 'not fit for a water-closet mat', should be free to print the work of great writers side by side with obscenities.

It was at the invitation of the Coldstream Guards, tendered by Lord Mulgrave, that the Dickenses went from Niagara to Montreal to play in garrison theatricals. With delight Charles took over the duties of stage manager and started drilling the actors in the manner of Macready. The pieces chosen were *A Roland for an Oliver*, *A Good Night's Rest* and *Deaf as a Post*. Owing to the shortage of young ladies, Kate

had to take a part and her husband said she played 'devilish
well'.   They stayed at Rasco's Hotel and were very kindly
treated by their military hosts, who put carriages and boats
at their disposal.   On the night of the performance, the band
of the 23rd Regiment played in the foyer.   Dickens was one
of the four gentlemen carrying lighted candles deputed to
meet the Governor-General, Sir Charles Bagot, on his arrival.
The Commander-in-Chief, Sir Richard Jackson, also attended
the opening performance which was 'strictly by invitation'.
One other performance was given 'to prevent heart-burnings
in a heart-burning town'.   Among the officers acting were
Lord Mulgrave, the Hon. Paul Methuen, Captain Willoughby
and Captain Granville.

Most English travellers coming from the United States
relapsed with satisfaction into the extremely English atmosphere of Eastern Canada.   Dickens alone among English
visitors expressed himself 'appalled' by the Toryism of
Toronto.

During his travels Dickens had become the owner of a
white Havannah spaniel, the gift of Mitchell, the American
comedian.   First named Mr. Timber Doodle, a name
changed later to Mr. Snittle Timbery, this little dog lived to
be very old and accompanied the family in all its migrations,
including visits to Italy and Switzerland.   The society of
'Timber' and the display of Maclise's group-portrait of the
Dickens children made hotel rooms less chilling and impersonal.   Nat Willis, who had not seen Dickens since his
Furnival Inn days, had been specially interested when they
met again to see what the children looked like.   In vain did
Willis beg Mrs. Dickens to give him the portrait-group as a
souvenir.   'Imagine!' she wrote to Maclise, 'the impudence
and audacity of such a request!'   One of Mr. Putnam's jobs,
on arriving at any place they were to spend the night in, was
to open the rather big box containing the picture (15 inches in
diameter) and set it up on a side-table, after which ceremony
Dickens would take up his accordion and play 'Home, sweet

Home'.   Nine years later, when the number of children had
been doubled, Charles Dickens wrote to Mr. Putnam:

> The picture of the four we had when in America hangs
> in our dining-room at home.   It is in a gay round frame
> now and has these many years forgotten the sliding of the
> box you used to take off before you set it up on a side table
> at each of the four and twenty thousand inns we stayed in.
> I wonder whether you recollect the inn at Hartford where
> the levee would not go away—or at Newhaven where they
> kicked the staircase to express their impatience—or at
> Columbus where they came arm in arm at midnight—or
> at St. Louis where we had a ball—or at Pittsburg, or at
> Philadelphia where a little hatter with black whiskers did
> the honours.   I feel as if I should like to see all those places
> again.[1]

Distance of time had blurred the sharpness of the original
impressions and invested them with a mildly humorous
effulgence.   Not till Dickens, twenty years later, re-crossed
the Atlantic to expose himself to the immense fatigues and
excitements of a reading tour was he reminded that constitu-
tionally he was no American.

[1] 332. II. N.L.

Chapter 12

HOME AGAIN

*It was home. And though home is a name, a word, it is a
strong one: stronger than magician ever spoke, or spirit
answered to, in strongest conjuration.* CHARLES DICKENS

BY the end of June Mr. and Mrs. Dickens were back in
London. Both of them had been home-sick for months
and the satisfaction of settling down into their own comfortable groove made them glow with happiness. 'How we
enjoy our home and everything connected with it!' piped
Charles to an American friend. It was good indeed to be in
one's own study again, good to arrange one's books, paper,
pens, and specially good, after bleak experiences in hotel
rooms, to resume friendly contact with the inanimate furnishings of private life.

Against the return of their parents the four children had
been fetched from Clarence Terrace by their uncle Frederick
and had been tucked up in bed at Devonshire Terrace. 'We
quickly had them up,' said their father, 'little Charley was so
excited that he fell into convulsions. Except for this mishap
the meeting went off merrily. Kate was all smiles as she
cooed to the baby, and Charles, as soon as he could disengage
himself from the clinging arms of the little girls, ran across into
Regent's Park to see Macready, who had had charge of the
whole family for six months. He found his friend sitting in
a dark room by an open window looking out at the trees.
Never, never could Charles thank his dear Macready enough,
the children were 'heartily well' and 'delighted beyond all
means' to see their parents. Then followed an eager talk
about America.

Among the family faces greeting the arrival of the travellers
was that of Kate's sister, little Georgina Hogarth, who had
been in close touch with the children during their temporary
orphanhood. Georgina could tell Kate about her darlings,

recount the changes that had taken place during her absence, and the details of growth and behaviour precious to mothers the world over. It was plain that 'aunt Georgy' had won the love of the infant quartet, and it seemed only natural and convenient that she should continue her ministrations and make her home with Charles and Kate. Perhaps it flitted through Kate's slow mind that her presence might put an end to all the dreams and the talk about Mary to which she had listened so patiently these five years past. Georgina was the same age as Mary had been when she became an inmate of Doughty Street, and was sufficiently like Mary in appearance to be mistakable for her at a short distance. What now began to happen might have been predicted by anyone outside the home circle. Always thinking of Mary as as much part of himself as 'the beating of my heart', Charles after a few weeks began to 'see the spirit of Mary shining out in Georgina', and to find old times coming back 'so that the past can hardly be separated from the present'. This new emotional sublimation was to prove a source of vague contentment to Dickens and, after Georgina had matured to womanhood, a source of subconscious irritation to her placid sister. For the time being, however, no family could have appeared more completely happy and pleased each with the other.

Invitations reached Dickens by every post. Lord Lansdowne was early in the field with a dinner of welcome at which Moore, Rogers and Luttrell were fellow guests, and Forster assembled a party at Greenwich at which the Inimitable made a come-back and expanded like an anemone in a sun-warmed pool. With good companions like Talfourd, Maclise, Barham, Stanfield, Cruikshank, Monckton Milnes, Hood and Procter, he could throw discretion to the winds and give vent to his pent-up feelings about America. The comfort of associating with men who could not possibly misunderstand him and whom he could not possibly offend was in itself bliss; indeed to be with such people was to have the self-respect that had been so aggravatingly frayed by transatlantic treatment and criticism, completely restored.

With Lady Holland, too, he spent an evening soon after his arrival. He found that she had fitted up some of the lower rooms at Holland House in which to give dinners 'as of yore'. But there was not much 'yore' about it, for into the first-floor rooms, the scene of all her brilliant entertaining, she never entered. 'I had a strange sense', writes Dickens, 'of their being dark and vacant overhead.' In spite of Sydney Smith being 'in greater force than ever', it was a ghost-haunted evening, and as he watched the gouty hobble of the Canon of St. Paul's, and the sad expression of his hostess when not actually talking, he asked himself who would or could take the place of these rare personalities when they too stepped into the shadow. Life was a sad business, perhaps 'the saddest dream that was ever dreamed'.

One evening Tom Beard was pressed to come to Devonshire Terrace and 'eat breast of venison at half-past five sharp' in order to listen to the first chapter of *American Notes* being read aloud by Forster. Dickens was pining for literary encouragement. The tour had been a great strain; he only realised what a strain as he rapidly revived his experiences in a travel-book for autumn publication. The welcome he had received in London and the company he was keeping made it extremely hard to buckle to work and especially to concentrate on America. Someone must tell him that the book was worth persevering with, otherwise he could not manage to put good work into it, the truth being that the subject made little or no demand on the creative power that all the while was bubbling up within him and demanding its proper outlet. To his intimates he said, 'I feel my power now more than ever I did, I have a greater confidence in myself than ever I had'. He gave the impression in conversation of being bored to death with the United States, and to cross-examiners of his opinions would say, 'I went there expecting greater things than I found'.

In his first days in London he composed a letter to the *Athenaeum*[1] reporting on his efforts to secure international

[1] July 7, 1842.

copyright. He had interested certain transatlantic authors sufficiently to persuade them to draw up a petition for signature by the whole body of American writers. Among these authors were Washington Irving, Fenimore Cooper and Prescott, men as well known in England as in their own country. This petition had been presented by Mr. Clay to Congress and by Congress had been referred to a Select Committee, but in order to discount any advantage that might accrue to authors therefrom, the publishers of Boston had hurriedly passed a resolution to the effect that no change in the existing law was needed. And they justified their attitude by stating that if English authors were invested with any control over the republication of their own books, it would no longer be possible for American editors to alter and adapt them to the American taste. Dickens went on in his letter to say that Mr. Prescott, who could be relied on to behave like a gentleman and man of letters, was most indignant over the action of the publishers. It was high time, he urged, that English authors made some combined stand. As for himself, he was resolved never to enter into any negotiation with any American publisher for transmission of early proofs and was willing to forgo all profit derivable from such a source. In America he had come across newspaper editors and proprietors whose journals were almost entirely made up of the republication of popular English works. He had even read papers describing the success of his books which, over the page, contained scurrilous attacks on himself. The situation was intolerably unjust. He would like to stress the fact that so far he had been fighting single-handed, but now looked to all writers to rally to his support. Miss Julia Pardoe, the popular historian, read the letter in the *Athenaeum* and at once wrote to Dickens to ask how she could protect her own books. Little comfort was derivable from the reply:

> The existing law allows them [the Americans] to reprint any English book without any communication whatever with the author. . . . My books have all been reprinted on these agreeable terms. . . . Sometimes one firm of pirates

will pay a trifle to procure early copies and get so much the start of the rest as they can. . . . Directly it is printed it is common property and may be reprinted a thousand times.[1]

The great financial interests bound up with the pirating of English books were well able to protect themselves against the pen-pricks of even famous writers. Firms like Lea and Carey of Philadelphia and their rivals in New York had not, at the bidding of a Fenimore Cooper, abandoned the advantages gained by pirating the works of Scott, Byron, Leigh Hunt and Moore. The works of Dickens were almost as good a proposition as the Waverley Novels: there was a fortune latent in them.

For an American publisher at this time the only expense connected with the acquisition of a new English book was empowering an agent to dispatch an advance copy by the fastest ship available. Partly owing to the fact that no royalties had to be paid and partly to the large size of the original impression, American booksellers could produce books more cheaply than English publishers. In England a Waverley novel was printed in three volumes for 31s. 6d.; in Philadelphia it appeared in two volumes for 8s. 6d. and a few weeks later in a cheaper edition for 4s. 3d. Scott's *Life of Napoleon* was printed in nine volumes in England at 94s. 6d. In America it was published at 20s. It was never assumed by American book merchants that the sale of any work would go on quietly from year to year or even from month to month as in England. Demand was stimulated by clever advertisement and rose with extraordinary suddenness. Every publisher worth his salt made a speedy turnover and then scrapped remainders ruthlessly. They had no interests to consider but their own.

Fearful of possible reprisals by English firms, booksellers had asked Congress for protection against the competitive dumping of books printed in England, specifying the Bible as a case in point. It was alleged that between seven and eight hundred thousand Bibles had been imported to the States, and a means to keep them out was sought and oddly enough found, not in a direct embargo, but in the adoption for all schools and places of worship of Noah Webster's edition of the James I. Bible. When this was promulgated as the orthodox American version of Holy Scripture all imported Bibles automatically became worthless. From this instance and from other records of the day we may deduce that publishing, as practised in America, could be as exciting and cut-throat an enterprise as any that flourished in that prosperous land. Dickens had little idea of what he was up against in attacking the book-selling trade. He saw himself as the champion of an un-popular crusade on behalf of justice to authors and did not realise that the dragon of big business was immune from missiles slung by a mere scribbler. How unbelievable would it have seemed to him that all the great Victorian novel-ists would be in their graves before justice came into her own.

Dickens's thoughts were now straying towards journalism. We find him writing to Lady Holland[1] to say that he hears that the *Courier*, formerly a Whig and more recently a Tory evening newspaper, is to be incorporated in the *Globe*. Had he been in England earlier in the year, he would have put himself in touch with the leaders of the Liberal party and made proposals to them for saving the paper, 'nailing the true colours to the mast and fighting the battle staunchly and to the death'. What does Lady Holland think about it? Would she be in favour of an evening paper of the kind? Could she perhaps sound Lords Melbourne and Lansdowne, Mr. Stanley and a few more? Of course he could do this himself but would rather trust her to find out how the land lies. With an obvious bid for editorship, he says that he feels confident that he could establish an organ that would do good service and command immediate attention. A few days later[2] he writes again to Lady Holland, who has evidently sounded Mr. Stanley and perhaps others, telling her that she may be right, but that the Liberal party had very seldom erred on the bold side, adding, 'The notion of this newspaper was bred in me by my old teaching'. He begs to send her a volume of Longfellow's poems and an eagle feather from Niagara. And there the scheme for editing a daily paper ended until revived a few months later in another form.

August and September were spent at Broadstairs completing *American Notes*. In Captain Marryat Dickens had a companion with whom he could discuss each chapter as he completed it. Marryat liked the book and was full of praise for the humorous way in which his friend had treated his subject. Few writers concurred in this opinion. Thackeray, who did not like *American Notes*, was asked to review the book for the *Edinburgh*, but he refused, saying, 'I cannot praise it and I will not cut it up. . . . It is like the worst part of *Humphrey's Clock*, what is meant to be easy and sprightly is vulgar and flippant . . . the book is at once frivolous and dull.' Authorship with its implicit surrender to the judgments of others is not by any means a wholly enjoyable profession. Dickens never read reviews of his own books, saying that if he did so it would gouge all the writing heart out of him, for, taking them all in all, reviewers were good natural sadists.

Just as he had finished the *Notes* he learned that he was being attacked in the United States for a letter allegedly written to the *Chronicle* in which he had criticised hospitality tendered to him while in America. Headlines 'Dickens is a Fool', 'Dickens is a Liar' flared across the columns of the New York papers. In an effort to counter this slander he wrote a weak defensive foreword to his new book to the effect that he had always been prejudiced in favour of America and that to represent him as viewing America with ill-nature 'was merely to do a very foolish thing'. To Jonathan Chapman, Mayor of Boston, he wrote more forcibly, explaining the true integrity of his attitude:

> Because I claim to have been kindly received in America by reason of something I had done to amuse its people and

prepossess them in my favour; and not with reference to
something I was not to do; therefore I write about its
people and write freely.   And as I have never been deterred by hopes of approbation or visions of greatness from
pointing out abuses at home, so no amount of popular
breath shall blow me from my purpose, if I see fit to point
out, what in my judgment are abuses abroad, and if my
being an honest man brings down caprice and weathercock fickleness and the falsest kind of insult on my head,
what matter it to me—or to you—or to any man who is
worth the name and being right can look down on the
crowds and whistle while they hiss.[1]

American Notes is a dull book and mainly concerned with
visits to public institutions which are contrasted with their
counterparts in England.   For these institutions he expressed
measured admiration.   The charity of the people themselves
seemed to him better than private charity: he had noted that
the 'charity children' wore neither badge nor livery and that,
contrasted with the regimented infants of England, 'their
individuality seemed unimpaired'.   Hospitals for the Insane,
Houses of Reformation, Prisons, Deaf and Dumb Asylums,
those terrors of the ordinary tourist, were dealt with sym-
pathetically, for they were of compelling interest to one who
himself had been an underdog.   Taking as his text advertisements from a Washington gazette concerning the sale of
slaves, he, to conclude with, delivered a broadside against
slavery.   One notes that Dickens's last transatlantic excursion was to the Academy of West Point; his last vision of
America that of the Catskills and the Tappan Zee; his last
thoughts, like his first, of Washington Irving.

He was careful to explain to Mr. Tagart, his new Unitarian
friend, that when he determined to tell the truth about
America, he determined also that he would not from that
time read any American paper, pamphlet or book or review
in which he had reason to suppose (from the very fact of its
being sent him) there might be the least allusion to himself.

[1] 483. I. N.L.

I do not mean to say that it requires a Roman fortitude to exercise this self-denial. But I have beaten by these means every free and independent citizen who has written to annoy me, and judging from the number of packets I return to the Post Office unopened, I should say their name is legion.[1]

On neither side of the Atlantic was *American Notes* much appreciated by the general reader. Much of it was written with deference, surnames were omitted, opinions were watered down, the copyright controversy ignored; nevertheless four large editions sold before the end of the year and put a much-needed thousand pounds in his pocket.

News reached Dickens as he was leaving Broadstairs that Longfellow was on the point of landing in England. He at once dispatched a note to Dover saying, 'Your bed is waiting, the door gapes hospitality', and presently had the pleasure of welcoming the American poet on his own threshold at Devonshire Terrace. In a letter to Charles Sumner Longfellow said, 'I write this from Dickens's study, the focus from which so many luminous things have radiated. The raven croaks from the garden and the ceaseless roar of London fills my ears.' The visitor spoke much of Dickens's vogue in Germany and of German poetry. He gave his host the works of Freiligrath, the translator of 'Lady Clara Vere de Vere' and other Tennysonian poems. He also spoke of Herder's translations of popular verse, Herder who regarded poetry as a kind of Proteus among peoples breaking out in ballads and songs. Dickens listened to his outpourings and then pushed *American Notes* into his hands. Longfellow read it straight away and said, 'It is good-natured and severe'. The chapter on slavery struck him as 'grand'.

Longfellow's days in London were soon filled with engagements. Sam Rogers journeyed from Broadstairs to book him to breakfast on a Tuesday and dine on a Wednesday, and Dickens pinned him for several meetings with writers who included Tennyson, Browning and Bulwer Lytton. One morning 'Boz' and 'Fuz' carried Longfellow off to Rochester, where, defying the prohibition of the janitor, they overleapt gates and barriers and explored the castle ruins. A far less agreeable excursion was arranged to inspect the worst slums of the Borough. Maclise, who made a fourth on this occasion, was so overcome by the odours and the dirt that he vomited and had to remain outside in the street while the others, stronger-stomached, examined the squalid houses.

After a fortnight of crowded experiences Longfellow started for Bristol to catch the steamship *Great Western*. 'Boz' and 'Fuz' escorted him to Landor's house in Bath, where he dined and spent an evening in brisk discussion. They then accompanied him to his port of embarkation. In a letter to Dickens reporting safe arrival he said that as he lay on his back he 'soothed his soul with songs'. 'In *The Slave's Dream* I have borrowed one or two wild animals from your menagerie.' These verses were printed in a thirty-page pamphlet soon after his return.

As soon as Longfellow had sailed, Dickens, Maclise, Forster and Stanfield set out on a Cornish tour. They hired a conveyance in Devonshire, and from Thackeray we have a pen-and-ink sketch of four top-hatted gentlemen in full-skirted overcoats tightly wedged into a landau. During the trip Tintagel, Land's End and St. Michael's Mount were visited as well as old churches, caverns by the sea-shore and tin mines. Maclise made many sketches, and out of one of them, the waterfall at St. Wighton's Keive, near Tintagel, developed an oil painting. It was shown at the Academy of 1843 and in the same exhibition was hung Maclise's portrait of Harrison Ainsworth. Dickens liked the original sketch of the waterfall, and when Georgina posed as model for the Academy picture he determined to acquire it. Before it was completed he wrote to Tom Beard:

I am very anxious for many reasons to possess a little picture which Maclise is at this moment painting: and I know he would either insist on giving it to me or would

HOME AGAIN 193

set some preposterous price upon it which he can by no
means afford to take.[1]

Beard was instructed to inform the artist that 'a Mr. S. of
such-and-such a place in Sussex' would like to purchase a
small picture, 'The Girl at the Waterfall', for a hundred or
a hundred and fifty guineas. This subterfuge was made
necessary by the open-handedness of Maclise who insisted on
giving his beloved Bozzes anything of his they admired and
had refused to take payment for the sketch of the four children
or for the portrait of Kate. Stanfield also sketched busily
during the tour. One of his drawings is that of the Logan
Stone with Forster perched on top of it and Dickens and
Maclise rocking it from below. This sketch and the picture
of Georgina at the waterfall are included in the Forster
Collection.[2] Dickens, always highly suggestible, caught
something of landscape technique from his friends and described the antics of autumn-scattering leaves, the piling-up
of clouds and the lighting-up of fields and coast-lines by
sunburst or lightning. These effects, which as we shall
presently see were made use of in *Martin Chuzzlewit*, caused
Taine to say that Dickens was a landscape painter. Much as
the author longed to set his new novel by the Cornish shore,
he could not contrive to do so and somehow found himself
accepting an inland village in Wiltshire as substitute. By
arranging to open his story in the autumn he could, however,
make use of his landscape jottings of the plough-patterning
of the ruddy earth, the browning hedgerows, the berries like
clusters of coral beads, the sun-glints and the vagaries of the
huffy wind.

Once again ensconced in Devonshire Terrace, Dickens
resisted distractions gay or grave with all his might and distractions were not always amusing, for celebrity brought
with it human claims. For instance, William Hone, a most
indigent writer, sent a message by Cruikshank to say he was

[1] 495. I. N.L.　　　[2] Victoria and Albert Museum.

H

dying and that having read no books but those of 'Boz'
since he had lain ill, he aspired to shake hands with their
author 'before he went'.   So to Tottenham Dickens felt
bound to go, just as a month later he felt bound to attend the
funeral of this fellow craftsman.   But claims or no claims, he
somehow had to find the seclusion necessary for work, for his
publishers, Chapman and Hall, were pressing him for the date
of delivery of the first instalment of his new novel.   Once he
had given an undertaking to hand it in in January 1843, and
regularly thereafter monthly, he had to refuse all invitations.
Even Miss Coutts had to be notified that her always-tempting
dinners must be declined.   A note from her found him

> in agonies of plotting and contriving a new book; in which
> stage of the tremendous process, I am accustomed to walk
> up and down the house, smiting my forehead dejectedly;
> and to be so horribly cross and surly that the boldest fly
> at my approach. . . . Seriously, unless I were to shut myself
> up obstinately and sullenly in my room for a great many
> days without writing a word, I don't think I should ever
> make a beginning . . . the lapse of every new day only gives
> me stronger reasons for being perseveringly uncomfortable,
> that out of my gloom and solitude something comical, or
> meant to be, may straightway grow up.[1]

And so Dickens shut himself up in his study to write, only
emerging for food and exercise.   Just occasionally something
came along that pricked his curiosity, such as Maclise's news
that a young artist called Frith had done some charming
sketches of the girls in *Barnaby Rudge*.   It appeared, too,
that he had made genre designs for illustrating *Gil Blas*,
Kenilworth and the *Vicar of Wakefield*.   Fired by Maclise's
account Dickens seized his pen and wrote:[2]

> My dear Sir,—I shall be very glad if you will do me the
> favour to paint me two little companion pictures; one
> a Dolly Varden (whom you have so exquisitely done

    [1] 487. I. N.L.   [2] 489. I. N.L.

already), the other a Kate Nickleby.—Faithfully yours always, CHARLES DICKENS.

P.S.—I take it for granted that the original picture of Dolly with the bracelet is sold.

Frith, who was very young at the time, was enchanted to receive the letter. He and his mother cried over it and they read it so often that it was a wonder that anything was left of it. He got to work at once making a picture of Dolly Varden tripping through the woods and looking back saucily at her lover. For Kate Nickleby he fixed on a scene at Madame Mantalini's, with Kate figuring as a seamstress, 'the point being at the moment when her thoughts wander from her work, as she sits sewing a ball-dress spread upon her knees'. Directly the pictures were finished Frith invited Dickens to come and inspect them. A day for this visit was fixed and the artist awaited in 'very trembling expectation' the arrival of the man he regarded as superhuman. A knock sounded on the studio door and there on the step Firth saw a pale young fellow with long hair surmounted by a tall white beaver. His right hand was extended in a frankly cordial way and in his left he clasped a formidable stick. The portrait sketches were on the easel and the artist waited 'in an agony of mind' for the verdict. Charles Dickens sat down and looked at them closely and then a few minutes later said, 'All I can say is that they are exactly what I want. I'm very much obliged to you for painting them.' Before leaving he asked Frith whether he would be at home on the following Sunday afternoon as he would like to bring his wife and his sister-in-law to see how well the work had been carried out. Sunday came and it found Frith at the open door of his studio when a smart curricle driven by Dickens dashed up. 'I was not accustomed to curricles,' he says naïvely in his diary, 'the bright steel bar in front gave the turn-out a very striking appearance.' A groom jumped to the head of the spanking bays when the two-wheeled carriage halted and the ladies floated into the studio and gushed over the pictures, which

were entirely to their taste.   That Charles and what he called
his 'brace of petticoats' made an attractive trio we can see
from Maclise's sketch done at this time, which shows three
profiles one behind the other giving the effect of a set of
triplets.   With all the air of a grand seigneur 'Boz' bestowed
on Frith the sum of forty pounds and thanking the artist took
his deparure in the same flourishing style in which he had
arrived.   Frith, aged twenty-three, wondered rather wist-
fully whether he, when he had reached the age of thirty, would
be as successful as his patron, but it was to be twelve years
before he caught the public eye with 'Ramsgate Sands' and
twenty before 'The Railway Station' had to be gated from the
pressure of enraptured crowds at the Royal Academy.   He
lived long enough to see his portraits of Kate Nickleby and
Dolly Varden sold at Christie's, after Dickens's death, for
thirteen hundred guineas.

Pricked out of concentrating on his book by Lord Londonderry's pamphlet, *A Letter to Lord Ashley* (attacking the Mines
and Collieries Bill), Dickens hurriedly reviewed it in an
anonymous letter addressed to the assistant editor of the
Morning Chronicle, Charles Mackay.[1]   Lord Londonderry
fiercely resented any interference with labour conditions as he
was opening up new collieries and constructing a harbour at
Seaham.   He was indignant that the 'disgusting pictorial
woodcuts' accompanying the Report of the Commissioners
should have found their way into the boudoirs of refined and
delicate ladies who were weak-minded enough to sympathise
with these 'victims of industry'.   Adopting a gawkily satirical
tone, Dickens rejoiced that the noble Marquis has chosen to
express his views in pamphlet form, partly because he writes
very badly and partly because he has laid himself open to
criticism.   He was particularly incensed by the noble Lord's
attitude to Dr. Southwood Smith, the most high-minded of
commissioners.   Measures like the Mines and Collieries Bill
cost a world of trouble to bring to birth, they must not be
strangled by the Herods of the peerage.[2]   That Lord London-

[1] 484. I. N.L.   [2] *Morning Chronicle*, October 20, 1842.

derry should take occasion to remind the public that not all men are born to read and write 'carried within it his condemnation'. Dickens did not add that when he himself had read the Report, he had broken down and sobbed.

Except for occasional interruptions Dickens now worked steadily. His new novel was named for the grandfather of the hero and its cumbrous title was:

> The Life and Adventures of Martin Chuzzlewit, His Relatives, Friends and Enemies. Comprising all his Wills and his Ways; with an Historical Record of What he Did and What he Didn't; showing, moreover Who inherited the Family Plate, Who came in for the Silver Spoons and Who for the Wooden Ladles. The Whole forming a Complete Key to the House of Chuzzlewit. Edited by 'Boz'. With Illustrations by 'Phiz'.

It was published in twenty monthly numbers with forty illustrations in all, and was dedicated to Miss Coutts 'with the true and earnest regard of the author'. There are many well-known characters in this book, among them Mr. Pecksniff, as great in his way as Tartuffe, and Mrs. Gamp, one of the most popular figures ever created by a novelist.

The figure of Mrs. Gamp first came to Dickens when he was lodging in 'a sequestered farm house' at Finchley where he 'buried himself' for a whole summer month to get away from interruptions. From the moment he introduced his readers to Mrs. Gamp's little room over the bird-fancier's shop in Holborn the monthly sales rose. When he had got a firm hold of his story, Dickens moved the family to Yorkshire for the rest of the summer months and in 'the leafy lanes' round Castle Howard Mrs. Gamp blossomed as a humorist. Dickens, who exulted in his creation, asked Forster what he thought of the woman and then wrote to Professor Felton asking the same thing and adding:

> Heaven! such green woods as I was rambling among, down in Yorkshire when I was getting that done last July. For days and days we never saw the sky but through green

boughs; and all day long I cantered over such soft moss and
turf that the Horses' feet scarcely made a sound upon it.
We have some friends in that part of the country who are
the jolliest of the jolly, keeping a big old country house
with an ale-cellar something larger than a reasonable
church.[1]

One would have thought after seeing the tepid reception
accorded to *American Notes* that Dickens would have left
America and its inhabitants alone.   But this was not the case:
he selected certain figures to typify some American characteristics just as he had selected certain figures to typify some
English characteristics.   Mrs. Jellyby, Mr. Pecksniff, Mr.
Bumble have their pendants in Mrs. Hominy, Elijah Pogram
and Jefferson Brick, though the American figures do not rival
the English figures in vitality and stature.   The author
allowed Martin and Mark great licence in conversation: they
said all the things he had felt and could not at the time express
about the bad manners, ignorance and conceit of the Americans he had knocked up against in hotels, river-boats and
trains.   Scoffing at the levee imposed on strangers, Dickens
said no single word in palliation of the attacks he made.   In
fact he made the ordinary Yankee appear a quite odious
creature.

It probably was not the character drawing that offended
transatlantic taste so much as the obvious seriousness of the
charge against America made by the stranger who talks with
Martin in the dining-room at Mrs. Pawkins's boarding house
in New York:

'I believe [says the stranger] that no satirist could breathe
this air.   If another Juvenal or Swift could rise up among
us to-morrow, he would be hunted down.   If you have
any knowledge of our literature and can give me the name
of any man, American born and bred, who has anatomised
our follies as a people and not as this or that party; and who
has escaped the foulest and most brutal slander, the most
inveterate hatred and intolerant pursuit, it will be a strange

name in my ears. In some cases I could name to you, where a native writer has ventured on the most harmless and good-natured illustrations of our vices or defects, it has been found necessary to announce that in a second edition the passage has been expunged, or altered, or explained away, or patched into praise.'

In a gratuitously offensive mood Dickens chooses to close a chapter with observations of his own on Tom Moore, whose reflections at Washington forty years earlier had been expressed in the lines:

> Rank without ripeness, quickened without sun,
> Crude at the surface, rotten at the core.

Sydney Smith read *Martin Chuzzlewit* with great amusement and wrote twice while the work was in progress: 'I believe you will excuse me for saying how very much pleased I am with the first number of your new work. Pecksniff and his daughters and Pinch are admirable—quite first rate painting such as no one but yourself can execute,' and again, 'Excellent! nothing can be better. You must settle it with the Americans as you can, I have only to certify to the humour and power of description.'[1]

How little Dickens understood America may be gauged by the great surprise he evinced when told that *Martin Chuzzlewit* had been destroyed on the stage in New York, having been cast (to the great delight of the audience) into the witches' cauldron in a burlesque of *Macbeth*. No English people of that day understood America; we have only to read the books of Mrs. Trollope, Miss Martineau and Captain Marryat to find this out. To them the manners and customs of the Americans seemed either very humorous, very provincial or very provoking. Carlyle summed up the feeling generated in America by *Martin Chuzzlewit* when he said it caused 'all Yankee-doodledum to fizz like one universal soda-water bottle'. Somewhat flustered by the commotion he was responsible for, Dickens wrote to Forster:

[1] January and July 1843.

Martin has made them all stark staring raving mad across the water. . . . Don't you think the time has come . . . to state that such public entertainments as I received in the States were either accepted before I went out, or in the first week after my arrival there: and that as soon as I began to have any acquaintance with the country, I set my face against any public recognition whatever but that which was forced upon me to the destruction of my peace and comfort—and made no secret of my real sentiments.[1]

It was too late for explanations. Dickens had to stand by what he had written and learn by experience how foolish it was to hold a nation up to ridicule.

It was Macready's turn now to go to the United States and before his departure a farewell dinner was given to him at the Star and Garter, Richmond. Marryat, Dickens, Stanfield, Forster, Barham, Maclise, Landseer and six others were present. Dickens, who had every intention of going to Liverpool and bringing Mrs. Macready home after her husband had sailed, proposed from the chair the only toast. He spoke so movingly that Macready broke down in tears. Forster had just told the actor that he had written a very strong letter to Dickens endeavouring to dissuade him from accompanying him to Liverpool, and Marryat that evening took occasion to warn Dickens that Macready would suffer from his attention—the *Nickleby* dedication was damaging enough. Dickens, acting upon his friends' advice, wrote to Macready:

I have lately had grave doubts of the propriety of my seeing you on board the steamer. It will be crowded with Americans at this time of the year and believe me they are not the people you suppose them to be. So strongly have I felt that my accompanying you on board would be, after the last *Chuzzlewit*, fatal to your success and certain to bring down on you every species of insult and outrage, that I have all along determined within myself to remain in the hotel and charge the landlord to keep my being there a secret.

[1] John Forster, *Life of Dickens*, vol. i. p. 308.

But this morning I have heard from Marryat to whom Stanfield had chanced to mention our Liverpool design, and he so emphatically and urgently implores me for your sake not even to go to Liverpool, that I instantly renounced the delight of being among the last to say 'God Bless you!' for when a man, who knows the country, confirms me in my fears, I am as morally certain of their foundation in truth and freedom from exaggeration as I am that I live.

If you but knew one-hundredth part of the malignity, the monstrous falsehood, the beastly attacks, even upon Catharine which were published all over America, even while I was there on my mere confession that the country had disappointed me, confessions wrung from me in private society before I had written a word upon the people, you would question all this as little as I do. Soon after you receive this I hope to come across to Clarence Terrace to shake you by the hand.

In a private talk with Macready Dickens begged him never to champion him when he hears him abused, never even to admit the friendship between them, never to contradict, never to take offence, and then added, 'I wish I could *un*-dedicate *Nickleby* until you come home again!'

Chapter 13

PIRATES AND PUBLISHERS

*Novelty, pleasant to most people, is peculiarly delightful
to me.*   CHARLES DICKENS

THE working background of Charles Dickens's life
throughout 1843 was *Martin Chuzzlewit*. Though he
toiled at this book from four to six hours a day there are
many indications in the correspondence of this date that his
mind was opening to new impressions, and that America had
in some ways broadened his sympathies and changed his
judgments. In his leisure time he took more interest than
heretofore in books, partly because in his efforts to entertain
Longfellow he had come in contact with poets and prose-
writers and partly because he was reading more. Though
Dickens never strictly speaking became what we call a literary
man, he managed to enjoy the work of some of his contemporaries, Browning and Tennyson for instance, but one does
not find him praising the novels of Bulwer Lytton or
Thackeray. As he walked along the shore at Broadstairs he
repeated cadences from *The Dream of Fair Women* and exclaimed to a friend, 'I have been reading Tennyson again and
again, what a great creature he is!' From reading this poem
there arose in his mind visions of the bottom of the sea, of
'queer creatures, half fish and half fungus, looking down into
all manner of coral caves and seaweed conservatories and
staring in with their great dull eyes at every open nook'. . . .
'Who but Tennyson could conjure up such a close to the
extraordinary series of pictures?'

> Squadrons and squares of men in brazen plates,
>   Scaffolds, still sheets of water, divers woes,
> Ranges of glimmering vaults with iron gates,
>   And hushed seraglios.

As Landor would say, it was 'most wonderful'. *The Dream,*

The Lady of Shalott and other poems had just been revived and republished by an author who had had all the writing heart taken out of him ten years earlier by Lockhart in a review in the *Quarterly* and was now for the first time being recognised as an important poet. When sending a set of his own books to Tennyson Dickens wrote:

> For the love I bear you, as a man whose writings enlist my whole heart and nature in admiration of their Truth and Beauty, set these books upon your shelves believing that you have no more earnest and sincere homage than mine.

Sufficiently curious about poetry to experiment with it himself, Dickens now wrote a prologue in verse for *The Patrician's Daughter*, 'a drama in modern dress', by J. Westland Marston due for a production at Drury Lane. He was sure that a spirited prologue would give the play a send-off. 'Get the curtain up with a dash,' he said to Macready, 'and begin the play with a sledge hammer blow.' Macready consented to speak the lines which went to show that the present was as worthy as the past to be the theme of tragedy:[1]

> Awake the Present! Shall no scene display
> The tragic passion of the passing day?
> Is it with man, as with some meaner things,
> That out of death his single purpose springs?
>
> . . . . . .
>
> Awake the Present! Though the steel-clad age
> Find life alone within its storied page,
> Iron is worn at heart by many still.
>
> . . . . . .
>
> Learn from the lessons, of the present day
> Not light its import and not poor its mien;
> Yourselves the actors, and your homes the scene.

Despite the prologue Marston's first play was a failure. He decided to read his second, *Strathmore*, aloud in a hall before venturing to get it staged. Dickens and Forster went to the rehearsal, and Forster told Marston straight out that he

[1] Prologue. *Sunday Times*, December 11, 1842.

was reading 'like a parrot, a confounded old parrot'. 'You *must* let us know,' he said testily, 'what character you are impersonating.' Marston tried again, turning his head from one side to the other when the characters changed, but he mouthed the words in the same dull monotone. When the small audience had drifted away Dickens said, 'Give me the book, I'll show you how you ought to do it!' He read the act through aloud and automatically impersonated each figure to the life. Thus did he, rather to his surprise, discover himself to be a born entertainer who, merely by reading aloud, could vivify characters of any age.

Another play that Dickens concerned himself with at this time was *The Blot in the 'Scutcheon*, which he read in manuscript. He told Forster that he found it 'Lovely, true, and deeply affecting', and charged him with a message to Browning to the effect that there was no man living and not many dead who could produce such a work. Its heroine of fourteen who, by allowing herself to be seduced by the very man proposing formally for her hand, incurs 'punishment inexorable', for having sinned against the honour of her house, made a strong appeal to him despite the artificiality of the plot. He was particularly touched by the youth of the heroine and by the repeated line, 'I had no mother', in which she excuses her foolish surrender. Nothing interested Dickens more at this time than successes honestly won by writers and painters. To novices worried by cruel reviews he said:

> When I first began to write I suffered intensely from reading reviews and I made a solemn compact with myself that I would only know them for the future from such general report as might reach me. For five years (1843) I have never broken this rule once, I am unquestionably the happier for it.

He was not always quick in recognising the work of friends. For example, when Bulwer Lytton's *Duchesse de la Vallière* had been hissed off the stage, the mortified author arranged that his next drama, *The Lady of Lyons*, should be produced

anonymously at Drury Lane.   Macready of course knew by
whom it was written, but Dickens, who was at the first night,
did not, and in an excited rush to congratulate his friend the
actor-manager on the great success of the performance he
met Bulwer Lytton in a passage and asked him what he
thought of the play.   'Without our friend,' replied Bulwer
Lytton gravely, 'it might have been a hideous failure.'   Believing him to be jealous Dickens retorted, 'You should be
the first to acknowledge a young writer's success!'

Mrs. Cowden Clarke, whom we have already met gushing
over Dickens's appearance at the Macready dinner four years
earlier, now was introduced to Dickens by Leigh Hunt at the
house of Mr. Tagart, the Unitarian minister.   They took to
each other at once and were soon talking and laughing as if
they were old friends.   They looked at illustrations in *Punch*
—Mr. Punch as Caius Movius seated among the ruins of
Carthage, Mr. Punch swimming in the sea near a bathing
machine.   The tears ran down Dickens's cheeks and Mrs.
Clarke had the, to her, deeply moving experience of seeing
'those large, dark-blue eyes, fringed with magnificent long
thick lashes, yes—those orbs now swam in limpid, liquid
suffusion'.   It was to Mrs. Clarke a memorable occasion as it
opened to her the doors of 1 Devonshire Terrace.

Owing to the constant companionship of Maclise, Stanfield
and Landseer, Dickens could not help hearing what contemporary painters were doing and almost in spite of himself he
was obliged to take a lively interest in art.   The Pavilion in
Buckingham Palace gardens was, at this time, being decorated,
by order of Prince Albert, with frescoes by Etty, Stanfield,
Maclise, Landseer, Leslie and Sir William Ross, the miniaturist.   One morning in September 1843 Macready summoned Rogers, Forster and Dickens to meet him at the
London Library for the purpose of seeing the frescoes.   They
all strolled across the Green Park to the Palace where they
found Mrs. Dickens waiting to accompany them to the
Pavilion.   Her dear Daniel Maclise had painted two of the

pictures, a design for Undine and a repetition of his 'Scene from Comus', and there was no painter who appealed to her so much both as an artist and as a friend.

On several occasions this year Dickens was persuaded to speak in public, notably at the Printers' Pension Society dinner at the London Tavern in March 1843. In toasting the Press, 'that wonderful Archimedes lever which *has* moved the world', he apostrophised it as 'the fountain of knowledge and the bulwark of freedom, the founder of free states and their preserver!' an eulogium that he would never have bestowed on the House of Commons.

At the Manchester Athenaeum a few months later he sat on a platform with Disraeli and Cobden and told his audience how glad he was that amid all the clank and roar of machinery the mind was not altogether forgotten. The Athenaeum with its cheerful rooms, instructive lectures and six thousand books gave opportunities for blameless enjoyment. He would not rake up the arguments against its existence or pay heed to 'the wicked axiom' that 'a little learning is a dangerous thing'. That was arrant nonsense, he would like to carry people who thought like this to certain jails and night refuges he knew of and convince them that ignorance was the prolific parent of crime and all misery. Refusing an invitation from Lord Brougham to go on to Cumberland for a visit, he says he cannot possibly spare the time, every minute of which he is devoting to the inspection of jails. How he longs to be a police magistrate so as to get a chance to show all classes the vital importance of education!

In his speech he confessed that his own heart died within him when he thought of all the immortal creatures condemned to tread a path, not of primroses, but of jagged flints and rough stones cemented together by this most wicked axiom. If only 'the dragon ignorance could be chased from every hearth, self-respect and hope would reign in every heart'. He is looking down on bright eyes and beaming faces, he will not forget the scene, and they, for their part, must remember that 'the more intelligent and reflective society becomes in the mass the more confidently will writers throw themselves on the feelings of the people'.

It was at Manchester that the idea came to Dickens of 'throwing himself on the feeling of the people' in a short story, *A Christmas Carol*. The first of his famous Christmas moralities, it is possibly the most read of all his works. The hero, Ebenezer Scrooge, is the type of the frozen-hearted in all lands. This miserly man, whose better nature had withered, is visited on three successive nights, by three spirits, the ghosts of Christmas past, present and future. Christmas past takes him back to his childhood, Christmas present to the home of his clerk Bob Cratchit, and Christmas future to a deserted grave-yard. The Christmas scene at the Cratchits', the good cheer, the affectionate family atmosphere and above all the courage of Tiny Tim, the cripple, appealed to young and old. When Scrooge's health is drunk in the fifteen-shillings-a-week household the very pitch of magnanimity is reached and Tiny Tim's voice piping 'God bless us every one' is felt by the old curmudgeon to be a call to which he must respond. Christmas future shows him a corpse lying under a sheet in an empty room and then a neglected grave headed by a stone bearing his own name. Must this really happen to me? Scrooge asks himself. Is it impossible to redeem the past? As his nature melts with compassion the spirit trembles and dissolves and Scrooge, with heart new-born, learns to become the good master, the good friend, the good man.

The story took him only a month to write and it was brought out by Chapman and Hall with four coloured illustrations by John Leech. It sold well and its author expected to make a good round sum, but to his annoyed surprise, instead of the anticipated thousand pounds, his publisher handed him £500. 'I never was so knocked over in all my life!' he said to a friend. Lord Jeffrey who was very much interested in his earnings wrote, 'I want amazingly to see you rich and independent of all irksome exertions'. In a way it was Dickens's own fault, for he had insisted that Chapman and Hall should publish *A Christmas Carol* on 'commission terms', under which an author was charged with the full cost of the book and received the entire proceeds of the sale, the publisher taking no more than a fixed percentage on the total amount realised by the sales. The result in this case proved so unsatisfactory to the author that it made him consider breaking with Chapman and Hall.

Another bad knock was the pirating of the story in a twopenny weekly, *Parley's Illuminated Library*, in which it appeared as 'A Christmas Ghost Story re-originated from the original by Charles Dickens, Esq., and analytically condensed expressly for this work'. Engaging Talfourd as his counsel, Dickens moved for an injunction against Lee and Haddock to stop publication. The injunction was granted by the Vice-Chancellor, Sir J. Knight Bruce, and in the application, drafted by Talfourd, the words appeared, 'You use my ideas as gipsies do stolen children; disfigure them and then make them pass for their own'. To Lady Holland Dickens wrote telling of the pirating of the *Carol* and how he had been plunged into six Chancery suits; it has put his work back and he dare not come and see her till things are straightened out.

> I took Serjeant Talfourd out of his own Court to lead my Chancery cases. Knight Bruce understood the matter so perfectly and appreciates the piracy so well, that he did not require to hear Talfourd at all, which I think was a prodigious disappointment to the Serjeant, who had made up his mind for a great speech.

The Vice-Chancellor said the case was one of 'peculiar flagrancy'. Lee and Haddock moved to dissolve the injunction and filed an affidavit to the effect that when they had abridged and re-originated *The Old Curiosity Shop* and *Barnaby Rudge* the plaintiff had not interfered. In the *Carol* they contended that they had made great improvements and important additions, for example Tiny Tim had been given a song of sixty lines to sing. Far from being a colourable imitation of the plaintiff's work, it had been 'unhinged and put together again' while 'incongruities had been tastefully remedied'. Knight Bruce decided the injunction should be proceeded with, but when Dickens claimed £1000 damages the defendants took refuge in bankruptcy, and the rueful author had to pay £700 for his own costs. Later on when urged to proceed against fresh infringements of copyright he refused, saying:

> My feeling is that it is better to suffer a great wrong than to have recourse to the much greater wrong of the Law. I shall not easily forget the expense, and anxiety, and horrible injustice of the 'Carol' case, wherein in asserting the plainest right on earth I was really treated as if I were the robber instead of the robbed.

Other disagreeable experiences connected with publishing occurred in 1843–4. One of them, the meagre sale of the serial *Martin Chuzzlewit*, also involved him in financial difficulties. Monthly publication enabled Chapman and Hall to gauge readers' reactions to the work in progress, and they found that the average sale of the first six numbers was less than half that of *Oliver Twist* and *Nicholas Nickleby*. It so happened that Dickens dropped into their office one afternoon in June when William Hall was indiscreet enough to refer to the disappointing sales of the story. And then, as if that were not enough, to add that he hoped it might not be necessary to put the penalty clause into effect and get Dickens to refund some of the money they had over-advanced. Dickens flung himself out of the office and going to Forster said, 'I am bent on paying Chapman and Hall down and when I have done that, Mr. Hall shall have a piece of my mind.' 'Publishers are bitter bad judges of an author,' observed Forster.

It will be remembered that by the agreement come to between Chapman and Hall and Dickens in September 1841 the publishers were paying him £150 a month until a new novel was produced. Then supposing the author's share in the profits on the new book (in this case *Martin Chuzzlewit*) should not amount to the total of the various sums of £150 paid him monthly during the year 1842, there should be a repayment to the publishers of the amount of the deficit. The repayment clause was to come into force, if necessary, after the publication of five numbers of *Martin Chuzzlewit* when £50 might be deducted from each subsequent monthly payment until their earlier investment was repaid.

Though the sales rose with the introduction of Mrs. Gamp, they did not rise sharply enough to prevent Messrs. Chapman and Hall putting into operation the clause empowering them to lower the monthly stipend. When the blow fell in July Dickens was enraged and poured scorn on the 'scaly-headed vultures', saying he could have nothing further to do with such monsters of shabbiness. 'I am rubbed in the tenderest part of my eye-lids with bay salt . . . and a wrong kind of fire is burning in my head, I don't think I can write.' He was in a fever to find another publisher. John Forster temporised and advised him to do nothing final about breaking with Chapman and Hall, at any rate until he had been away to Broadstairs and had thought the matter over in all its bearings. This counsel may not have been entirely disinterested for John Forster was literary adviser to Chapman and Hall and intended to remain so.

The more Dickens cogitated the more irritated he became. He already had debts to pay off and was incurring more all the time. Devonshire Terrace with its staff of servants, its entertainments, its carriage and horses, its rent, its rates, to say nothing of four children to educate and another baby on the way, and on top of all this the unceasing demands for cash from Alphington, where his parents were also running up debts, made life almost unbearable. Drastic economies must be planned and means of earning more money discovered. Though it might be unwise to break with Chapman and Hall before *Martin Chuzzlewit* was completed, Forster really must sound other firms; it was always possible that Bradbury and Evans the printers might care to act as publishers. Forster temporised once more and persuaded his friend to talk things over in detail with Tom Mitton and anyway to wait till

Christmas was past before making any change. It might then be sensible to let Devonshire Terrace and go abroad to economise.

Putting his personal troubles on one side, Dickens at Christmas 1843 organised a party at Clarence Terrace, the home of his friend Macready. Macready, as we know, was touring America and the object of the entertainment was to give Mrs. Macready and the children as jolly a Christmas as possible. By one of the guests, Mrs. Carlyle, it was called 'the most remarkable party that I ever was at in London'. Dickens, who had been practising legerdemain for weeks, gave a display of conjuring with Forster for accomplice. All in a minute a plum pudding was cooked over a fire in Stanfield's tall hat and, to the astonishment of children and grown-ups alike, handkerchiefs turned into comfits and bran into guinea-pigs. Helen Faucit, who was there (at the moment acting Juliet), tells of one of the games—'Proverbs'. A proverb was selected and the company by question-asking had to guess what it was. 'The devil is never so black as he's painted' was the saying chosen by Helen Faucit. Maclise challenged her for the second word which she had to insert into her reply. She could not think of an answer when Dickens crept behind her and whispered, 'What did you say last night to the Nurse when she was keeping you in that cruel suspense?' Helen Faucit jumped up and said angrily to Maclise, 'What devil art thou that thou dost torment me thus?' When she tried to thank Dickens afterwards for his prompting, he said, 'Oh, the words must have come into your head. How should *I* have thought of them?'

After a champagne supper crackers were pulled, toasts given and country dances romped through. Everyone, including Thackeray, Maclise and Jerdan, 'capered like maenads'. Dickens failed to induce Mrs. Carlyle to waltz with him, but Forster seized her by the waist and whirled her round the room. 'For the love of heaven let me go!' she cried. 'You are going to dash my brains against the folding doors.' Whereupon Forster bellowed, 'Your brains? Who

cares about brains here?' 'The thing', according to Mrs.
Carlyle, 'was rising into something not unlike the Rape of the
Sabines', when suddenly someone shouted, 'Twelve o'clock!'
and all the guests rushed to the cloak-room. 'It was just a
little knot of blackguardly literary people who felt themselves
above all rules and independent of the universe', she added by
way of commentary. One would like to know the verdict of
the Macready children on the fun provided for them by the
high-spirited grown-ups. There were more junketings of the
same guests at Devonshire Terrace on Twelfth Night when
Dickens appeared, all in black, as a magician, with Forster,
all in 'fiery-red', as another magician. Between them they
produced a séance calculated to send at least 'fifty people into
fits'.

In February Dickens fulfilled an engagement to speak at a
Mechanics' Institute soirée in Liverpool. When he arrived
at Radley's Hotel, he found T. J. Thompson waiting for him.
Together they dined, wined and sat over the fire talking, and
next morning went to inspect the lecture theatre in which the
speech was to be made. They ran into Captain Hewett of
the 'Britannia', who carried Charles off for a drink to 'the old
ship' which lay at the same berth as she had done when they
had embarked for America. Charles was sorry Kate was not
there too; it certainly seemed very strange to be on board
again. He was glad to think on what friendly terms they still
were with the captain; they had had him to stay in London,
and Kate had taken him to Drury Lane. Captain Hewett was
now invited to the soirée.

Dickens took the chair at 7 P.M. and, as he told his wife
afterwards, 'spoke up like a man and distinguished himself
considerably'. To his delight his clothes had been remarked
on; he had heard people saying, 'What is it? Is it a waistcoat? No it's a shirt!' and so on, and this he took to be very
gratifying and complimentary. The clapping of hands and
stamping of feet had struck him as 'thunderous and awful'.
Expressing high admiration for the civic spirit of Liverpool
in tackling ignorance and shedding light in dark places,

Dickens complimented the founders of the Institute on their
11,000 books and their roll of 3000 members, soon he believed to be swelled to 6000. It delighted him to know that
women and girls were to be given the same chances as men
and boys. Once again he struck the new classless note: 'I
look forward from this place as from a tower, to the time
when high and low, rich and poor, shall mutually assist,
improve and educate each other.' Adding that he would
give to all the means of taking out a patent of nobility, he
ended his speech by quoting lines from a poet 'who uses his
great gifts for the general welfare':

> Howe'er it be, it seems to me,
> 'Tis only noble to be good.
> Kind hearts are more than coronets,
> And simple faith than Norman blood.

A programme of music formed part of the evening's entertainment and in his role of chairman Dickens, reading from a
paper put into his hand, said:

> I am requested to introduce to you a young lady whom
> I have some difficulty and tenderness in announcing—Miss
> Weller—who will play a fantasia on the pianoforte.

The audience exploded with laughter and, as the performer
came shyly forward, Dickens looked towards her and saw the
'angel face of a girl standing out alone from the whole crowd'.
His heart bounded in his breast. What could he do to make
amends for the discomfiture he had caused her? Pulling himself together he tried to reassure her by whispering in her ear
that he hoped some day she would change her name and be
very, very happy. Next morning he walked off to ask her to
bring her father to luncheon and, thinking it would be nice to
write something in her album, made up verses as he went
along. Miss Weller, unlike most young ladies of his acquaintance, did not produce an album so he posted her the following lines to explain the joke of the evening before:

> I put in a book, once, by hook and by crook
> The whole race (as I thought) of a 'feller',

Who happily pleas'd the town's taste, much diseas'd
And the name of this person was Weller.
I find to my cost that one Weller I lost,
Cruel Destiny so to arrange it!
I love her dear name, which has won me some fame,
But, Great Heaven! how gladly I'd change it.

At luncheon with Thompson as fourth guest, Dickens realised
that they both had fallen for the girl's charm.   Surprised by
the warmth and suddenness of his own reaction—he had felt
nothing like it since Beadnell days—Dickens wrote, 'What a
madman I should seem if the incredible feeling I have conceived for that girl should be made plain to anyone.   Her
face will be always in my sight . . . her green fur-trimmed
dress must be preserved in lavender.'   He watched Thompson enviously, for though he was an older man and a
widower, he was 'irretrievably' in love.   As for himself 'the
angel's message in her face' smote him to the heart.   Would
that he could step into Thompson's shoes!   When Thompson told him how fathoms deep in love with Christiana he
was, Dickens wrote, 'my lips turned white' . . . 'the whole
current of my blood stopped', but mastering his strange
emotion he advised Thompson (who was uncertain whether
to propose to so young a girl) not to hesitate, after all he has
means and is irresistibly impelled towards her.   It is true that
he has only known her a few days, but then can he not say to
himself 'hours with her are like years of common women'?
He urges Thompson to win her, marry her, and 'join us in
Italy'.   'Do not crucify yourself lest in so doing you crucify
her.'   Thompson acts on his advice and Dickens congratu-
lates him on his 'Noble Prize'.

Two nights after the Liverpool meeting Dickens spoke at
a conversazione for the Birmingham Polytechnic Institution.
The Town Hall was crammed to the roof by some 2000
persons.   When he showed himself the whole company rose,
'rustling like the leaves of a wood'.   The ladies had hung the
walls with artificial flowers and on the front of the great
gallery facing him was WELCOME BOZ in letters six feet high,

while behind his head 'immense transparencies' were suspended, 'representing several fames in the act of crowning several Dicks'.

In his speech he welcomed the Polytechnic idea as being neither sectarian nor class and as something in which honest men of all degrees and every creed may associate. It was an idea that might even prevent men working at machines from degenerating into machines. The note he sounded was as before, 'all for each and each for all'. In answer to a vote of thanks in which gratitude and admiration for his books was included, he said:

> So long as I can make you laugh and cry I will. . . . To you, ladies of the Institution, I am deeply and especially indebted. I sometimes think (and he pointed to the balcony) there is some small quantity of magic in that very short name and that it must consist in its containing as many letters as the three Graces.

His financial disappointment over *A Christmas Carol* and *Martin Chuzzlewit* combined with Forster's unwillingness to negotiate with Bradbury and Evans or any other new publisher, caused him to give Tom Mitton a free hand to deal with his business affairs, begging his friend especially to familiarise himself with all agreements, contracts and other documents. A tentative approach to Bradbury and Evans revealed that, though a little alarmed, they were not averse to taking over the publication of future works provided Mr. Dickens was able to come to an arrangement with Chapman and Hall that did not involve them in trouble. To understand this we must bear in mind that Bradbury and Evans was a printing firm, printers indeed to Chapman and Hall and in no sense their rivals as publishers. Tom Mitton handled the situation with competence and matters were settled up before Dickens went abroad. Chapman and Hall's balance was paid off and the whole question of the stock-on-hand of the books gone into. In losing Dickens Chapman and Hall lost their best author and the founder of the fortunes of their house, but as he walked out, Thackeray walked in with his *Irish Sketchbook*.

Thackeray, who was just off to the Middle East, promised further sketches which were to appear as *Cornhill to Grand Cairo*. Carlyle soon became one of their authors and was quickly followed by the Brownings and Arthur Clough. John Forster, though he could not control Dickens, certainly managed to serve the firm that employed him well.

When the transfer from one publisher to another was completed Dickens wrote to Bradbury and Evans to explain what he wanted in the way of an advance to enable him to live in Italy:

> I will begin with the statement of the amount in which I must desire to become indebted to you. The balance payable to Chapman and Hall will be £1500. The sum I shall require for my anticipated expenses will be £1500. I owe you already £500 and against this entire sum of £3500 I propose to place to your credit, when the account for the subscription for the completed *Martin Chuzzlewit* is rendered, £500. . . . But in addition to this sum of £3000 which will then be left, I may require for anything I know, in the spring of next year, £500 more. . . .

Now for the repayment of advances we must look of course to the following heads:

(1) First the new Carol and the new next Christmas issue of the old one.

(2) The Magazine or Journal and the mutual relations we may agree upon respecting it, I would suggest that it should be commenced within six months.

(3) The best working of the copyrights in existence.[1]

Oliver Twist he states is his own unconditionally and it has not so far been published in a single volume. *A Christmas Carol* is also his own unconditionally. In *Pickwick* his interest is one-third of the copyright. He can only sell his share to Chapman and Hall and they can only sell their share to him. He has no power to appoint other publishers for this work. *Nicholas Nickleby* will become entirely his in November 1844, that is in seven months' time. He then will have the right to buy the stock at cost price. As for *Master Humphrey's Clock*, i.e. *The Old Curiosity Shop* and *Barnaby Rudge*, he owns half the copyright. In *American Notes* he owns three-quarters of the copyright and in *Martin Chuzzlewit* three-quarters of the copyright. The *Sketches* bought from Macrone by Chapman and Hall for £2250 must remain the property of Chapman and Hall till March 1845, and then if the book has paid for itself, half the copyright must be surrendered to him.

To make a long story short, Bradbury and Evans advanced him a lump sum of £2800 in return for a fourth share of any book he should write during the next eight years.

Business affairs, especially negotiations with publishers, always irked Dickens terribly and by the time matters were fixed up with Bradbury and Evans he had fretted and fumed himself into a state of intense irritation which nothing but an escape abroad could now allay. When the final agreement was signed and he was put in possession of a lump sum of money, he heaved a sigh of relief; at last he was free to let his house and make the economies called for by his debts.

Having begun to learn Italian and having played with the idea of going to Italy, he was thrilled at meeting Mazzini with the Carlyles. Dickens at once became disposed to be the friend of the political refugee from Italy. On being told that Mazzini's correspondence was subject to censorship by order of the Home Secretary, Sir James Graham, he by way of protest took (June 1844) to writing on the back of his envelopes, 'It is particularly requested that if Sir James Graham should open this, he will not trouble himself to seal it'. From 1837 on, Mazzini had been teaching boy compatriots in London and since 1839 had been correspondent of revolutionary committees in Malta and Paris. He was subjected to the usual police supervision. Both Carlyle and Dickens, however, protested against 'this turpitude', the first in a letter to the *Times*, and the second in a letter to the Home Secretary. Espionage they hated, it was unenglish, and the idea that the

information obtained by the censor might be passed on to
the Neapolitan Government was abhorrent to them both.
Carlyle championed Mazzini as 'a man of genius and virtue',
'a rare man worthy to be called a martyr soul'. The matter
was hotly debated in Parliament and Sir James Graham's
authority called in question. In the opinion of Lord Denman
and other peers, the subject was a very grave one. They
were emphatic that England should not be made the police
office of any foreign state whatever.[1]

For the Italian Relief Committee Dickens offered to draw
up an appeal, the forerunner of the countless appeals for
exiles with which two wars have familiarised us. 'The
English people, distinguished for generosity and love of
justice among all the nations of the earth', are urged to welcome to England, the land of the free, the fighters for freedom,
'noble spirits who because of their protest against bigotry and
despotism are refugees in an alien land'. Some people
affected to take no interest in the refugee question. 'And
what is Mazzini?' asked Lady Holland (July 1844). 'A
revolutionary man and the head of young Italy,' was Carlyle's
reply.

Dickens was this year invited to the Royal Academy dinner.
Mr. Brookfield, always a little sniffy about him, wrote to his
wife:

> Dickens spoke shortly, and well enough, but it had a
> very cut and dried air and was rather pompous and shapely
> in its construction and delivered in a rather sonorous deep
> voice. Not a jot of humour in it. He looks like Milnes,
> same height and shape, still longer hair, but not his de-
> moniacal good humour of expression.[2]

Just at this time R. H. Horne, author of *Orion*, published
A New Spirit of the Age. Twenty years had gone by since
Hazlitt's *Spirit of the Age* had appeared and a new set of men,
he asserted, animated by a new spirit, were impressing themselves on the public mind. Horne led off with seventy-six

[1] *Parliamentary Debates*, 2nd series, Hansard, lxxv.
[2] *Mrs. Brookfield and her Circle*, May 13, 1844.

pages on the most representative of the new men, Charles Dickens, and accompanied his essay by so grim a study by Margaret Gillies from the Maclise portrait as to cause the victim to exclaim, 'Why I look like the man in the iron mask!' With some particularity Horne compared Dickens with Hogarth and noted that 'le célèbre Cruikshank' often would illustrate a book without due reference to the original, thereby turning credible human beings into caricatures, which was deplorable as 'the delineation of characters' was so very much the most prominent and valuable portion of Mr. Dickens's works. His tremendous reputation had been achieved in eight years. Life was being lived at high pressure; Mr. Dickens was manifestly the product of his age, a genuine emanation of its aggregate and entire spirit. He was not an imitator of anyone but an author of unexhausted originality.

Chapter 14

ITALY

A man who has not been in Italy is always conscious of an inferiority. SAMUEL JOHNSON

PLANS for going abroad were now laid to take effect from the concluding number of *Martin Chuzzlewit* due to appear in July. When consulting Lady Blessington on the merits of foreign localities, Dickens wrote that, having made up his mind 'to decamp, bag and baggage, for a twelvemonth', he purposes establishing his family in some convenient place from which he can 'make personal ravages on the neighbouring country'.

Both Lady Blessington and Count d'Orsay had advised him to go to Italy where living was cheap and the climate good. They thought 'he should set up his nest at Pisa'. Later advice from Landor recommended Genoa as preferable to Pisa and suggested that an effort should be made to secure Lord Byron's villa, Casa Saluzzi, at Albaro, the seaside suburb of the city. Inquiry revealed that this house was in a ruinous state and that the ground floor had been converted into a 'third-rate wine-shop'. Il Paradiso, the Blessingtons' house, was not available, so Angus Fletcher, who was buying marbles at Carrara, was instructed to select another house which, if possible, should be at Albaro. Mr. Kindheart had little capacity either as a sculptor or as an agent and none at driving a bargain, but he found the Villa Bagnerollo and was empowered to rent it for three months, during which period Dickens counted on him and his marbles being accommodated on the garden floor so as 'to make company' for the family. It was only after arrival that Dickens found he could have had the Doria Palace, set in beautiful woods to the west of the city with grounds running down to the sea, complete with pictures and furniture, all for £40 a year. The banker to

whom he was accredited had advised Fletcher to take it, but
Fletcher had been told to rent a house at Albaro, and rent a
house at Albaro he did for four times its proper value, with
the result that it soon became to Dickens 'the detestable
Bagnerollo'. It was an annoying mistake, but Mr. Kindheart
was certainly not a business man.

Before plans were completed Devonshire Terrace was let
to 'a desirable widow', who insisted on moving in at once.
Owing to her importunity the family had to transfer to furnished rooms. Writing to Lady Holland from 9 Osnaburgh
Terrace,[1] Dickens tells her that as he is in the throes of
Chuzzlewit, he has to avoid all dining-out and walk for hours
among streets and fields. The book should be finished 'by
the end of this week' and he will call on her on Saturday,
12.30 P.M., to say good-bye. It was at 9 Osnaburgh Terrace
that Mr. and Mrs. Charles Dickens gave their farewell dinner.

This dinner was a great worry to Dickens and he consulted
Forster as to whether he should drop it, transfer it to the
Clarendon, or take Kate's advice and give it at the Star and
Garter at Richmond? Could it be done, he wondered, for a
couple of guineas apiece at the Clarendon? 'In a matter of
importance I could make up my mind. But in a matter of
this kind I bother and bewilder myself and come to no conclusion whatever. Advise, Advise!' Forster told Charles
to throw over the party, but Kate cleverly managed to arrange
that it should take place in the hired house, which pleased
Charles much better. The list of guests included Lord
Normanby, Lord Denman, Sir John Easthope with his wife
and daughter, Sydney Smith, the Macreadys, Babbage, Lady
Osborne and daughter, Dr. Southwood Smith, Dr. Quin,
Thomas Chapman and his wife, and of course Forster. A
rather significant list in so far as it shows that Dickens had no
intention of quarrelling with those who might be thought to
have treated him shabbily, Easthope and Chapman, and how
real was his friendship with his fellow philanthropist and
novelist, Lord Normanby. A few days later Lord Normanby

[1] June 10 1844.

tawdry and as part of an utterly dead past. Mass in the cathedral at Avignon was attended by a few aged crones and a baby in arms while a dog ran up and down the aisle. There was nothing to claim his interest in these junk-like buildings and their ghosts except the ex-votos, which at least must have been offered up by living, overflowing hearts. How different were the packed Protestant churches of the New World with their attentive, intelligent congregations and their well-lit, well-polished interiors!

From Lyons the party travelled by steamer down the Rhone, past Valence where Napoleon studied, past Avignon with its papal palace, prison of Rienzi whose story Bulwer had romanced over and Miss Mitford had dramatised. During a visit to the offices of the Inquisition, Dickens noticed a wall frescoed, as if in irony, with the story of the Good Samaritan. This horrified him into buying a guide-book from the custodian wherewith to make himself acquainted with other aspects of history in Avignon.

A night at Aix-en-Provence proved 'hot, clean and comfortable', and thence the *berline* rolled on through clouds of dust to Marseilles. There it was hoisted aboard a steamer, the 'Marie Antoinette', and the family, freed from its confinement, loitered on deck and watched the coast slide by. Nice, San Remo, Genoa, the sea journey was all too short.

On the quay at Genoa horses were once again harnessed to the vehicle which they dragged to a house among the vineyards at Albaro. There in the courtyard of the Villa Bella Vista the young family unpacked itself, a little disconsolate, for the approaches to the House of the Beautiful View were mournful, the lanes leading to it neglected, and the rusty entrance gates as they swung back into a shabby little garden rank with weeds had creaked ominously in their ears. Was it really possible to settle in such a place, the grown-ups wondered silently. To Dickens's private eye the building looked like a deserted jail, a pink jail. Pink jail! ha ha! that was not too bad a name for it.

Inspection revealed 'a square hall like a cellar' and 'a

cracked marble staircase' leading to the *sala*—an enormous
room with a vaulted roof.   On the walls were pictures, on the
floor a vast immovable sofa and some stiff chairs upholstered
like the sofa in crimson brocade.   It certainly was not a home
from home, and one member of the party, at least, thought
with longing of spick and span Devonshire Terrace with its
cosy armchairs, pile carpets, neatly draped windows and
admirable lavatories.   What could the Bella Vista beds be
like? Kate asked herself.   How dismaying it was to come so
far and to have so much to contend with!   There could be
no point in disparaging the place before the children and the
servants, they must all see the *bella vista* at once.   United by
a common impulse the whole party began to lean from the
eleven windows of the *piano nobile*.   Fortunately the view
was eminently praisable.   One could see from the grassed-
over terrace, on to which the windows gave, the sea, other
villas, other gardens, and mountains in the background.
Near at hand three cows were quietly munching vine-leaves
and Kate heard a voice, it may have been Mr. Kindheart's,
saying that they were yielding plenty of milk.   For the rest,
—lizards, rats, scorpions, fleas and flies were in occupation of
the many empty rooms.   By day they were advised the
shutters must be shut against the sun and by night the windows against the mosquitoes, by night too they might be
troubled by the singing of frogs.   'Timber', being nearest to
the floor, fell an immediate victim to the fleas, had to be
shaved and was so ashamed of the appearance he then presented that he nearly died of grief, or so his master said.   Bella
Vista decidedly was not a house after Mrs. Dickens's heart, it
would be out of the question to spend the winter there: all one
could hope was that the children would take no permanent
harm from camping in this alien environment.

I think that even young Mr. Dickens's spirit may have
quailed at the prospect before him—but he reminded himself
that he was the breadwinner, that he had come there on purpose to write and must shut himself away from domestic
worries.   It was for Kate to wrestle with callers and trades-

I

men and vermin, he must go on with his Italian and rescue
his books from the Customs.   It would never do for the plays
of Voltaire or Ruskin's *Seven Lamps of Architecture* to be
confiscated.   Having worked diligently at Italian in London
with one Mariotti, he immediately engaged 'a little patient
revolutionary officer, exiled in England during many years'
to come three times a week to read and speak Italian with him.
He began on *I Promessi Sposi*.   'How charming and what a
clever book!' he observed in a letter to Samuel Rogers.   In
between his studies he bounced off to see the sights of the
city, among them the newly painted, regilded Church of the
Annunziata, and standing there before the altar, looking up at
the three domes, he was turned 'giddy by the flash and glory
of the place'.   It seemed to him that 'every sort of splendour
were the perpetual enactment in these Italian churches.
Gorgeous processions pour from them.   There is illumina-
tion of windows on festal nights.'   For a moment he thought
the Church more alive than it was in France, but this impression was evanescent.   What fun it was to watch the
marriage brokers, queer old women and queer old men,
operating in out-of-the-way corners of streets.   How strange
to see sedan chairs 'gilded and otherwise' plying for hire; but
then as he was soon to realise they were not part of a dead past,
they were a necessity of daily life, for the entrances to many
palaces were in *salite* which no wheeled vehicle could reach
and ladies were forced to use these means of conveyance.
All about him in Genoa Dickens saw walls mouldering,
frescoes peeling, a city crumbling to decay.   Its 'squalid
mazes' were packed with 'filthy people' and every fourth or
fifth man he passed was 'a repulsive-featured religious'.   To
balance these uglinesses there were everywhere delicious green
figs, green lemons, green almonds, and with these ingredients
added to 'rare Hollands' he found that very good punch
could be contrived.   He managed with the help of the French
consul to dive into local society and so was introduced to
Byron's friend, the Marquis di Negri, the owner of a fine
house and a heavily grottoed garden, who entertained freely.

Agreeing with Kate and the rest of his suite that the Bella
Vista could only be regarded as a summer perch he diligently
sought other accommodation, and found it within the walls
of Genoa itself. Thus after enduring the pink jail for three
months, the family transferred to the Palace of the Fishponds,
the Palazzo Peschiere, than which no lovelier residence could
be found in all Italy. Dickens described it to Forster as
'something larger than Whitehall multiplied by four'. The
Dickens family took possession of the *piano nobile* and a
Spanish duke lived below them. All Genoa could be seen
from the terraces and the sweet scents from the garden induced in 'Boz' a dream of happiness. One of the great new
pleasures he shared with Kate was a box at the opera which
cost them almost nothing. The opera-house was so close
to the Peschiere that they could go and sit there 'with no more
trouble than in their own drawing room'.

After moving into Genoa they got to know some of the
foreign residents and with their introduction to the De la
Rues was initiated a period of great mental agitation for Kate.
Charles's interest in hypnotism was undiminished and such
experiments as he had made on his wife and others had given
him great confidence in his powers. Mr. De la Rue was a
Swiss banker carrying on business in Genoa, who, with his
English wife (an 'affectionate, excellent little' woman, according to Dickens), lived elegantly in a charming apartment at
the top of the Palazzo Rosso. It soon became plain to Kate
that Mrs. De la Rue had taken a marked liking to her Charles
and was bestowing on him her confidences. From the first
moment of meeting, Dickens was conscious that some magnetic attraction was drawing them towards each other and
creating between them a state of deep sympathy. Soon Mrs.
De la Rue was telling him that, in spite of all appearances to
the contrary, she, being the victim of delusions, was a very
unhappy woman. She was haunted, it seems, by a phantom
that spoke to her and a crowd of gory entities which pursued
her with veiled faces. Charles was moved by her distress
and convinced that he could banish the delusions by means of

hypnotism. Mr. De la Rue, he was assured, was anxious that he should make the experiment. And so it came about that Kate had to watch a peculiarly intimate relationship establishing itself between her husband and this stranger, a relationship necessitating one, if not two, meetings a day. Kate cogitated over the situation, was it or was it not love at first sight? or was it what it was alleged to be, the merely magnetic attraction that was a prerequisite of treatment of this nature? Charles was always at Mrs. De la Rue's beck and call and kept urging her to have no reticences with him, insisting that it was dangerous and might invalidate the cure if she kept any secret from him. For the hundredth time Kate wished herself back in Devonshire Terrace, where life was plain-sailing and held no disagreeable surprises. Of course she had been told by Charles that 'poor little Mrs. De la Rue' had been haunted by spectral forms whose faces she could never see, and that he was sure that in the end he could help her to control and finally to dispel these phantasms. Listening to such tales with what sympathy she could muster, Kate lived on tenterhooks, and things were not made easier by the fact that somehow Dickens found himself inhibited from writing. When he did settle down to compose a short story, it was full of spirits and goblins.

It was a disappointment to Dickens to find Genoa so im-possible a place to write in, what could be the matter with him? was it merely that he felt strange or was it the clanging of the innumerable bells that was driving him mad? The day was to dawn, however, when he suddenly felt inspired by the bells and knew he could make them work for him. Down on paper went the heading of a short story *The Chimes*. His attitude of mind had changed, he welcomed the clangour, 'Let them clash upon me now from all the churches and con-vents. I see nothing but the old London belfry I have set them in.' And thus amid the faded grandeurs of an Italian palace he focussed his imagination on a London ticket-porter and his sufferings. 'In my mind's eye, Horatio,' he wrote to Forster, 'I like more and more my action of making in this little book a great blow for the poor.' Continuing in the same strain he said, 'I am in regular ferocious excitement with *The Chimes*! get up at 7: have a cold bath before breakfast and blaze away wrathful and red hot until 3 P.M. or so when I usually knock-off for the day.' When working under emotional strain his hair went lank, his head hot, his face pale, his eyes hollow and brimming with tears. 'I have had a good cry,' he wrote, 'I am worn to death. I was obliged to lock myself in when I finished it yesterday for my face was swollen for the time to twice its proper size and was hugely ridiculous.'

Begun on October 10, *The Chimes: A Goblin Story* was finished on November 3, and so much does Dickens think of it as an achievement that he feels compelled to try and realise vividly the effect on others of what he has accomplished. He must go to the Cuttris Hotel in the Piazza, Covent Garden, for a few nights and Forster must assemble his friends at his house in Lincoln's Inn Fields so that he may try the story out on them by reading it aloud. 'I believe', he wrote to Mitton, 'I have written a tremendous book and knocked the *Carol* out of the field.'

Leaving Kate, Georgy and the children at the Peschiere, Dickens set out by slow stages for London. He crammed a lot of sightseeing into his journey, which took him through Stradella where he lay at 'a galleried inn'; then to Piacenza 'a brown, decayed, old town . . . deserted, solitary, grass grown, with ruined ramparts': from thence he posted to Parma noting its bustling streets and, in the Farnese palace, its desolate crumbling theatre. It depressed him to see the boxes sagging, the festoons dangling and blue sky showing through gashes in the roof. In Parma, too, the neglect of the cathedral upset him, the whole building seemed to mourn the rotting of the Correggio frescoes in the cupola. The melancholy induced by painted figures fading away on walls was, he felt, akin to the melancholy induced by the fading of human forms from our lives. Dickens tired his couriers out. Up by candlelight and sightseeing at lightning speed till dark, he barely left himself time to jot down any impressions. At

Modena, a town of 'sombre colonnades and brilliant skies', he pushed through leathern doors into 'a crooning High Mass'. How strange it was to him to find again as he had found in France and in every stagnant Latin town 'the same heart beating with the same monotonous pulsation, the centre of the same torpid, listless system'. At Bologna he came on the tracks of 'Milor Beeron', dead these twenty years past. 'Milor Beeron had approved of the matting' in his room; 'Milor Beeron never touched milk'. The ancient town arcades, the rich churches with their drowsy masses and tinkling bells, and the Great Meridian on the pavement at San Petronio awakened in Dickens a sadness as of withered romance. Life had ebbed from Italy. Ferrara struck him as more solitary, more depopulated, more deserted, than any city of the solemn series. Grim Ferrara, with the grass growing in its silent streets—Ariosto's house and Tasso's prison did not redeem for him a place which, from its appearance, might have been ravaged by pestilence.

Venice transported him. Venice the magnificent, stupendous reality, utterly beyond the scope of pen or pencil, the wonder, the sensation of the world, now part of him for ever. He is frantic in his admiration for Tintoretto's 'Assembly of the Blest' or Paradise: as for Titian's 'Assumption' it is for him the 'culmination of beauty'. Always one notices his bankruptcy in analogy—in order to heighten his praise of a gallery of pictures he will say 'Hampton Court is a fool to 'em'. From Venice he made for Verona and Mantua, then Milan, where his wife and sister-in-law met him, bringing with them his correspondence; they all three spent a couple of days seeing sights together, then Kate and Georgy returned to Genoa and the author went on to sledge over the Simplon and so by way of Fribourg, Strasbourg and Paris to London.

Forster was surprised his friend should think the journey worth while, though he knew better than anyone that Dickens was compelled by inner tension to come and get, if he could, a vivid sense of the effect his work had on his friends—he calls it 'that unspeakable restless something' which made him feel like a full balloon—obliged to go up. Forster also knew that he was expected to provide the audience, to give a dinner for Dickens and then inquire of him casually would he perhaps care to read his new Christmas story aloud to the other guests. Impulse has no prevision and to those who do not share it always seems to be mad, but to exclude it may be to stifle vitality and development. In Forster's well-regulated life there was no room for anything so anarchical as impulse, but he was a good enough friend to Dickens to fall in with demands made upon him. After talking things over in London the idea of dinner gave way before a plan for issuing a summons for a 'special purpose on Monday, December 2 at half-past six'. Dickens made a list of those to be invited: Carlyle of course was indispensable, so was his wife, for *her* judgment would be invaluable. Maclise must come and perhaps his sister. 'Stanny' and Jerrold he would particularly wish for, and Edwin Landseer, Blanchard, Harness, Fonblanque and Fox must also be thought of.

In the end no women came, but a company of ten more or less distinguished men settled themselves down to listen for two hours to the Goblin Story. The audition took place in Forster's rooms at 58 Lincoln's Inn Fields under the 'Verriolike ceiling' described in *Bleak House* as ornamenting Tulkinghorn's chambers. Maclise sketched the scene drawing rays of light over the reader's head, and Forster described the sketch when alluding to the incident, but added no personal impression:

> The reader may be assured (with allowance for a touch of caricature to which I may claim to be considered myself as the chief and very marked victim) that in the grave attention of Carlyle, the eager interest of Stanfield and Maclise, the keen look of poor Laman Blanchard, Fox's rapt solemnity, Jerrold's skyward gaze, and the tears of Harness and Dyce the characteristic points of the scene are sufficiently rendered. All other recollection of it is lapsed and gone; but that at least its principal actor was made glad and grateful sufficient further testimony survives.

Barham of *The Ingoldsby Legends* is not shown in the sketch though he must have been present, for he gave such an enthusiastic account of the first reading to his friends that a repetition had to be arranged for.

In this informal reading we may sense the germ of all the public readings of later years. Dickens always, like a true actor, had the desire to see himself mirrored in the eyes of his audience. So invigorated did he feel by appreciation of his performance that he arranged with Forster to act a play as soon as he returned home from abroad.

The Chimes, a little volume, was brought out by Chapman and Hall as the Christmas Book of 1844. Lady Blessington wept over the story and found herself obliged to defend the author from 'the charge of wishing to degrade the aristocracy'. Brookfield told his wife[1] that '*The Chimes* was as utter trash as was ever trodden under foot'. Twenty thousand copies of the book were sold at once, giving Dickens a profit of £1500 which for the time being satisfied him.

Forster wrote to Dickens, after he left, to express his grief that he had had so tempestuous a journey for such brief enjoyment, to which he replied that the visit had been one of happiness and delight to him.

> I would not [he wrote] recall an inch of the way to you or from you, if it had been twenty times as long and twenty thousand times as wintry. It was worth any travel—anything! With the soil of the road in the very grain of my cheeks, I swear I wouldn't have missed that week, that first night of our meeting, that one evening of the reading in your rooms, aye, and the second reading too, for any easily stated or conceived consideration.[2]

Macready, who had just returned from America, could only attend the first reading in Lincoln's Inn Fields as he had to rush over to Paris for a brief Shakespeare season. Dickens promised to fall on him 'with a swoop of love in Paris'. And so he did, on his way back to Genoa. Macready was playing

[1] March 12, 1845.　　[2] *Life of Dickens*, vol. i. p. 372.

Hamlet, Macbeth, King Lear, Othello, Virginius by Sheridan Knowles, and the greatest of all his parts—*Werner*. The performance of the twelve-day season took place at the Salle Ventadour, a building usually devoted to Italian Opera. In Paris Dickens plunged headlong into theatrical and literary society, hobnobbing daily with Macready's acquaintances, Théophile Gautier, Louis Blanc, Victor Hugo and Alexandre Dumas. Dumas gave them a box for his play, *Christine*, and they saw a great deal of Régnier of the Théâtre Français and of Louis Bertin, editor of the *Journal des Débats*, and son of its founder. Dickens also made friends with Paul Delaroche, 'court painter to the decapitated sovereigns Lady Jane Grey, Mary Queen of Scots and Charles I in his coffin with Cromwell raising the lid'; with Delacroix too, painter of dramatic battle-scenes and shipwrecks, he fraternised, while from the lips of Michelet and Quinet he heard all the gossip about Guizot. Macready made him known to Comte de Vigny, author of *Cinq Mars*, and to Mr. Bowes, whose memory in England is perpetuated in the Bowes Museum, Barnard Castle. It was a most stimulating experience and crowded with new contacts. He found it hard to tear himself away, but when he did go he went with the determination to return to Paris as soon as an opportunity offered. To get back to his family in time for Christmas he had to set out in snow by *malle-poste* for Marseilles. A thaw supervened and the horses literally 'waded' to the coast. Detained at Marseilles by stress of weather he, after delays impatiently endured, took the steam-packet *Charlemagne*, and ran through heavy seas to Genoa where the chimes once more 'rang sweetly in his ears'.

Writing to Mrs. Macready to tell of his snowy journey, the traveller says:

I was so cold after leaving you and dear Macready in Paris that I was taken out of the coach at Marseilles in a perfectly torpid state and was at first supposed to be luggage, but the porters not being able to find any directions upon me led to a further examination and what newspapers call 'the vital spark' was finally discovered under a

remote corner of the travelling shawls which you were
pleased to approbate in the Hôtel Brighton. After that I
passed three days of waking nightmare at Marseilles. . . . It
may have been two, but I crowded into the space the
noisome smells of a patriarchal life. After that I was so
horribly ill on board a steamboat that I should have made
my will if I had had anything to leave, but I had only the
basin and I couldn't leave that for the moment. That
suffering over I rushed into the arms of my expectant
family. Their happiness is more easily conceived than
described. . . .

Re-united at the Peschiere, the Dickens family did their
best to generate the Christmas spirit. This was made easier
by the thoughtfulness of Miss Coutts, who had sent her
godson, Charley, a sugared cake weighing ninety pounds.
No Twelfth Night confection had ever been seen in Genoa
before, and when it was sent to the pastrycook's to have its
sugar ornaments repaired after its journey, it stood on exhibition for customers to wonder at, together with its bon-bons,
crackers and Twelfth Night figures complete. Twelfth
Night festivities over, Mr. and Mrs. Dickens quitted Genoa
for Rome.

Mrs. De la Rue, who had missed him terribly during his
five weeks' absence, begged him before he started for the
Eternal City on no account to go alone to Trinità dei Monti,
for she had been through her first sinister adventure there and
was solicitous lest Dickens, after treating her, might not
attract the same evil phantoms to himself. During the long
drive southwards Kate realised that Charles was worrying
about his 'patient' and wondering what bad effects separation
from him might not entail. It soon transpired that he was
giving her absent treatment and concentrating his thoughts
upon her. What could Kate with her matter-of-fact Scottish
mind think about her husband's absorption in another woman
except that he must be in love with her?

Breaking their journey at Spezzia, they made a detour to
the marble quarries of Carrara to visit Angus Fletcher who

had gone there to lodge with an English marble merchant, Mr. Walton. He took them to the local opera-house to hear *Norma*, and on their return to the Walton villa they were serenaded by a chorus of marble workers. Pisa was the next stop: the moon was shining on the famous tower which looked 'all awry in the uncertain light'. Next morning on visiting the group of buildings of which it formed a part, they found 'a grave, retired place set in a verdant carpet of turf' and Dickens observed that monuments clustering together as if shrinking from the ordinary transactions of the town 'have a singularly venerable and impressive character. It is the architectural essence of a rich old city, with all its common life and common habitations pressed out, and filtered away.'

Of course Dickens climbed the Leaning Tower, and in so doing got the sensation of being on a ship that had heeled over: the view upwards through the slanted tube struck him as most curious. On the walls of the fretted cloisters lingered ancient frescoes looking down on grassy graves filled with soil brought from the Holy Land six centuries earlier. The impression made by the *campo santo* on his mind was one of solemn, unforgettable loveliness.

After visiting Leghorn, 'made illustrious by Smollett's grave', they returned to Pisa and hired a *vetturino* and his four horses to drive them through Tuscany to Siena. Siena with its old palaces dreamy and fantastic seemed 'like a bit of Venice without the water', but Dickens was no wholehearted admirer of beauty in decay because these cities were identified in his mind with a vague notion of a tyrannous past and, like the Tower of London, evoked visions of rat-infested dungeons, racks, torture chambers and the headman's axe. As Mr. and Mrs. Dickens drove over the desolate, dangerous Campagna, they strained their eyes for Rome and when they saw the great cupola it put them disappointingly in mind of London! 'There it lay, under a thick cloud, with innumerable towers, and steeples, and roofs of houses, rising up into the sky, and high above them all, one Dome!'

On closer acquaintance Rome failed to impress these

tourists: the shops, the people, the equipages were so ordinary, no flicker of grandeur was anywhere to be discerned. Charles wrote unhappily to Forster, 'It is no more my Rome, degraded and fallen and lying asleep in the sun among a heap of ruins, than Lincoln's Inn Fields is'.

The measure of what one gets from sightseeing is governed by the amount one brings to sightseeing. Dickens brought very little. The educational and cultural background necessary to the understanding of the past was almost completely lacking and his reactions are sometimes silly and often shallow. In the paucity of his analogies the paucity of his general mental equipment is only too evident.

Perhaps he could not apprehend great monuments in their majesty or integrity because there was nothing to link them up with human joys and human tears. On first submitting himself to the overwhelming vastness of St. Peter's he missed the *vox humana*. 'I felt no very strong emotion. I have been infinitely more affected in many English cathedrals when the organ has been playing and in many English country churches when the congregation have been singing.'

They stood there, this little couple from England, gaping up at the Dome and half stunned by the size of the building, till Dickens said, 'We've been here an hour, let us go to the Coliseum'. There he found his paralysed imagination begin to work again, peopling the tiered seats with faces and the arena with a whirl of strife and blood and sand. Never could he be more 'moved and overcome by any sight not immediately connected with his own affections and afflictions'.

Walls and arches overgrown with green, corridors open to the day, long grass growing in the porches, trees in the ragged parapets, birds nesting in chinks and crannies, all this he saw as he climbed to the upper walls and looked down on the triumphal arches of Constantine, Severus and Titus, on the Forum and the Palace of the Caesars, ruin, ruin, ruin all about him, here was his Rome at last! In such a mood he wandered out along the Appian way, out on to the open Campagna with its broken aqueducts, its broken temples, its broken tombs,

sombre and desolate beyond all expression. Here indeed
was the Rome of his imagination, the city he had pictured
when, as a boy, he had visited the Roman bath in London.

One of the first diversions indulged in by the Dickenses
was to take part in the Carnival. They hired a carriage, and
filling it with nosegays and sugar plums, wore their wire
masks and started tossing their flowers and volleying their
confetti. Charles gives a lively description of the draperies
and banners on the Corso, of scaffoldings turned into glittering bowers, of the battle of the tapers which he enjoyed to the
utmost, extinguishing other people's lights, keeping his own
burning and jeering 'Senza moccolo!' So lively is his
description that Germans have compared it with Goethe's
account of his experience on a similar occasion.

Presently they decided to leave Rome for the rest of Lent
and to return in time for Holy Week. Georgy was due to
meet them in Naples, coming direct from Genoa by sea and
bringing with her letters from England and news of the
family. At Naples Charles excited himself to fever-pitch
over his mail and, when the boat came in from Genoa,
watched the unloading of the mailbags through a telescope.
On having the De la Rue letters put into his hands, he read
them avidly, only to learn how adversely his departure had
affected his poor little patient. Impetuously he sent an
express letter by the return boat urging her husband to bring
her to Rome for further treatment. Relieved in mind by this
decision, he set to work to see the sights with a will. He and
his ladies went to Pompeii, Herculaneum, Monte Cassino
and other places. They made the ascent of Vesuvius (Kate
and Georgy in litters) and they explored Naples itself very
thoroughly. To Dickens it was not nearly so beautiful a city
as Genoa. When he had tired his ladies out with orthodox
sightseeing, he spent his time investigating lazzaroni and slum
life. The slums he walked through were so squalid that
'those of Saffron Hill seemed genteel' by comparison. He
visited the burial sites or pits covered by flat stones into
which uncoffined paupers were nightly thrown and they made

the congested graveyards of London seem almost decent.

Just before Holy Week the sightseers returned to Rome, putting up at the Hotel Meloni where Mrs. Dickens found that the De la Rues had also reserved rooms. As soon as they arrived Dickens began to mesmerise his patient daily. Her worst moment in the twenty-four hours was between one and two in the morning, as Kate soon had reason to know. She and her husband had gone to bed one night as usual, expecting to sleep till dawn, when Kate awoke to find Charles, with all the candles lit, pacing up and down the room in indescribable terror. He continued pacing up and down till he had mastered his emotion and then went back to bed. It was 1 A.M. A night or two later, at the same hour, Mr. De la Rue came knocking on their bedroom door in great distress and insisted that Charles should rise at once and come and treat his poor wife, who had had an extra bad seizure. Dickens went with him and, in his own words, found Mrs. De la Rue 'rolled up into an apparently impossible ball. . . . I only knew where her head was by following her long hair to its source.'[1] Though he had no experience of phenomena of the kind, Dickens boldly treated her by means of strokings and passes and in fifteen minutes had the satisfaction of seeing her relax, unwind herself, and resume her normal posture.

Charles on the whole regretted having been persuaded to attend the long ceremonies of Holy Week and counselled travellers to visit Rome at any other moment of the year than this. He saw the Pope being 'carried about like a Guy Fawkes', the Washing of the Feet, and the slow Good Friday 'knee-shuffle' up the Scala Santa, 'ridiculous and unpleasant in its unmeaning degradation'. For him that was the keynote of it all, the meaninglessness of the Church, and its infamous taste in draping architectural features in 'impertinent frippery'. The Bambino of the Ara Coeli came in for scathing abuse and so did the frescoes representing the tortures of martyrs. Less irritating experiences are recorded of excursions to Albano, the Ville d'Este, the ruins of Tusculum, as well

as strolls through the Vatican Galleries and the Barberini
Palace, walks in the Catacombs, and to conclude with an
indulgence in the 'vice anglais,' a public execution.   Dickens
and De la Rue set out in good time for the scene of punishment.   Anxious to miss nothing of the spectacle, they got
places in a kind of wash-house looking straight on to the
seven-foot scaffold on the top of which stood the guillotine.
After noting every detail of the religious procession with its
black-draped crucifix, Dickens watched the victim closely.

> The young man kneeled down below the knife.   His
> neck fitting into a hole made for the purpose, in a cross-
> plank, was shut down by another plank above; exactly like
> the pillory.   Immediately below him was a leathern bag.
> And into it his head rolled instantly.
> The executioner was holding it by the hair, and walking
> with it round the scaffold, showing it to the people, before
> one quite knew that the knife had fallen heavily, and with a
> rattling sound.
> There was a great deal of blood.   When we left the
> window, and went close up to the scaffold, it was very
> dirty. . . . A strange appearance was the apparent annihila-
> tion of the neck . . . the body looked as if there was nothing
> left above the shoulder.

After writing this strictly objective account of what his eyes
had seen, Dickens commented sadly that no one seemed to
care, there was no manifestation of disgust, pity, indignation
or sorrow; it was nothing but an ugly careless, filthy, sicken-
ing spectacle.

In Rome Dickens saw something of Father Prout (Francis
Mahony) an old friend whom he provisionally engaged as
correspondent for the *Daily News* to take effect in the new
year.   Father Prout says that they ratified this 'solemn
compact at the Milvian bridge, a spot that had witnessed many
occurrences more important to mankind', with a handful of
cigars.   He pressed them on Dickens with the assurance they
had been 'blessed by the Pope', though they really had just
been bought at Torlonia's shop in the Corso.   'I trust', he

wrote later on, 'that you found their efficacy in traversing the pestilent Campagna.'

On all excursions and on some of their more casual sight-seeing the De la Rues now went everywhere with the Dickenses, and when they came to leave Rome travelled with them in the same carriage. Charles gave his patient treatment 'sometimes under olive trees, sometimes in vineyards, sometimes in the travelling carriage, sometimes at wayside inns during the mid-day halt'. By degrees the delusions faded and by the time the party got back to Genoa Mrs. De la Rue was in a better state of health than she had been in for years.

Florence was one of the cities visited by this strangely assorted party. There they found Lord and Lady Holland at their beautiful villa, Careggi de' Medici, at the moment being frescoed by a shy young Englishman, George Watts, who took refuge in a pavilion when visitors appeared. Lord Holland invited the English colony to meet the great 'Boz', and in this way Dickens saw jovial Mrs. Trollope and her son Augustus. In fulfilment of a promise to Landor, Dickens went to Fiesole and inquired for Landor's villa. From the convent wall on the height a peasant girl pointed out 'La Villa Landora', and Dickens, visiting it, plucked an ivy leaf from the wall and posted it to England. Before leaving he had asked Landor what he should bring him from Italy. 'An ivy leaf from Fiesole,' was the reply. He also made acquaintance with Mrs. Landor with whom he had a pleasant conversation.

In April Charles Dickens and his ladies returned to Genoa to spend their last two months abroad. Mrs. Dickens was not on speaking terms with the De la Rues, and Dickens, in order to explain away a very embarrassing situation, told them that she was subject to nervous breakdowns, a fiction that he employed later on to cover other awkward dilemmas.

Notes on the sights he had seen had now to be sorted and written up, but somehow Dickens found his imagination had stopped working, maybe because he had tried to observe

too many unfamiliar things. His genius, which in any case
nourished itself on past experience and was retrospective in
nature, was as it were anaesthetised by his overdose of present
experience. The kaleidoscope of the changing Italian scene
had been too much for him and he was to discover from
experience that environment of the right kind was quite as
essential to his genius as freedom from financial worries. It
became obvious that he could not afford too much novelty,
or too great and prolonged an effort to assimilate foreign
matter.

Combining his letters to Forster with his own notes, he soon
had *Pictures from Italy* in shape. Arrangements for publishing in book-form were postponed for the time being as his
wish was to bring the *Pictures* out serially if he could manage
it. Eventually Bradbury and Evans produced them in a neat
blue-cloth volume with illustrations by Samuel Palmer. The
last page was embellished with a design showing the gather-
ing-in of the grape harvest and the last paragraph, which
might have been written by a Victorian bishop, ran as follows:

Let us not remember Italy the less regardfully, because,
in every fragment of her fallen Temples, and every stone
of her deserted palaces and prisons she helps to inculcate
the lesson that the wheel of time is rolling for an end and
that the world in all great essentials gets better, gentler,
more forbearing and more hopeful as it rolls.

The author was quite satisfied with the terms given by Bradbury and Evans: they were certainly treating him better than
Chapman and Hall had done, especially in the matter of this
small, occasional book *Pictures from Italy*. He was no
longer worrying about money and wrote orders to Mitton
for the doing-up of Devonshire Terrace against his return.
These orders give one an idea of the manner in which living
in palatial surroundings had affected his taste. He had been
taken with the Italian habit of imitating the graining of wood
in paint and of ornamenting ceilings. The skirting board of
the drawing-room was to be painted to look like satinwood,

the ceiling was to blush pink, wreaths of flowers were to be limned round the gas chandeliers and a flock paper of blue and gold or purple and gold was to be hung on the walls. The estimate he received for the redecoration was such 'a staggerer' that, instead of carrying out his original intention of getting the room done as a surprise for Kate, he told her of his plans and she at once modified them into mere cleaning of walls and a repainting of windows and doors.

By June the party at the Peschiere was packing up. To escape the 'miseries of moving' Dickens went to stay with the De la Rues at the Palazzo Rosso, leaving Kate to wrestle with the situation. Soon the whole family set out for Brussels, where Jerrold, Maclise and Forster were due to meet them. Maclise, who had come from Paris, was full of the new French paintings which had enraptured him, and Dickens was full of his travels which enabled him to talk with familiarity of the Farnese Hercules, the Laocoön and the glorious frescoes in Venice. It was a very happy reunion and the week they spent together was devoted to intensive sightseeing. After a year's absence from London Dickens went back to Devonshire Terrace a far more restless man than he started out. He was conscious of an inner drabness caused by unidentified discontent and felt the need of dramatising his life somehow or another. The eleven months that were to elapse before his second flight abroad were months of experiment, but not of novel-writing.

Chapter 15

DAILY NEWS AND ROSEMONT

*Which of us is happy in this world?   Which of us has his
desire? or having it is satisfied?*   W. M. THACKERAY

EVER since *The Chimes* audition, Charles Dickens had been
promising himself the fun of appearing on a London stage,
and so almost as soon as he returned from Italy he mobilised
his friends and arranged that they should, between them, act
Ben Jonson's comedy *Every Man in His Humour*.   Forster,
Cruikshank, Jerrold, Lemon, Leech, Cattermole, Maclise,
Frank Stone, T. J. Thompson and his brothers Frederick
and Augustus Dickens were all roped in, but Maclise fell away
before rehearsals began.   Though more than a little scornful
of amateurs Macready was persuaded to coach them, at the
same time noting in his diary that the whole troupe 'seemed to
be under a perfect delusion as to their degrees of skill and
power in an art of which they do not know what may be
called the very rudiments'.   The actor-manager was rather
exasperated one day on going to a theatrical costumier's to
find Dickens ruffling it in doublet and hose in front of a
mirror.   He confided to his journal: 'It is ludicrous the fuss
the actors make about this play'.   Some of the rehearsals took
place at 90 Fleet Street, where Dickens, Jerrold and Wills
were secretly working at plans for founding the *Daily News*.
Fuss or no fuss, in his capacity of stage-manager, property-
man, prompter and actor, Dickens managed to keep his team
hard at work and happy, with the result that he could present
a well-rehearsed, workmanlike performance on the night.

A man from the *Daily News* office went to the Royalty
(better known as Miss Kelly's theatre) on September 20 to
help Dickens, Lemon and Jerrold with the final arrangements.
Dickens and Lemon took off their coats and set to work to
number the seats in the boxes and dress circle.   'Boz' wore

his puce-coloured velvet waistcoat and into the pockets put tacks and bradawl, while in his hands he carried a hammer. Jerrold kept on his coat as he was preparing a fire on the stage with slacked lime and red tinsel. 'Lemon, will this do?' he shouted, and Lemon shouted back, 'The smoke's all right, but a little more tinsel would improve the fire!'

Admission to the performance was by printed card of invitation and each member of the cast had thirty to thirty-five tickets. Even Macready was obliged to admit that the despised amateurs scored a considerable success. 'Captain Bobadil' played by 'Boz' was outstandingly good, or so the critics said. Leslie, the American painter, admired him so much in this part that he asked him to sit for him as Bobadil. On November 15 the same company, with Maclise (half fainting from stage fright), repeated its performance for charity in Prince Albert's presence. This time they acted in the St. James's Theatre as the Royalty would not hold all the peers and peeresses who applied for boxes and who found awaiting them play-bills printed on white satin. It delighted Dickens that the Duke of Devonshire should travel two hundred miles from one direction and Alfred Tennyson the same distance from another direction in order to be present. Charles Greville reported that the audience was 'cold as ice', and Lord Melbourne was heard by everyone in the interval saying, 'I knew this play would be dull, but that it should be so damnedly dull as this I did not suppose.' Thackeray, it appears, had offered to help by singing between the acts, and had received a rebuff which hurt him very much.[1] The proceeds of the performance were given to Dr. Southwood Smith's nursing home, The Sanatorium, in Devonshire Terrace.

For Dickens, play-acting was as near heaven and complete self-realisation as anything he ever did. We shall see the urge to act (growing stronger in the next two years) suppressed for novel construction, and in the end dominating him by making him act his own stories to vast appreciative audiences. Life

[1] G. Waterfield, *Lucie Duff Gordon*, p. 101.

has a way of going in cycles and we return on ourselves and our early loves sometimes to find them more attractive than ever and sometimes to find them utterly distasteful.

In October 1845 another baby was born, a sixth child, and a fourth son. This event filled Dickens, as every addition to his family now did, with apprehension about the future. How could he make more money? How could he hope to support so large a household? To have a whole family dependent on the slender thread spun by a master spider was madness, the mere thought of his responsibilities made him restless. Would the floating of another weekly periodical perhaps ease the worries that beset him? Would a three-halfpenny magazine with some such name as 'The Cricket' meet the case? Forster threw cold water on the suggestion and urged him to concentrate on a story: it was a far quicker way of making money. Why could he not write a tale called 'The Cricket' for the Christmas market? Dickens fell in with this suggestion at once and sat down to write *The Cricket on the Hearth: A Fairy Tale of Home*, inscribing it to Lord Jeffrey 'with the affection and attachment of his friend the author'. It was garnished with woodcuts from drawings by Maclise, Doyle, Leech, Stanfield and Landseer, but this did not save it from being savagely attacked in the *Times*. Forster warned his friend that this must do him great harm, but found Dickens so angry and so fixed on his own opinions and in his admiration for his own work, as to be impossible to talk to on the subject. Rather exasperated by his attitude, Forster jotted down the reflection that 'this partial passion would grow on him till it became an incurable evil'. Dickens, however, knew his public: they liked the little book as much as he did, and read it rapturously. Caleb Plummer, who made the life of his blind daughter beautiful by wielding 'the only magic art that still remains to us, the magic of devoted, deathless love', won the hearts of readers, as did Mrs. Peerybingle, and her nurse-maid, Tilly Slowboy. The sales of *The Cricket* doubled those of his two other Christmas tales. Dramatised for the Keeleys at the Lyceum for Christmas 1845, a fortnight later versions of it were being played at twelve London theatres.

During the autumn weeks when Kate was laid up, Georgy inevitably played a more active part in Charles's life: they took long country walks together and he discussed with her his journalistic plans and worries. They talked much of Dan Maclise for whom both Kate and her sister had a great weakness, and they talked of themselves. What is one to make of the cryptic sentence (referring to Georgy) in a letter to Mrs. De la Rue, 'I have left that matter where it was; trusting to its wearing itself out, on her part, in due course'. Who was in love with whom? All that autumn Dickens was immersed in the hitherto hushed-up activities connected with the founding of a new daily newspaper. Though Forster knew all the ins and outs and was at his elbow throughout, he states that it does not come within the plan of his biography to record the episode in detail and that in principle he disapproved of it. For six months Dickens now devoted his best energies to seeking information on how to conduct a paper; how the foreign departments of papers like the *Herald* and *Morning Chronicle* were run; how the mail service from the Far East worked; how information from correspondents in Ceylon, Aden and Malta was transmitted. He was plodding away industriously at plans in September 1845 when he called rehearsals of *Every Man in His Humour* at 90 Fleet Street (in a second-floor room overlooking St. Bride's spire), but exactly how he came to shoulder this work at all has never been clearly explained.

The actual inception of the paper may be said to have lain in the conversation between Dickens, Paxton, and Bradbury and Evans (and probably Forster) in the spring of 1844, referred to in the last chapter. When on his return from Italy Dickens reopened the subject he learnt from his publishers that the firm was agreeable to putting up capital and that Joseph Paxton (who had made money during the railway boom) was willing to stand in with them. Dickens then mentioned two personal friends of his own living in the north of England, Sir William Jackson and Sir Joseph Walmsley, who might both be counted on for financial backing. Sir Joseph, who had hailed Dickens publicly as 'the best friend to progress and reform yet seen in English fiction', was the parliamentary champion of Liberalism in the north, and was regarded by Cobden as the foremost organiser of the party, a man who had managed to bring together middle-class and Chartists without setting them by the ears. This object, we should note, was from the first the policy of the *Daily News*.

For some months after his return from abroad Dickens was absorbed and excited by the scheme, which involved him in many interviews and business meetings, and gave him a feeling of great importance. He rushed down to Derbyshire at a minute's notice (a day or two after the birth of his fourth son) on 'matters of great moment connected with *my* scheme', and discussed with Paxton 'the stunning venture'. Writing to Tom Mitton, he said:

> Paxton has command of every railway influence in England and abroad except the Great Western and he is in it heart and purse. One other large shareholder is to come in; and that is to be a house which has the power of bringing a whole volley of advertisements upon the paper always. The commercial influence that will come down on it with the whole might of its aid and energy; not only in the City of London, but in Liverpool, Manchester, Bristol and Yorkshire, is quite stunning. I am trying to engage the best people right and left.[1]

Fixing his own salary as editor at £2000 instead of the £1000 allotted for the purpose by Bradbury and Evans, Dickens at once took a high-handed line in dealing with his colleagues, announcing that he could not be depended on to be in the office himself: 'When I am not there I shall have a sub-editor to whom I can hand over the management with perfect confidence. . . . On these terms I am willing to become the head and leading principle of the thing',[2] and on these terms,

[1] Unpublished letter (W. Dexter).
[2] 714. I. N.L.

owing to his great drawing power, they accepted him, but how soon they must have regretted it! Some of his letters at this time show lack of nerve, almost panic, when certain City failures take place that he thinks may affect the stability of the backers of the paper, and this nervousness he imparted to his staff, some of whom tried to get back to their original jobs. A week or two later he was in good heart again and boasting of having received a proposal for a second sub-editor 'which will drive Sir John Easthope raving mad'. There was a growing fear in the minds of Bradbury and Evans that he was a very difficult, if not an impossible, man to work with or control.

If we glance at the political situation in England in the summer of 1845, we shall see why it must have appeared to Radicals the moment of all others to float a new paper in which their gospel could be preached. To both Protectionists and Free Traders a great shock had been imparted by the famine in Ireland, and Whigs and Tories alike felt impelled to try and cope with the crisis. Important political leaders were reported to be modifying their views on the Corn Laws, and it was widely rumoured that Sir Robert Peel himself was converted to the idea of Free Trade. When Lord John Russell's letter to his constituents in London, announcing that the time had come 'to put an end to the whole system of Protection', appeared in the *Times*, Peel realised that on this issue the Whigs were prepared to make common cause with the anti-Corn Law League. His Foreign Secretary, Lord Aberdeen, told Delane confidentially that Peel, if he could not secure agreement in the cabinet, would resign. Next day the *Times* carried a statement to the effect that the cabinet would summon Parliament to meet in January to propose the total repeal of the Corn Laws. This broke the Government as no cabinet agreement on the subject had been arrived at. Two days later Peel resigned and Lord John was sent for by the Queen, but as he could not form an alternative Government Peel was sent for again and reconstituted his cabinet, bringing in, as one of the new team, Mr. Gladstone, Secretary for the

Colonies, who had no seat in the House. Parliament was summoned to reassemble on January 22 and on the preceding day the *Daily News* made its well-timed first appearance.

Dickens had collected his staff regardless of expense. 'Critics, leader-writers and reporters were offered terms so favourable that seceders from existing newspapers were numerous. . . . Editors and publishers were angry and disturbed as some of their best writers were being drawn away.'[1] Eyre Crowe, Paris correspondent of the *Morning Chronicle*, and Thomas Hodgkinson of *The Economist* are examples of this. Among the leader-writers was W. J. Fox, M.P., golden-tongued apostle of untaxed bread. Forster was a permanent leader-writer, and with him were working W. H. Wills, F. Knight, Leigh Hunt, Charles Mackay and Father Prout, soon to become 'our Rome correspondent'. Provincial intelligence, military and naval news, the City, sport and commerce were all in charge of the best men Dickens could get hold of. Douglas Jerrold, Albany Fonblanque, Mark Lemon all supported him personally to the utmost of their ability. Perhaps he was unwise to put his father in charge of the reporting staff with Laman Blanchard, William Hazlitt, Jerrold, J. A. Crowe and a dozen others under him, for though energetic and good-tempered he was by this time very bulky and rather old for all-night work. His father-in-law, George Hogarth, was made musical and dramatic critic: his uncle, John Henry Barrow, whom he failed to get sent out to India, became a sub-editor: and Lady Blessington was engaged for six months at £500 to supply 'exclusive intelligence of a social kind'. The price of the *Daily News* was 5d., as against the 7d. charged by the *Times* and most other dailies.

On January 17 the printing machines were 'christened' in the presence of a party of ladies and gentlemen, and the machine against which the wine bottle was dashed was named 'Perseverance'. A dummy paper was then printed with the date January 19. Dickens by this time was installed in an editor's room on the third floor, 'up aloft in Whitefriars'.

[1] Violet Markham, *Paxton and the Bachelor Duke*, p. 169.

He had in the early autumn insisted that this room should be 'properly furnished' as he intended to occupy it 'every day'. The office furniture was installed together with shelves of Hansard, 'Annual Registers', 'Mirrors of Parliament', 'State Trials', Shakespeare's works, the Bible, 'a complete set of the classics' and a fair supply of dictionaries and works of reference.

On the eve of the appearance of the *Daily News* its prospects had been discussed at dinner by Eyre Crowe, Henry Reeve, C. W. Dilke, Forster and Dickens. Dilke and Reeve walked away together. 'I foresee,' said Reeves to his companion, 'your knowledge will some day be invoked to remedy the mischief done by Dickens's genius to this new paper,' a prophecy that was realised in fact three months later. On the day of its appearance W. H. Russell, opening the first copy, was delighted to see it 'ill-printed and badly made up'. The *Times* had nothing to fear from this upstart radical organ.

In the opening number of the paper the editor wrote:

> The principles advocated by the *Daily News* will be principles of progress and improvement, of education, civil and religious liberty and equal legislation—principles such as its conductors believe the advancing spirit of the times requires, the condition of the country demands, and justice, reason, and experience legitimately sanction.

The leading article was by W. J. Fox (who had agreed to write four leaders a week) and the number contained a report of Mr. Cobden's meeting at Norwich of the evening before, a long review of railway affairs, two gossip columns, a critical article on music by George Hogarth, 'Voices from the Crowd' by Charles Mackay and the first of Dickens's 'Travel Letters'. After the paper had been dispatched, the staff, much elated at getting it out ahead of the *Times*, assembled to drink success to the enterprise. Next day, when the Queen made her speech in person, enormous efforts were made by John Dickens to keep his men moving briskly in and out of the Gallery. It was an exciting sitting to all newspaper men, for Peel made it quite clear that he was a convert to Cobden's views, and this gave Disraeli his great opportunity of denouncing him as one who had betrayed his party and his principles.

What happened to Dickens now cannot be explained by any ordinary standards of behaviour. Two days after Peel had made his great speech the editor began to flag in energy. A week later he wrote to Forster, 'I have been revolving plans in my mind this morning for quitting the paper and going abroad again to write a new book in shilling numbers'. Suddenly he lost all interest in the paper and ten days later, without apparent compunction, resigned. For weeks past he had been looking on the *Daily News* as a thing of his own creation to be dealt with exactly as he saw fit. Whether his collapse was due to adverse criticism or whether he had all along meant just to launch the paper and then hand it over to Forster, no one can now say. It would seem that, as in Boston, he had one of those curious nervous and temperamental breakdowns which overtook him whenever things became vexatious or disappointing. The hostility evoked by his copyright speech in Boston had drained him of vitality, and difficulties connected with his wholesale bribing away of men from other journals must have arisen in the *Daily News* office. He hated to realise that he was making enemies. If it is hard to believe that Dickens ever seriously intended to remain editor, it is equally hard to imagine what could have induced him to undertake a job that he had no intention of carrying to its conclusion. He complained of being 'worn out', but no one knew better than he the penalties of office work, and to those collaborating with him during the autumn and winter of 1845 he appeared to enjoy good health and to be putting his whole heart into the venture. It is clear from the Nonesuch *Letters* that there was serious friction between him and Mr. Bradbury, the controller of general expenditure, salaries and staff qualifications. Dickens complained to Mr. Evans of his partner's 'interposition between me and almost every act of mine at the newspaper office', which is 'as disrespectful to me as it is injurious to the enterprise'. He complained, too, that his father had been treated with rudeness and ended by saying that Bradbury was far worse than Easthope to deal with, which was saying a great deal. The net result of all this friction was that Forster found himself in Dickens's shoes and Dickens found himself a free man, except that he was under an engagement to write two articles on capital punishment and some 'Travel Letters' for the newspaper he had abandoned.

Dickens had always taken extreme interest in capital punishment, but though he had considerable experience of executions he had hitherto made no use of his observations except in *Oliver Twist* when he described the scene of Fagin's hanging as follows:

> Day was dawning. . . . A great multitude had already assembled; the windows were filled with people, smoking and playing cards to beguile the time; the crowd were pushing, quarrelling and joking. Everything told of life and animation, but one dark cluster of objects in the very centre of all—the black stage, the cross-beam, the rope, and all the hideous apparatus of death.

For the *Daily News* he now defined his attitude to the death penalty, declaring that nothing human ingenuity could devise worked such ruin as a public execution. Out of 167 persons who, being sentenced to death, had been questioned by a clergyman, only three had not been present at a hanging. Further, Dickens said that some natures feel themselves heroes at a public execution: it almost seems to console them for dying, therefore the glamour and distinction of a public death should be denied them. The crowd attracted on these occasions is always criminal. When standing close to a scaffold in Rome, Dickens was wearing a shooting-jacket and he could feel its many pockets being systematically gone over by thieves, but as the pockets were empty he pretended to notice nothing. An execution must be condemned as an utterly useless, barbarous, brutalising sight, and the sympathy of all beholders, who have any sympathy at all, is certain to be always with the criminal and never with the law. From studying comparative statistics, he is able to state that wherever capital punishments are diminished in number, there crimes diminish in number too. In bringing his three letters to a close, Dickens expressed his genera conclusions quite plainly:

> I beg to be understood to advocate the total abolition of the Punishment of Death as a general principle, for the advantage of society, for the prevention of crime. . . . I am the more desirous of being so understood, after reading a speech made by Mr. Macaulay in the House of Commons in which that accomplished gentleman hardly seemed to recognise the possibility of anyone entertaining an honest conviction of the inutility and bad effects of Capital Punishment in the abstract . . . without being the victim of 'a kind of effeminate feeling'. Without staying to enquire what there may be that is specially manly and heroic in the advocacy of the gallows or to express my admiration of Mr. Calcraft, the hangman, as doubtless one of the most manly specimens now in existence, I would simply hint a doubt whether this be the true Macaulay way of meeting a great question.

Victor Hugo, writing at this time in Paris, condemned all executions, public or private. Dickens returned to the charge three years later after attending the hanging of Mr. and Mrs. Manning at Horsemonger Gaol,[1] a spectacle witnessed from a neighbouring house. 'We have taken', he wrote to Leech, 'the whole of the roof (and the back kitchen) for the extremely moderate sum of ten guineas or two guineas each.' Dickens arranged that his party should sup at the Piazza Coffee House, Covent Garden, at 11 P.M. He then wandered about for some hours in the streets among the poor folk to gather impressions. At the site of the gallows there was a dense sea of heads and above them the roof-tops black with people. Men and women were fainting around him. That evening he wrote his famous letter to the *Times* saying

[1] November 13, 1849.

that the wickedness and levity of the immense crowd could be imagined by no man and could be presented in no heathen land under the sun.

Some people like to think that it was owing to Dickens's protests that executions in public were prohibited, and this may be partially true as we are notoriously slow about reforms, but it was not for twenty years (1868) that a law was passed ordaining that the death penalty be carried out behind prison walls.

The Dickenses' fourth son was nearly six months old when they decided to have him christened at St. Marylebone and give a party afterwards. For some reason or other, possibly because of the choice of godfathers, the tongues and pens of the literary folk of the day got busy on the event. To Father Prout it was a rhyming occasion:

> What eye but glistens
> And what ear but listens
> When the clergy christens
> A babe of 'Boz'.

Edward FitzGerald wrote to his friend Edward Barton[1] that Tennyson had been standing godfather to one of Dickens's children, Count d'Orsay being the other godfather, and that the poor child had been named 'Alfred d'Orsay Tennyson', which to his mind proved clearly enough that 'Dickens was a snob'. 'For what', he went on to say, 'is Snobbishness and Cockneyism, but all such pretensions and parade? It is one thing to worship heroes and another to lick their spittle.' And kindly Robert Browning, writing to Elizabeth, who was so soon to marry him in the very church in which Master Dickens was baptized, wonders if she knows why it is that Alfred Tennyson has been dining with Dickens to meet celebrities.

What do you suppose caused all the dining and repining? He has been sponsor to Dickens's child *in company with Count d'Orsay* and accordingly the *novus homo* glories in

---

[1] *New Letters of E. FitzGerald*, p. 122.

the praenomina Alfred d'Orsay Tennyson Dickens . . .
You observe: Alfred is common to both the godfather and
the devil-father. . . . When you remember what the form
of sponsorship is, to what it pledges you in the Church of
England—and then remember that Mr. Dickens is an
enlightened Unitarian,—you will get a curious notion of
the man, I fancy.

Monckton Milnes also joined in the ribaldry and made jokes
appropriate to the occasion. 'The baby', he said, 'is in good
truth not *the* Alfred of either personage, but of Mr. Alfred
Bunn', Alfred Bunn being the manager of Drury Lane and
the butt of the wits who nicknamed him 'Laureate Bunn'.
Contemporary opinion, especially if it is of a humorous
nature, is often stifled by the blare of praise that goes up on
the death of a great writer, and it is only in the by-paths of
private correspondence that we savour the actual verdict of
the hour. Until one has actually read with one's own eyes
Alfred d'Orsay Tennyson Dickens, the entry in the baptismal
register at St. Marylebone, one can hardly believe that any
parent could saddle a child with such names.

Alfred Tennyson had been much in the public eye this year
over a sparring match he had been engaged in with Bulwer
Lytton. At Christmas 1845 Bulwer Lytton had published
The New Timon anonymously. It was a novel in verse
dealing with life in London. Certain lines in it have sur-
vived, as, for example, 'Stanley, the Rupert of Debate' and
'Languid Johnny, grown to Glorious John'. 'School-miss
Alfred', however, was treated with contumely. Bulwer
Lytton wrote of his verse as

> Out-babying Wordsworth and out-glittering Keats
> Where all the airs of patchwork pastoral chime
> To drowsy ears in Tennysonian rhyme.

He also animadverted on the pension Tennyson had recently
been given (on the recommendation of Hallam) by the
Government[1] and spoke of him as 'belonging to a wealthy

[1] He had been given a Civil List allowance of £200 a year which enabled
him to travel abroad.

family'. Tennyson, of course, soon heard from Forster and others who the author of this attack was, and at once riposted with *The New Timon and the Poets*, which Forster insisted must appear in *Punch*. After a reference to 'Old Timon and his noble heart', Tennyson let fly at *The New Timon*:

> So died the Old; here comes the New!
> Regard him—a familiar face;
> I *thought* we knew him!—What, it's you—
> The padded man that wears the stays!
>
> Who killed the girls and thrilled the boys
> With dandy pathos when you wrote!
> O Lion, you that made a noise
> And shook a mane *en papillottes*!

Before deciding to transfer the household abroad Charles Dickens made one more effort to secure a regular stipend by applying to a leading member of the Government to be appointed a police magistrate for London. He was decidedly rueful when his application was turned down, for what excellent copy such experience would have provided! Life now took on for him the semblance of a waking nightmare in which his heavy commitments, his inability to write, his bills, his health all oppressed him by turns. Was the very ground under his feet giving way beneath him? had he really no foothold on present or future in spite of all his work and all his celebrity? Harassed by the possibility of 'failing health or fading popularity', he would from time to time tell Forster that he felt giddy and could scarcely see. It soon became obvious that there was only one sensible course to pursue, and that was to let his London house and once more take the family abroad. He tried to get Kate to agree to his renting the Peschiere again, but she refused, as the following characteristic letter written to his 'dearest' Mrs. De la Rue shows:

I need not tell *you* that *I* want to go to Genoa? But Mrs. Dickens, who was never very well there, cannot be got to contemplate the Peschiere though I have beset her in all kinds of ways. Therefore I think I should take a middle course for the present, and coming as near you as I

THE HOSTESS OF DEVONSHIRE TERRACE
by Daniel Maclise, R.A.

A MUSICAL EVENING AT ROSEMONT
"The Duet," by Frank Stone, A.R.A.

could, pitch my tent somewhere on the Lake of Geneva, say at Lausanne, whence I could run over to Genoa immediately.

My Diary of March the 19th 1845 is lying open on my desk, and looking at it I see this entry—*Madame D. L. R. very ill in the night. Up till four* . . . what a miserable Devil I seem to be cooped up here, bothered by printers and stock-jobbers, when there are bright Genoas (with bright patients in them) and ruined coliseums in the world!

I talk to all the nice Italian boys who go about the streets with organs and white mice and give them mints of money *per l' amore della Bell' Italia.*[1]

Once the decision had been made to settle at Lausanne, Charles was miraculously relieved of all untoward symptoms and, as soon as Sir James Duke applied to rent Devonshire Terrace for twelve months, his spirits rose enough to enable him to take the chair at the first banquet of the General Theatrical Fund Association and thoroughly to enjoy himself.

This Association had been founded seven years earlier for granting permanent pensions to poor, retired or invalid actresses and actors, singers and dancers. Dickens, in his speech, explained that the promoters of the fund had worked hard and without advertisement, and that in his opinion the Association should now be placed on a sound financial footing. Covent Garden and Drury Lane each had their pension funds, both richly endowed and of long standing. To qualify for help under these funds it was necessary, in the case of Drury Lane, to have played there for three consecutive seasons. As for Covent Garden, it was but a vision of the past. 'The human voice is rarely heard within its walls save in connexion with corn or the ambidextrous prestidigitation of the Wizard of the North.' In like manner Drury Lane was being conducted with a sole view to the opera and ballet, 'in so much that the statue of Shakespeare over the doors served as emphatically to point out his grave as his bust did in the church of Stratford-upon-Avon'. It was really impossible for the profession generally to hope to qualify for the Drury Lane and Covent Garden benefits, for its oldest and most distinguished members had been driven from the boards, on which they had earned their reputation, to theatres to which the General Fund alone extended. Those to whom he spoke must not let them pass from the footlights into gloom and darkness. Speaking for himself, he could truthfully say that he had never been in any theatre 'without carrying away some pleasant association, some favourable impression'.

A week or two before leaving England Dickens had a long talk with Miss Coutts on the desirability of establishing a rescue home for girls. He thought that if such a home were run in conjunction with an emigration scheme financed by Government, the girls, after re-education, would make excellent wives for colonists. Clarifying his recommendations by putting them down on paper, he said that the training must aim at making the girls useful and happy and be mainly domestic in character. It would be advisable to link up with the governors of prisons as no machinery was in existence to help females serving short sentences. Almost invariably they were forced back into bad ways. For his own part he would very much like to be entrusted with some share in the supervision and direction of the institution proposed. To this end he will make it his business to examine every scheme of the kind operating in Paris where he feels much valuable knowledge may be acquired. He will tabulate the information he collects so that Miss Coutts may grasp it at once. A year later when Dickens was once more settled in London we shall find him helping Miss Coutts to organise and administer a rescue home known as Urania Cottage, Shepherd's Bush. Made doubly impatient to escape from London and the claims of friends by the sense that a new story was rapidly forming itself in his mind, he left England with Switzerland as his goal.

With the circumspection to be expected from the father of a large family, Charles Dickens piloted his party to Ostend, and then shepherded them to a river steamer on the Rhine. There was something patriarchal about the movement of two ladies, six children, four servants and a dog, and the patriarch in question was just thirty-four and still looked very young. At Mainz a German came aboard and addressing Mrs. Dickens in good English said: 'Your countryman Mr. Dickens is travelling this way just now our papers say. Do you know him or have you passed him anywhere?' Explanations followed and the stranger, Josef Valckenburg, soon found himself talking to the great 'Boz' whose books had made such a furore in Germany, books which, as he pointed out, were at that moment being read by many people on the steamer. Charmed by the stranger's civility, Dickens apologised for not being able to understand or speak German. He was politely told by Mr. Valckenburg that he need not regret it, for 'even in a small town like ours where we are mostly primitive people and have few travellers I could make a party of at least forty people who understand and speak English as well as I do'. Mr. Valckenburg, a wine merchant, came from Worms, a city Dickens was to visit and to describe as 'a fine old place, greatly shrunken and decayed in spite of its population, with a picturesque old cathedral standing on the bank of the Rhine and some brave old churches shut up and so hemmed in and overgrown with vineyards that they look as if they were turning into leaves and grapes'.

It was no news to Dickens that his books were widely known in Germany and in steady demand, for the first instalment of *Pickwick*[1] issued in five small volumes had had a great sale, and before the last volume appeared a German version of the *Sketches* was printing as *Londoner Skizzen*.[2] In the same year *Nicholas Nickleby* was published[3] and *Oliver Twist* advertised. Even the *Memoirs of Grimaldi* had been trans-

[1] 1837-8.   [2] 1838.

[3] 1838-9. *Leben u. Abenteuer des Nicolaus Nickleby*, von Boz mit Federbezeichnungen nach Phiz, 1838-9 (Braunschweig, Georg Westermann), green covers on English model, slightly reduced in size. In the last of the twenty numbers appears an advertisement of *Oliver Twist, oder die Laufbahn eines Waisen Knaben.*

lated twice in 1839. R. H. Horne[1] did not think the German translations as accurate as they might have been and specially commended the Italian translations *Oliviere Twist* of Gianbattista Basaggio published in Milan, and the *Nicolas Nickleby* of E. de la Bedollière. By 1843 some of Dickens's books had appeared in Dutch and Russian.

The chief ground for the popularity of *Pickwick* in Germany was what the Germans call its *Behaglichkeit* for which we have no word, a radiating kindliness arising out of solid comfort and the enjoyment of things in common. Georg Freytag in *Ein Dank für Charles Dickens* said that *Pickwick* was like a ray of sunshine in Germany at a time when conditions of life were dreary in the extreme and characterised by complete absence of warmth and good nature in literature as well as in private and public life. 'The joyful conception of life,' he writes, 'the unending cosiness, the brave good sense that shines through the comic treatment was as moving to Germans of that day as a melody from home that strikes unexpectedly on a wanderer's ear.' No similar, happy, national life was observable anywhere among his compatriots; in fact Germany, like Italy, was in his time little more than a geographical expression.

German readers sensed in Dickens's pages the outcropping of a tender vein of sympathy, and the glowing of a heart that brought him much closer to the ordinary man and woman than the elegance and learning displayed by their own classical and romantic writers. High-born ladies and gentlemen were at a discount in the newly crystallising strata of society that were in process of becoming self-conscious. The mere fact that Dickens's books are formless, unconventional and styleless must have recommended them to the reader of few books, who only understood life as an ordinary day-to-day business in which kindness counts as the chief good. There is another point which may account for the immediate welcome accorded to the works of 'Boz', and that is that there is something distinctively German about his excursions into the

[1] *Spirit of the Age*, p. 76.

world of phantasy.   He had certainly read Hoffman's *Tales*,
The Golden Pot in particular, for we may notice that the
knocker in *A Christmas Carol* which changes into Marly's
dead-alive face, and yet remains a knocker, has its counterpart
in this tale.   His friend Carlyle had translated some of the
Tales and was for ever talking, to anyone who would listen,
of Germany and German books.   George Eliot, George
Lewes and William Thackeray all learnt German well, but as
a language it was not much better known among the generality
of Englishmen than it had been at the turn of the century when
Sir Walter Scott, Matt Lewis, Taylor of Norwich, Words-
worth and Coleridge were among the few studying the
language.

For nearly ten years Dickens had been in correspondence
with Germans about the translations of his books and during
that time had become very well known in German literary
circles by name and reputation.   Dr. Flügel had presented
him with a copy of his German-English dictionary, and Dr.
Künzel in 1838 had asked him for biographical particulars to
be included in the Brockhaus Conversations-Lexikon.   In
1841 he had even invited his co-operation in an Anglo-
German magazine to be called *Britannia*.   In wishing success
to this magazine Dickens avowed that 'next to his own
people he respects and treasures the Germans'.   He goes so
far as to say that he honours and admires them more than he is
able to express and that he realises that, because of their great
mental gifts and their culture, Germans are the chosen people
of the earth.   Never was he prouder than when he learned for
the first time that his writings had been warmly taken up in
Germany.   'God bless you and your work', he concluded.
'By heaven, I wish I could speak German even badly.   If I
could I should be with you in six months.'[1]

Bernhard Tauchnitz had commenced his famous series of
English books in 1841 with *Pelham*, which was followed by
Pickwick the same year and by *American Notes* the next.   In

[1] Ellis N. Gummer, *German Romance and Specimens of its Chief Authors*:
C. D. to K., September 13, 1841.

1843 this enlightened publisher visited authors in England and generously arranged to pay them a fee though no international copyright existed to oblige him to do so. In return Dickens offered to supply him with early corrected proofs of future works which would enable him to publish in Germany at the same time as the book came out in England. Ten works by 'Boz' were issued in a Tauchnitz edition between 1843 and 1846. Tauchnitz had no monopoly, for several Germans firms specialised in translations while others again went in for imitations such as Stolle's *Deutsche Pickwickier* and Hesslein's *Berliner Pickwickier*.

The novels of Dickens and the friendly, get-together spirit he engendered were even welcomed by the editor of the *Rheinische Zeitung*,[1] Karl Marx. The mere fact that 'Boz' never attempted to conceal or palliate the unpleasant truth that conditions in England were bad, quite as bad as Lord Ashley's reports testified and as Friederich Engels reported, lifted the novelist, in Marx's esteem, into the category of social reformers, despite the fact that the methods of betterment he indicated were extremely vague and hopelessly sentimental. Engels thought of Dickens as 'a member of a great spiritual family united in all lands in spite of the hindrance of language'.

Taking the train at Strasbourg, the Dickens family journeyed to Basle and thence by road to Lausanne. On the way they stopped for a few hours at Schloss Riedenburg near Bregenz, a four-square fortress commanding wonderful views. Here they were entertained by Charles Lever who was renting it from Baron von Pöllnitz and was busy writing *The Knight of Gwynne* and corresponding with Hayman. At Lausanne the Dickenses all lodged at the Hôtel Gibbon (which they were amused to hear pronounced 'Jibbone') till they found in 'Rosemont' a villa to suit them. It was 'a doll's house' with enough bedrooms for the whole party and a colonnade supporting a balcony, all to be rented at £10 a month. It had the advantage of seclusion without loneliness,

[1] 1841–2.

and the riot of roses in the garden was enough, Dickens said, 'to smother the whole establishment of the *Daily News*'. The bowers and pavilions in the grounds put him in mind of the Chalk Farm tea-gardens of his childhood, except that these were far more beautiful. The branchy places, bright flowers and singing birds, the walks, the views, the people delighted him and, best of all, 'there was not a monk or priest to be seen in the streets crammed with bookshops'; in fact there was but one Catholic church, all the others were used as 'packing warehouses'. There is no mention in his letters of any of his literary predecessors at Lausanne, Gibbon, Rousseau, Shelley or Byron, though one apprehends that, as at Albaro, Charles Dickens liked to consider himself the heir of those English writers who had the love of Europe in their blood.

Deciding to make a room with a view over Leman his study, he set his table at the balcony window to await the arrival of the fighting frogs and the writing equipment which were as 'indispensable to his work as blue ink and quill pens'. When the box containing his particular treasures was de-livered at the villa he took out a book and said to the watching family, 'Now whatever passage my thumb rests on, I shall take as having reference to my work.' The book was *Tristram Shandy* and opened at these words, 'What a work it is likely to turn out! Let us begin it!'

Next morning he took the plunge and wrote the first slip of *Dombey and Son*, 'the study in pride' he had discussed with Forster in London. It was two years since he had finished *Martin Chuzzlewit*; he was out of practice and to begin with the new book progressed but slowly. In a letter to Forster he said:

> You can hardly imagine what infinite pains I take or what extraordinary difficulty I find in getting on FAST . . . the difficulty of going at what I call a rapid pace is pro-digious. I suppose this is partly the effect of two years' ease and partly of the absence of streets and numbers of figures. I can't express how much I want these. It

seems as if it supplied something to my brain, which it cannot bear, when busy, to lose. For a week or a fortnight I can write prodigiously in a retired place (as at Broadstairs) and a day in London sets me up again and starts me. But the toil and labour of writing, day after day, without that magic lantern is IMMENSE. . . . I wrote very little in Genoa (only *The Chimes*) and fancied myself conscious of some such influence there—but Lord, I had two miles of streets at least, lighted at night, to walk about in; and a great theatre to repair to every night![1]

Dickens, as Forster points out, never thought lightly of his work, but he was not self-important about it, though it was his paramount interest and essential life. Even now it is not generally recognised on what difficult terms, physical as well as mental, Dickens held the tenure of his imaginative life, or the high price he had to pay for his triumphs and successes. 'I hold my inventive faculty', he said, 'on the stern condition that it must master my whole life, often have complete possession of me, make its own demands upon me and sometimes for months together put everything else away from me.' In being delicately balanced, easily cast down and equally easily elated, Dickens was sharing the lot of most imaginative writers, and, however steadily he might be working, he was liable at any time to be overcome by 'an extraordinary nervousness almost impossible to describe'.

His system of work was always the same. Just before 10 A.M. he sat at his writing-table; sometimes he wrote much and sometimes nothing, but whether he wrote much or nothing he did not leave his table before 2 P.M. The quietude of Rosemont was in one way favourable to industry, but after a day at the desk it would become almost unbearable to the author, who would tear over to Geneva for a night or two to wander about the streets.

In Geneva he had the strange experience of meeting two American ladies at dinner, a mother and daughter, who habitually smoked cigars, cigarettes and hookahs. Dickens con-

[1] 782. I. N.L.

fessed himself 'ridiculously taken aback' when the daughter
smoked six to eight cigars on end, for he had never seen any
woman, not even a gipsy, smoke before, and it opened up
vistas of what he 'might be in for when his own daughters
were full grown'.

English people came and went at Lausanne. The Tal-
fourds appeared and so did Mrs. Charles Brookfield; Harrison
Ainsworth and his daughters turned up at an hotel, as did the
T. J. Thompsons. The hub of English life was the house
of Henry Hallam, a summer resident. 'Good Heavens, how
Hallam did talk!' said Dickens after an evening spent in his
company, 'I don't think I ever saw him so tremendous.'
Then Lord Vernon, the Dante scholar, arrived and the Ladies
Taylor, 'fair and charming daughters of Lord Headfort'. All
English people, whether they were travelling to economise or
travelling to educate their families, expected to be received at
Rosemont. Among the English living in Lausanne were the
former member of Parliament for Ipswich, William Haldimand, and his sister Mrs. Marcet, the educationalist, who was
very lively and a dear friend of Sydney Smith and Sam Rogers.
Apropos of Sydney Smith's jokes, Mrs. Marcet told Dickens
that when she had stayed with him at his parsonage at Combe
Florey she had complimented him on the excellence of his
ham. 'Ah yes,' he said, 'ours are the only true hams, all the
rest are shems and japhets.' And Dickens in return told her
that the Canon had said he was 'the richest author that had
ever browsed on the commons of literature'.

Haldimand was a great benefactor to the blind asylum at
Lausanne and took Dickens there several times. At Haldimand's house Dickens also met M. de Cerjat, a Swiss citizen
with an English wife, who became a lifelong friend and
regular correspondent. Here, too, he first met the Watsons
of Rockingham Castle, Northamptonshire, who were spending the summer in a villa by the Lake. With both the Watsons Dickens also formed a lasting friendship. As Richard
Watson was a Liberal and had represented his county during
the Reform debates, there were reminiscences to be gone over

CHARLES DICKENS

and public figures to be discussed. Both men wondered why Lord Grey (whom Dickens had always disliked) and unassuming, friendly Lord Lansdowne had proved equally incapable of attaching a single young man to their party, and then they passed on to discuss the demerits of Disraeli. With some of these companionable people the Dickenses made excursions to the Great St. Bernard, Chamonix, Chillon and other places later to be worked into the texture of *Little Dorrit*. We never hear of visits to the Villa Diodati in search of Milton or Byron, or of Madame de Staël's Coppet, Voltaire's Ferney or even Rousseau's Bosquet de Julie—all so accessible by land and water; but then Dickens's interests were never consistently literary though they were consistently human and nearly always contemporary.

When in London Dickens had tried to persuade Alfred Tennyson to share a house at Lausanne with him for the summer, but the poet had declined to do so, and had explained his refusal to his confidante, Elizabeth Barrett, by saying that he found Dickens's sentimentality highly irritating, and that if he had been foolish enough to accept, 'it was a sure thing they would quarrel and part and never see one another any more'. That summer, however, in company with his publisher Moxon, Tennyson set out for Switzerland, making a bee-line for Leman quite as much to see his uncle Henry Hallam as his friend Dickens, and thus found himself at Lausanne.

Sprightly Mrs. Brookfield has something mocking to say about this tour with Moxon. One day while they were walking together Alfred said, 'Moxon, you have made me very unhappy by something you said at Lucerne'. It was the unfortunate remark, 'Why, Tennyson, you will be as bald as Spedding before long!' Poor Alfred brooded over it and 'put himself under a Mrs. Parker, who rubs and pulls out dead hairs at 10/- an hour. Fancy the Queen's pension being spent like this! but really his hair is such an integral part of his appearance it would be a great pity if he should lose it.'[1]

See *Mrs. Brookfield and her Circle*.

Wandering up the Rosemont road one golden evening, Tennyson was surprised to hear a girl's voice singing 'The Queen of the May' to a piano accompaniment.   Open stood the French window of the villa from which the sound came, and he stood listening till the song ended.   Charley Dickens well remembered that evening of fading twilight when his sister Mamie sat at the piano and tall Alfred Tennyson 'strolled in among them through the window that opened on to the lawn, as if the odd coincidence were quite a matter of course'.

In turning over the pages of *Early Victorian England*[1] I came on an illustration, evidently chosen as of typically period interest, showing a group of persons in evening dress listening to a piano duet.   The original, from which the reproduction was taken, was a painting by Frank Stone that had been exhibited at the Royal Academy of 1847 under the title of 'The Duet'.   As I looked closely at this elegant Victorian gathering I realised that, though the bevy of ladies, gentlemen and children were unmistakably English, the room in which they were sitting was foreign.   Their setting was a neat French salon.   The cornice-moulding, the curtains, the bookcase with its bust, the *guéridon*, the portraits, the furniture were French.   Why, I wondered, should these English people be living in a foreign house, and why should children be included in an evening party unless they formed part of a family picture?   The small child on the tabouret was playing with a white dog, the sort of dog given to Dickens in America. Could it possibly be Mr. Timber Doodle? was my first query and then tumbling after came other queries: Could the child be Francis Jeffrey Dickens?   Could the tall man with the steeple head leaning chin-in-hand on the piano possibly be Alfred Tennyson?   Could the whole group, instead of being anonymous assistants at a *soirée musicale*, be identified as the Dickens family at Rosemont?

Reference to the Dickens letters quickly established the fact that Frank Stone had visited Rosemont.   On inquiry at the Rischgitz Institute a portfolio of Dickensiana was pro-

[1] Edited by G. M. Young.

duced in which was the photograph of an engraving with a note supplied by Marcus Stone, son of Frank Stone:

'The Duet' by Frank Stone

(introducing Tennyson, Dickens, and the latter's dog and Miss Hogarth one of the figures seated at the piano).

Though no locality was indicated in this note, the furnishing of the room made it obvious that it was a contemporary snapshot of an actual Victorian family abroad and that it was in this cultivated, prosperous, happy *milieu* one could establish Dickens! Stone had evidently made a sketch of the incident on the spot and had built it up into an oil painting later, just as later on he did studies of the Dickens children in the verandah at Bonchurch.

Dombey and Son was by now developing steadily and Dickens read the first numbers aloud to Mrs. Marcet and a few chosen friends. 'The old lady', observed the author, 'was so devilish cute' that she realised at once that he intended to kill Paul. As he sensed his auditors gripped by interest so tense as to flower into apprehension, Dickens began to enjoy himself vastly and read better and better. The sensation he derived from their sympathy was so delightful that it occurred to the author that, 'if it were not *infra dig.*', it would be most pleasurable to read to larger audiences 'from one's own books', and incidentally that a great deal of money might be made that way. He mentioned his idea to Forster and then pushed it to the back of his mind whence it emerged again when his need for money became more acute.

In September Dickens began to apply himself intently to his new Christmas tale *The Battle of Life*, 'cordially inscribed to my English friends in Switzerland'. It is the story of a girl who gives up her sweetheart to her sister, and some people have read significance into the theme. *Dombey* of course had to be laid aside, though it put him out to have to interrupt a story that was now going well and in sales was outstripping *Chuzzlewit* by more than twelve thousand copies a number. In forcing himself to work at *The Battle of Life*

Dickens found his writing going 'all awry', and his health too, but somehow with the help of a visit to an hotel in Geneva he managed to finish it. The *Times* repeated its *Cricket* performance and gave it a very bad notice which he foolishly read. 'I see the good old *Times* is again at issue with the inimitable B. Another touch of a blunt razor on B.'s nervous system. . . . Dreamed of "Timeses" all night. Disposed to go to New Zealand and start a magazine.'

By mid-November the Dickens household had been established at Rosemont for six months: it was long enough for one to whom city streets were an inspiration. If *Dombey* was ever to be finished he must get to a big city, not necessarily London; Paris would serve his purpose, so to Paris the family journeyed in three carriages, a *fourgon* and a cabriolet, taking five days to cover the distance. To begin with they put up at the Hôtel Brighton. On the evening after their arrival Dickens took 'a colossal walk' and found the brilliance and brightness of the streets frightening. He then set about looking for a house to rent for the winter. That of the Marquis de Castellane was bizarre enough to attract Dickens's fancy. It was 48 rue de Courcelles in the Faubourg St. Honoré, and Sir Henry Bulwer while at the British Embassy had occupied it and had had the walls of one room painted to look like a grove of trees brightened by bits of glass stuck in among the leaves. Dickens described it as 'a Paris mansion in miniature with courtyard, garden and Concierge's lodge complete with a cordon to open the door'. The bedrooms were so small as to be comparable to opera boxes and their partitions were almost as frail. Charley remembered his father saying, 'It was something between a baby house, a shades, a haunted castle, and a mad kind of clock, and not to be imagined by the mind of man. One room is a tent, another room is a scene at the Victoria. The upstairs rooms are like fanlights over street doors. The inventor got frightened at what he had done and went away.'

The month of December was intensely cold and the water in the jugs froze at night, but the house had the merit of providing Dickens with something new in the way of experience. He soon was to find out that it was not a place in which he could write. Taking a dislike to the upstairs room he had chosen as a study, he would come down disconsolate to the drawing-room and, finding no corner that suited him, would sit there stubbornly for hours getting perhaps half a dozen lines on to paper. Dejectedly he took to wandering about the streets and to looking in frequently at the Morgue, for he never knew in advance what would set him working again and had to take his chance and often waste time waiting for the moment of kindling. The French people with whom Dickens came in contact impressed him at first unfavourably; they could not hold a candle to the Swiss for reliability. He came to change his views when he knew them better, but to begin with he found them indifferent, careless, procrastinating and their semi-sentimental devotion to Liberty seemed to have nothing in it of American vigour or purpose. Possibly they were fit for nothing but soldiering, but what, he asked himself, could he expected from a people bled white by the great Revolution and the Napoleonic wars?

So dull did he find himself in Paris that he went over to London for a week before Christmas to arrange for a cheap double-column edition of his books with new prefaces, a series to be dedicated to 'the English People'. Part of his time was spent at rehearsals of *The Battle of Life* which had been rapidly dramatised for the Keeleys by Albert Smith. He found that in the copying of the parts the whole play had been reduced to 'insufferable nonsense'. He put this right and could not resist waiting for the first night at the Lyceum. It went very well and the house accorded him an ovation.

During this short visit he had to wrestle with his brother Frederick who was anxious to marry Christiana Weller's sister. In spite of stiff opposition by the families on both sides the wedding took place two years later and turned out disastrously. He also found time to swoop on Gore House for 'a heart-to-heart talk' with Lady Blessington. Charley was a spectator at this dinner, and in his Reminiscences says:

As we sat down to dinner there was a vacant chair next to mine. 'It is only the Prince,' explained Lady Blessington to my father, 'he is always late,' and indeed some minutes passed before a sallow, rather sullen, heavy-looking man came in and after kissing Lady Blessington's hand and taking very little notice of the rest of the company, who, for their part, seemed to be content to take very little notice of him, sat down by my side. The newcomer took very little part in the general conversation, but talked to me pleasantly enough about my school life and recent stay in Paris, and then very soon after dinner after an interval of moody silence took himself off.

Charley's father also watched the man he had so often seen there 'biding his time', the man who through circumstance had assumed a new significance, the self-contained, reticent person nicknamed Prince Taciturn, soon to be the ruler of France.

Returning to the family for Christmas he resolved to shut himself up in order to write, but found it extremely difficult to refuse the invitations of Mrs. Norton's brother, Charles Sheridan, and, of course, he could not shirk entertaining the Watsons who arrived in Paris for the New Year. With Lord Normanby, the British ambassador, he also dined; their friendship was of old standing and they had a constant link in Lord Mulgrave with whom Dickens had crossed the Atlantic five years earlier. Though the ambassador was informal and friendly in private intercourse, he seemed harassed by the political situation and weighed down by responsibility and apprehension about the future. Louis Philippe's reign was tottering to an inglorious close and it was his duty to report to his government every fluctuation in the political barometer. Was monarchy doomed in France, and if so what president would or could take over supreme authority? Those of us who have read Lord Normanby's memoirs and official reports may see expressed in them an intelligent observer's reactions to events. Our policy at the moment was far from rigid. Palmerston as Foreign Secretary (in Lord John Russell's government) in writing to Lord Normanby had laid down,

'Our principles of action are to acknowledge whatever rule may be established with apparent prospect of permanency, but none other'.

Dickens at this time was going to the opera so frequently and dining out so constantly that he began to wonder whether he had ever had anything to do with a book called *Dombey* or ever sat over a chapter of it day after day until he began to think it the only reality in life and to mistake all the realities. for short-lived shadows. Sometime he jerked himself into refusing an invitation. For instance, when Lord Albert Conyngham invited him to a masked ball he declined the invitation as it 'would play the very devil with my to-morrow's occupation'. Paul Dombey was about to die and Dickens was miserable, his head ached; he says he took 'prodigious pains' over the child's end. When it was over he wrote to Miss Coutts: 'Between ourselves, Paul is dead. He died on Friday night about ten o'clock and as I had no hope of getting to sleep afterwards I went out and walked about Paris until breakfast next morning.' How could any-one combine moods of this kind, moods necessary to creation, with the routine of dining out? As it was, the printers found he had underwritten *Dombey* by two pages, and he had to hurry over to London to make good the deficiency.

We shall see when we come to examine the novel in detail how differently it was received by different readers. Henry Hallam, writing to Mrs. Brookfield, said: 'Everybody is pre-tending that the death of Paul Dombey is the most beautiful thing ever written. Milnes, Thackeray, and your uncle own to tears. I am so hardened as to be unable to look on it in any light but pure business.' Thackeray strode into the *Punch* office, and, flinging down his number on Mark Lemon's desk, said, 'There's no writing against this, one hasn't an atom of a chance; it's stupendous'. The Dickens family felt out in the cold. 'I am certain', Charley was in the habit of saying, 'that the children of my father's brain were much more real to him at times than we were.'

Forster joined his friend in Paris on the day of Paul's death. The climax reached, Dickens was only too thankful to put work aside to entertain 'Fuz'. The two friends spent an exciting fortnight together, going to a play each night and consorting with authors, actors and such celebrities as were accessible to visitors. The aged Chateaubriand was one of the great figures to whom they paid homage, but the author of *Les Mémoires d'outre-tombe* was an ailing man, and Dickens, having but little in common with him, was hard put to it to find subjects of conversation. It was easier to get on with Alphonse de Lamartine whom he had learned to like at Albaro. Madame de Lamartine's salon was a meeting-ground for foreigners, she herself being English. With Alexandre Dumas, Eugène Sue, Théophile Gautier, Alphonse Karr and Amédée Pichot Dickens conversed, for he now spoke, as Lamartine tells us, fluent French though with a heavy English accent. Macready's friend Régnier gave him the freedom of the green room at the Français where on Molière's birthday he saw his *Don Juan* revived.

The Frenchman who made the greatest impression on Dickens was Victor Hugo. Not only was he the most influential literary figure of the day, but also, as Louis Philippe had recently made him a peer of France, the political man of the moment. Dickens describes him as under middle height with pale face and an intense sweetness of expression combined with keen intellectuality. He spoke warmly of the English and their literature and showed a flattering appreciation of the works of 'Boz'. Writing to Lady Blessington[1] in the afterglow of his wonderful visit Dickens says that the home of Hugo was crowded with armour, tapestries, coffers; it was not an ordinary apartment, it was more like 'an old palace wherein old golden lions played at skittles with ponderous old golden balls'. The romantic setting seemed more like a chapter from one of his books than the furnishings of real life. It interested Dickens very much to hear that Madame Hugo was loved by Sainte-Beuve and Julie Drouet,

[1] January 24, 1847.

CHARLES DICKENS

the actress, by Victor Hugo, and that no one of their friends took these arrangements amiss.

The author of *Hernani*, *Ruy Blas*, *Lucrezia Borgia*, those operas without music, at this time a man of forty-five, was living on the first floor of 37 rue de la Tour d'Auvergne, a big solitary house backing on to the Palais-Royal with windows looking out over a panorama of Paris. By way of a deserted courtyard one approached the flight of steps that led to the door of an apartment crammed with antique treasures. So great a variety of objects could not be grasped all in a moment. Cordova leather adorned the walls of the *salle d'attente*, Gothic tapestry, and folios standing on lecterns, an anteroom. The salon with its blue damask walls, its Venetian negroes, its white satin upholstery, its bust by David, its glass pictures, made a sumptuous impression. So did the dining-room with its carved oak, gleaming lustre-ware, tapestry and glass 'all assembled', as Théophile Gautier says, 'by the patient fantasy of the poet'. To Dickens the scene resembled 'some gloomy vast old theatre' or some equally gloomy vast curiosity shop. 'I was much struck', he told Lady Blessington, 'by Hugo himself, who looks like a genius as he is every inch of him, and very interesting and satisfactory from head to foot.' The antique setting Victor Hugo had chosen for himself was in no way indicative of a conservative temper. He was already at work on *Les Misérables*, that epic novel on the sufferings of the poor, and he had already declared for a League of Nations and a Republican United States of Europe.

Most of the contacts made by Dickens in Paris during this visit were with men of letters and of the theatre. He did not meet their wives or go to their houses. It was not till nine years later, after two French-talking summers at Boulogne, that he was able to take his place as *grand écrivain* at the parties of George Sand, Madame Viardot, Madame Scribe and Madame Scheffer. By then his novels had been serialised in *Le Moniteur* and were so widely read that compliments were showered on him by shopkeepers and hotel clerks.

At this time Kate was unable to accompany him on excursions to the environs and Georgy was his constant companion. As the new baby was expected in April Dickens, though his own house was still in the possession of Sir James Duke, transported his family to London in March. This necessitated his renting a furnished house, 3 Chester Place, where a fifth son, Sydney Smith Haldimand, was born.

Just at this time (1847) Lord Jeffrey bobbed up again with inquiries about Dickens's earnings and on receiving a full statement wrote, 'I am rather disappointed I must own, to find your *embankment* still so small'. He really cannot make out why this should be, as the public had paid at least £100,000 for his books. Is it due to mismanagement? improvident arrangement with publishers? or careless control of their proceedings? His young friend must secure *independence* though he is far from 'grudging him the elegancies and indulgences suitable to his tasteful liberal nature'. He feels paternal anxiety on Dickens's behalf—or will his young friend call it the caution of senility? He is not in any way a father confessor, but he would dearly like to know whether Dickens has ever felt the promptings of prudent avarice, pride of purse or the like? Dickens answered the questions for a while, but as Jeffrey continued to importune him with a kind of cross-examination he stopped replying to his letters. A year later we find Jeffrey writing that as he is the godfather of a Dickens child he does not wish to 'grow quite out of acquaintance'. 'You really must take a little notice of me now and then.' In the month of his death, January 1850, he informed Dickens, 'Living or dying, I retain for you, unbated and unimpaired, the same cordial feelings of love, gratitude and admiration as for these many years past'.[1]

Just at the time *Dombey and Son* was coming out in its green covers *Vanity Fair* was being issued in yellow covers and there was a kind of rivalry between the books, though *Vanity Fair* only sold 7000 as against *Dombey's* 25,000. Carlyle spoke of the relief he found it to turn from Thackeray's 'terrible cynicism' to the cheerful geniality of Dickens. He

[1] *The Dickens Circle*, p. 432.

preferred Charles Dickens to Thackeray as a man, for Dickens always treated him with deference whereas Thackeray would oppose his opinions or even 'practise persiflage on him'. The name of Thackeray was really unknown to the British public as he had chosen hitherto to write as 'Michael-Angelo Titmarsh'. *Catherine*, *Barry Lyndon* and the *Snob Papers* for *Punch* were published under this name.

Abraham Hayward, writing to Thackeray about *Vanity Fair*, said:[1] 'Don't get nervous or think about criticism or trouble yourself about the opinion of friends; you have completely beaten Dickens out of the inner circle already'. Mrs. Carlyle wrote in the same strain: 'Very good indeed. Beats Dickens out of the world.' Thackeray laughed and forwarded the letters to Mrs. Brookfield.

Early in 1847 Thackeray wrote some parodies on contemporary writers entitled *Punch's Prize Novelists*. In April appeared 'George de Barnewell' (Bulwer Lytton), then 'Codlinsby' (Disraeli). These were to be followed by some kind of a 'Boz' skit, but the proprietors of *Punch* (Bradbury and Evans) would not permit such an outrage. It is certain that Dickens intervened on his own behalf.[2] In a way he was easy game for a parodist, as Anthony Trollope, in *The Warden*, was to show.

[1] November 1847. [2] 80. 35. D.

Chapter 16

THEATRICALS

Man is an embodied paradox, a bundle of contradictions.
C. C. COLTON

DURING the three months now spent at Chester Place Dickens worked steadily at *Dombey and Son* and dined out more than he had ever done. Sometimes he went out as a bachelor and sometimes with Georgina, who, as a companion, suited him better and better. By this time she was twenty-one and had become more sure of her power to charm and amuse: the tears literally ran down Charles's cheeks when she started mimicking the people they met. Entries in diaries show that during the weeks after the birth of Sydney Smith, Charles and Georgy were always about together. One night it would be a dinner with Forster to meet the Macreadys, Régniers, Stanfield and Maclise, and another night it would be a dinner-party at Chester Place for a play. Lord Ellesmere's rhymed translation of *Hernani* was being presented with Fanny Kemble in the principal part (a part in which she had played sixteen years earlier at Bridgewater House). In Dickens's box at the St. James's Theatre sat the Régniers, Harrison Ainsworth, Maclise, Jerrold and Stanfield. Two evenings later Charles and Georgy, Forster, Maclise and the Régniers dined together again in the company of Landor. As soon as Mrs. Dickens was about again, her husband took her to a large party at the Macreadys' to meet the Lord Advocate and Mrs. Rutherford, Mr. and Mrs. Carlyle, Eastlake, Panizzi, Rogers, Miss Jewsbury, Edwin Landseer and Jenny Lind. These dinners now formed the natural conclusion of Dickens's writing day, a day that often lasted from six to eight hours. Before transporting his family to Broadstairs at the end of June, Charles and Kate dined with the Douglas Jerrolds at Putney Heath where once again the

Macreadys and Maclise turned up; this time they foregathered
to meet the perennially penniless Leigh Hunt for whom they
were devising a benefit performance. Hardly had their plans
been perfected than Lord John Russell to some extent fore-
stalled them by giving Leigh Hunt a Civil List pension of
£200 a year. This caused the would-be helpers to abandon
all idea of playing *The Merry Wives of Windsor* in London,
but to implement their scheme for paying off Leigh Hunt's
debts by giving performances of another play in Manchester
and Liverpool only. For this purpose *Every Man in His
Humour* was revived and most of Dickens's original cast
rallied to his support, the only new names being those of
Augustus Egg and George Henry Lewes, at that time living
with his wife, later to become Mrs. Thornton Hunt. Rehearsals were carried on at Miss Kelly's Theatre with 'Boz' in
supreme control.

The company played at Manchester on July 26, where
Dickens delivered a prologue written by Talfourd, and at
Liverpool on July 28, when Forster spoke another prologue
composed by Bulwer Lytton. The tour was very good fun,
and the amateur company did themselves so handsomely that
though takings were good, clear profits amounted to but
£400. The meagreness of this sum set off against the energy
and time expended rather disappointed Dickens, who now
planned to add to it by writing a narrative of the tour. The
theme was suggested to him by the condition of Mrs. Leech,
who, touring with her husband, nearly had her baby in the
train and only just succeeded in reaching the Victoria Hotel,
Euston Square, before it was born. 'What a tremendous
chance', wrote Dickens to Mark Lemon, 'that Leech's little
girl was not born on the railway!' In 'Piljian's Projiss,[1] or
Mrs. Gamp and the Strollers' the humour and the character-
isation are alike heavy. Mr. Wilson the wigmaker and Mrs.
Gamp meet on the departure platform as the players assemble
and Mr. Wilson points out the celebrities. 'George the
Crookshank who draws for *Punch*' is one of them, and Mrs.

---

[1] Written August 1847, and preserved in Forster's *Life*.

Gamp says with a sniff 'which I never touches on account of
the lemon!' a joke involving another member of the cast,
Mark Lemon.   Frank Stone and Augustus Egg are explained
as 'well-beknow'd at the Academy as sure as stones is stones
and eggs is eggs'.   John Forster figures as 'a resolute gent,
apperrently going to take the railway by storm, his weskit
very much buttoned up, his mouth very much shut, his coat
a-flying open and his heels a-giving it to the platform'.   He
is quickly followed by Mrs. Gamp's 'beeograffer . . . a wild
gent that's been tearing up and down with a great box of
papers under his arm a-talking to everybody very indistinct
and exciting himself something dreadful'.   'That's the
Manager!' cries Mr. Wilson the wigmaker.

This is an aspect of Dickens's humour that appeals as little
to present-day readers as his Victorian treatment of birth and
death generally.   Perhaps it is just as well that 'Mrs. Gamp
and the Strollers' remained a rough sketch, as the dragging in
of characters from earlier books or rather their resuscitation—
of which Mr. Pickwick and Sam Weller in *Master Humphrey's
Clock* are examples—is not satisfactory.

Dickens seldom read the work of foreign writers, but oɪ
Hans Andersen's *Fairy Tales* he made an exception and they
were relegated at once into the class of 'special favourites' that
included the works of Washington Irving and Oliver Goldsmith.   The first man to introduce this Danish author to
English readers had been William Jerdan who, in his capacity
of editor of the *Literary Gazette*, was able to advertise his
merits.   In response to a complimentary letter sent to the
author he had received an effusion from Andersen expressing
love of English books and English authors, naming 'Scott,
Bulwer and Dickens' as among those he most cherished.

How much I should like to shake the hand of Boz [he
wrote].   When I read his books I often think I have seen
such things and feel I could write like that.   Do not misunderstand me. . . . I do not know how better to express
myself than to say that what completely captivates me seems

to become part of myself.   As the wind whistles round his bell-rope, I have often heard it whistle on a cold, wet autumn evening, and the chirp of the cricket I remember well in the cosy corner of my parents' humble room.

And so with Jerdan's encouragement, the fairy-tale teller began planning a visit to England.   The welcome prepared for him ensured that, as soon as he reached his hotel in Leicester Square, he should find himself an honorary member of the Athenaeum Club.   Calling on Count Reventlow, the Danish Minister, next morning, he was told he must present himself at Lord Palmerston's party that evening in order to be introduced to his English admirers.   Eagerly Hans Andersen asked whether he would meet Jenny Lind at the reception, but the Count could hold out no hopes that 'the Lind' would be there; she lived in retreat at Brompton, refusing all invitations, so if he really wanted to see her he must go to Brompton.   To Brompton he hied, and was greatly comforted to be received 'like a dear brother' and promised easy access to the opera house whenever he wished to go there.

At Lord Palmerston's house Andersen was overcome to find himself the centre of attraction, smiled on and complimented by ladies in sparkling tiaras and billowing satin gowns. Each looked to him a queen and each had something ravishing to say about his tales.   When his English gave out, he took refuge with his revered patron, the Duke of Saxe-Weimar, and talked to him in German.   Andersen thought the English women around him 'flower-like and lovely', and at Lady Paulet's ball, given to celebrate Queen Victoria's birthday, he described them 'standing like rose-petals in the press'. Vainly at these parties did he crane his neck looking for 'Boz': there was no 'Boz' to be seen.   William Jerdan told him that Dickens was with his family at Broadstairs, and that Lady Blessington was contriving a meeting for the two authors at Gore House.   No less anxious to meet Andersen than Andersen was to meet 'Boz', Dickens had written to Lady Blessington 'I *must* see Andersen', and she at once made

it her business to see that he did so.   To the Duke of Saxe-
Weimar Andersen wrote of this happy meeting:

> At Lady Blessington's I made the acquaintance of
> Dickens. . . . He is just what I thought he would be.   We
> understood each other at once, clasped each other's hands
> and talked English—I unfortunately not well, but as I said
> before we understood each other.[1]

The Dane, who was accustomed to very simple surroundings at home, found the Gore House hospitality over-
whelmingly palatial.   His host, Count d'Orsay, tried to put
him at his ease by rallying him in a 'very jolly' way, and he was
allowed to admire in silence all the 'very fine' flowers, pictures
and statues.   A second meeting grew out of the first, and this
time Dickens brought with him to Gore House a set of his
books, each volume inscribed 'To Hans Christian Andersen
from his friend and admirer Charles Dickens'.   He also
warmly invited him to come and share 'the crowded family
life' at Broadstairs.

Andersen spoke in enthusiastic but limited terms to
Dickens and Jerdan of the English literature that had 'enriched his fancy and filled his heart'.   Those who have read
his biographical sketch, *The Improvisatore*, will remember
how as a little boy he made his dolls perform Shakespeare's
tragedies in a toy theatre, and how on first arriving in Copenhagen he would spend his few pennies in getting a Scott novel
and, while reading it, would forget hunger and cold.   Stories
of this kind show that Hans Andersen was in the true tradition
of those who lead the inner life of imaginative authors, for
whom the world is the shadow show and the life of the mind
the only reality.   Dickens, too, understood this life very
well, for, when he was clothing his imperishable figures in
flesh, the world in which his own body moved became remote
and insubstantial.

Just before recrossing the channel Hans Andersen dined

[1] For this and other excerpts see F. Crawford, *Correspondence with Grand
Duke of Saxe-Weimar, Dickens*, etc., 1891.

with Dickens at Broadstairs and next morning his host walked over to Ramsgate to see his boat leave. Andersen recorded the farewell:

> We pressed each other's hands and he looked at me so kindly with his shrewd sympathetic eyes, and, as the ship went off, there he stood waving his hat and looking so gallant, so youthful and so handsome. Dickens was the last who sent me a greeting from dear England's shore.

No one could say that gawky, easily confused Hans Andersen had ever looked young, though equally no one could say he had ever grown up. From the financial angle his visit was a success, for Bentley, with whom he had stayed in Kent, arranged to publish seven of his fairy tales as *A Christmas Greeting to my English Friends*, and fourteen of his new stories under the title *A Poet's Day Dreams*. The latter volume was dedicated to Dickens.

> I feel a desire, a longing to transplant in England the first produce of my poetic garden as a Christmas greeting and I send it to you, my dear noble Charles Dickens, who by your works have been previously dear to me and since our meeting have taken root in my heart.

During the ten years that went by before Hans Andersen revisited England, he kept up a desultory correspondence with Dickens. None of these letters have survived, save a note in which Dickens assures him that he lives fresh in his remembrance and that everyone is asking when he is going to make everyone happier and better by writing a new book. 'We feel jealous of Stockholm and jealous of Finland and we say that you ought to be at home and nowhere else with a quill in your hand and a goodly pile of paper before you.'

The Dickens family remained at Broadstairs till early in September 1847 and then reinstalled themselves in Devonshire Terrace, of which they had but two years further lease. Dickens had waited with some impatience to regain possession of his own house, for in Broadstairs, unless it was pouring

with rain, he could not get half an hour's peace to work on
Dombey. The place had become an inferno of excruciating
organs, fiddles, bells and glee-singers. He now had no
worries about money, for *Dombey* was selling far in excess of
what he had anticipated. 'The profits of the half-year are
brilliant. Deducting the hundred pounds a month paid six
times, I have still to receive two thousand two hundred and
twenty pounds, which I think tidy.'

The autumn simply flew by at Devonshire Terrace.
Dombey absorbed most of Dickens's waking hours and on
account of *Dombey* he postponed for a twelvemonth the
writing of a Christmas story, *The Haunted Man*. He spoke
at Leeds on December 1 at the Mechanics' Institute, and was
rather surprised at the giant advertisements of his lecture that
met his eyes in the streets. Speaking with a heavy cold on
him, he said he looked to Institutions such as this to refine
and improve the social edifice. He rejoiced to see in the
report that French and German were being taught as well
as drawing and chemistry. 'The Creator having breathed a
mind into men must have intended them to be educated.'
These words evoked a warm response.

A domestic Christmas was followed by a journey to
Scotland with Kate to open the new Athenaeum in Glasgow.
He had promised to speak on 'the friendships we make with
books'. As they were travelling to Glasgow by rail from
Edinburgh Kate was taken suddenly ill with a miscarriage
and could not attend the meeting, at which Charles praised
Athenaeums in general, partly because they were initiated by
working men and partly because they aimed high in teaching
Spanish, Italian, French and German as well as music, mathematics and logic. He ended his speech by hoping that money
for more books would soon be raised. Mr. Alison proposed
an enthusiastically supported vote of thanks. In writing an
account of this occasion to Georgy, Charles casually mentioned Kate's mishap and then described the packed meeting
at which 'the Inimitable did wonders. His grace, elegance,
and eloquence enchanted all beholders.' Whenever he uses

the word 'Inimitable' we know that he is in the highest spirits, and it is no surprise to find him telling Georgy, 'I have never enjoyed myself more completely'. They were staying with the Alisons who, Dickens tells us, lived 'in style' in a handsome country house outside Glasgow with everything very pleasant about them. Kate was kept in bed and Dickens, 'treated as a person of great distinction', ate a 'gorgeous state lunch with the Lord Provost and City Council' and was entertained at a banquet in the evening. After two nights Kate was supposed to be well enough to travel, but she collapsed in Edinburgh and had to take to her bed again. This gave Dickens the opportunity of sightseeing and of a good gossip with Lord Jeffrey. Macaulay had just lost his seat in the House of Commons and people said no one else could possibly have lost it, and that he had gone out of his way to be disagreeable and get himself disliked. He also heard from Lord Jeffrey that Sheridan Knowles, the author of two highly successful plays, *Virginius* and *The Hunchback*, had just made a declaration of bankruptcy before him. Easily moved to compassion by the troubles of authors, Dickens at once cast about him for ways and means of help-ing the poor fellow. There was a scheme afoot for buying Shakespeare's house at Stratford-on-Avon in order to pre-serve it as a national monument. He had attended the committee called by Payne Collier in August at the Thatched House Tavern in St. James's Street, and now discussed with Lord Jeffrey the possibility of installing Knowles at Stratford as curator, but, as his friend drily observed, Sheridan Knowles quite recently had rather compromised his position as a literary figure by having become a Baptist minister. This might well prove an obstacle to his appointment as custodian of a literary shrine.

Dickens's sightseeing centred on Sir Walter Scott. Lord Jeffrey showed him the memorial, which seemed to him 'like the spire of a Gothic church taken off and stuck in the ground'; Abbotsford was also inspected, and there he was shocked by 'the vile glass case' containing the clothes last

worn by Sir Walter. It depressed him deeply to be shown
an old white hat 'tumbled and bent and broken by the uneasy,
purposeless wandering hither and thither of his heavy head.
It so embodied Lockhart's pathetic description of him, when
he tried to write and laid down his pen and cried, that it
associated itself in my mind with broken powers and mental
weakness.' Clothes, both his own and other people's,
always meant a great deal to Dickens, and one calls to mind
his insistence to Cattermole on the pathos to be conveyed to
readers by Nell's bonnet and shawl. Clothes affect some
people in a very peculiar way and Dickens was particularly
sensitive in his reactions to their appeal.

On returning to London he found that the Borough
Council of Stratford-on-Avon had made themselves responsible for the purchase and conservation of the Shakespeare House, so he concentrated on collecting money to
endow a curatorship. Even if Knowles did not directly
benefit, some other writer might be chosen for the post.
Jumping at once to the idea of a theatrical production, he
summoned his cast together to choose a play. He was very
bright and lively on his return from Scotland, but the prospect
of acting was not the only cause of exhilaration, for the end
of *Dombey* was in sight and he had time to let his mind play
on other matters. The abdication of Louis Philippe, King
of the French, threw him into the wildest spirits. What
had happened to Lamartine? and what would d'Orsay do?
Forster (to whom he talked) said that now, of course, d'Orsay
would rush back to Paris. 'But not at all,' retorted Dickens,
'Monsieur le Comte is still giving dinners at Gore House!'
The explosion of democracy in France went so completely to
his head that he declared he would renounce his native tongue
for 'the language of gods and of angels'. Vive la France!
Vive le Peuple! Plus de Royauté! Plus de Bourbons!
Plus de Guizot! Voilà les sentiments du citoyen Charles
Dickens! Historian friends of his were also convulsed by
the news. Henry Hallam ate no breakfast and paced up and
down his dining-room, an empty plate pressed against his

heart, and Carlyle wrote in his journal, 'Louis Philippe is flung out; he and his entire pack with a kind of exquisite irony driving off in a street cab!' What Dickens thought of the London repercussions we do not know; he does not allude to them in any letter of the date. But, absorbed as he was in concerns theatrical, he cannot have ignored the fact that when the Chartist petition was presented in April no private carriages were to be seen on the streets, or that the gates of Green Park and Constitution Hill were closed and the iron shutters of Apsley House bolted. Emerson, who was in London at the time, took notice of everything and made a point of attending the meeting convened by the Chartists in London to receive the report of the deputation they had sent to Paris to congratulate the French Republican Government. At this gathering the 'Marseillaise' was as lustily sung as at Abolition demonstrations in the United States. Like other intelligent Americans Emerson was horrified by the depths of tragic poverty revealed in the streets of Liverpool and London and, in view of the general smugness of the propertied classes, it was hardly possible to believe such miseries could be terminated without a revolution. Emerson, on Carlyle's advice, went on to Paris to see how things were for himself and found all the enthusiasts for the new regime 'bearded like goats and lions'. Having satisfied his curiosity, he returned to London to deliver six lectures at the Portman Square Literary and Scientific Institution on the Laws of Thought, Politics and Socialism, Poetry and Eloquence, and kindred subjects.

Though Emerson had come to London in October 1847, Dickens did not play any part in welcoming him. He was the house-guest of the Carlyles and the particular charge of Mrs. George Bancroft, who took him to see Rogers and other men of letters before he set out for the north to deliver the lectures that were the reason for his coming to England. In this connection one may mention that George Bancroft, the Harvard historian, had been appointed minister to the Court of St. James in 1846. He had, as we know, been a kind friend to Dickens during the American tour, but now he saw nothing of him and there is no allusion to him in the many available letters of this date. It is doubtful whether any Bostonian wished to see much of the writer of *Martin Chuzzlewit*. It was not till Bancroft was on the point of leaving for America a year later that an entry appears in his diary for April 19, 1849, 'Dine at Mr. Charles Dickens'. On May 8 he returned the civility by asking Dickens to breakfast in company with the Duke of Argyll, Hallam, Macaulay, Milman, Bunsen and Frothingham. There was no resumption at any time of the friendliness generated in Boston in 1842.

On May 4, 1848, Forster, at Dickens's request, invited him to meet Emerson at his rooms in Lincoln's Inn Fields. Carlyle was also of the party of four and was greeted by his host in a stentorian voice as 'My Prophet!' which surprised the American guest. The conversation turned on the shameful lewdness of the London streets and Carlyle had a good deal to say about whoredom generally and the wickedness of our so-called civilisation. Carlyle said that chastity in the male sex was as good as gone and Dickens endorsed this opinion. Emerson protested that it was quite otherwise in America and that men of good understanding and education went to their nuptial bed as virgin as did their brides.[1] Dickens replied that incontinence was so much the rule in England that if his own son were particularly chaste, he should be alarmed on his account as if he could not be in good health. Emerson's heart did not go out to garrulous Dickens as it had done to the sensible, quiet-mannered Alfred Tennyson with whom he had had such charming talks.

The play chosen for the Shakespeare Curatorship Fund was *The Merry Wives of Windsor* and it was to be followed by *Animal Magnetism, Love, Law and Physic, A Good Night's Rest* or some other farce. Most of the old cast took parts and there was one important newcomer, Mrs. Cowden Clarke, who asked to be allowed to play Dame Quickly to Dickens's

[1] R. W. Emerson, *Journals*, vol. vii. p. 441.

Master Shallow. She found Dickens a very businesslike
stage manager. He usually sat at a small table to one side of
the stage and sometimes would stand with back to the footlights to watch entries and exits. The amateurs opened their
series of nine performances at the Haymarket on April 15 and,
after visiting Manchester, Liverpool, Birmingham and Edinburgh, ended it in Glasgow on July 20. The announcement
for the first night ran as follows:

THEATRE ROYAL, HAYMARKET

AMATEUR PERFORMANCE

in aid of

THE FUND FOR THE ENDOWMENT OF A PERPETUAL
CURATORSHIP OF SHAKESPEARE'S HOUSE

> To be always held by some one distinguished
> in Literature and more especially in Dramatic
> Literature, the profits of which it is the in-
> tention of the Shakespeare House Committee
> to keep entirely separate from the Fund now
> being raised for the purchase of the House.

Directors of Arrangements: John Payne Collier,
Charles Knight, Peter Cunningham, and the London
Shakespeare House Committee.

Stage Manager: Mr. Charles Dickens.

Evening dress in all parts of the House.

The Carlyles took seats for this performance and Mr. Carlyle
watched Dame Quickly's performance with great interest.
When the curtain went down Carlyle was heard to say, 'A
poor play, but *plaudite, plaudite!*' In Mrs. Cowden Clarke
we have a better chronicler[1] than Mrs. Gamp, for her recollections are natural and charmingly expressed. She and
her sister, Emma Novello, accompanied the troupe on tour
and always travelled in the same compartment as Mr. and Mrs.
Dickens and Mark Lemon. Dickens made a habit of getting
to the station early and greeting his 'strollers' as they turned

[1] C. and M. Cowden Clarke, *Recollections of Writers.*

GEORGINA HOGARTH (circa 1850)
by Augustus Egg, R.A.

" My little housekeeper Miss Hogarth "

CHARLES DICKENS, AGED 46
by W. P. Frith, R.A.

up with 'a beaming look', which affected the railway officials
so benignly that they took every possible care of his whole
company.   Mrs. Clarke goes on to tell of

> the delightful gaiety and sprightliness of our manager's
> talk, the endless stories he told us, the games he mentioned
> and how they were played.   The bright amenity of his
> name at various stations when he showed to persons in
> authority the free pass-ticket which had been previously
> given in homage to Charles Dickens and his party.   The
> courteous alacrity with which he jumped out at one
> refreshment room to procure food for somebody who
> complained of hunger. . . . His indefatigable vivacity,
> cheeriness and good humour from morning to night, all
> were delightful.

The way in which he acted amused her very much:

> In *Love, Law and Physic* he used to tuck me under his
> arm with the free and easy familiarity of a lawyer patronis-
> ing an actress whom he chances to find his fellow traveller
> in a stage coach. . . . It is something to remember having
> been tucked under the arm by Charles Dickens and had
> one's hand hugged against the side! one thinks better of
> one's hand ever after.

And it was not only on tour that she found the company of
Dickens delightful; she also loved going informally to the
house in Devonshire Terrace and being treated as one of the
family.   Altogether she outlines one of the most attractive
pictures of Dickens that has survived.   Charles, to her
thinking, showed up well in his own family, especially with
the smallest children, and she looked on it as a much enjoyed
privilege to be allowed to share the intimate life of his home.

> On one of the quiet occasions [she writes] when Mr. and
> Mrs. Dickens, their children and their few guests were
> sitting out of doors in the small garden in front of their
> Devonshire Terrace house enjoying the first warm summer
> evening I recollect seeing one of the little sons draw
> Dickens apart and stand in eager talk with him. [Dickens
> a few minutes later told her what the child wanted.] 'The

L

little fellow gave me so many excellent reasons why he
should not go to bed so soon that I yielded the point and
let him stay up half an hour later.'

All this to her was far more delightful than being bidden to
one of the 'brilliant dinners' at Devonshire Terrace, dinners
at which large companies assembled and everything was done
in 'superb style with a bouquet of flowers beside the plate of
each lady present'.   Sometimes she dined alone with them
before the opera, for which Miss Burdett Coutts often lent
them her box.   It was a great treat to be taken to hear Jenny
Lind in *La Sonnambula* by Mrs. Dickens, to whom she became very much attached.   Kate at this time was in great
good looks and made an elegant figure in clothes of the latest
fashion.   Maclise's third portrait of her conveys a distinctly
mondaine impression.

Just before Dickens moved to Broadstairs in the late
summer he made an excursion down the Thames evidently in
high spirits and in holiday mood.   He had several reasons for
being pleased: the sales of *Dombey* for one, and the success of
the theatrical tour for another.   The total realised, when all
expenses had been deducted, was £2551, of which Sheridan
Knowles received a share and John Poole, author of *Paul Pry*,
a lesser share.   As we have learnt, Knowles had already been
assisted with a Civil List pension, and now Poole was also
allocated an income by the ever sympathetic Lord John
Russell.   With the money provided by Dickens they could
now pay their debts and make a fresh start.   It was a very
satisfying reflection to the contriver of the theatrical scheme.

Dickens was always fond of down-river and up-hill excursions as his many journeys to Greenwich and Hampstead
testify.   This summer he went to look for a Chinese ship
reported to be moored in the Thames near Blackwall Tunnel.
In a casual letter to Forster (afterwards expanded into an
article for the *Examiner*) he described what he had seen and
what he advised his readers to do.   They should drive down
to the Blackwall railway, where, for a matter of eighteen-

pence, any one of them can reach the heart of the Chinese Empire in no time. 'In half a score of minutes the tiles and chimney pots, backs of squalid houses, frowsy pieces of waste ground, narrow courts and streets, swamps, ditches, masts of ships, gardens of duckweed and unwholesome little bowers of scarlet beans, whirl away in a flying dream and nothing is left but China.'

Gingerly he climbed aboard, wondering at the frailty of the craft that was so unlike a ship of any kind.

> So narrow, so long, so grotesque; so low—in the middle; so high at each end, like a Chinese pen-tray; with no rigging, with nowhere to go aloft; with mats for sails, great warped cigars for masts, gaudy dragons and sea-monsters disporting themselves from stem to stern and in the stern a gigantic cock of impossible aspect defying the world. . . .

And then the Chinese figures lounging on deck, who on earth could guess them to be mariners?

> Imagine a ship's crew, without a profile among them, in gauze pinafores and plaited hair; wearing stiff clogs a quarter of a foot thick in the sole; and lying at night in little scented boxes like backgammon men or chess-pieces, or mother of pearl counters.

More surprising was the cabin with its swinging lanterns, its figure of Chin Tee of the eighteen arms curtained in a celestial Punch's show; the threads of smoke from joss-sticks, the tissue umbrella. Dickens wondered what would happen in a storm at sea. Would all the cool and shiny little chairs and tables continually slide and break each other, and if not why not? And the Mandarin passenger, what was he think-ing about as he lay sick on a bamboo couch in a private china closet of his own signing autographs for curious visitors? Would he or anybody else on the voyage ever read those two books printed in characters like bird-cages and fly-traps? There was matter enough for reflection in this vision of a static civilisation. 'Finality in perfection', he called it, and commented, 'no blade of experience grown in centuries, what

a contrast was the perfect junk with all its exquisiteness to the
river it floated in'. And yet to English minds the river-
banks were mighty in their signs of life, enterprise and progress. One might look at it that way or one might take it
in another way, and Dickens was most struck, not by the
signs of progress, but by the mimic eyes painted on the prow
of the junk to help it find its course across the seas, and could
not but ask himself whether we ourselves do not grope along
relying on conventional eyes that have no sight in them.
The cameo-like quality of this sketch is an example of that
singleness of sight which enabled him on occasions to achieve
effects with a true economy of words. Parallel effects are to
be found scattered through all his books: an exemplary paragraph from *David Copperfield* reads thus:

> The water was out over the flat country, and every sheet
> and puddle lashed its banks, and had its stress of little
> breakers. When we came within sight of the sea, the
> waves on the horizon, caught at intervals above the boiling
> abyss, were like glimpses of another shore. . . . The people
> came to their doors all aslant and with streaming hair.

'If thine eye be single, thy whole body shall be full of light'
is a text of special application to writers. Dickens's eye was
not always single. It was, as Taine discovered, sometimes
multiple, which may be why, in spite of felicitous examples of
perfect prose, we have to admit that in the main the body of
his work is styleless. His extraordinary fertility of invention
often got in his way. Pullulating with power and variety,
he was constrained to surrender himself to life as it poured
through his brain. For a serial worker there was no time to
do otherwise.

Chapter 17

HOUSEHOLD WORDS

Nullum magnum ingenium sine melancolia.

IN the desultory frame of mind induced by holiday-making with the family at Broadstairs, Dickens could not apply himself to serious novel-writing. Instead, he snatched at the opening given him by Cruikshank's shilling sets of plates, 'The Bottle' and 'The Drunkard's Children', to preach on temperance.[1] Drunkenness to him had always been 'the great national horror', but Cruikshank's plates would do no good at all; why, even Hogarth had not ventured to depict the progress of a drunkard because he knew that the causes of drunkenness lay so 'far down in sorrowfulness and human misery' that he could never bring them 'fairly and justly into the light'. The real origin of the vice was to be found in the desire to forget 'disgusting habitations, bad workshops, scarcity of light, air and water'. In fact 'the disastrous condition of England' was at fault, and it was folly to preach against the gin-shop when the conditions of existence made the gin-shop irresistible. His deep desire to change English life and to get rid of complacency and shams made Dickens long for a pulpit from which to expound his ideas of reform. This pulpit he was eventually to construct for himself in *Household Words*, a magazine intended to find its way into all the poorer houses in the land.

Before planning to carry out this scheme, he had to fulfil his pledge to produce another Christmas book and another full-size novel. To write the Christmas book, which had been simmering in his head for a long time, he went to Brighton and there conjured up another Scrooge in Mr. Redlaw and another Cratchit family in the Swidgers, with the Tetterby's and their Moloch of a baby thrown in, as it were,

[1] *Examiner*, July 8, 1848.

for luck. Redlaw, a studious man, is haunted by painful memories of a great wrong done him in early life. Interviewed by a spectre, the presentment of his gloomy past, a kind of second self, he is offered the power to forget with the penalty attached that he will make everyone he meets oblivious not only of past unhappiness, but of kindnesses and benefits received. This gift turns out to be destructive of all human relationships, and the moral of this story, *The Haunted Man, or the Ghost's Bargain*, is that it is better not to seek forgetfulness. In less than a fortnight Bradbury and Evans got a letter from Brighton saying, 'I finished last night, I've been crying my eyes out over it, not painfully but pleasantly— these last three days'. Tenniel, Leech, Stanfield and Stone were at once called in to illustrate the little book, while Mark Lemon, to steal a march on the pirates, hurriedly dramatised it for the Keeleys to present at the Adelphi. Eighteen thousand copies were sold in the first week of publication, and the success was celebrated by a book-dinner at Devonshire Terrace.

The Haunted Man may be taken as a pointer to the way Dickens's mind had been working. He had sought by some stratagem to induce forgetfulness of his own past which held incidents he had never breathed a word of even to Kate. Having at the time of his engagement emerged victorious from a hard struggle to become independent, he had seen no reason to expose the details of his squalid upbringing to anyone. Respectability being the master-key to Victorian society, he must have thought his past connection with jails shaming and have believed that if people knew his story it would prejudice his chances of success, and cause him to sink in the esteem of the Hogarths. To the world he was just a successful journalist blossoming into a super-successful novelist and, as far as the people he entertained or associated with were concerned, had no past. This was not at all the way he felt about himself; he was desperately conscious of his past; it was for ever pushing itself forward in one way or another, and he was for ever pushing it back into what he hoped might be oblivion, but after wrestling with the problem in *The Haunted Man* he could promise himself no comfort in a ghost's bargain. It was quite a while before the idea of coaxing the past to display itself in all its hatefulness and humiliation and pinning it down on paper, as one pins butterflies to a setting board, occurred to him. Forster says that it was a chance question that put the notion into his mind. Dickens's belief that the secrets of his boyhood were unknown was shattered by a man called Dilke, a fellow clerk of his father's at Somerset House. Dilke one day inquired of Forster whether the little boy, Dickens, he had seen at Thomas Barrow's lodging in Gerard Street was not the famous 'Boz'. He then went on to say that he had once walked with John Dickens to a warehouse near the Strand, and had tipped a small boy, working there, half-a-crown and had received in return a very low bow. Forster at once asked Dickens whether he remembered Mr. Dilke. As no reply of any kind was forthcoming, his questioner judged that he must have put his finger on a sore spot. Weeks later, Dickens told Forster that he had unwittingly touched on a matter so painful that 'even to the present hour' he 'could never lose the remembrance of it while he remembered anything'. Soon after this talk he began to write down the account of that part of his childhood which hurt him most. The notion of writing a complete autobiography flitted across his mind, but he soon abandoned it in favour of using such parts of his manuscript as suited him in a new novel, the novel we know as *David Copperfield*. With Forster he now talked over many things he did not care to write about, and from time to time said, 'How much I suffered it is utterly beyond my power to tell'. The actual autobiographical material was only seen by Forster after his friend's death.

The fact that his parents, at the time of his worst humiliation, were living happily in the Marshalsea with 'every bodily comfort to hand' had made his own circumstances appear all the more forlorn. He had seen that they had money enough to live in the best prison style, but that they gave him no help until he insisted on getting himself lodged near enough to the prison to take meals with them. This callousness was for him an unforgivable offence. And even when they were released these same parents had made no immediate move to free him from servitude. But one happy day his father had given him a note to hand to James Lamert which, when read, made Lamert turn on him sharply saying it would now be impossible to keep him in the factory. 'With a relief so strange that it was like oppression, I went home', wrote Dickens in his confession; but from that hour till the hour of writing a quarter of a century later no word of his experience was ever breathed by him, and his parents remained as dumb as himself.

What exactly was it that made this facing up to the past so painful? Why did those six weeks spent in the blacking factory hurt so much in retrospect? Why did he mind the fact that his parents lived in the Marshalsea when he was able to make such good use of the Marshalsea in his books? Was he unusually sensitive? Was he peculiarly proud? Was he deeply ashamed of the discreditable hand-to-mouth existence in which his mother had involved him and in which she would have liked to keep him? Was he always measuring himself and his defective education against the more fortunately born friends he made? Was he consumed with self-pity? Was he in fact compartmented from the rest of the world?

The answer to those questions is to be found to some degree in all of us. There are certain things in our lives that, if we are sensitive, we never get used to, which, in other words, never become retrospective but are eternally present. I will give one instance from personal life. As a child of ten I was cleaning a box in which a dormouse lived, and in throwing the hay and food crumbs into the fire I emptied out the sleeping dormouse and heard its one squeak as it fell into the red heart of the coals. It is as vivid and horrifying to me now as it was decades ago, and it enables one to understand why Dickens's childhood never became retrospective, but remained an ever-present reality. The Beadnell romance and the death of Mary Hogarth fell into the same category of experience, for Dickens had in an extreme degree a faculty that we only have in a lesser degree. Because of it he never, in spite of all his warm friendships, his high spirits, his acting, his huge successes, was a truly happy man.

When beginning *David Copperfield*, Dickens had the usual difficulties in hitting on a good title. This time he began with 'Mag's Diversions' and ran through a gamut of 'Copperfield Disclosures', 'Copperfield Survey', 'Copperfield's Confessions', 'Copperfield's Entire', till he finally decided on the title we know.

The Devonshire Terrace household being keyed up over the imminent arrival of a new baby, Dickens ran down to Norwich on New Year's Eve 1848 to get his story started. Leech and Lemon accompanied him and they visited Stanfield Hall, scene of the murder of Isaac Jermy, Recorder of Norwich. To Dickens 'the place seemed to invite such a crime: it had a murderous look about it'. Before going on to Yarmouth he saw the jail in which the murderer Rush was imprisoned and the place of execution which 'we found fit for a gigantic scoundrel's exit'. At Yarmouth he bought a shawl of local make to take home to his wife. After an enjoyable walk to Lowestoft and back he returned to London on January 10. Having got himself into a writing mood he did not lose it even in the commotion caused by the birth of a sixth son, Henry Fielding, on January 13. Immersed in work, he accepted the event calmly, and carried on with his social life with Georgy at his side. At the end of January (1849) Forster and Dickens went as usual to Bath to dine with Landor on his birthday. In thanking them for this visit their host wrote, in his huge sprawling hand:

My thanks were not spoken to you and Dickens for your journey of two hundred miles upon my birthday. Here they are not visible upon the surface of the paper, nor on any surface whatever, but in the heart that is dictating this letter. On the night you left me I wrote the following:

DYING SPEECH OF AN OLD PHILOSOPHER

I strove with none for none were worth my strife.
Nature I loved, and next to Nature, Art;
I warmed both hands before the fire of Life;
It sinks and I am ready to depart.

On his return from Bath, Charles took Kate to Brighton as he always found it possible to work there and the bracing air was good for both of them. The first instalments of *David Copperfield* appeared in May 1849, and at a dinner the following month, at which Mrs. Gaskell, Thackeray, 'Phiz', Mr. and Mrs. Tagart and Mr. and Mrs. Carlyle were his guests in Devonshire Terrace, it delighted their host, when asking after Carlyle's health, to get the reply, 'I am a lone lorn creatur and everythink goes contrairy with me'. Mrs. Gummidge, like her forerunner Mrs. Gamp, was in a fair way to becoming a national figure.

In June he was working at top speed most of the day and in the evening walking about fields in the neighbourhood of London. One evening was spent with Professor Owen at Richmond. A rather faddy young man, Mountstuart Grant Duff, records meeting him there. Dickens struck him as 'singularly unprepossessing' and a little vulgar. This may have been because he was in an 'inimitable' mood and chattered away about Gore House, d'Orsay, and the 'squabbles' that went on at Holland House. There was, of course, every reason at the moment to talk about Gore House, for everyone had been to the auction there and it was estimated that 20,000 people had come to gape. Lady Blessington's friends had been observed as they walked round the rooms by d'Orsay's French valet, who wrote an account of the people he recognised. 'M. Thackeray est venu aussi; et avait les larmes aux yeux en parlant. C'est peut-être la seule personne que j'ai vue réellement affectée à votre départ.' It was one of the last letters Lady Blessington received before her death.

Dickens somehow managed to combine great social

activity with heavy work. Forster chronicles dinner-party after dinner-party at Devonshire Terrace this year. Besides the old stagers like the Macreadys, Sam Rogers, Edwin Landseer, Stanfield, Talfourd and Fonblanque, we find the names of Julius Benedict, Lord Strangford, the Procters, Sir James and Lady Graham, Mrs. Norton, Lady Dufferin, Lord and Lady Lovelace, the Milner Gibsons, Mowbray Morris and Horace Twiss and their wives, Lady Molesworth, Charles Babbage, the John Delanes, Isambard Brunels, Thomas Longmans, Lord Mulgrave, Lord Carlisle and others listed as guests. He also went about a great deal and everywhere his infectious high spirits made a success of almost any party. He was not above giving hosts the humblest assistance. John Millais, asked by a friend to describe 'the dance at Mrs. Collins's', says, 'It was a delightful evening . . . there were many lions, amongst others the famous Dickens, who came for about half an hour and officiated as principal carver'. At this time, whenever Dickens was held up over a chapter, he would run down to the sea for recreation. Near-by beaches having become noisy and crowded, he had to seek some more secluded place to which to migrate with the family in the summer. Rather opportunely, a clergyman friend, James White, who had retired from his profession to write Scottish historical tragedies in the Isle of Wight, offered to let him a house next his own at Bonchurch. At first sight Dickens fell in love with the place, the 'prettiest he had seen at home or abroad'. Conveying the family to this paradise, he rollicked through picnics at Shanklin, dinners at Blackgang Chine, and tea-parties in Lady Jane Swinburne's garden where his own youngsters played with a red-headed boy called Algernon. Till two o'clock each day he remained shut away writing, but in the afternoon laid himself out to amuse the children with excursions, games and conjuring tricks. Charley remembered continual outings and picnics. John Leech commemorated one of them in *Punch*, 'Awful appearance of wops at a picnic party'. Old friends like Talfourd, Leech or Browne, were bidden to share his enjoyment, but suddenly the rose-tinted glasses turned black; the life became 'hateful', and the place 'a mortal mistake'. Depressed and tearful, he found himself succumbing to a desire to sleep by day or waste precious hours in languor. He blamed the climate. Bonchurch was 'a smashing place', far more disagreeable than 'hot and dirty Naples', 'feverish New York', 'raving Paris' or 'exciting Genoa'. 'A year here and I should die of prostration', he gasped. To pacify himself he began to plan his magazine pulpit, now called 'the Dim Design', then, in a new state of intense irritation, suddenly whisked the entire family to the Albion Hotel, Broadstairs. There he recovered his spirits and finished the seventh number of *David Copperfield*.

In *Mr. Brown's Letters to a Young Man about Town* appearing in *Punch*, *David Copperfield* was highly commended: 'How beautiful it is . . . there are little words and phrases in his books that are like personal benefits to his readers'. The writer of *Mr. Brown's Letters* was Thackeray who was generous-spirited enough to tell a friend that 'the green chap had beaten the yellow chap of this month hollow'. And the yellow chap was *Pendennis*, his own autobiographical novel!

In November 1849 Charles went with Kate to Rockingham Castle to stay for the first time with the Watsons. He was very much impressed by its situation and 'its bastion-like entrance, dating from the days of King Stephen', but even more impressed by the great honour and consideration paid him by his host and hostess. He was in 'inimitable' form, got up theatricals, conjured and danced till three in the morning. With Mrs. Watson's cousin, Mary Boyle, he struck up a great friendship. Mary Boyle was two years older than Dickens, fair, blue-eyed, and only five feet high. The tradition in the Boyle family to this day is that Dickens was a naughty man to make love to great-aunt Mary. Like Dickens, Mary Boyle loved acting, and together they staged scenes from *The School for Scandal* and concocted a duologue from *Nicholas Nickleby*. Soon to become 'my dearest

Meery', this young woman was to prove a faithful friend and loving worshipper. To express her constancy to him, she arranged that buttonholes should be provided for him at every public reading and was clever enough to keep this up even during the second American tour. As she herself puts it, 'I now took the hand that for twenty successive years was ever ready to grasp mine in tender friendship and whose pressure still thrills my memory'.[1] It is always said that Dickens took his descriptions of Chesney Wold, the ancestral home of the Dedlocks, from 'green-hearted Rockingham', but *Bleak House* had yet to be written.

Meanwhile at the back of his mind 'the Dim Design' was taking shape. It had begun to define itself as a weekly magazine in which contributors, however distinguished, would be nameless. It would include a serial novel, good poetry, and essays on subjects 'such as knight-errantry, piracy, savages or the sangraal'. Associated with the publication would be 'a Shadow', who would know everything and would comment on everything. The 'Shadow' would haunt the London streets, the churches, the theatres, the prisons, the House of Commons itself: it would talk about what it saw and, when anything new or startling happened, it was hoped that people would wonder what the 'Shadow' would have to say about it. To Dickens it was 'an odd, unsubstantial whimsical new thing, a sort of previously unthought-of power going about . . . the "Thing" at everybody's shoulder'. He wondered whether the paper itself might not be called *The Shadow*. Forster thought this a silly idea and insisted that the word 'Household' should be incorporated in the title. *Household Words* was at last decided on and an office rented in Wellington Street, Strand. There, as his chief helper, was installed his former employee on the *Daily News*, W. H. Wills, an experienced man who had been assistant-editor of *Chambers's Journal* for three years (1842–5), and there, as editor, or as he preferred to call it, conductor, Dickens him-

[1] *Mary Boyle: Her Book*, p. 231.

self settled in to work. We have it from one of the staff, Garett Dumas, that the editor would arrive about 8 A.M. and dictate while pacing up and down the room. One of his tricks was to comb his hair on arrival, a process he repeated again and again, sometimes a hundred times in a morning. By 11 A.M. he had tired himself out and usually went off to the Garrick Club. The office book for *Household Words* shows that R. H. Horne was engaged at five guineas a week, but left after three months, and that both Charles Knight and G. A. Sala were contributors, as well as young George Meredith. It is clear that John Dickens and George Hogarth were also included on the permanent staff.[1] Half the magazine was the property of Dickens (who paid himself £500 a year as conductor); one-quarter was allocated to Bradbury and Evans; one-eighth to Forster; and one-eighth to Wills, who drew a salary of £8 a week. In time *Household Words* became a valuable property soon to be known as the training-ground for the rising generation of writers. On no one was Dickens's influence more stamped than on young Sala, the creator of the miscellaneous leader, the pen-and-ink impressionist doing sketches of Paris and later of Petersburg.

The first number, dated March 30, 1850, exuded in its foreword a matey, get-together spirit. The editors aspired to be the good comrade of persons of both sexes and all ages, a cherished member of every household in the land. The magazine announced itself as 'the gentle mouthpiece of reform'. Among its more immediate and practical objectives were the removal both of the paper tax and the light tax. It was hoped that through its agency greater and lesser folk would be brought to better acquaintance and kindlier understanding. All countries and nations were to be dealt with, 'for nothing can be a source of real interest to one that does not concern all the rest'. The editor thinks he can hear voices, 'encouraging voices', that say 'Go on!' and he responds, 'We go on cheerily!'

The editorial 'Word' is followed by the first chapter of

[1] March 6, 1850: letter to Wills.

Lizzie Lee by Mrs. Gaskell, a short and dismal serial opening with a Christmas corpse and this an Easter number!   In
true miscellany style, 'Valentine's Day at the Post Office',
'Abraham and the Fire Worshippers', 'The Amusements of
the People', 'Incident in the Life of Mademoiselle Clairon'
and a bundle of 'Emigrants' Letters' are included in the
number.   These items and others were printed in twenty-
four pages of double-column small type.   The presentation
was poor and the material makes dull reading, but if we refer
to contemporary opinion we shall find nothing but praise.
To Edmund Yates the first numbers of *Household Words*
appeared to be 'perfect models of what a magazine intended
for general reading should be'.   Dickens's own work was
considered 'admirable', the dawning Sala 'excellent', the
antiquarian lore of Peter Cunningham and Charles Knight
'interesting'.   Forster was praised for 'trenchant criticism',
Wilkie Collins for 'first fruits', Horne for his descriptive
powers, Adelaide Procter for her poetic pathos, Henry Spicer
for his odd humour and the 'Roving Englishman' for the
value of his observations.

Not altogether satisfied with his first number, Dickens tried
to infuse more sentiment into the second, for taking all in all
'the lay-out lacked heart'.   To make good this deficiency he
wrote *A Child's Dream of a Star* which he could make tender
because it concerned his newly dead sister, Fanny, with whom
as a child he had often wandered in a churchyard under the
stars.   One of the functions assumed by the editor was to
clip and improve all contributions so as to give a strictly
family atmosphere to the whole.   Mrs. Gaskell found the
editor's blue pencil very trying and protested, only to be told
that he had made the cuts in perfect good faith and would not
willingly do anything to cause her a minute's vexation; but he
continued to use his pencil.   Miss Jewsbury, Miss Berwick
(A. Procter) and Mrs. Linton also objected, and George
Eliot would never write for him at all.   Elizabeth Lynn (Mrs.
Linton) was inclined, Dickens thought, to imitate Balzac
and her story *Sentiment and Action*, though paid for, was held

up as 'not quite wholesome'. So adversely was the conductor affected by Holm Lee's tale about an unhappy marriage, *Gilbert Massenger*, that he returned it for fear of 'waking too painful emotions'. Emily Jolly, author of *The Wife's Story*, was encouraged to persevere as in her he thought 'a great writer was coming up'. The complaints Dickens received from the ladies he edited only seem to have made him more artful in his emendations, for we find remarks in his letters to the effect that he has cut Miss Martineau in such a way that she will never see the changes. Dickens by degrees evolved a pattern of his own for serial publication. He explained it from time to time in letters to contributors. Movement and action were essential in a first instalment and the early introduction of plot was important. Writing to Bulwer Lytton over his *Strange Story*, the conductor explained his method:

> For the purpose of weekly publication the divisions of the story will often have to be greatly changed. . . . I think I have become by dint of necessity and practice rather cunning in this regard; and perhaps you would not mind my looking to such points from week to week.

It has been calculated that in the weekly serials Dickens tried to arrange for an episode every ten pages and in the monthly serials every eighteen pages. Mrs. Gaskell never learnt to accept his rulings and was infuriated when *North and South* was cut. When it came out in volume form, she explained how she had been obliged to hurry on events. In those days authors had no second copy to refer to and it is doubtful whether Dickens ever let them see the proofs. By the third number the conductor had devised a threepenny monthly supplement called a *Narrative of Events*. This was a valuable publication, edited by John Dickens, giving excellent condensed reports of proceedings in Parliament as well as chronicling the principal law-suits and the important books. There was no editorial or other comment. Opening with a Narrative of Parliament and Politics, it went on to Law and Crime, Accident and Disaster, Social, Sanitary and Municipal

Progress, Obituaries, Colonies and Dependencies, Foreign Events, Literature and Art, Commercial Record, Stocks and Shares and Emigration Figures. Dickens defined the purpose of the *Narrative* as 'another humble means of enabling those who accept us for their friend to bear the world's rough-cast events to the anvil of courageous duty and then beat them in shape', a rigmarole of a typically Dickensian type.

Household Words showed signs in the fourth number of becoming even more 'matey' in spirit: it was suggested that with a little goodwill and a little good-humour society might be reformed. 'Supposing', wrote the editor, 'we were all of us to come off our pedestals and mix a little more with those below us, would it do any harm or would it be productive of great and lasting good?' . . . 'Supposing a Watt, a Jenner, a Brunell, a Stevenson or a Hogarth were to sit in the House of Lords, would any one of them really disgrace our Old Nobility?' These 'Supposings', which cover many subjects, are often surprisingly modern and always full of good sense. Dickens is revealed in them as a typical nineteenth-century reformer, and the ideas that he put forward half humorously, half seriously, but always with deep conviction, are ideas that subsequent generations of men have adopted and made applicable to daily life. Thinking it rank folly to exclude whole classes from the management of public affairs when there was such a wealth of ability to draw on, Dickens, with a fraternal instinct rare if not unique in his day, urged those in power to say to the powerless, 'Come, brothers, let us take counsel together and see how we can best manage. . . . Let us all improve ourselves and all abandon something of our extreme opinions for the general harmony.' Having mocked at stock politicians in *Nicholas Nickleby*, he now tried a more direct form of pressure. The people had been fooled long enough. If the country was to be properly run, everyone must henceforth put their shoulders to the wheel. 'Supposing', he asked, 'that governments were to consider public questions less with reference to their own time and more with reference to all time?'

Secret diplomacy was one of the questions tilted at in 'Supposings'. The editor wondered whether the world would not get on a great deal better if the Foreign Office were shut up for three days a week. Diplomacy, after all, was a form of conspiracy and half the time of the Foreign Secretary was taken up with bringing about situations that must result in wars, an idea pushed to its cynical conclusion by Adolf Hitler when he wrote, 'An alliance that does not comprise the intention of war is senseless and worthless'.

Household Words had a good deal to say about education and illiteracy. 'The Schoolmaster at Home and Abroad' must have been written either by Thomas Hughes, the author of *Tom Brown's Schooldays*, or by someone who had read his reports on continental education. It is filled with comparative statistics: 'Taking the whole of northern Europe including Scotland, France and Belgium, there is one child to every two and a quarter of the population acquiring the rudiments of knowledge, while in England there is only one such pupil to fourteen inhabitants'. This meant that a quarter of the population could neither read nor write and that half the children of England attended no place of instruction. These shameful facts were viewed callously by the Government of the richest nation in the world, and it was left to private philanthropy to run schools, 'ragged' schools at that, to save children from the perils of the streets. In all the German states as well as in the Scandinavian countries all children from six upwards were being educated, and taught cleanly ways, with the result that their appearance equalled that of middle-class children in England. Abroad, people usually read and spoke correctly, and had good manners.

Dickens commented on so many important subjects and advocated so many reforms that it would take more space than can be spared in a biography of moderate length to deal with them adequately. It is necessary to compress, even suppress, much of the material available.

In 'Pet Prisoners' the editor drew attention to the contrast in diet between the new model prison of Pentonville and the nearest workhouse, St. Pancras. Why, he asked, should paupers be treated less well than criminals? Why should a man in prison receive 28 ounces of meat weekly and a man in the workhouse 18? The same discrepancy was noticeable in other rations: 140 ounces of bread against 96, 112 ounces of potatoes against 36, and so on. About the man who is neither pauper nor prisoner—the free labourer—he has something even more serious to say. Wages at 12s. a week worked out at £31 : 4s. a year. A prisoner cost £34 to maintain, therefore a free labourer with young children to support, rent to pay, and clothes to buy, had, for the maintenance of himself and family, between £4 and £5 a year *less* than the sum spent on keeping one man in a model prison. Dickens wrote in 1850 and half a century later agricultural workers were still earning a pittance of 12s. a week. It has taken two wars to raise their standard of life. Whirlwinds of Westminster dust were being scattered in men's eyes, 'but it cannot blind us to the real state of things'.

The 'Happy Family' articles or 'Comments by the Raven', are for the most part Dickens's own. His study gave on to the garden in which Grip, the raven, lived. As he watched it cocking its head in a knowing way he made it pass remarks on current events. For example, Grip attacked the conventional practices at funerals by describing a typical *cortège*.

> What a scene it was. First of all two dressed-up fellows came, then a hearse and four, then two carriages and four, then horses with plumes and feathers on their heads and black velvet on their backs, and then there was a fellow in the procession carrying a board of them like Italian images, and then there were about five and twenty or thirty men often red in the face with eating and drinking, dressed up in scarves and hat bands and carrying fishing rods, I believe.

The raven's master was careful to leave instructions in his will that his own burial ceremony should be as plain as possible and include but two mourning coaches.

English railways were not immune from censure. Their discomfort was contrasted with the high degree of comfort

achieved on the continent, but then, as the editor wryly
observed, 'foreign trains were not run in the interests of share-
holders'. In an article called 'Lungs for London' (which
may be by Wills) attention was drawn to the jerry-building
of the moment:

> Bricklayers spread webs and meshes of houses with
> powerful rapidity in every direction, suburban open spaces
> being entombed in brick and mortar mausoleums, the
> Lungs of London are undergoing congestion.   Finsbury
> and Islington have suffered most.   Within my recollection
> Clerkenwell Green was the right colour.   Moorfields,
> Spafields and the East India Company's fields were adorned
> with grass, and he must be young indeed who cannot re-
> member cricket playing in White Conduit, Canonbury,
> Shepherd and Shepherdess, Rhodes and Laycock.   Thanks
> to the window tax and the bricklayer fresh air will be
> thoroughly bricked out.   A bath for Finsbury is too urgent
> a demand for dense population to allow of much time being
> wasted in knocking at the door of the Treasury.   The
> public must bestir *themselves*.

Many of the wrongs attacked by Dickens remained wrongs
for generations, some of them still endure.   The spirit of
Household Words is the spirit of reform: its slogan is to inspire
people to become alert and active in bringing about their own
salvation.

Henry Morley, founder of Morley College, was a contributor and wrote articles accusing employers of not providing adequate protection for operatives against machines.
Miss Martineau, on behalf of the National Association of
Manufacturers, was put up to reply.   Morley then attacked
the editor for printing her 'misstatements'.   It seemed that
the editor had not read her disclaimer before it went to press.
Put into a very bad temper by the incident, he wrote, 'I do
not suppose there was ever such a wrong-headed woman
born—such a vain one or such a humbug'.

For the next twenty years Dickens was to be a magazine
editor.   Later on his controllership loosened into a general
overseership and the spade-work was all carried out by Wills,

who was continually exhorted to keep *Household Words* imaginative.

One would have thought that work on *Household Words* and the writing of *David Copperfield* provided employment enough for one spring, but almost as soon as the magazine was launched Dickens took Kate and Georgy to Knebworth for a week to discuss a new scheme propounded by Bulwer Lytton for improving the lot of writers and artists. The scheme took Dickens's fancy and he hurled himself into plans for producing money to finance the undertaking, and as a consequence we shall presently see how much of his priceless time was squandered on theatrical productions.

In June Dickens went to Paris with Maclise to see pictures and plays. They stayed at the Hôtel Windsor, but the weather was far too hot for them to enjoy being cooped up in theatres. 'I am half dead', he wrote, 'and have nothing on but a shirt and a pair of white trousers.' Ostensibly he had timed his visit to see Rachel in her last performance of 'Lucretia' before she came over to London for the season, but his sense of anxiety about *Household Words* made him feel after two days that he had been absent for a year. On his return he commissioned Augustus Egg to paint him a portrait of Georgina. It is a small circular picture of considerable charm and shows a girl in profile bending over needlework.

As Kate was expecting a baby in August, Dickens arranged for his sister-in-law and the rest of the family to go to Broadstairs for the hot months while Kate remained in London. As soon as the new baby was born, Dickens joined the Broadstairs party, and it is now for the first time that we find him talking of 'my little housekeeper Miss Hogarth'. It was the first occasion they had kept house together. Who could have foreseen that in seven years' time Kate would have been eliminated from her position as wife and mother and that her sister would be installed as permanent housekeeper in her stead?

The year ended with the 'extra' Christmas number of

Household Words for which Dickens wrote *The Christmas Tree*. It is a kaleidoscope of burning tapers, sparkling ornaments and changing pictures of angels talking to shepherds, travellers following a star, a baby in a manger, and scene after scene in the life of Jesus. A whispered message may be heard coming from the branches of the Tree, 'This in commemoration of the law of love and kindness, mercy and compassion. This in remembrance of ME.' For Christmas 1851 Dickens in like mood wrote *What Christmas is as we grow older*. At Christmas we should shut out from our firesides—Nothing. We must welcome the dead, the living, all whom we love. 'Lost parent, dear child, dear husband, wife, brother, sister, we will not discard you. You shall hold your cherished place in our Christmas hearts and by our Christmas fires, and in the season of immortal hope and on the birthday of immortal mercy we will shut out Nothing.'

Chapter 18

THE GUILD OF LITERATURE AND ART

Every reform was once a private opinion.
R. W. EMERSON

THE Guild of Literature and Art, planned at Knebworth in the spring of 1850, was in essence a scheme for persuading authors and painters to band themselves together in their own interests.[1] It was proposed that each member should take out a life-policy at some recognised insurance office, and that those who through ill-health or age were uninsurable should be elected as associates of the Guild and share, if indigent, in the benefactions of the Fund to be accumulated by the founders. Certain land in the vicinity of Stevenage was by the generosity of Bulwer Lytton to be made over to the Guild, and moneys to be derived from certain theatrical performances as well as the copyright in certain plays were to be ear-marked for building houses and endowing the Guild. The scheme, as at first outlined, resembled the prospectus of a provident society and, as such, was not smiled on by the people it was designed to benefit. The promoters, however, were so convinced that the Guild was wanted and that they could by forging ahead with their plans make certain of eventual popularity among writers and artists, that coldness and indifference on the part of writers and artists did not discourage them.

In considering the lot of authors of the past and the means of benefiting authors of his own day, Dickens was haunted by these lines of Goldsmith:

> The men who to mankind most good have brought
> Have had the world's worst evils to endure;
> Nor till the world, for which its fools have thought,
> Thinks for itself, can wisdom bring the cure.

[1] See *Household Words*, May 12, 1851.

Nothing seems to have touched him more than the acute poverty in which many writers lived and the want of appreciation accorded to them by their contemporaries. Every time he went into Sam Rogers's house he used to glance at Milton's receipt for *Paradise Lost*, and remind himself that great Dr. Johnson sold his rights in *Rasselas* to pay for his mother's funeral. It was a bad tradition that must at all costs be broken with.

When staying with Bulwer Lytton in the spring, Dickens had suggested that it might be well to advertise the nascent Guild to their friends by playing *Every Man in His Humour* in the banqueting hall at Knebworth. It would not take long to rehearse, he could get his old cast together, and the clothes were still in good condition. Would it not be a good plan to prepare to give three representations in the autumn as soon as he had got *David Copperfield* off his hands? Bulwer Lytton welcomed the idea and was more than ready to put his house at the disposal of the actors. So in November the troupe arrived with all their properties. *Animal Magnetism*, a farce by Mrs. Inchbald, was to be included in the programme and in this Kate Dickens was to act, but, as she sprained her ankle at the last moment, Georgy took her part. Fired by the theatrical atmosphere, Bulwer Lytton set to work to write a play for Guild production in London, while Dickens and Mark Lemon concocted another.

It was a good moment to launch a scheme of the kind, for the Great Exhibition (to be opened by the Queen on May 1, 1851) would draw crowds of visitors to London many of whom would have money to spend. In February, Dickens, a shivering figure in furs, was piloted over the vast glass building which was only partially roofed. He observed that it did not look as if it could possibly be finished in time and Paxton replied, 'I think it will, but mind I don't say it will'. When the structure was completed and filled with exhibits, Dickens found it even more unattractive and uninteresting than when it was half finished and empty, and this despite the fact that homage had been paid to his genius in statues of Oliver Twist and Little Nell, both of which were conspicuously displayed.[1]   In deference to the demands of his family he visited the Exhibition twice, wandered miserably through its avenues for a short time, then left saying that his 'eyes refused to focus' and that he felt 'used-up' and bewildered. To Mrs. Watson he wrote, 'It is to me terrible duffery'.

> I have a natural horror of sights and the fusion of so many sights in one has not decreased it.   I am not sure that I have seen anything but the fountain and perhaps the Amazon.   It is a dreadful thing to be obliged to be false, but when anyone says, 'Have you seen?' I say 'Yes,' because if I don't I know he'll explain it.

The Guild committee, agreed that in spite of the spending capacity of holiday crowds they should aim at economy in their London productions, hired the Hanover Square Rooms so as to avoid the expenses of a regular theatre.   In the provinces they hoped to secure concert halls for their purpose.   Someone suggested that it would be well to begin their campaign in a private house and try to get the Queen to patronise the scheme in person.   This idea was warmly taken up and discussed, with the result that Dickens was deputed to approach the Duke of·Devonshire and ask him whether he would lend Devonshire House for the first performance of *Not So Bad as We Seem*, a new play by Bulwer Lytton.   In a carefully composed letter he threw himself on the Duke's 'generous attachment to Art and Letters', explaining that no trouble would be incurred by him should he accede to the request, and that no damage would be done since, by means of a transportable stage, light scenery and new mechanism, any room could be made to serve as a theatre at a few hours' notice.   The opening of Devonshire House for this purpose would render the success of the scheme certain.

---

[1] By Hughes Ball of Boston (English born).   He is said to have executed an Oliver Twist in marble for Chatsworth, but no trace of it exists.   His Little Nell was removed in 1852 to the Athenaeum, Boston.

Within a couple of hours of dispatching this appeal Dickens received from the Duke a charming letter placing his services, his subscription and his house at the disposal of the Fund. He added that he had long wished to know Dickens better, having so far only met him in crowded rooms.   With all the enormous energy that on occasion he could put forth, Dickens now set himself to make the performance perfect of its kind. His old cast rallied gladly round him and attracted to its ranks new members.   The newcomer who concerns us most is young Wilkie Collins who had been sounded by Augustus Egg as to whether he would take the part of Smart, valet to Sir Robert Wilmot (played by Dickens), in *Not So Bad as We Seem*.   Egg then invited Dickens and Collins to meet at his home, Ivy Cottage in Black Lion Lane (Queen's Road), and this initiated the friendship that was to squeeze Forster out of his position as Dickens's unique confidant.   Collins, generally portrayed with a bushy beard, at this time was a clean-shaven man in spectacles, with hands and feet so small that he took women's sizes in gloves and shoes.   This quiet rather smug-looking young person, with his taste for coloured ties and waistcoats, charmed Dickens as no young man had charmed him for years.   Soon he became the indispensable companion of his more frivolous hours.

Dickens, as we know, was autocratic as a stage manager and he now urgently exhorted all players to put their backs into rehearsals.   Macready was permitting them to use Covent Garden for this purpose and was even going to watch them at work.   The later rehearsals would be taken at Devonshire House when the stage had been erected and the scenes assembled.   These scenes were in course of painting in the studios of Stanfield, David Roberts and Landseer.   The manager's desire was that the production should reach perfection in every detail.

The cast, when the first rehearsal was called at Devonshire House, were delighted with the 'condescension' of the Duke in permitting them, in their 'common cabs', to drive through his wooden gates in Piccadilly, and in giving them 'splendid luncheons' which he himself attended and at which his 'foot-men waited equally on all'.[1]   Some of the players made an unfortunate mistake on the first day they set foot in the house, for on seeing a tall elderly gentleman in black examining the stage, they had ordered him out of the way.   It turned out to be the Duke.

Paxton, with great efficiency, put the theatre up, arranged for the seating of the audience, and for the masking of the pictures by hoardings covered with crimson velvet.   A special box was built for the Queen, and her chair, raised above the floor, was set in a bower of magnolias, jasmine and roses while the sides and arches were hung with tendrils dotted with stephanotis on which shimmered dew-drops of crystal and opal.   There was a profusion of candles, and scented oil was provided for the lamps.[2]   Dickens as a stage manager was consulted about every detail and Thackeray compared him to Goethe in the theatre at Weimar.   Helpers worked with a will and soon Dickens could write to the Queen's equerry to inquire what date would suit her Majesty for the first night.   He also asked the Duke of Devonshire whether it would be in order to charge three guineas for each seat. The answer he got encouraged him to ask more, and every seat was sold at the £5 printed on the ticket of admission.   A second performance took place ten days later to console would-be ticket-buyers for the first, and on this occasion two guineas was charged.

Just when Dickens had completed all his arrangements, he was overtaken by a run of great misfortunes.   Kate, who had been very poorly, was recuperating at Malvern with Georgy for company.   Charles, who had taken her there, was paying her another visit from which he was recalled almost at once to London by the news of his father's serious illness.   He was just in time to see him alive, and then had to postpone all rehearsals till the funeral was over.   A few days after they had been resumed, Charles, under very great

[1] R. H. Horne, *Bygone Celebrities*.
[2] *Gentleman's Magazine*, February 1871.

pressure, consented to fulfil an old standing engagement, that of taking the chair at the annual dinner of the General Theatrical Fund which they said would be a financial failure without him.   Just before leaving Devonshire Terrace for the dinner he ran up to the nursery to say good-night to baby Dora who had always been a rather ailing child.   Before he had concluded his appeal for the Theatrical Fund little Dora had fallen into convulsions and by the time he got home she was dead.   It was a terrible shock.

Forster at once offered to go down and break the sad news to Kate at Malvern, taking with him a letter from Charles, who had to arrange for the child's funeral.   Next morning the harassed producer wrote to the Queen's equerry begging that the first performance be postponed till some date between May 13 and May 20.   May 16 was chosen.   This was the occasion when Rosina Bulwer, always apt to be spiteful about her husband's friends, especially where Forster and Dickens were concerned, made the malicious comment, 'Oh, Mr. Dickens makes a habit of acting with a dead father in one pocket and a dead baby in the other'.

Meanwhile the Duke had studied *Not So Bad as We Seem* carefully and told the author that he liked it, but that in rehearsal Forster was liable to be rather loud-voiced and vulgar.   Frank Stone, on the other hand, made a grave, dignified Duke of Middlesex, and Dickens, though hearty enough to be a sea captain, played the fop about town with credit.   In the production he found much to praise; the clothes were gay and correct; the snuff-boxes the better for being real; on the whole the picture of high-life in the reign of George I was exact.   The Duke cautioned Dickens about possible gate-crashing, and Bulwer Lytton, nervous lest his wife should force her way in as an orange-girl or get someone to transfer a ticket to her, arranged for personal passes to be issued even for dress rehearsals.   On the first night every window on the stage or in the property room had to be left wide open by the Queen's wish, and no farce followed the play as 'the Queen got very restless about midnight'.   Orders were given that everyone must be seated by 8.45 P.M. and must sit quiet while the Duke's private band (composed for the occasion of students from the R.A.M.) entertained the company with a specially composed overture by Mr. Coote.

Dickens had been under considerable strain, and at the first performance felt terribly unwell.   He was alarmed, as he played his part, to see his legs and ankles swelling up rapidly. Somehow he got through the evening and was rewarded for his immense pains by immense applause led by the Queen herself.   At the second performance at Devonshire House ten days later he was himself again, and played in *Mr. Nightingale's Diary*, the farce concocted by himself and Lemon.   It is worth noting that in this farce Dickens took several parts, throwing himself whole-heartedly into each. The play was set in Malvern Wells and he impersonated an old woman in trouble over a missing child, a sexton with a quavering voice and a complacent smile, a *malade imaginaire*, a waiter and so on, six characters in all.   Arthur Helps, who knew him well, said, 'When he read or spoke, the whole man read or spoke'.   *Mr. Nightingale's Diary* was the forerunner of all the later 'Readings'; it gave him the conviction that he could impersonate as many people as he chose.

Macaulay, after attending the first performance of Bulwer Lytton's play, wrote at once to the author asking whether he had no misgivings about the Guild it was proposed to found. Would he not be wise to form a list of the thirty best writers, strike off all who required no assistance, all who required assistance and were receiving state pensions, and then see who was left?   Twenty-five out of the thirty were bound to fall into one or the other class and the Guild would then be left to support second-rate writers or even failures.   No letters could at this time damp Bulwer Lytton's ardour for the scheme, though Macaulay was in the long run to be justified in his apprehensions.

The two performances at Devonshire House were followed by three at the Hanover Rooms, all of which were well

attended.   The short London season was, however, but the
prelude to a campaign organised for the following year, a tour
in which Derby, Sheffield, Nottingham, Sunderland, New-
castle, Manchester and Liverpool were included.   The Duke
of Devonshire continued to support them and at Derby sat
among the audience while scene-shifters peeped through
cracks to get a look at him.   The Duke also graced the
Sheffield performance and asked Dickens to come and stay at
Chatsworth, but the author had to rush home 'lest there
should be no *Bleak House* for October'.   The enthusiasm
displayed by the audience in the Free Trade Hall in Liverpool
put 'Boz' in mind of the nights he had spent at the opera in
Genoa and Milan.   He wrote to Bulwer Lytton about it:[1]

> I left Liverpool at 4 o'clock this morning and am so
> blinded by excitement, gas, waving hats and handkerchiefs,
> that I can hardly see to write; but I cannot go to bed
> without telling you what a triumph we have had. . . . I
> sincerely believe that we have the ball at out feet and may
> throw it up to the very Heaven of Heavens.

Manchester was equally rapturous.   Four thousand people
stood and cheered and most delightful of all a stage-carpenter
told him, 'It's a universal observation in the profession, sir,
that it was a great loss to the public when you took to writing
books'.   Bristol showed 'prodigious enthusiasm'.   Birmingham gave them the warmest of welcomes.   'We have won
a position for the idea,' trumpeted Dickens.   'We carry the
fiery cross!   I have been so happy I could have cried.'
Kate and Georgy, who toured with the company, shared in
the excitements of the experience.   The tour closed with a
Manchester banquet at which Dickens and Bulwer Lytton
explained the aims of the Guild.   They were glad to announce
that a sum of £4000 had been made by means of plays, and
Bulwer Lytton (just returned as a Tory for the county of
Hertford) told his audience of his intention of introducing a
bill into Parliament to incorporate the Guild which relied for

[1] February 15, 1852.

its support on the adherence of all writers and artists.   In
1854 he carried this bill through Parliament and the Guild was
incorporated.[1]   Its objects were as follows:

1. To aid those of its members who follow Literature or
   the Fine Arts as a profession, and obtain the insurances
   upon their lives;
2. To establish a provident sickness fund for its members;
3. To provide dwellings for its members and to grant
   annuities to them or their widows.

One of the several weak features of the bill was that it could
not become operative for seven years, which gave more than
enough time for the enthusiasm that generated the scheme to
evaporate.   We shall assist later on in this book at the
opening of the first Guild houses.

Having followed the fortunes of the Guild in 1852, we
must now revert to the year 1851 in order to record the
evacuation of Devonshire Terrace by the Dickens family and
the hunt for another London home.   For most of the summer
of this year Dickens made a point of sleeping in the country
whenever he got the chance, partly because the lease of his
house had come to an end and partly because of the crowded
condition of London.   Fort House, Broadstairs, was rented
by him and the family moved there in May.   It was from Fort
House that he came up for the *Copperfield* banquet in June.
Given at the Star and Garter at Richmond and remarkable in
so far as women writers were for the first time bidden to the
feast, it is said to have been 'the pleasantest of all the book-
dinners'.   Thackeray and Alfred Tennyson were among the
guests.

Now that Dickens was a world figure many of the foreign
visitors to the Exhibition brought with them letters of introduction to 'Boz'.   'Boz', however, was not able to do much
for them as he could not occupy Tavistock House till October.
Tavistock House, Bloomsbury, belonged to his friend Frank

[1] In 1897 another Act was passed dissolving the Guild and bestowing its
funds on the Royal Literary Society.   The houses were sold for £2000.

Stone and he was only lured to live so far from a park by
the idea that the big studio or some other room would be
easily convertible into a small theatre.   As with Devonshire
Terrace, he saw to all the furnishing himself, ordering
curtains and carpets, arranging for glass mirrors and console
tables on the landing and planning bookcases between study
and dining-room, complete with dummy book-backs bearing
titles that it had amused him to invent.   Here are some of
them:

> *Five Minutes in China* (3 vols.)
> *Forty Winks at the Pyramids* (2 vols.)
> *Abernethy on the Constitution* (2 vols.)
> *History of the Middling Ages* (6 vols.)
> *The Quarrelly Review* (4 vols.)
> *Lady Godiva on the Horse*
> *Hansard's Guide to Refreshing Sleep*
> (as many vols. as possible).

He enjoyed getting in to the new home and was observed
while doing so by a German author, Theodor Fontane, who
sauntered in the garden in front of Dickens's house, fervently
wishing that the air that blew there would communicate to
him the secret spirit of London.   'Dickens', he wrote, 'lives
in a charming garden-surrounded building standing between
St. Pancras and our house.   I have not yet had the courage to
look him up, and I probably never shall have it, as he is
so overrun by Germans.'[1]   He was also overrun by other
foreigners.   A Frenchman made the excuse of admiration
in calling on him.   'Your fame and the universal sympathy
you inspire doubtless expose you to innumerable intrusions.
Your door is always besieged, you must be visited every day
by princes, statesmen, scholars, writers, artists and even madmen.'   'Yes, madmen! madmen! Madmen! they alone
amuse me,' shouted Dickens, and pushed his visitor out by
the shoulders.[2]

[1] *Ein Sommer in London in 1852.*
[2] *The Dickensian*, vol. ix, p. 156.

The use made by Dickens of the material to hand in the city of London had, as we have already seen, been a cause of envy and admiration to all literary Germans.   More than ever did they seem to feel themselves provincials.   Auerbach said, 'Dickens had the luck to be born an Englishman.   What are we?   Always, always provincials.   What has Freytag done? what have I done?   We have dealt with provincial life.' Time and again the complaint went up that Germany had no national existence, no centre of national culture, no focus of modern life.

Household Words seems to have had an immediate influence in Germany, for Gutzkow produced a publication with the same kind of title—'Conversations by the Household Hearth', but then everything Dickens wrote now had its repercussions abroad.   *Soll und Haben* by Freytag is under his influence, and Gustav Frenssen says of *Pickwick* in his diary: '*Pickwick* is a wonderful work produced with dynamic power'.   Comparing Dickens with Balzac, Frenssen found the Frenchman's work 'rather hollow'.

So much for Dickens's German admirers.   His own belief in German education was such as to cause him to send his eldest boy, Charley, straight from school to Leipzig and a younger boy to Hamburg.   The results were not what he had hoped for.

When the Duke of Wellington died, Charley, at the moment a wet bob at Eton, entreated his father to take him to St. Paul's for the funeral.   By the good offices of the Duke of Devonshire six permits for the Cathedral were secured for 'Mr. Dickens and family'.

Reporting on the ceremony to Miss Coutts, Dickens said:

The whole public has gone mad about the funeral of the Duke.   I think it a grievous thing, a lapse into barbarous practices and a most ludicrous contrast to the calm good sense and example of responsibility set by the Queen Dowager . . . a pernicious corruption of the popular mind just beginning to awaken from the long dream of inconsistencies, monstrosities, horrors and ruinous expenses

M

that has beset all classes of society in connexion with death. I shall try and present the case in *Household Words*; at present I might as well whistle into the sea.

Trading in Death appeared in *Household Words* in November.[1]

A panegyric on the dead Duke was delivered in the House of Commons by the leader of the Conservative Party, Disraeli. His speech reminded some reporters of something they already knew and the *Morning Chronicle* made a scoop by hunting up Thiers's oration on Marshal Mortier and printing it in parallel columns with Disraeli's speech: they were identical. Pleased with their astuteness, they went on to extract from *Venetia* the character of Lord Cadurcis and printed it side by side with the character of Lord Byron drawn by Mr. Macaulay in the *Edinburgh Review*, in which all contributors were anonymous. The explanation offered by Disraeli was that he copied anything that struck him and did not know afterwards whether he had written the extracts or not. Macaulay ignored the incident.

In reading through Dickens's letters it is a continual surprise to see how much time and consideration he gave to Miss Coutts's many projects of social reform. Whether it is the furnishing of the little house of rescue at Shepherd's Bush or the uniform to be worn by its inmates or the leaflet to be handed by the police to women on the streets, he was always at her service, and all the time he was helping with the Urania Cottage scheme, he was writing *David Copperfield*. He explained in his leaflet that Miss Coutts, as she watched the girls on the pavements by her house, had been troubled and moved and was now resolved to make a home for them, a place where they can be taught household work. She wishes to give them a chance to begin life afresh and hopes to restore them to society in a place where no one will know of their past and where they will be able to find husbands. 'Leave prison, leave your present life!' urged Dickens. 'Resolve to begin anew, but don't, if you are not resolved and

[1] November 27, 1852.

not serious, take up the space another girl might occupy. Whether you accept or reject the offer think it over'[1]—signed, Your Friend.

Miss Coutts, as eager to abolish slums as to save girls, decided (since no government would take action in the matter) to rehouse ten thousand slum dwellers of Bethnal Green. With Dickens she discussed what form the building should assume. Dickens was of opinion that tenement houses offered the best chance of good air and green open spaces.

I have no doubt [he wrote] that the large houses are the best. You never can, for the same money, offer anything like the same advantage in small houses. It is not desirable to encourage small carpenters or builders to run up small dwelling houses. If they had been discouraged long ago London would be an immeasurably healthier place than it can be made in scores of years to come. If you go into any common outskirts of the town now and see the advancing army of brick and mortar laying waste the country fields and shutting out the air, you cannot fail to be struck by the consideration that if large buildings had been erected for the working people instead of the absurd and expensive walnut shells in which they live, London would have been about a third of its present size and every family would have had a country walk miles nearer to their own door. Besides this, men would have been nearer to their work . . . there would have been thicker walls of separation and better means of separation than you can ever give (except at preposterous cost in small tenements) and they would have had gas, water, drainage, and a variety of other humanizing things which you can't give them so well in little houses. Further, in little houses you must keep them near the ground and you cannot possibly afford such sound and wholesome foundations (remedying this objection) in little houses.[2]

As a result of Dickens's advice Miss Coutts paid for the erection of tenement buildings in Bethnal Green.

The problems raised by rehousing and sanitary reform had

[1] *The Dickensian*, 1926, p. 199.   [2] 388. II. N.L.

interested Dickens passionately ever since he had got to know
Dr. Southwood Smith.   At a dinner of the Metropolitan
Sanitary Association presided over by Lord Carlisle at
Soyer's Symposium[1] (Gore House) Dickens proposed a toast
to the Board of Health coupled with the name of Lord
Ashley and expatiated on the sufferings of the suburbs without
water, pleading earnestly for the poor man for whom 'cleanli-
ness must be legislated for before godliness'.

> Give him and his a glimpse of heaven [he pleaded].
> Give them water, help them to be clean.   Take the body
> of the dead relative from the room where the living live
> with it, and where such loathsome familiarity deprives
> death itself of awe.   Then, but not before, will they be
> brought willingly to hear of Him whose thoughts were so
> much with the wretched and who had compassion for all
> human sorrow.

On the same theme Dickens at this time also wrote an article
for *Punch*, 'Dreadful Hardships'.   It never appeared in
Punch as it was considered better to refer to the matter in a
cartoon.   To say that Dickens was always working for
social reform is almost to understate his constant attitude to
human suffering and human degradation.   He did more than
work, he put his whole being into it, and where the poor and
helpless were concerned his tenderness of heart was unsur-
passed.

[1] May 10, 1851.   See Spielman's *History of Punch*.

Chapter 19

COOKERY AND BOULOGNE

His genius was his fellow-feeling with his race; his mere personality was never the bound or limit to his perceptions.

JOHN FORSTER

As soon as he was comfortably established in Tavistock House, Dickens began work on a new novel. The book was some time settling into its permanent name as he wanted the title to indicate that it was the story of 'a house that got into Chancery and could not get out'; eventually it became *Bleak House*. Written primarily to draw attention to the abuses of Chancery practice, he based the case of Jarndyce and Jarndyce on the notorious Jennings case which had been, at intervals, before the Court for ninety years. He also made use of a case supplied him by a correspondent which figures in the fifteenth chapter as the Gridley case. In the preface he is careful to state that the facts set out in the book are substantially true and even within the truth.

The success of *David Copperfield*, so largely due to self-portraiture, encouraged Dickens, in *Bleak House*, to be a little bolder and to incorporate among its characters two well-known literary men, who recognised themselves in its pages, and one, if not two, literary women who did not see themselves as others saw them. These experiments were really an extension of that method of romanticising familiar things in which Dickens used to say his art consisted. Some readers professed to be shocked that he should make use of friends in this manner, but they must have been people unacquainted with the fact that the imagination does not work in a vacuum and that most novelists, and certainly all great novelists, create capital from the material of their own experience. Dickens's masters, Smollett, Fielding and Goldsmith, had modelled their characters on themselves, their womenkind

325

or their friends; even Scott had been no exception to this practice. There is, however, an unwritten code which novelists must not ignore: the likeness must never be photographic, for in that case, as Forster points out, it becomes mere reporting and may result in 'a radical wrong to the victim'. The line of demarcation being really an aesthetic one, it is in practice hard to define. According to contemporary opinion, it was not overreached in the case of Landor and considerably overreached in the case of Leigh Hunt.

Landor at this time was still living at Bath, worshipping Dickens, and in process of dedicating his latest book to him, but Leigh Hunt was in London and the conductor was constantly dealing with him as the contributor of dull articles[1] to *Household Words*. Admittedly the portrait of Skimpole is a far less agreeable one than that of Boythorn, but then Dickens liked Leigh Hunt less than he liked Landor and preferences will out. Lawrence Boythorn is described by Jarndyce, who had been at school with him, as

The most impetuous boy in the world, and he is now the most impetuous man. He was then the loudest boy in the world, and he is now the loudest man. He was then the heartiest and sturdiest boy in the world and he is now the heartiest and sturdiest man. He is a tremendous fellow . . . there's no simile for his lungs. Talking, laughing, or snoring they make the beams of the house shake . . . but it's the inside of the man, the warm heart of the man, the passion of the man, the fresh blood of the man . . . that I speak of.

There is nothing unattractive about this description; one is drawn to Boythorn rather than repelled, and when he comes into the room he is even more likeable:

He was not only a very handsome old gentleman— upright and stalwart as he had been described to us—with a massive grey head, a fine composure of face when silent . . . he was such a true gentleman in his manner, so chivalrously polite his face lighted by a smile of so much sweet-

[1] See 'Lounging in Kensington', 'Gore House', etc. etc.

ness and tenderness, and it seemed so plain that he had nothing to hide but showed himself exactly as he was . . . that really I could not help looking at him with equal pleasure as . . . he smilingly conversed with Ada and me, or was led by Mr. Jarndyce into some great volley of superlatives, or threw up his head like a bloodhound, and gave out that tremendous Ha, ha, ha!

And here is the description of Harold Skimpole, in other words, the portrait of Leigh Hunt, that gave so much offence:

> He was a bright little creature, with rather a large head; but a delicate face, and a sweet voice, and there was a perfect charm in him. All he said was so free from effort and spontaneous, and was said with such a captivating gaiety, that it was fascinating to hear him talk. . . . He had more the appearance of a damaged young man, than a well-preserved elderly one. There was an easy negligence in his manner and even in his dress (his hair carelessly disposed, and his neckerchief loose and flowing, as I have seen artists paint their own portraits) which I could not separate from the idea of a romantic youth who had undergone some unique process of depreciation.

Stressing as it does the eternal wish to be youthful that led Hunt to such posing at sixty-five, this presentation was cruel, but it may have been the character study in irresponsibility that hurt him most:

> I am constantly being bailed out, like a boat; or paid off like a ship's company. Somebody always does it for me. *I* can't do it, you know, for I never have any money; but Somebody does it. I get out by Somebody's means, I'm not like the starling: I get out. If you were to ask me who Somebody is, upon my word, I couldn't tell you. Let us drink to Somebody. God bless him!

Though Leigh Hunt was considerably offended by these passages and by the description of Skimpole's life in the Polygon, he did not quarrel with his bread and butter, but went on inviting his 'dear Dickens' to his house in Hammersmith. Several letters of refusal are printed in the Nonesuch *Letters*, but no acceptances.

The organising, pamphleteering Mrs. Jellyby was said by some contemporaries to be a caricature of Harriet Martineau, who had written twenty-five tales illustrating aspects of Political Economy. Mrs. Jellyby is breathlessly described in *Bleak House* as

> a lady of remarkable strength of character, who has devoted herself to an extensive variety of public subjects, at various times, and especially to the subject of Africa with a view to the general cultivation of the coffee berry *and* the natives, and the happy settlement of our superabundant home population in Borrioboola-Gha on the left bank of the Niger.

Possibly Dickens as 'conductor' of *Household Words* had his contributor, Harriet Martineau, as much on his mind as Leigh Hunt at the time he wrote this book, for there is a hint of her in Mrs. Pardiggle, 'a School lady, a Visiting lady, a Reading lady, a Distributing lady, and on the Social Linen Box Committee and many general committees', but then Harriet Martineau's activities were so multiple that she might well be split up into several persons. Neither Mrs. Jellyby nor Mrs. Pardiggle gave offence to anyone, for Harriet Martineau did not recognise herself in either character. But Mrs. Hill, the original of Miss Mowcher in *David Copperfield*, protested against being guyed.

Forster was fussed by the likenesses when he went over the *Bleak House* manuscript, and made Dickens change the Christian name of Skimpole from Leonard to Harold, and modify certain sentences in which the portrait was, in his opinion, too particular. The practice of drawing from life, as we shall see in *Little Dorrit*, was henceforth persevered in by Dickens. As a prolific author writing to schedule he was driven to employ a realistic technique based on experience.

The fly-wheel of the story of *Bleak House* is the Court of Chancery: all cogs move in connection with it. Principal and lesser persons alike are all drawn insensibly into the machinery and are one by one lethalised by the monster operating as Justice and Equity. The villain of the piece is the Law, protector of the Vested Interest. The Lord Chancellor and his Court represent the apparatus of evil. And not only were real institutions and real people depicted in this book, but real places like Chancery Court, Belgrave Square and Forster's chambers, and real scenery from Rockingham, observations on trees, and the behaviour of light, clouds and shadows. *Bleak House*, though it demanded great concentration, did not give its author so much trouble to construct as *Dombey and Son* had done. It was dedicated to his colleagues in the Guild of Literature and Art, and illustrated with forty plates by 'Phiz'. 'Browne has done Skimpole and helped to make him singularly unlike the great original', wrote Dickens to Forster.

That it was not favourably reviewed is no matter for surprise. Few of Dickens's novels ever were, and this time he was told that as a writer he had every fault and as a reformer tilted against windmills. In this connection it is well to remind ourselves of the words written by Landor to Edith Southey on the subject of reviewing in general: 'In my father's library was the *Critical Review* from its commencement; and it would have taught me, if I could not even at a very early age teach myself better, that Fielding, Sterne, and Goldsmith were really worth nothing'.

Lord Denman, Chief Justice of England, who disapproved of *Bleak House* on account of its central theme, attacked it as it came out on the minor issue of Mrs. Jellyby, saying that it would discourage efforts to put down slavery, and Miss Harriet Martineau followed suit. These attacks had no effect on general readers, who showed their appreciation by buying nearly twice as many copies of *Bleak House* as they had done of *David Copperfield*.

During the summer of 1851, Kate Dickens, who was as usual expecting a baby, had taken to her pen and beguiled the months of comparative inactivity by putting together a

cookery book entitled *What shall we have for Dinner?* [1]
Writing as Lady Maria Clutterbuck, Kate, in a foreword,
explained that the late Sir Jonas Clutterbuck had, in addition
to a host of other virtues, enjoyed a good appetite and excellent digestion and that he had been kept in a state of connubial
bliss by a wife who studied his food:

> Sir Jonas was not a gourmand, although a man of great
> gastronomical experience. Richmond never saw him more
> than once a month and he was a rare visitor to Black-
> wall and Greenwich. Of course he attended most of the
> Corporation dinners as a matter of duty and now and then
> partook of a turtle feast at some celebrated place in the
> City; but these dinners were only exceptions, his general
> practice being to dine at home.

His relict believed that by her study of his appetite she had
been enabled to 'secure possession of his esteem unto the last'.
Female confidantes had told her that their daily life had been
embittered by 'that surplusage of mutton or redundancy of
chops that drives men to the club'. To rescue her friends
from such domestic suffering she has consented to give to
the world her bills of fare. And the really awful secret of
this little book was that the bills of fare it contained were all
taken from dinners given by Mr. and Mrs. Dickens! Charley
in his 'Reminiscences' says: 'My mother published under the
name of Lady Clutterbuck a book of our daily bills of fare at
Tavistock House'.

In reading it one learns odd things about Victorian dishing-
up and about the sequence of viands. Dressed crab was
served at the end of a meal: cod's head went with soles, smelts
with turbot. It was advised that a leg of mutton be stuffed
with oysters, eggs and minced onions. Most menus conclude with toasted cheese or bloaters. Calling to mind the
atmosphere of his home, Charley Dickens later exclaimed,
'How many meals began with milk punch and ended with

---

[1] *What shall we have for Dinner?* Satisfactorily answered by numerous
Bills of Fare for from two to eighteen persons by Lady Maria Clutterbuck.
Bradbury and Evans, 1851.

toasted cheese I cannot tell you!' Reviewers, though they praised the book, wondered how long any man could survive the consumption of so much toasted cheese.

Some of the recipes were *à la Soyer* after the famous cook who at the time of the Great Exhibition had set up a restaurant, Soyer's Symposium, in Gore House. There is not much difference in fare between small dinners and large. A dinner for six to ten persons would consist of

Carrot Soup
Turbot with Shrimp Sauce
Lobster Patties
Stewed Kidneys
Roast Saddle of Lamb
Boiled Turkey
Knuckle of Ham
Mashed and Brown Potatoes
Stewed Onions
Cabinet Pudding
Blancmange and Cream
Macaroni

A dinner for eighteen would have two of all courses. Two soups, two fishes, followed by many *entrées* such as Mushroom Patties, Pork Cutlets, Oyster Curry, Lamb's Fry or Grenadine of Veal. These were succeeded by Forequarter of Lamb, Boiled Chicken and Tongue, New Potatoes, Spinach, Salad Larded Capon and Roast Pigeons. Then came Asparagus, Italian Macaroni, Ice Pudding, Brunswick Sausage, Anchovies and Cheese.

The sweets in all the menus are dull and limited and it is obvious that Sir Jonas, alias Mr. Dickens, could not have been a sweet-tooth and that Lady Maria, alias Mrs. Dickens, took more trouble to provide savouries than sweets.

To supplement this account of Victorian feeding we will look at what Nathaniel Sharswell Dodge had to say about Dickens at this time:[1]

---

[1] See an American scrap-book presented to the Boston branch of the Dickens Fellowship in May 1939.

The personal habits of Dickens were those of the average English gentleman. He was abstinent from breakfast to about half an hour before dinner. This was his working time. He told me that four hours at his desk and four hours afield—on foot or on horseback—rarely in a carriage —was the rule of his working life. He took brandy and seltzer before dinner, drank, as everybody drinks in England, sherry with his meals and port with dessert, sat long at table; enjoyed his cigar; spent an hour perhaps in the drawing room at the conclusion of the evening and then retiring to his study, read, smoked, and sipped brandy-and-water till his bed time at midnight.

Perhaps the cookery book and the American vignette are not really so side-tracking to our narrative as they may at first sight have seemed to be, for they bring home to us the normal habits of the well-to-do people of the time and show us what it might otherwise be difficult to understand, why so many of the early Victorians aged so young. By forty, Mrs. Dickens had become fat and lethargic and her husband's arteries were hardening fast. Lady Maria Clutterbuck's book makes it clear that every well-to-do household expected to be regaled daily as at a City banquet and spend what to us would be an inordinate time at table.

The advent of a seventh boy gave no joy to either parent. To a lady asking to be godmother to one of his children Dickens at this time replied with sardonic humour, 'May I never have the opportunity to give you one'. To another he wrote: 'My wife has presented me with No. 10. I think I could have dispensed with the compliment.'[1] Again he says, 'I have some idea of interceding with the Bishop of London to have a little service in Saint Paul's beseeching that I may be considered to have done enough towards my country's population'.[2] Frankly he writes to Mark Lemon: 'I don't congratulate you on the Baby, because I can't bear to be congratulated on my own Babies'. Kate penned a note her-

[1] 394. II. N.L.   [2] 416. II. N.L.

self to Bulwer Lytton asking him to stand godfather to the newcomer and attend the christening dinner.[1]   Charles asked Forster to be the other godfather.   Mrs. Brookfield tells that 'Fuz' came in late to dinner begging ten thousand pardons and explaining that he had had to act as godfather 'to one of Dickens's children'.   Whereupon Douglas Jerrold observed, 'I hope that if you gave the child a mug it was *not* your own'.

We do not know what Mrs. Dickens's thoughts on child-bearing were, but her husband was desperately tired of the babies he seemed to think she alone was responsible for.   He was wearied, too, by the eight children who swarmed over the house, of whom only Charley was at school, but this did not prevent him from doting on the little boys so long as they were little.   Like Queen Victoria, he ceased to be quite so fond when the children grew to years of discretion.

The year 1852 saw the passing of old friends, for Watson, d'Orsay and Mrs. Macready all died during its course.   'The tremendous sickle', as Dickens put it, was 'cutting deep into the corn around him' and he realised that his own blade had ripened.   Rather out of heart and intensely occupied with the Guild tour in the north of England, he, almost absentmindedly, rented a house at Dover for the children from July to September.   Kate and Georgy went on tour with him and as soon as the children could be sent back to their home in London Dickens took a trip with his wife and sister-in-law to Boulogne.   Of course he fell in love with the ramparts, as Isabel Arundell had done that same summer when she first set eyes on Richard Burton.   He was also greatly taken by the fisherfolk and indeed by everything about the place. Why was it that these foreigners were so much more alive and interesting than the dull inhabitants of Dover?   Why were they able to display such individual fancy in their gardens and their houses?   Why could they express life as they did? 'Please God', he wrote to Forster, 'I shall be writing on these ramparts next July.'[2]

Kate and Georgy agreed with him that it would be a great

deal more amusing to spend a summer in France than among their own compatriots, so they decided to rent a house recommended to them by a Swiss friend, the Château des Moulineaux. Facing the ramparts and unfinished cathedral of the Haute Ville, it stood clear of the town on a terraced hillside of fir-woods. It was an amusing place with five summer-houses and fifteen fountains—a veritable children's paradise. The mere idea of spending a summer in these delightful surroundings put Dickens into tearing spirits and he became at once 'the Sparkler of Albion', which was the equivalent of the Inimitable in England and America.

The family got back to Tavistock House at the end of October and the autumn was devoted to work on *Bleak House* and *Household Words* and to the society of his old cronies, Leech, Lemon and Maclise. Christmas was spent by the family together, but for Twelfth Night (1853) Dickens went to Birmingham with Kate, where a dinner was given in his honour. Beforehand in the rooms of the Society of Art in Temple Row a presentation took place of a silver-gilt salver and a diamond ring. In accepting them Dickens solemnly promised to remove his own old diamond ring from his left hand and in future wear the Birmingham ring on his right where its grasp will keep him in mind of his very good friends in Birmingham. The gathering adjourned to Dee's Hotel for the banquet of two hundred and twenty guests, among them 'many distinguished Royal Academicians'. Dickens, speaking in reply to a toast, rejoiced that the age of patronage and venality was over. It is the people of England, he stated, who have set writers free from the shame of the purchased dedication, the dependence at my Lord Duke's table one day and at the sponging-house the next, and from all the scurrilous and dirty work of Grub Street. Who now may be said most to encourage the dissemination of the writings of Macaulay, Wellington, Layard or Tennyson? Why, the working men of England!

And my creed in the exercise of my profession is that Literature cannot be too faithful to the people—cannot too ardently advocate the cause of their advancements, happiness and prosperity. I have heard it sometimes said that Literature has suffered by this change, that it has degenerated by being made cheaper. I have not found that to be the case: nor do I believe that you have made the discovery either.

He went on to deride 'the coxcombical idea of writing down to the people', a remark that elicited warm applause: his whole speech was punctuated with quick approval. Delighted with the appreciation of this Midland audience and the generosity of their gifts, he offered to return at Christmas to read two of his stories aloud.

All through February and March he worked steadily. Something of a sensation was caused by an anonymous article in *Household Words* describing life in a workhouse in which it was alleged that the youths in these institutions were 'positively kept like wolves'. It was said to be by the conductor.

At the Royal Academy banquet on April 30 Dickens was bracketed with Dean Milman to reply to the toast of 'Literature'. He did so quite shortly. Addressing the President, Sir Charles Eastlake, whose crimson-velvet chair had been placed in front of the picture of the year, 'The Victory' by Stanfield, he congratulated him and his better half (not visible on this occasion) for their tasteful writings. On the following night Mr. and Mrs. Dickens dined with the Lord Mayor. Mr. Justice Talfourd proposed 'Anglo-Saxon Literature' with allusion to Charles Dickens as having employed fiction to awaken attention to the condition of the oppressed and suffering classes. 'Mr. Dickens replied playfully', says Mrs. Beecher Stowe who faced him at the table. Earlier in the proceedings Vice-Chancellor Wood, who spoke in the absence of the Lord Chancellor, had made a sort of defence of the Court of Chancery, not distinctly mentioning *Bleak House*, but evidently not without reference thereto. The explanation of the Law's delays was the inadequate number of judges. More had now been appointed and unnecessary delays would be done with. This item of intelligence was quizzically treated by 'Boz' as he rejoiced in the good news. The incident showed that the Chancery Bar was not insensible to his representations. In this respect Mrs. Stowe thought the English remarkable; everything met with the freest handling, but nobody took offence. Dickens had gone on unmercifully exposing all sorts of weak places in the English fabric, public and private, yet nobody cried out upon him as the slanderer of his country. 'He could go on serving up Lord Dedlocks to his heart's content.' In this respect Americans, she thought, had much to learn from English people. Mrs. Stowe, moving off with the ladies after dinner to the reception-room, was introduced to Mrs. Dickens, who, to her eyes, appeared 'large, tall, well-developed and high-coloured with an air of frankness, cheerfulness and reliability'. Other distinguished Americans were visiting England at this time, including Dickens's dear friend Professor Felton for whom he gave a dinner at the Trafalgar, Greenwich, after which Stanfield displayed to the guests the glories of the Hospital.

Cranford was appearing in *Household Words*. Dickens was extremely pleased with it and told Mrs. Gaskell she could write as much as she liked for his magazine. Miss Lynn was still sending in stories such as *Marie's Fever* which seemed to him (and probably were) 'imitations from the French', she having worked for some time in Paris. In such time as he could spare from his own work Dickens now took on himself the arranging of a benefit for Miss Kelly and served, in company with the Dukes of Devonshire, Beaufort and Leinster, on a committee got together for the purpose. Writing to Régnier, he said the audience would be of the *élite* and that if he could arrange to come over with his company and play *Le Bonhomme de Jadis* it would be a very great help. Régnier consented and the play was fixed for June 15, by which time Dickens, having fallen ill, had escaped from London to Boulogne.

Dickens was doing work for Miss Coutts by day and diverting himself in the evening with table-turning when he was suddenly taken ill. The weak kidney that had given him trouble as a boy and the sharp pain in his side from which he had suffered in the blacking factory once more laid him low. With a head feeling as if it would split, he cut free from all engagements and dashed off to Boulogne with Kate and Georgy, leaving the family to follow three weeks later with the London carriage, horse and groom. For relaxation he read a manuscript, 'Anne Rodway', on the journey, a new story by his dear young friend Wilkie Collins, and it made him shed those half-pleasurable tears that were never far from the surface. It was delightful to think that Collins was going to join him for the summer and live in the Tom Pouce pavilion in the garden of the Château des Moulineaux, and that 'Pumpion' (Frank Stone) too would come over with his family. How he revelled in his French 'doll's house'; Rosemont too had been a 'doll's house'. It was charmingly situated and 'the best place I have ever lived in abroad'. He got on capitally with the owner, portly M. Beaucourt, who displayed the improvements he had thought out with the intense pride of a property owner.

The château was approachable by thirty-six stone steps set tribune-wise from the road. Its hall was almost all of glass, the dining-room looked like a conservatory, and every room had a mirror over the mantelpiece. Dickens being particularly partial to mirrors, it was a house after his own heart. A map of the property hung on the wall, giving the impression that it was about the size of Ireland: on it were marked the bridges of Austerlitz and Jena, the cottage of Tom Pouce, the Hermitage, and the Bower of the Old Guard. The many clocks in the house ticked away busily, keeping what Dickens said must be 'correct Australian time which sometimes would vary nine or ten hours from the French norm'.

The Dickens children were enraptured by their setting, but in a different way from the grown-ups: they liked the goldfish in the pond and the rose-alleys running in all directions. It was a wonderful playground. Old and young alike were pleased, and the oldest person there was Charles Dickens aged

338 CHARLES DICKENS

forty-one and feeling very much the Sparkler.

Mary Boyle came with Peter Cunningham to this abode of bliss. She describes the approach to the steps as 'an avenue of hollyhocks'. How greatly privileged she felt at being taken for long walks alone by Charles, walks which would have been far more enjoyable if Georgy had not occasionally insisted on coming too.

Bleak House allowed itself to be written easily in this happy place. 'We had a little reading of the final double number here the night before last and it created a great impression', wrote the author to Forster. The book was finished by August 27 and the dinner in honour of its completion was given at Boulogne and attended by John Leech, Mark Lemon, Frank Stone and Wilkie Collins.

After working steadily for the best part of a year, the author's heart leapt to think that he could soon go for a carefree holiday and cut loose from the family. Before doing so he dictated to Georgy the last instalments of his *Child's History of England* (originally undertaken for the instruction of his own children), which since January had been appearing in *Household Words*. Like Macaulay's *History*, it concluded with the Revolution of 1688. Forster gives no account of this rather deplorable production. Dickens had far better have left the teaching of history to tutors than disfigure his narrative with phrases like these: Henry VIII was 'a corpulent brute, grunting and growling in his own fat way like a royal pig. A disgrace to human nature. A blot of blood and grease on the history of England.' And again: 'There was a bad fever raging in England and I am glad to write the Queen took it and the hour of her death came. . . . As Bloody Mary this woman has become famous and as bloody Queen Mary she will ever be justly remembered with horror and detestation' in Great Britain. James I 'who wrote of witches' was alluded to as 'His Sowship'. The book comprises some 150,000 words and must have been an adaptation of some other history intertwined with the expression of personal opinions. In its shallow, vituperative judgments it is a little reminiscent of Hawthorne's contribution to English history for schools (1836). A few words about the accession and marriage of Queen Victoria are tacked on at the end of the book.

All work for the moment polished off, Dickens summoned his two young friends, Augustus Egg and Wilkie Collins, inseparables since the Devonshire House rehearsals, to go with him on holiday. He was in 'Sparkler' form and prepared to enjoy himself enormously. The party had rooms at the Falcon Hotel, Lausanne, but Chauncey Hare Townshend insisted on putting them all up at his villa, Mon Loisir, just above Rosemont. Dickens renewed acquaintance with the Haldimand and Cerjat circles and then went on by way of Chamounix to Milan, where he started talking Italian volubly and rushed excitedly to the Scala only to find the performance 'execrable'. 'It is so strange and like a dream to me to hear the delicate Italian once again—so beautiful to see the delightful sky and all the picturesque wonders of the country, and yet I am so restless to be—half desperate to begin some new story.'

The railroad from Turin took Dickens within twenty miles of Genoa, where he lost no time in getting in touch with the De la Rues, T. J. Thompsons and Yeats Browns. Mrs. De la Rue, though still suffering from delusions, refused his offer of further treatment. Old friends hardly recognised the soberly clad figure with black vest and black cravat who presented himself at their doors. Dickens found the Thompsons living in a ruinous Albaro-like palace at Nervi on the road to Portofino. Christiana had lost her glamour and now showed herself too engrossed in oil painting to be able to spare much time for two untidy little slips of girls,[1] crop-headed and stockingless, who were being taught arithmetic by their father, in 'a billiard-room with all manner of messes in it'. Mrs. Yeats Brown said Mrs. Thompson had far better have stuck to her music than work at painting which she was no good at. Visiting the Peschiere, he found it had been

[1] Lady Butler and Mrs. Alice Meynell.

turned into a school for girls and that all the painted gods and goddesses had been covered up. A tour of the gardens revealed their state of complete neglect.

On the ship that transported the Dickens party to Naples he found handsome, courteous Sir Emerson Tennent, M.P. for Belfast, his family, and a number of tourists. All complained of the P. & O. service. It was bad and overcrowded (forty per cent more first-class tickets sold than there were berths) and all hoped that it might soon be superseded by an Italian or French service. 'It would serve the exploiters right to be pinched out,' said one passenger. At Naples, which he had always thought one of the most detestable places on earth, Dickens met Henry Layard, who was travelling with Lord and Lady Somers. With Layard he climbed Vesuvius again and explored Pompeii. Long political discussions with this new friend caused him to write, 'I am more than ever confirmed in my conviction that one of the great excuses for travelling is to encourage a man to think for himself and be bold enough to declare it'.

Henry Layard was Dickens's great discovery on this trip. Layard had made a name for himself over his excavations at Nineveh and his book describing them sold very well. He was at this time busy revising Kugler's *Italian Painters* and making tracings in outline of Italian pictures. He spoke Italian, for his youth had been spent in Italy. The two men took to each other at once. There was but a difference of five years between them and each confided to the other that his principal preoccupation was hunting for solutions to the problems that riddled the social life of their country. Dickens was planning *Hard Times* and Layard, newly elected Liberal M.P. for Aylesbury, was hoping to cut a figure in the House of Commons as a serious reformer. They discussed the writings of Carlyle and agreed as to the hopelessness of solving political, much less economic problems by Downing Street methods. More and more did Dickens feel it laid upon him to strike a great blow for the poor and Layard thought that in Dickens he had found a man whom he could trust to advise him and whom he could look up to in the perilous days to come.

On arriving in Rome Dickens sought out J. G. Lockhart, who was, as he told Kate, 'very weak and broken':[1]

One bright day [in Rome] I walked about with him for some hours when he was dying fast, and all the old faults had faded out of him and the now ghost of the handsome man I had first known when Scott's daughter was at the head of his house, had little more to do with this world than she in her grave, or Scott in his, or small Hugh Littlejohn in his. Lockhart had been anxious to see me all the previous day (when I was away on the Campagna) and as we walked about I knew very well that *he* knew very well why. He talked of getting better, but I never saw him again.

In St. Peter's Dickens found David Roberts and Louis Haghe painting. He knew them well, for they had both helped him over scenery for *Not So Bad as We Seem*. Sending Egg and Collins out sightseeing by themselves, he took long walks alone cogitating on a story for the Christmas extra-number of *Household Words*, to which he always gave his most careful personal supervision, even if he did not actually write the entire number.

When the party left Rome for Siena, a two days' drive, they did so with some trepidation, as to expose oneself at night to the malarial air of the Campagna was a serious risk. Dickens writes in a half-scared way of marshlands and deserted plains where shepherds shut themselves up in stuffy huts at night with families languishing from fever. He hired a light carriage, the sooner to get out of the danger zone, but had to pass a night at Bolsena on the fringe of the Campagna. There in great mouldering rooms the party snatched a little fitful sleep. By Bologna and Ferrara they at last reached Venice, where the Inimitable appeared at the Opera in perfect evening dress while spindle-legged Collins, with his spec-

tacles, moustache and dirty gloves, cut no better a figure than
scrubby Egg with his little black beard and his undistinguished
air. From Venice Dickens posted his contribution to the
Christmas number.

During this tour Charles's letters to Kate are particularly
affectionate, solicitous and intimate, and as his travels have
evoked old memories, he, on reaching Turin, wrote at some
length suggesting that nine years having gone by, she ought
to patch up the differences that had arisen when they were
living at the Peschiere, when by her strange behaviour she had
constrained him to make a painful declaration of her state of
mind to the De la Rues which De la Rue had had too much
delicacy and gratitude ever to allude to.

> Whatever made you unhappy in the Genoa time had no
> other root beginning, middle or end than whatever has
> made you proud and honoured in your married life, and
> gives you station better than rank, and surrounded you
> with many enviable things. . . . Your position beside these
> people is not a good one, is not an amiable one, or a
> generous one—is not worthy of you at all. . . . You have it
> in your power to set it right. . . .
>
> Nine years have gone away since we were in Genoa.
> Whatever looked large in that little place may be supposed
> in such a time to have shrunk to its reasonable and natural
> proportions. You know my life and character, and what
> has had its part in making them successful; and the more
> you see of me, the better perhaps you may understand that
> the intense pursuit of any idea that takes complete posses-
> sion of me is one of the qualities that makes me different,
> sometimes for good; sometimes, I dare say, for evil, from
> other men.[1]

This letter plainly refers to the hypnotic treatment of Mrs.
De la Rue. Kate now acted on his suggestion and wrote in a
friendly way to the woman of whom she had been so jealous
and whose interest in her husband she was now persuaded she
had misunderstood during the miserable months at Genoa.

[1] W. Dexter, *Mr. and Mrs. Dickens*, p. 227.

The holiday-makers reached London in mid-December just in time for Dickens to keep Christmas with his family and make good his offer to read his Christmas stories aloud in Birmingham.   Mr. and Mrs. Dickens were entertained before the readings at the Hen and Chickens Hotel and Mrs. Dickens was presented with a silver flower-stand.   A red pulpit, like a Punch and Judy stand without the top, was provided for Mr. Dickens's convenience in the Town Hall and from it he read *A Christmas Carol* on December 27 and *The Cricket on the Hearth* on December 29.   Next day he read the *Carol* again to a specially summoned audience of working men and their wives.   In a few introductory words he said how important he thought it that the working man should take his share in management; indeed it seemed to him essential to the healthy life of the community that he should do so.   As, in his opinion, no class could of itself do much for the good of the community as a whole, the fusion of all classes must be aimed at, co-operation between employers and employed stressed, and common interests defined.   In this way only could the stamping out of exploitation be achieved.   In the Mechanics' Institute set up in their midst he sees a temple of concord, a model edifice for the whole of England.   In conclusion he read three verses from a favourite poem.

> And should my youth, as youth is apt, I know,
>   Some harshness show,
> All vain asperities I day by day
>   Would wear away
> Till the smooth temper of my age should be
> Like the high leaves upon the Holly Tree.
>
> And as when all the summer trees are seen
>   So bright and green,
> The holly leaves a sober hue display
>   Less bright than they,
> But when the bare and winter woods we see
> What then so cheerful as the Holly Tree?
>
> So serious should my youth appear among
>   The thoughtless throng,

So would I seem among the young and gay
      More grave than they
That in my age as cheerful I might be
As the green winter of the Holly Tree.[1]

These Birmingham readings brought home to Dickens
that whenever he pleased he could with his sympathy and his
mimetic power not only draw large audiences but could hold
them spell-bound.   This was a consoling reflection, for
should his writing faculty fail him, as sometimes he feared it
might, he would have another means of livelihood at his
command.

[1] R. Southey, 1798.

Chapter 20

THE CONDITION OF ENGLAND

*All things considered, there never was a people so abused as
the English at this time.*   CHARLES DICKENS

THE year 1854 opened with rehearsals of Fielding's burlesque *Tom Thumb*, played by the Dickens and Lemon
children on Twelfth Night at the 'Theatre Royal', Tavistock
House.   Mark Lemon took the part of the giantess Glum-
dalca, and Dickens that of Gaffer Thumb.   The acting of the
children, especially of Henry Fielding aged four, was amus-
ingly grave, so much so that one of the spectators, Thackeray,
rolled off his chair with laughter.

Dickens began writing *Hard Times* this month, and as he
was finding it uphill work fixing the setting to his fancy, he
went off to Preston to get first-hand impressions of a strike.
It was annoying that Peter Cunningham should paragraph
him in the *Illustrated London News* and give the public to
understand that the book was to be written on the spur of the
moment and deal specifically with Preston.   This in no way
corresponded with facts, for he had been turning the subject
over in his mind for months and making notes for the book.
Only now that he saw his way to printing the first instalment
in *Household Words* (in April) was he going to Preston just
to see what a strike looked like.   It was a Saturday, and he
was disappointed to find the scene neither tragic, dramatic nor
even pathetic, though the lock-out had been in operation for
twenty-three weeks.   Owing to the cold furnaces, skies were
clear, streets empty and people moping indoors.   As there
was nothing to do and nothing to see, he went to *Hamlet* at
the local theatre, and sat through the performance feeling he
would have done quite as well to 'sit within doors and mope'
as the workmen were doing.   On the Sunday morning he
attended the meeting of delegates in the Cock-pit and was

impressed by their fortitude, good sense and restraint in speaking.   On the Monday he went to see the strike pay distributed and then to an open-air meeting at which the whole assembly sang

> Awake, ye sons of toil! nor sleep
> While millions strave, while millions weep
> Demand your rights; let tyrants see
> You are resolved that you'll be free.

Preston was reputed to be a model town, but Dickens found it a place so 'nasty' that he became more than ever set on lifting the working people out of the dreary districts into which industrialism had forced them.   It was all very well for Lord Derby and Mr. Bright to call such places 'centres of manufacturing industry'; he would follow Cobbett and Carlyle in calling them 'hell-holes'.   It was quite certain that capitalists could make their own fortunes in these places, and it was equally certain that they did not make the fortunes of their employees.   The writing of *Hard Times* drove him 'three-parts mad', for being no economist he found it uncongenial work trying to animate his narrative by expounding the falseness of certain accepted economic doctrines such as that of the law of supply and demand: it obliged him to try and rival the pedagogic efforts of Miss Martineau.   To Macaulay, Dickens in this book seemed to be heading for 'sullen socialism'.

Coketown, the scene of his story, and the country round were described graphically and formed the background for a satirical picture of the employers Bounderby and Gradgrind. Ruskin, who read each number eagerly, said that its value was impaired by displaying Bounderby as a monster instead of a worldly employer and Stephen Blackpool as a saint instead of an honest employee.[1]   He thought, however, that the author had succeeded in proving that the principle of buying in the cheapest and selling in the dearest market was a vile practice conducive to the suppression of all that was best in man. Intent on keeping humanity human, Dickens said that his

[1] *Unto this Last*, pp. 14-15.

satire was directed against those who think in figures and averages. They seemed to him 'representatives of the wickedest and most enormous vice of our time'. In writing a book so contrary to his own instinctive genius, Dickens was taking his stand alongside Carlyle, Kingsley, Hood, Mrs. Gaskell, Charlotte Brontë, George Eliot and other writers who resented the exploitation of the powerless. Persevering in this uncongenial work 'for righteousness' sake' made Dickens more than usually short-tempered and restless. Virtue is always a disagreeable task-mistress, and in order to complete his weekly instalments he had rigidly to deny himself to all visitors and to refuse all invitations.

Edmund Yates was one of these visitors. Ringing at the doorbell of Tavistock House, he was ushered by a footman into the drawing-room, a large room at the back of the house. Presently Miss Hogarth came in and greeted him pleasantly, saying that Mr. Dickens was too busy to see him but that if he was the son of Frederick Yates (the actor) he would receive him on Sunday at 2 P.M. On the Sunday he found Dickens in a room on the first floor. Yates saw no trace of the 'Maclise view' of him, indeed he was already looking like the Frith portrait painted years later. His bearing was hearty, almost aggressive. 'God! how like your father!' he exclaimed and then began to talk about the old Adelphi. Yates sent him a copy of *My Haunts* and marked him down as godfather for the child he was expecting in the autumn. Dickens dined with him in November 1854 for the christening of his son. We see from the account of this interview that Georgy was playing the part of receptionist to a great author. There is no doubt that she had great charm of manner and nothing very much to do.

As Dickens worried away at *Hard Times* he felt overwhelmed by the number of things that were wrong with England. One of the principal wrongs he held to be the landed system of the country at large. To his mind it was responsible for many 'locked-up social evils', evils that remained unexposed because the land was its own legislator.

If only the people could grasp this plain truth they would 'make themselves heard like the sea all round this island'. Often he talked with Layard in this strain. Layard, he said, was 'the most useful man in England, and his speeches should be broadcast at every market cross, in every town hall . . . up in the very balloons, and down in the very diving bells'. He can help support him in the press, for Lemon of *Punch* is ready to back him, so is Shirley Brooks of the *Illustrated London News* and *Weekly Chronicle*, and as for his own *Household Words*, Layard may count on him as being 'Damascus steel to the core'. In carrying out this pledge he told his readers baldly that unless they seriously set about improving the houses of the poor they would be guilty before God and man of wholesale murder. He cautioned working men not to be tricked by speakers calling themselves reformers who are merely angling for parliamentary votes, but to go on organising trade unions. Working men should never lose sight of the basic fact that but for them the world would not go round. They must see to it that their exertions shall not in the future be devoted to the maintenance of a workless, extravagant upper class whose interest it was to focus public attention on foreign rather than domestic affairs. The House of Commons was still, for Dickens, the ash-heap of his youth, and its members sifters and resifters of cinders. 'It appears to me,' he said, 'that Parliament is become just the dreariest failure and nuisance that ever bothered this much bothered world.'

The English and French declaration of war on Russia at the end of March 1854 filled Dickens and his friends with despair, put an end to social planning, and forced Lord John Russell to withdraw in April the new Reform Bill he had introduced in February. So the people were to be made fools of again, 'made to sing their own death-song in "Rule Britannia" and allow their own wrongs and sufferings to be obscured by cannon-smoke and blood-mists!' Everyone Dickens knew was already contributing to the Patriotic Fund 'without giving a thought to the wretchedness engendered by cholera, of which in London alone an infinitely larger number of English people than are likely to be slain in the whole Russian war have miserably and needlessly died'. 'I feel', he sighed, 'as if the world had been pushed back five hundred years.' Layard, who had been attaché to our embassy in Turkey under Stratford Canning, made ready to go to Constantinople, thence to take his chance of getting on to the Crimea. When British and French troops landed near Sevastopol in September he managed to get aboard the *Agamemnon*, and from her main-top witnessed the battle of the river Alma.[1] To his experiences and the effect of his reports on Dickens we shall return later.

Before doing so we must see how Dickens tried at Boulogne, during the summer months of 1854, to fight against ever increasing restlessness and depression. He had rented another of M. Beaucourt's houses (the Villa du Camp de Droite), for the family and in these congenial surroundings quickly polished off *Hard Times*. At Boulogne, however, he seemed closer to the war than at home. Buglers sounded calls at all hours, his favourite walks were ploughed up by baggage waggons, and sixty thousand soldiers were in camp near Wimereux. When the Prince Consort came over to inspect the troops, Dickens ran up a Union Jack with a tricolour atop of it. On the day of the review he went for his usual walk and, returning by the Calais road, found himself face to face with the Prince and Louis Napoleon. He snatched off his wideawake, whereupon the Emperor swept off his cocked hat, and Prince Albert did the same. The Emperor appeared more solid than in the old days at Gore House, but this may have been the effect of uniform. He looked tired and 'stooped in the manner of Albany Fonblanque'. That night an *entente cordiale* was celebrated in Boulogne, English sailors and guardsmen could be seen everywhere dancing, drinking and embracing French soldiers in the streets. Dickens contributed to the gala effect by lighting

[1] September 20, 1854.

one hundred and twenty wax candles in his seventeen front windows, thereby earning the applause of M. Beaucourt. Prince Albert's September review was followed in October by the Emperor's review at which the storming of the Malakoff redoubt was announced, as it happened prematurely, but the men were not to know that! The cheering of the troops on parade sounded very feeble to Dickens, who said, 'fifty English throats could have made more noise than those French divisions'. The Empress sat her grey horse 'capitally', looked charming, and when the Emperor handed her the dispatch, 'kissed it with as natural an impulse as one could wish to see'

In England Nathaniel Hawthorne, from his consular post at Liverpool, noted the rejoicing over the same news of victory. When it turned out to be incorrect, he wrote, 'I am glad of it . . . it is impossible for an American to be otherwise than glad. Success makes an Englishman intolerable . . . an Englishman in adversity is a very respectable character.'[1] Hawthorne's reflections on the Englishmen he came in contact with during his residence in our country are worthy of note, as they are representative of educated American opinion of the day.

> An Englishman [he says] likes to feel the weight of all the past upon his back; and moreover the antiquity that overburdens him has taken root in his being and has grown to be rather a hump than a pack . . . he appears to be sufficiently comfortable under this mouldy accretion.

When Dickens returned to London, he found the clubs buzzing with Crimean stories. William Russell, the *Times* correspondent, was sending home highly disquieting and damaging reports. The shameful organisation of supplies, it appeared, was causing great hardship on troops in the field, and the condition of the lazar-house at Sevastopol was described by Cobden as 'unutterably shocking'; but Layard said, what could be expected of a government so conscience-

---

[1] Henry James, *Life of Hawthorne*, p. 153.

less as to 'go on vacation for eight weeks without once summoning a cabinet meeting'? Why, ministers had paid less attention to the affairs of the country than a merchant did to his business! Dickens of course was in full sympathy with Layard's strictures and reflected ruefully on the Boodle-Buffyism that made such a state of affairs possible. His friend Sir Joseph Walmsley told him he never would forget the gloom of these weeks 'when each man asked the other with whom did the fault lay, was it with the commanders abroad or with the government at home?' Cobden had told him that the French had covered themselves with great glory, adding, 'I am sorry to say nothing but discredit and shame attaches to us . . . crowds of officers, including the Duke of Cambridge and Lord Cardigan, have slunk home, boys had been left in charge of boys, for there were few grown men out there.'

After Christmas Roebuck in the House of Commons moved that a committee be appointed to inquire into the conduct of the war. His voice faltered when he told how an army of 54,000 men had left England a few months earlier, how only 14,000 of these were still alive of whom but 5000 were fit for duty. In face of an overwhelming vote of censure the ministry resigned on February 1, and by February 16 a new government had been formed with Palmerston as prime minister in place of Aberdeen. Dickens at once took his political skit, *The Thousand and One Humbugs*, out of a drawer and brought it up to date. 'Parmastoon has newly succeeded Abbadeen (or the Addled) who has for his misdeeds been strangled with a garter.' It amused him to read through his old satire; it should now see daylight in *Household Words*. Dickens had a particular distrust of Palmerston, the statesman he called 'the glib vizier'. Palmerston, who had been in office before he was born and who had been joining governments in some capacity or other as long as he could remember. Palmerston with his traditional policy of suspicion of Russia, encouragement of Poland, support for Turkey, backing of Italian Liberals, and the whole balance of power box-of-tricks that he was such an adept at conjuring with. Reluctantly did the new prime minister grant an inquiry into the conduct of the war and on assuming the premiership fuse the offices of Secretary for War and Secretary at War, giving the post to Lord Panmure over whom he could exercise the tightest control. Palmerston's hatred and distrust of Russia, which set the course of opinion in England for generations, was so strong that Dickens felt he might carry on the war for years. As Cobden said:

> If our ignorant clamourers for the 'humiliation of Russia' are allowed to have their own way, look out for serious disasters to the Allies! No power ever yet persisted in the attempt to subjugate Russia that did not break in pieces against that impassive empire . . . the Russians can beat all the world at endurance . . . we exaggerate the power of a naval blockade . . . Russia has resources we cannot touch.

It is extremely strange in reading patriotic war speeches to see how the idiom of one war always fits another war. At a dinner of the London Commercial Travellers Schools,[1] Dickens was asked to propose the health of the army in the Crimea. He said, 'It does not require any extraordinary sagacity in a commercial assembly to appreciate the dire evils of war'. War paralysed enterprise, enfeebled trade, beat down the peaceful arts, but 'there are seasons when the evils of peace are immeasurably greater and when a powerful nation by admitting the right of any autocrat to do wrong, sows by such complicity the seeds of its own ruin and over-shadows itself in time to come with that fatal influence which great and ambitious powers are sure to exercise over their weaker neighbours'. Even Dickens placed the guilt on 'one man who had plotted against mankind. One man having effaced peace and justice, forces us to fight in the cause of human freedom.' All wars seem somehow to be the same war.

At Christmas-time Dickens gave readings of the *Carol* at Bradford, Reading and Sherborne, at which place Macready

[1] December 30, 1854.

was living in unhappy retirement. For his own children he arranged some theatricals, *Fortunio and his Seven Gifted Servants*, by Planché. This performance, over which he took infinite trouble, gave him the desire to produce a play for grown-ups during the summer. Play production was the most satisfying recreation of all. Still the prey of restlessness, he made plans for going to Paris, warning Régnier that he was about to hurl himself in company with his young friend Wilkie Collins into all the 'diableries of that delightful city'.

Just as he was packing for Paris Maria Beadnell made an unexpected come-back. Going through the pile of letters he found waiting for him one evening at Tavistock House, he recognised her handwriting on an envelope. 'Three or four and twenty years vanished like a dream. I opened it with the touch of my young friend David Copperfield when he was in love.'[1] What a relief to turn from war and hell-holes to personal romance again. Eagerly he told Maria in a hastily written note:

> You cannot remember more tenderly than I do. I hardly ever go to the city, but I walk up an odd little court at the back of the Mansion House and come out by the corner of Lombard Street. . . . I forget nothing of those times. . . . I shall be charmed to have a long talk with you.[2]

Explaining that he was on the point of starting for Paris, he was tripped up by the word 'Paris'. The very word evoked memories of a day 'when my existence was entirely uprooted and my whole being blighted by the Angel of my soul being sent there to finish her education'.

This reply gave intense pleasure to Maria, who obviously took it as evidence that he still secretly adored her above all others. Another letter, written from the Hôtel Meurice, also seemed to be under the spell of the old enchantment. The little blue gloves he once matched for her, does she remember? Has she not read in one of his books a faithful reflection of his

[1] 625-6. II. N.L.   [2] 626. II. N.L.

N

passion for her? Perhaps on laying down the book she may have thought, 'How dearly that boy must have loved me!' or perhaps, 'How vividly this man remembers it!'

Yet another note reached her a week later written from Tavistock House. It seemed to show a wish for intimate friendship. She had 're-opened the way to a confidence which . . . may be between ourselves alone'. Mrs. Winter's dull heart glowed at the language used by her old lover:

> My entire devotion to you and the wasted tenderness of those hard years which I have ever since half-loved, half-dreaded to recall made so deep an impression on me, that I refer to it a habit of suppression, which now belongs to me, which I know is no part of my original nature, but which makes me chary of showing my affections even to my children except when they are very young.[1]

Maria Winter could not handle such correspondence at all and made the fatal mistake of accusing her ex-adorer of having 'exaggerated' his feeling for her. This hurt Dickens, who retorted:

> I don't quite apprehend what you mean by my over-stating the strength of the feeling of five-and-twenty years ago. If you mean of my own feeling, and will only think what the desperate intensity of my nature is, and that this began when I was Charley's age; that it excluded every other idea from my mind for four years, at a time of life when four years are equal to four times four; and that I went at it with a determination to overcome all the difficulties which fairly lifted me up into the newspaper life, and floated me away over a hundred men's heads, then you are wrong, for nothing can exaggerate that. I have positively stood amazed at myself ever since! And so I suffered, and so worked, and so beat and hammered away at the maddest romances that ever got into a boy's head and stayed there, that to see the mere cause of it at all, now, loosens my hold upon myself. . . . No one can imagine in the most distant degree what pain the recollection gave me in *Copperfield*. And, just as I can never open that book as

I open any other book, I cannot see the face (even at four-and-forty) or hear the voice without going wandering over the ashes of all that youth and hope in the wildest manner.[1]

There can be no doubt that in the Maria Beadnell romance lay the clue to much that we do not understand in Dickens's behaviour.

A few days later Kate Dickens, who knew nothing of these letters, called on Mrs. Winter at Charles's request and asked her to dinner, arranging that their carriage should fetch her and her husband to Tavistock House. The disillusionment of this meeting, even if we had not Georgy's confirmatory comments to rely on, was obviously complete. Dickens, however, chose to pull himself together and visit Mrs. Winter as if to make quite sure that the Maria Beadnell he once knew had no physical existence. The glass eyes of little 'Jip' stared at him in the hall and he watched his hostess adding brandy to her tea. There was nothing more to say and no action to be taken. A month later Dickens, in reply to Maria's suspicion that he never wants to see her again, fends her off with, 'Whoever is devoted to an art must be content to deliver himself wholly up to it. I can't help it, I must go my own way whether or no.'[2]

He talked to her of Spain, Greenland, the North Pole, Constantinople, saying he was driven by a demon of restlessness. 'You say that once upon a time I was not like this—now it has become myself, and my life.' Unwilling to abandon hope, Maria offered, somewhat obtusely, to come and see him on a Sunday and he replied that he would be out of town for many Sundays. And from henceforth fatuous, foolish Maria was transferred to the crucible of Dickens's imagination, whence she was to re-emerge in the guise of Flora Finching in *Little Dorrit* and he to figure as Arthur Clennam.

On his way to Paris Dickens got out of the train at Chatham to look at the house which in boyhood he had

[1] 626-35. II. N.L.   [2] 649. II. N.L.

dreamed of possessing—Gad's Hill.   He had heard through
Wills that it would shortly be in the market, as his contributor, Eliza Lynn, had been left the property by her father,
but could not afford to live there.   Comprising a medium-
sized house and one hundred and twenty acres of land, it was
altogether a place after his own heart and he at once made up
his mind to buy it as soon as the oppotrunity offered, for to
make one of his dreams come true would be to achieve the
height of happiness.   In Paris Dickens and Collins went to
two and three theatres a night and dined at all the best
restaurants.   Dickens was pretending to be quite as young
and sportive as his companion and able to enjoy everything
quite as much, but in reality he was for the first time feeling
his age.   He toyed with the idea of settling permanently in
la ville lumière and in long walks by the Seine cogitated how
to make his new book an attack on the bureaucracy of
England.   One day there flashed into his mind the word
'circumlocution'.   In a moment he knew he had *le mot de
l'énigme*.   This was the book in embryo.   The organisers of
circumlocution followed automatically—giving themselves
the wonderful name of Barnacles, Tite (undislodgeable) Barnacles.   He could now get on swimmingly with the story.

Neither editorial duties nor work on his new novel were
enough to fill the empty spaces of a life which somehow, in
spite of its success, was beginning to seem a failure.   With
infinite trouble he began arranging plays for Tavistock
House.   The theatre at least never lost its attraction.   Wilkie
Collins had written *The Lighthouse*, 'a Domestic Melodrama
in two acts', and he would produce that.   It contained an
excellent part for him, that of the lighthouse keeper, Aaron
Gurnock.   He would get 'Stanny' to paint a drop scene of the
Eddystone as the action took place inside the lighthouse.
Three performances[1] were given and delighted guests
crowded into 'the smallest theatre in the world'.   The plays
were followed by excellent suppers at which speeches were

---

[1] Saturday June 16, Monday 18, Tuesday 19: *The Lighthouse* and *Mr.
Nightingale's Diary*.

made. On one of the nights Lord Campbell pleased his host and the company generally by declaring he would rather have written *Pickwick* than be Lord Chief Justice of England or a peer of Parliament.

The play was repeated on Tuesday July 10 at Campden House for the Bournemouth Sanatorium for Consumption. In this house, which was owned by a Colonel Waugh, there was a miniature theatre, complete with pit, boxes, stage and footlights which delighted Dickens, but Kensington knows it no more.

And all the time he was organising these entertainments he kept in touch with the member for Aylesbury who was as active as ever in attacking bureaucracy and demanding administrative reform. Dickens stuck closer and closer to Layard. Whatever it cost him, he would support him in his campaign. When a meeting was organised at Drury Lane[1] at which Layard was to denounce maladministration in Government offices, Dickens promised to be on the platform at his side, but could not manage to get there. Quoting from blue-books issued by the Sevastopol commissioners, Layard referred to 'records of inefficiency, records of indifference to suffering, records of ignorance, records of obstinacy', all casting shame on us and our system of government. The Civil Service was grossly over-staffed, every member of the Service was busy making work for another member and passing things on. He accused Lord Palmerston personally of an attitude of levity towards the sufferings of the people of England.

Greatly offended by the attack, the Prime Minister contemptuously alluded in the House to 'the private theatricals staged at Drury Lane' by Layard. Dickens, who had pledged himself to speak at another meeting at the same theatre, under the chairmanship of Samuel Morley, took this reference up in his speech:[2]

> The noble Lord at the head of the Government [he said] wonders why Mr. Layard accuses him of habitually joking

when the country is plunged in deep disgrace and distress. He turned his period with a reference to 'private theatricals' at Drury Lane. . . . I will try and give the noble Lord the reason for these 'private theatricals'.

The public theatricals which the noble Lord is so condescending as to manage are so intolerably bad, the machinery so cumbrous, the parts so ill-distributed, the company so full of 'walking gentlemen', the managers have such large families and are so bent on putting those families into what is theatrically called 'first business'—not because of their aptitude for it, but because they *are* their families— that we find ourselves obliged to organise an opposition.

Explaining his own position on the platform, Dickens said:

This is the first political meeting I have ever attended. . . . By literature I have lived and through literature I have been content to serve my country. . . . In my sphere of action I have tried to understand the heavier social grievances and to help to set them right. The country is silent, gloomy, England has never found an enemy one-twentieth part so potent to effect the misery and ruin of her noble defenders as she has been herself. . . . Discord is piled on the heaving basis of ignorance, poverty, crime. There is no understanding of the general mind in Parliament . . . the machinery of government goes round and round and the people stand aloof.

He has joined the Society for promoting Administrative Reform because men must get together over good citizenship. It is hoped to influence the House through the constituencies, but he has not the least hesitation in saying that he has scant faith in the House of Commons as at present existing.

As he looked back to the years when he served his apprenticeship in the gallery he saw little change in the House itself; certain things indeed were exactly the same. Now as then, personal altercation, *i.e.* the retort courteous, the quip modest, the reply churlish, the reproof valiant, the countercheck quarrelsome, the lie circumstantial and the lie direct were of immeasurably greater interest to the House of Commons than the health and education of a whole people.

The Society for Administrative Reform had come into existence because the well-being of the country was of more importance for the future of England than the maintenance of
unmeaning routine and worn-out conventions.   The association does not seek, as its enemies say, to set class against class,
but to bridge the gulf between governed and governors.

After this plunge into political controversy Dickens
retired to his desk again.   If direct attack did not make
'Twirling Weathercock' see the error of his ways, maybe the
indirect attack he was planning in *Little Dorrit* might be of
service.

Folkestone this summer proved almost intolerable owing
to the vulgarity of trippers.   Determined to absent himself
from England in the autumn, he crossed with Georgy to
France in order to find winter quarters for the family in Paris.
Writing to 'dearest Catharine', he reported that he had had
an 'awful job to find anything at all to suit them, for Paris is
perfectly full'.   He had managed, however, to secure 'two
apartments—an *entresol* and a first floor with a kitchen and
servants' room' at seven hundred francs a month.   'You
must be prepared for a regular continental abode', he wrote;
'the front apartments all look on to the Champs Elysées . . .
the situation almost the finest in Paris and the children will
have a window from which to look on the busy life outside.'
A more comfortable apartment in the rue du Faubourg St.
Honoré had been rejected because the children's rooms would
have looked on to a dull courtyard, and that would never have
done.   He and Georgy will try and get the apartment into
running order at once so that they may be ready to receive
the family as soon as may be.   The servants must join him at
once and Kate must cross to Boulogne and stay there with the
children till the rooms are ready.   Charles and Georgy and
the servants moved in to 49 Avenue des Champs Elysées.
During the first night Charles heard Georgy moving about,
got up, and asked what was the matter.[1]   'Oh, it's so dread-

[1] 697. II. N.L.

fully dirty. I can't sleep for the smell in my room,' replied Georgy. Next morning he exerted all his energy and persuasiveness to get the apartment 'purified'. It was like summoning a cast and assuming the role of stage-manager again. The porter, the porter's wife, the porter's wife's sister, a feeble upholsterer of enormous age and all his work-men—four boys. To these were added the co-proprietors of the apartment, an old lady, and a martial little man with a François Ier beard. 'It's not the custom,' objected the pro-prietor, but somehow Dickens got round them and they agreed to scrub and cleanse and even to provide new carpets. At last he could report that the place was exquisitely cheerful and 'as clean as anything human can be'. On receiving this encouraging intelligence Kate and the children joined him.

Chapter 21

LIFE ABROAD

The fuming vanities of Paris.
CHARLES DICKENS

THE plunge into Parisian life turned Dickens into a 'Sparkler' again. Blue as in Italy was the sky above the Elysian Fields, bright were the tossing fountains, the very heavens seemed to shine and, when the strains of martial music made themselves audible, 'all bloused Paris, led by the Inimitable', tripped along in a kind of hilarious dance. The younger members of the family took their pleasures more sedately and through the winter months spent many hours watching from their windows the moving panorama which to them was Paris. The apartment, over a carriage repository, had six windows facing the Avenue, each of them a vantage-point for sightseeing. One day they would see the Emperor and Empress driving to St. Cloud; another day the Emperor riding alone on horseback, looking so mortally ill that they would wish him in bed; yet another day a battalion of red-trousered Zouaves marching to the Barrière, stock on shoulder, preceded by their mascot, a black dog. Thoroughbreds ridden by dashing young men would prance along and elegant equipages roll by with white-harnessed black horses curvetting under their tight bearing-reins. In this wise did the wives of men who had made fortunes on the Bourse advertise their husband's success and display their own fine feathers and furs. Not less entertaining were the ladies of *ton* who, when the sun shone, floated by in their orange-coloured or russet shawls, the points of which spread over silky crinolines that, swaying, revealed glimpses of white stockings and glinting bronzed bootlets. It was the vogue that year to wear autumn tints, and Mamey and Katey were of an age to dote on the new fashions and, in so far as their

361

mother and father would permit, to dress themselves in the same sort of clothes.

The impression the family received from watching at these windows was of a gay world of almost fantastic wealth and luxury, and this impression was intensified when their father, returning from some bachelor dinner, gave them an account of the entertainment he had enjoyed. Charles Dickens, who always took colour easily abroad, became at this time floridly Parisian in gesture, and was given to talking voluble French at home. It was good practice for him and the children and qualified him for compliments from *convives*, who told him that he spoke 'the celestial language in a most angelic way'. Paris to him was a climate to bask in, almost a terrestrial paradise.

One evening he dined with the press magnate, Emile de Girardin, who lived 'in an opulence worthy of an eastern potentate', and was ushered through gorgeous drawing-rooms, lit with 'ten thousand candles in gold sconces', to a 'magnificent' dining-room whence, through plate-glass doors, one looked straight into the kitchen at cooks, in high white caps, stirring pans and basting viands. On the dinner-table, laid for eight, stood mounds of truffles and jugs of the best champagne. In reading the menu Dickens was puzzled by an item entitled *Homage à l'illustre écrivain de l'Angleterre*. This turned out to be a plum pudding far larger than any ever seen in England, served with a 'heavenly white sauce'. To watch the courses being carried through the glass doors fascinated him. The food was certainly 'the best ever tasted by mortal', but the wine was even more astonishing. With the third course was served a port 'costing at least two guineas a bottle', and after dinner a brandy 'buried these hundred years and more'. Exquisite coffee 'brought from the remote east in exchange for a quantity of gold dust' concluded the repast. Replete, the company returned to the drawing-room, where tables, moved by an unseen agency, arrived laden with cigarettes. Cool drinks 'flavoured by lemons fresh from Algeria and delicate oranges from Lisbon' next made their appearance and presently the guests, reposing on divans, ended a Luculline evening sipping 'caravan tea of finest quality from China. The lavishness, as Dickens explained to his family, was almost embarrassing to an Englishman, and the most amusing thing of all was that, in reply to the compliments he had paid to M. de Girardin on his marvellous entertainment, his host had replied, 'This is just nothing, Mr. Dickens, nothing at all. You must really come and *dine* another day.' And of course Mr. Dickens did so, accepting with alacrity an invitation to meet his friend Régnier, Jules Sandeau and other writers. This time it was not the wine that struck him most, for he was expecting that, but the cigars, 'five thousand inestimable cigars in prodigious bundles'. Such a display of riches was really stunning!

The difference in the wealth and standing of newspaper proprietors in England and France struck Dickens very much. M. de Girardin was the first press baron he had met. Not only was he the owner and editor of a powerful political organ, *La Presse*, but he was a pioneer in what we should call magazine journalism and made a bid in his weeklies to serve a large and varied public. They included the *Musée des Familles*, *Panthéon Littéraire*, *Journal des Connaissances Utiles*, *Journal des Institutions Primaires* and, most successful venture of all, the *Journal du Bien-être Universel*. It interested the French editor to compare notes with his colleague, the conductor and part owner of *Household Words*, whose notion of catering for the people was rather like his own. From his newspapers M. de Girardin had built up a fortune which he had been lucky enough to amplify on the Bourse. Even this magnate, it seemed, had had his political ups and downs. From 1834 to 1848 he had sat as deputy, but in the latter years he had resigned and had advised the King to resign too. At the moment of the revolution of 1848 *La Presse* was suspended and Girardin found himself consigned to prison by General Cavaignac. After spending eleven days in the Conciergerie, he was released, and got back on his incarcerators with a wildly popular pamphlet, *Le Journal d'un*

Journaliste au secret. From this successful man Dickens was able to pick up a good many ideas.

One of the many charms of Paris was that literary men were made much of by everyone connected with books and the theatre, and, unlike London, where nearly all writers were poor, writers in Paris were often very rich and always highly considered. Eugène Sue, for example, had a luxurious apartment crammed with pictures, statues, antiques and painted glass, hothouses full of flowers and fountains playing on gold and silver fish. And the joke in Paris was that Eugène Sue was believed to be the coiner of the famous mot, 'No one has the right to superfluities while anyone is in want of necessities'. A great fillip had been given to journalistic enterprise and trade generally by the war in the Crimea and authors in France did not seem to lead so parochial an existence as in England: they were sufficiently in touch with the world of affairs to improve the occasion and gamble on the Bourse.

It was rather head-turning to Dickens to be made so much of in Paris and to be entertained on a scale that even in America he had never experienced. The contagious cordiality of his reception by French people everywhere, and the fact that no explanatory introductions were ever required in any company, struck him most agreeably. A porter delivering a parcel would say pleasantly, 'Cette Madame Tojair. Ah! qu'elle est drôle, et précisément comme une dame que je connais à Calais.' As 'l'écrivain célèbre' Dickens had already burst into all homes, strangers would say, 'On connaît bien que Monsieur Dickin prend sa position sur la dignité de la littérature'. At long last he was recognised for what he was, the greatest novelist in the world. Why was it that his compatriots had never treated him in this way? And can we wonder that he took to Parisian life as a duck to water and felt himself the good comrade of all French authors?

The Dickens family were not allowed to waste too much time looking out of the window, for their father insisted on regular study hours and intensive cultivation of the French and Italian languages. Through Ary Scheffer, he secured for them as tutor Daniele Manin, ex-president of the Venetian Republic, 'best and noblest of unhappy gentlemen'. Dickens could not but reflect, as he looked on his seven sons in 'the banquet-hall' at No. 49 at Christmas 1855, that if he himself in youth had had half the advantages he was now bestowing on his children his life might have been entirely different!

The best and oldest friends Dickens now had in Paris were the Régniers whom he had so often entertained in London. Régnier, as on a previous occasion, made 'Boz' free of the green room at the Théâtre Français and it was through Régnier that he got to know Scribe, Auber and Alexandre Dumas. Kate Dickens managed to get on, after a fashion, with Madame Régnier and Madame Scribe too, but, unlike her husband, she was not electrified by contacts, nor did she in Paris acquire any vivacity of manner. Kate just remained what she had always been, amiable, placid and slow at the uptake, and she was at the great disadvantage of not daring to try and talk French. Great hospitality was shown to both of them by Sir Joseph Olliffe, physician to the British Embassy and the English colony in Paris. At Olliffe's house all birds of passage naturally perched and the doctor's parties were known for their pleasantness and informality.

With M. and Mme. Scribe, Mr. and Mrs. Dickens dined 'frequently', and at these dinners M. Auber was often present. By December Dickens spoke of Scribe as 'my particular friend'. Scribe not only had the charming apartment in Paris already alluded to but a château in the country as well, and his 'sumptuous carriage and magnificent span of horses' were admired by the Dickens family when they drew up at No. 49. Rather naïvely pleased with his possessions, Scribe would say to Dickens, 'All this I have earned with my pen, for, as you see, my dear Dickens, I began as a little law clerk'. And 'Boz's' heart went out to him, for had not he too begun as a little law clerk?

M. Auber could not have been more friendly. Dickens

describes him as 'a solid elderly little man having agreeable recollections of England' where he had once lived at 'Stock Noonton'. The first time they talked together he told of his meeting with the Queen of England, to whom he had been presented by King Louis Philippe, and of how the Queen had smiled and said, 'We are such old acquaintances through M. Auber's works that an introduction is quite unnecessary'. One evening the Dickenses were dining at a party that included both the Scribes and Aubers. It was the first night of the new opera *Manon Lescaut*, and though he had attended four hundred of his own first nights Scribe showed great fidgetiness towards the end of the meal, pulling out his watch from time to time and at last bouncing up and bolting from the table. Madame Scribe at once rose from her chair next to Dickens and, 'looking twenty-five though she had a son of thirty', laughed, curtsied to the company and ran after her husband. How wonderfully alert and alive these French women were; middle age and child-bearing seemed to have no effect on their vitality.

With rapidly increasing experience we find Dickens becoming a very bold critic of plays and developing a horror of the Comédie Française. He hated its dreary conventions, which, he said, were calculated to freeze the marrow. To him it was like 'a vast tomb such as you see in eastern legends where one goes to think of unsuccessful loves and dead relations'.

He saw *Le Paradis Perdu* at the Ambigu, a compound of Milton's epic and Byron's *Cain*. The wildest rumours had been flying about before the first night as to the nudity of 'our first parents', for all Paris had been ransacked in a hunt for a woman with brown hair falling to the calves of her legs. 'At last', says Dickens, 'she was found at the Odéon!' Going to a performance of *Comme il vous plaira*, he was much amused to watch the company sitting down as often as possible on as many trunks as possible: ' "gammon" was no word for it!' Macready, who attended a rehearsal, said the speech of the seven ages was delivered as a light comedy joke. Jacques married Celia and 'everything was as wide of Shakespeare as possible'. He counted Jacques sitting down seventeen times on roots of trees and twenty-five times on grey stones, and at the end of the second act he left saying, 'It must have been got up by patients in an asylum for idiots'. It was George Sand who had adapted it, though she told him privately that to adapt Shakespeare was to murder Shakespeare—adding with a shrug, 'As Paris would not accept him *au naturel*, something had to be done about it'.

It was the custom at the moment to suspend performances in theatres to admit of the reading of a bulletin on the war in the Crimea. To an Englishman it was surprising to note the complete apathy with which the French heard these announcements; the audience was 'stagnant as ditch-water'; even the claqueurs remained silent, the war seemed to be nobody's business.

At the Odéon Dickens sat out a play in verse, *Michel Cervantes*, which he pronounced to be 'an infernal dose of ditch-water': and at the Porte Saint Martin saw *Orestes* versified by Dumas. It was so bad as to be almost good. 'If I had not already learnt to tremble at the sight of classic drapery on the human form, I should have plumbed the utmost depths of terrified boredom.' Often he left before the end of a play. He would turn to Kate or Georgy saying, 'It is really unbearable. I shall go and walk two or three miles. You must tell me the end to-night.'

Making friends quickly was, as we know, a Dickens characteristic, and he found he could make delightful women friends in Paris without drawing down on himself the jealousy of anyone. He was greatly attracted to the famous contralto Madame Viardot, sister of La Malibran. 'Elle est parfaite,' he would say with his hand on his heart. 'Je suis son esclave.' Together they talked eagerly of writers and it was she who had been quick to arrange for Dickens the meeting with George Sand. Madame Viardot lived in the new quarter of Paris in a house so impersonal and bare that it looked as if she had moved in the week before and was to leave again the following week. The piano was shut, there was no music about and no books: it was the very last house one could associate with an opera singer, and when she told M. Boz that she had lived there for eight years he was more surprised than he could say. The dinner-party included the Ary Scheffers, the Sartorises, George Sand and 'a typical English lady' fresh from the Crimea, dressed *en paletot*, who smoked incessantly and monologued on her adventures. Dickens describes George Sand, who sat next him, as 'chubby, matronly, swarthy and black-eyed'. 'Chubby' does not seem a very happy adjective for that heavy, sleepy-lidded face with its strong Jewish features, but he further says, 'The human mind cannot conceive anyone more astonishingly opposed to all my preconceptions. If I had been shown her in a state of repose, I should have said the Queen's monthly nurse. *Au reste* she has nothing of the *bas bleu* about her and is very quiet and agreeable.'[1] At a disadvantage in not having read any of her books, whereas she had read all his, Dickens found that in conversation she took the initiative and had a little final way of settling his opinions for him which he took to have been acquired in the province where she lived and where he heard she dominated local society.

At the house of the great anglophile Amédée Pichot, director of the *Revue Britannique* and translator of *David Copperfield*, the Dickenses were also entertained. There, one evening, they renewed acquaintance with Alphonse de Lamartine, who always alluded to the English novelist as 'un des grands amis de mon imagination'. Lighter in hand than George Sand, he made a very unaffected and simple impression as he discussed the writings of Defoe and Richardson and their genius for minute detail in narrative. It was a tribute to Dickens when Lamartine said to Pichot that he had rarely met a foreigner who talked French so easily as 'ce cher Boz'.

Almost more gratifying than any social success was an article in the *Revue des Deux Mondes* which appeared in

[1] 733. II. N.L.

February 1856 entitled 'Charles Dickens, son talent et ses œuvres'. It was by Henri Taine and of high importance in placing Dickens for ever among the immortals. The French critic had found it difficult, he confided to a friend, 'de disséquer Boz', but after infinite pains he had done so.

At the time Taine wrote, literally nothing was known of Dickens's life-story, but that he was the son of a stenographer and himself trained to the same profession. Men spoke vaguely of an unhappy youth and of the great wealth and reputation that had come to him through the writing of serial novels. To know more they supposed they must wait till the day when 'M. Boz' published his memoirs. Forty volumes represented the inner history of genius, and as far as anyone knew they in no way depended on the circumstances of his outer life. As Taine sagely observed, 'On a beau être illustre, on ne devient pas pour cela la propriété du public.'

The author of the article had been reading *Martin Chuzzlewit* in the *Moniteur*. He notes the tendency to depict and the power of seeing in the manner of the camera's eye. With the description of a storm, taken by lightning, he illustrates his contention:

> The eye, partaking of the quickness of the flashing light saw in its every gleam a multitude of objects which it could not see at steady noon in fifty times that period. Bells in steeples with the rope and wheel that moved them; ragged nests of birds in cornices and nooks; faces full of consternation in the tilted waggons that came tearing past: their frightened teams ringing out a warning which the thunder drowned; harrows and ploughs left out in fields; miles upon miles of hedge-divided country, with the distant fringe of trees as obvious as the scarecrow in the beanfield close at hand; in a trembling, vivid, flickering instant, everything was clear and plain: then came a flush of red into the yellow light; a change to blue; a brightness so intense that there was nothing else but light: and then the deepest and profoundest darkness.

There was something definitely new about Dickens, and Taine thought that nothing comparable to this daguerrotype view had been either attempted or achieved by a novelist before. It struck him as astonishing, he felt the need to cover his eyes to shield them against this brilliant and extraordinary perception. To Dickens, Taine's dissection was a revelation. For the first time he had been taken seriously as a literary man by the leading critic of literature in France instead of being torn to pieces by anonymous reviewers.

Work on *Household Words*, which incidentally at this time carried many articles on Paris and France generally, obliged its conductor to make at least one journey a month to London. Sometimes he combined it with readings of *A Christmas Carol*. To please Mrs. Watson, he read it at Peterborough on December 18 from a 'tall pulpit of red baize', so tall that only his head and shoulders were visible. It was this experience that caused him to design and carry about his own reading-desk. The reading was a tribute to Mr. Watson's memory and a great occasion in Northamptonshire. A vote of thanks proposed by Mr. George Fitzwilliam was seconded by Lord Huntley. On December 22 Dickens read the *Carol* again at the Mechanics' Hall, Sheffield, and was presented with a service of table cutlery, a pair of razors and a pair of fish carvers, which he gratefully accepted as indicative of the skill of Sheffield hands and the warmth of Sheffield hearts.

Returning from London to Paris in February, he halted at Chatham in order to make final arrangements for the purchase of Gad's Hill. Though the Reverend James Lynn, who had lived there for thirty years, had died in 1855, his daughter Eliza was unwilling to give him possession before Lady Day 1857. An agreement to this effect having been reached, Dickens paid her the sum of £1790 and then put his dream castle out of his mind till he could live in it. Paris had certainly spoiled him for London, but thank God he would never have to look on London as his only home again.

In March he attended the annual general meeting of the Royal Literary Fund, really to indict the management, which was absorbing 40 per cent of the income. The house in Bloomsbury seemed to him inhabited by gliding ghosts engaged on mysterious occupations. What are these shapes about? To what end are their inquiries and confabulations directed? Do they seek to know whether an applicant deserves relief? It was plain to Dickens that the Fund was being pompously and badly administered at great expense instead of being simply administered at small expense. The secrecy to which it laid claim as its essential attribute was not preserved, for, through the 'two respectable householders' to whom reference must be made, the names of deserving applicants became perfectly well known to numbers of people. He begged the committee to decide what the Literary Fund was for and what it was not for. Was it a public corporation for the relief of men of genius and learning, or a smug, tradition-ridden, conventional society 'bent upon maintaining its own usages with a vast amount of pride, upon its own puffing at costly dinner tables and upon a course of expensive toadying to a number of distinguished individuals'. 'These are the questions', he told his audience, 'that you cannot this day escape from.' This speech was but one of the many efforts made by Dickens during his lifetime to raise the position of authors to a dignity accorded to them in France, but denied to them in England.

From this March outing he returned to Paris with an account of the burning down of Covent Garden, and with some 'pulverising', 'scarifying' *secret* news about Forster that excited Kate and Georgy to frenzy. Imagine old 'Fuz' getting himself engaged to Henry Colburn's widow and never telling them a word about it! Charles said you could have knocked him down with a feather when he first heard of it, and Kate and Georgy simply could not believe the news was true.

Once more Dickens settled down happily in Paris, where the delightful parties, the sympathetic conversation, the kindness and appreciation shown by the Parisians he most wished to be on good terms with made it difficult to concentrate even on *Little Dorrit*, the earliest issues of which had already surpassed those of *Bleak House*, for forty thousand copies of each number were being disposed of. 'It is a tremendous start', he wrote, 'and I am overjoyed at it.' In order to get his monthly fascicule completed within the prescribed fortnight he would walk round the walls of Paris, leaving it by the Barrière de l'Etoile and turning right one day and left the next. On the road he would often meet French regiments with bands playing airs from *Il Trovatore* and *Il Barbière di Siviglia* to which his thoughts jigged along in pursuit of the Tite Barnacle family and their antics at the Circumlocution Office.

In April Dickens dined with M. Hachette the publisher, in order to make acquaintance with his translators. It was, he commented, an 'odd sticky dinner' with salmon coming late on the menu and lobster following sweet. M. Hachette offered to pay him for French rights at the rate of £40 a month for a year, and Dickens was glad to acknowledge in a printed address to French readers of his books that M. Hachette had behaved throughout the negotiations in a 'spirited, liberal and generous manner'.

Almost as soon as he had settled in the Champs Elysées Dickens had been pounced on to pose for his portrait by Ary Scheffer, who on first seeing him said, 'You are not at all like what I expected to see; you are like a Dutch skipper.' Every day in November Dickens had to sit to this artist and the inaction drove him half distracted because the time wasted might have been given to writing. Ary Scheffer was a nice enough man and the people who frequented his house were delightful, but, as Dickens wrote to a friend, 'I can hardly express how uneasy and unsettled it makes me to have to sit, sit, sit with *Little Dorrit* on my mind and the Christmas business too . . . and the crowning feature is that I do not discern the slightest resemblance either in his portrait or his brother's! They both peg away at me at the same time.'

The sittings dragged on into the new year and made the sitter long to escape to the St. Bernard Hospice or somewhere equally remote. After a while the likeness became 'a nightmare portrait'; Dickens said it was very well painted with 'a fine spirited head that does not look at all like the original'. Wilkie Collins praised the picture and said Scheffer had been 'particularly successful with the eyes', which is untrue as they droop and lack vitality. One looks in vain for the confident alert expression of a man who has the world at his feet.

It was with fresh interest that Dickens attended the Royal Academy dinner in May, for he was able to tell Panizzi, whom he sat next, many details about French artists in Paris and the interesting work they were doing. London at the moment was celebrating the end of the Crimean War with illuminations and Dickens asked permission of Dean Milman to describe the scene from the top of St. Paul's for *Household Words*.

By the time the International Exhibition of art opened in Paris Dickens was very dissatisfied with the way English artists were painting. Frith, Egg and Ward seemed to him to come out best, but on the whole the work of his compatriots appeared to him lifeless, niggling and conventional. 'There is a horrid respectability about most of the best of them—a little, finite, systematic routine in them, strangely symptomatic to me of the state of England itself.' Of course there were bad French pictures, but the goodness of the good ones, their fearlessness, action, passion, left him lamenting that 'mere form and conventionalities usurp in English art, as in English government and social relations, the place of living force and truth'. And when we call to mind that Dickens had seen the work of Degas, Puvis, Manet, Courbet, Corot, Ingres, Millet and others, we are not surprised at his strictures. The exhibition attracted crowds of English visitors, including the Brownings, Thackeray, Owen Meredith, and many artists, among whom Dickens makes special mention of his friends Edwin Landseer and Charles Leslie. Several times he went to the English section and each time tried to praise and admire with 'great diligence', but it was of no use; his 'convictions as to their want of interest' remained unchanged.

More and more did Dickens seem to be drifting away from the insular point of view both of England and the continent.

The very thought of London now filled him with apprehension. 'I have never taken to it kindly since I lived abroad. Whenever I come back from the country now and see that great heavy canopy lowering over the housetops, I wonder what on earth I do there except of obligation.' He simply could not face the idea of returning to England for the summer: they must all go back to M. Beaucourt's château at Boulogne. There he felt more free than at Broadstairs, for he could don a workman's blouse, complete with leathern belt and cap, dawdle among the terraces and fountains, loaf on the pier and with regret observe the little seaport being vulgarised by 'insolent' English day trippers. And when the call came to him to work he could count on writing the next number of *Little Dorrit* without much trouble.

Although the Wimereux camp was by this time evacuated, an act was staged at the local fair showing the capture of the Malakoff redoubt—the key to Sevastopol—a triumph for French arms. Most French soldiers wore an English medal which they called 'The Salvage Medal', meaning that they got it for saving the English army. 'I don't suppose there are a thousand people in all France who believe that we did anything except get rescued by the French. . . . Nobody at home has yet any adequate idea of what the Barnacles and the Circumlocution Office have done for us.'

Cattermole and his family had also become tenants of M. Beaucourt for the summer—unsatisfactory tenants, as they could not pay their bills or their servants. In the end one of their sons had to act as cook to the whole family, who between them in the washing-up managed to break all the glass and china. In spite of this loss the good-hearted Beaucourts insisted that the poor little cook, Walter, should dine with them every day.

The outbreak of an epidemic known as 'Boulogne sorethroat' (really diphtheria) in late August sent the Dickenses hurrying back on Dr. Olliffe's orders to London. Gilbert à Beckett and his child had died after a few days' illness, and the *plage* had suddenly become desolate. The George

Hogarths, who were in possession at Tavistock House, were told to find other quarters at once and Dickens remained at Dover till he was certain they had cleared out, as 'he really could not bear the contemplation of their imbecility any longer'.

Both in Paris and Boulogne Wilkie Collins had danced in constant attendance on Dickens. Though he had not actually slept at 49 Champs Elysées, he had engaged a room at No. 63 so as to dine every day with the family, and when the transfer to Boulogne took place he occupied a cottage in the grounds. So indispensable had he become to the conductor of *Household Words* that in September 1856 he was appointed assistant editor at five guineas a week. Dickens admired Collins's stories at this time extremely and found him always ready to work for him. As the friendship grew ever closer we cannot but notice a falling-off in Forster's biography, and Forster as a married man was almost entirely superseded in intimacy and influence by the younger friend. It may be for this reason that the biography becomes a less reliable and almost a different kind of book, just as Dickens himself, under Collins's influence, became almost a different kind of man.

Chapter 22

ARCTIC CONCERNS

*Here, then, you have a tragedy, by its very origin, in mere
virtue of the accidents out of which it arose.*

DE QUINCEY

THREADING through the letters written by Dickens during
the spring and summer of 1856 are allusions to a play that
is being written by Wilkie Collins for Christmas production.
Miss Coutts and others were told it was 'a very special sort of
drama', and the family, who were to help act it, were kept on
the tiptoe of excitement as to its subject.   Ever since reading
Dr. Rae's Report on Sir John Franklin's last Arctic expedition, published by the Admiralty, Dickens had been haunted
by the tortures its members had endured before dying of
starvation.   He was particularly shocked by the paragraph in
which Dr. Rae said of the encampment in which they
perished:

> From the mutilated state of the corpses and the contents
> of the kettles, it is evident that our wretched countrymen
> had been driven to the last resource—cannibalism—as a
> means of prolonging existence.

Dickens maintained that Franklin's manly record of his own
sufferings and those of his men, all picked for character, gave
the lie to this monstrous inference, and he set himself to dis-
prove the paragraph and so remove from the minds of these
brave men's relations a most painful impression.   The task
he undertook was to write an article testing the story by the
most trying and famous cases of hunger and exposure on
record.   For a time he immersed himself in the stories of the
wrecks of the *Bounty, Peggy, Pandora, Juno, Medusa*, just as
Byron had done before writing canto II of *Don Juan*.
Dickens studied the records of those and other unfortunate
ships until he had familiarised himself with every possible

aspect of the horrors of shipwreck. These he talked over with Wilkie Collins, who in his turn wondered whether they could not be dramatised. With Dickens's help *The Frozen Deep* came to be written.

Still in holiday mood, Dickens, on his return from Boulogne in the first days of September, began to turn Tavistock House once again into a theatre. A meeting was summoned for October 20 of Stanfield, Lemon, Egg, Forster and other potential helpers at which the new play, *The Frozen Deep*, was read aloud. Dickens seemed delighted with the effect it produced and at once ordered a fair copy to be made for his own use. Then, after allocating the parts between friends and family, he told the members of the caste that each was responsible for copying out his or her lines. Rehearsals would take place every Friday in November, and later there might be more frequent repetitions. It was to be the most perfect amateur production imaginable.

At a cost of £50 and a clangour like that of 'shipbuilding in Chatham Dockyard', the schoolroom was converted into a neat theatre. Everything to do with the stage, even the hammering, put Dickens into the highest spirits, and when 'dear old Stanny' arrived with seventy pots of paint, a ball of string and an umbrella for measuring boards, backcloth and curtain, his mood became hilarious. At intervals he disappeared from view to get on with his *Little Dorrit* quota. In one of these retired moments he wrote to Macready:

Calm amidst the wreck, your aged friend glides away on the Dorrit stream, forgetting the uproar for a stretch of hours, refreshing himself with a ten or twelve miles' walk, pitches headforemost into foaming rehearsals, placidly emerges for editorial purposes, smokes over buckets of distemper with Mr. Stanfield aforesaid, again calmly floats upon the Dorrit waters.[1]

The autumn, as Charley, aged nineteen, recollected it, was 'one long rehearsal', during which hospitality was dispensed

[1] 815. II. N.L.

on the most lavish scale. Such abnormal quantities of meat were ordered in that the butcher thought he was but doing his duty to Mrs. Dickens (when she returned from a short rest-cure in the country) by calling to inquire if everything was in order. Kate had gone away to escape the worst of the noise, but now she and Charles put their heads together over the invitations to the play. There would be in all nearly four hundred guests to accommodate, which meant that the performance would have to be repeated four times. Just over ninety chairs could be placed in the auditorium each night, but the problem of seating 'was intensified by crino-lines'. It was obviously necessary to put up an extra room outside the house for cloaks and if necessary use it as an extension for standing at the back of the seated audience. January 6, 8, 12 and 14 were decided on for the nights, and the Duke of Devonshire was requested to name his own evening as Lord Lansdowne, Lord Houghton, Miss Coutts and Bulwer Lytton were to be invited to supper to meet him. Mrs. Dickens had a great deal of work to do in arranging for the grand refections that were to follow the acting as well as for the endless hospitality enforced on her by ever more frequent and prolonged rehearsals.

The better to imagine himself an arctic explorer, Dickens grew a beard instead of the neat moustache and tiny chin-tuft depicted by Ary Scheffer. Forster found this a very tiresome innovation since he had commissioned Frith to paint him a portrait of his friend for £50.[1] The artist was now told to hold his hand until such time as Dickens shaved again, but, after two years of waiting, he had to go ahead with the paint-ing, as the beard was evidently there for life. Wilkie Collins, who up to that time had been clean-shaven, also grew a beard for the part of Frank Aldersley which he never again removed. To get word-perfect in his Wardour lines Dickens used to walk of an evening along the Finchley Road to Willesden 'shouting his part to the great terror' of the localities he

[1] In 1859 he paid 300 guineas to Frith, 150 for the portrait and 150 for the copyright.

passed through. Clara Burnham was played by Mamey
Dickens and two other female characters were taken by Katey
Dickens and Georgy Hogarth. Francesco Berger, a Leipzig
friend of Charley Dickens, wrote the overture and incidental
music for the play.

The play was to be preceded by a prologue written by
Dickens. Forster was to speak it and could be heard mouth-
ing his words as he prowled about the house. It seemed to
Kate, when taken off her guard, that dear Macready must have
come to help them as of old.

The action of *The Frozen Deep* is set in the arctic regions
which, owing to the Franklin voyages, were now everyone's
concern. The two principal male characters in the play,
Richard Wardour and Frank Aldersley, are officers on two
ships of an arctic expedition seeking the North-West Passage.
Both are in love with the same girl, Clara Burnham, who
favours Aldersley. After two years of adventure and priva-
tion both men find themselves adrift on the same ice-floe.
Wardour, the stronger of the two, has Aldersley in his power
and could leave him to freeze to death. He saves him by
sacrificing his own meagre comforts and food, thus preserving
him for Clara, who, having been given a passage on the
Government relief ship, is awaiting them in Newfoundland.

On the first night Forster was ordered to recite the Prologue behind the scene and could be heard inviting an
audience keyed to the highest pitch of expectancy to

> Pause on the footprints of heroic men,
> Making a garden of the desert wide
> Where PARRY conquer'd death and FRANKLIN died.
>
> To that white region where the Lost lie low,
> Wrapp'd in their mantles of eternal snow;
> Unvisited by change, nothing to mock
> Those statues sculptured in the icy rock,
> We pray your company; that hearts as true
> (Though nothings of the air) may live for you;
> Nor only yet that on our little glass
> A faint reflection of those wilds may pass.

But, that the secrets of the vast Profound
Within us, an exploring hand may sound,
Testing the region of the ice-bound soul,
Seeking the passage at its northern pole,
Soft'ning the horrors of its wintry sleep,
Melting the surface of that 'Frozen Deep'.

The lighting effects were of a very special kind and de-
noted the passage of time. Day faded into evening, and
evening into night. The audience was entranced by these
unexpected novelties.

The first act makes us acquainted with four young ladies
living in Devon, each of whom has a lover serving with a
Polar expedition. Clara Burnham not only has her betrothed
out in the icy regions, but the rejected lover who has sworn
to kill him wherever and whenever they meet, though he does
not even know the name of his rival. Clara, haunted by the
fear that some mysterious influence may reveal them to each
other, tells her story to Lucy Crayford. As she does so, a
crimson sunset dies away to grey and Nurse Esther goes
about the house murmuring of scenes that come to her from
'the land o' ice and snaw'. She stands, as night falls, by the
misty blue of the window, describing to the young ladies her
bloody vision from the Northern seas. Lucy Crayford
shudders and calls for lights: Clara Burnham swoons.

The second act is set in the arctic regions. The stranded
men are in a hut deciding who is to go and seek relief.
Frank Aldersley is chosen by lot, and when somebody else
falls out Richard Wardour has to accompany him. Just
before they start Wardour discovers that Aldersley is his
hated rival.

The third act takes place in a cavern in Newfoundland.
The girls, smartly dressed in crinolines, their Scotch nurse,
and some members of the expedition are present, but neither
Wardour nor Aldersley. Presently a ragged maniac rushes
in and is given food and drink. He has escaped from an
ice-floe but is not too demented to recognise and be recognised by Clara Burnham, who suspects him of having

murdered her Frank   As soon as he understands this he goes off, returning a few minutes later with Aldersley in his arms to lay at Clara's feet.   'Often', he gasps, 'in supporting Aldersley through snow-drifts and on ice-floes have I been tempted to leave him sleeping.'   He has not done so and is now exhausted to death.   Wardour's distraught looks, his hysterical burst of joy at being able to prove himself no murderer, the melting tenderness with which he kisses his only love and then his 'fearfully fine' death under the Union Jack, reduced his audience to tears.   Everyone said it was a most touching and beautiful performance.

Dickens enjoyed the sacrificial role of Richard Wardour immensely.   No eye was dry when he bestowed upon the happily reunited lovers his dying benediction.   A hush followed the fall of the curtain and was maintained while the little orchestra, led by Francesco Berger at the piano, played the music specially written for the occasion.   Recomposed, the audience was led into a more cheerful mood by Buckstone's farce *Uncle John*, which prepared them for the champagne, oysters and other delicacies they were presently to enjoy.

'I am perfectly happy with the success', wrote Dickens next morning, and when all four performances were over and the stage in process of being dismantled he was pleased to be told, 'The play has been the talk of London these three weeks'.   How sore he was to think that two of his dearest friends, Mrs. Watson and 'Dan' Maclise, had missed it!

It is important at this point to note that during all the months of 1856 relations, according to the private correspondence, remained obviously normal between Charles Dickens and his wife.   There is no thought of separation in his mind or in hers.   Letters to 'My dearest Catharine' were written, when they were apart, about family affairs, all showing the ordinary confidence of a man in his partner.   She will be interested in the weather, in the Channel passage, in the Academy dinner, in what he said to Panizzi and what Webster said to him. A large lilac tree has been blown down in their Tavistock garden. He will see about a new passport. The house has had a thorough cleaning, every room has been scrubbed, aired, purified from roof to hall. Maclise has given him a funny description of Mrs. Henry Colburn which he proceeds to quote. It is safe for the boys to return to school at Boulogne, for the epidemic has ended. He fears she will have a rough passage taking them across the Channel and encloses a cheque. Writing after the first rehearsal of *The Frozen Deep* he tells her that the new cook 'is no good'. 'All love, and Forster's new house is excellently done up.' Again he says that 'the rehearsals are most satisfactory considering Mark Lemon has a rheumatic jaw and Berger a frightful cold'. This is the tone of all the letters of 1856.

Dearest 'Meery' Boyle danced the old year out at Tavistock House. With Charles as partner she romped through 'avenues' of guests in a country dance. It was but one of 'the innumerable evenings' spent at the house of enchantment 'where all that was eminent in Literature and Art or endowed with social and intellectual gifts was sure to find a welcome'. She was also present on Twelfth Night when *The Frozen Deep* was produced and a smiling, handsomely-gowned Mrs. Dickens received the guests while an excited Mr. Dickens was putting the last touches to Richard Wardour's expressive countenance. On three subsequent nights Mrs. Dickens beamed a welcome to her many guests.

In February 1857 Charles obtained possession of Gad's Hill and took Kate to Waite's Hotel at Gravesend, a house known for its comfort and good cooking. From there he intended they should both superintend the alterations needed in their new house, the changes in the garden, and the boring for water. While at Gravesend he went on working at *Little Dorrit* who was creating for herself a circle of warm admirers. Among the letters that reached her creator was one from Hans Andersen to say he was spell-bound by the book and found little Dorrit quite as lovable as little Nell.

I would and must admire you for the sake of this one book alone even if you had not previously bestowed upon the world those splendid compositions, 'David Copperfield,' 'Little Nelly' and the rest.   When I last spoke with you . . . in England you presented me with your published works. . . . I possess the latest books, but you must give me a copy of *Little Dorrit* when we greet each other again. God's blessing and delight be yours as you delight us all.

In this letter Andersen was obviously fishing for an invitation to stay.   He was thinking of coming over to London, but not for London's sake; no, it would be for Dickens's sake and for Dickens's sake alone.   Charles and Kate agreed there was nothing for it but to press him to come to them, tell him to make Gad's Hill his home and assure him that he may live as quietly there as in Copenhagen.   The fairy-tale author took his dear 'Boz' at his word, arriving on June 8 and (as we see from his letter to the Queen-Dowager in Denmark) he made a long stay.   'I have now been in England five weeks and have spent the whole time with Charles Dickens at his charming villa at Gad's Hill.'

Mrs. Dickens liked him and his childish dependent ways and took complete charge of him.   He thought her a 'charming chatelaine', and her 'womanly repose, china blue eyes and smile' made him associate her with the character of Agnes in *David Copperfield*.   Hans was very simple and Kate was simple too, there were no barriers between them and they talked much of the children.   How delightful it was to learn that the little boys were all called after poets and writers! What talents their names conjured up, and what fun it was to play in the hay with Edward Bulwer Lytton and Henry Fielding, Sydney Smith and Alfred Tennyson, and then to discuss their aptitudes with their mother!   The large field of clover close to the house made a good playground.   'The sons and I are often lying there', wrote Hans naïvely, 'there is a fragrance of clover, the elder tree is in blossom and the wild roses have an odour of apples so fresh and strong.'   He basked in the family life and saw no sign of any rift between his host and hostess: both personified for him 'the spirit of true amiability'.

One evening they strolled to the top of Gad's Hill and lay on the grass in a circle to watch the sun go down. The windings of the river turned into a ribbon of gold: ships stood out like black silhouettes: blue smoke curled over cottages: bells in the distance pealed, while near by the grasshoppers chirped. A great bowl of claret-cup, complete with its bunch of borage, circulated from hand to hand, and presently the moon came up round, red and large, mounting the heavens till it shone in clear purity and made the fairy-tale teller feel as if he were living in a midsummer night's dream. That evening his host was full of joy, very fresh, very impulsive. What a memory to take home to Denmark!

His first trip to London was made for the funeral of Douglas Jerrold whom he had got to know well during his former visit and who had died about the time he landed in England. Only a week before his collapse Jerrold had dined at a party given at Greenwich by William Howard Russell to meet Dickens, Delane and other old friends. When Jerrold died so unexpectedly Russell begged for an assurance from Dickens that he was not the cause of his demise. This Dickens readily gave him, telling him at the same time that he was planning help for Jerrold's widow. One gathers from the Jerrold side that this was not altogether a welcome intervention. But there was no gainsaying Dickens when he had made up his mind to theatricals. The proposed benefit offered a wonderful chance of reviving *The Frozen Deep*; he had other ideas, too, in his head such as reading the *Carol*, persuading Thackeray to give a lecture, and coaxing Wilkie Collins to co-operate in some way. Intentions seethed in his head; he would announce his decisions after the funeral. On the morning of the funeral Edmund Yates received a note from Dickens inviting him to dine that evening at the Garrick. Albert and Arthur Smith were to be of the party. They had all been to the ceremony at Norwood earlier in the day and Dickens spoke very strongly against the extravagant

way it had been conducted.   Mourners had worn bands of
crape round their arms with the initials D. J., and the car for
the coffin was like that provided for the Duke of Wellington.
After dinner he unfolded his plan for helping Mrs. Jerrold,
for whom he hoped to collect £2000.   Andersen was much
touched by his host's spontaneity and eagerness to help a
friend's widow and much impressed, too, to see the business-
like way Dickens assembled his cast, organised rehearsals,
and set up a committee office at the Gallery of Illustration in
Regent Street.   Notices headed 'In Remembrance of the late
Mr. Douglas Jerrold' appeared in no time announcing that on
Saturday, July 4, *The Frozen Deep* by Wilkie Collins would be
staged at the Gallery of Illustration privately for the Queen
and that other performances for the public would follow.

While this philanthropic activity was absorbing the time of
Dickens and his daughters, Andersen was taken about by
Mrs. Dickens, who, after driving her guest to the cemetery at
Norwood for the Jerrold interment, took him on to the
Crystal Palace for the first of the Handel festivals when *The
Messiah* was given before an audience of 12,000 persons.
The vast glass building seemed to Hans Andersen like an
Aladdin's palace, and when the music began to swirl round
him he told Kate he wanted to cry and ended by doing so.
From the concert hall they moved to the terrace and watched
the water 'from a thousand fountains blown in a sweepy veil
over gardens all sparkling in the sunshine'.   It amused him to
watch 'many little crinolined monsters reeling before the
spray'.   Another outing with Mrs. Dickens was to the
theatre to see the great Italian actress Ristori in the part of
Lady Macbeth.   He felt rather forlorn next day when Mr.
and Mrs. Dickens returned to 'dear' Gad's Hill leaving him
to the hospitality of his great admirer, Miss Coutts.   Miss
Coutts was not nearly so scaring to the nervous Dane as
were her 'proud servants' who understood nothing he said
His hostess talked German and he could explain to her what
they failed to understand, that his bed in her house in Stratton
Street was not to his liking as he was accustomed to sleeping

o

high on a mound of pillows. Miss Coutts smiled com-
prehension and, going up with him to his room, helped him
to remake the bed. He then confided to her that he could
not exist without soda-water, which she at once ran off to
fetch 'with her own hands'. His bedroom, 'the like of which
I have never seen before', had 'a bright fire, costly carpets and
windows giving on to a garden and Piccadilly'. That
evening in Miss Coutts's drawing-room he met the whole
fashionable world and next day his hostess drove him out to
her Highgate estate, Holly Lodge, to walk in the garden there.
This was all very gracious and very pleasant, but the fairy-tale
writer had not come to England to go to parties, shake hands
with smart people and receive compliments. It was Dickens
he wanted to be with all the time, just walking 'arm-in-arm'
with this greatest of living authors through the streets and
squares so remarkably described by him.

To the private performance of *The Frozen Deep* Andersen
was taken by Mrs. Dickens and it gratified him to see what a
select affair it was, only fifty persons present, and among them
the Queen, Prince Albert and the King of the Belgians.
Georgy Hogarth, who had by this time taken up a very
amicable confidential pose with Mrs. Winter, wrote to her new
friend, 'The Queen and Her party made a *most excellent*
audience'. Andersen expressed particular satisfaction with
the lovely hothouse flowers, provided by the Duke of
Somerset, but it seemed to him very odd indeed that his host
should excuse himself from presentation to the Queen.
Neither in Denmark nor in Germany could one brush Royal
personages aside in this way. The English were certainly a
very odd race and how they could endure the London air in
summer-time he could not think. To him it seemed 'very
coaly' and the June heat difficult to bear. How preferable it
would really have been to stay at Gad's Hill all the time, but,
if he had insisted on doing that, he would have missed those
wonderful walks through the streets with 'Boz'. One day
he had to submit to being taken to the house of Dickens's

lawyer, Mr. Ouvry, North End Lodge. Another day he was conveyed to Albert Smith's party at Walham Green, when the 'Glaciers of Mont Blanc' found great amusement in entertaining the 'Icebergs of the Frozen Deep'. Albert Smith was the author of *Christopher Tadpole*, who combined work for *Punch* with entertaining at the Egyptian Hall: Mark Lemon, editor of *Punch*, and other members of the staff were among the guests dining on the lawn and quaffing 'great goblets of champagne'. It was all very different from the frugality Andersen was used to at home.

To Andersen's first English friend, William Jerdan, Dickens confided that his guest got into embarrassing entanglements if left to himself in London and to fits of chagrin if left to himself in the country. One day they brought him up from Gad's Hill and had lost him at the London Bridge terminus whence he had driven away in a cab by himself. When he turned up he told them that as he passed through the new unfinished streets of Clerkenwell he made sure his driver was carrying him off 'to a remote fastness' to be robbed and murdered, and he had stuffed his watch, his pocket-book and all his money in his boots! Another day at Gad's Hill, Mrs. Dickens had found him, weeping bitterly, face down in the clover. Seeing that he clutched a newspaper she asked, 'Are any of your friends dead?' 'No, no,' faltered Andersen. He had, it appeared, been reading an adverse review, 'a perfectly nasty criticism', of his latest story. It was easy in a way to cheer him up for his sense of humour was that of a child. He could be made quite happy again by being asked to cut fairies and elves out of paper or mats with intricate lacy patterns. He also delighted in being dragged off by the Dickens children to gather flowers in the woods, of which he would make 'the strangest little nosegays'. Wilkie Collins had only to appear in a wide-awake for Andersen to manage, unobserved, to slip a daisy-chain over its crown. He then took Collins and the children to the village, where the wearer of the wide-awake was surprised to see everyone laughing at his appearance.

It was with a feeling akin to relief that Dickens one July day drove his friend to Maidstone and after embracing him affectionately put him in the train. Hans Andersen was tearful, and recorded, 'I travelled alone in the steam serpent to Folkestone. Dickens was like a dear brother to me to the last moment.'

The visit had been an outstanding success from the Dane's point of view; he had on the whole been happy, for the entire family had laid themselves out to amuse him, and Dickens had even invited his old enemy Bentley for a couple of nights to Gad's Hill for his benefit. When the great man was safely gone Dickens stuck a card up on the dressing-table mirror in the room he had used and on it was written, 'Hans Andersen slept in this room for five weeks which seemed to the family ages'.

One might have hoped for interesting impressions of Charles Dickens from so practised a writer, but there is nothing more than he set down at the time in his letters to the Queen-Dowager of Denmark and Henrietta Wulff, except for a short article of reminiscences published in *Temple Bar* after Dickens's death. Paris seemed terribly dreary to him after London; he said it seemed to him like 'a beehive without honey'. As time went on Andersen tended to become even to Dickens what he had long since become to his girls Mamey and Katey, 'a bony bore'. Many were the strangers who arrived on the Dickens doorstep with letters of introduction signed by Hans Christian Andersen. Eventually the friendship languished and died, maybe because Dickens got to know that Andersen gossiped by letter with his friend the Grand Duke about the Jerrold benefit, saying that Jerrold's son had protested against 'the hat being carried round' as his mother had not been left in 'straitened circumstances'.

Four days after Andersen left England Walter Landor Dickens sailed for India. With a good deal of forethought Charles Dickens was mapping out lives for his seven sons. Charley, after returning from Leipzig, had been, through the interest of Miss Coutts, entered to Baring's and through the

same interest an East Indian cadetship had been secured for
Walter Landor. Walter had at one time shown signs of
following in his father's footsteps, but his tutor was instructed
not to press him to write, 'the less he is encouraged to write
the better . . . and the happier he will be'. Though the
actual leave-taking shattered Dickens for a day or two, he
soon got over it and was able to preen himself on having
provided a career for a second son, even though the boy had
no inclination for the life he had been assigned to. A very
small figure in a uniform made to allow for development
appears pathetically in a faded photograph. The face that
looks out beneath the military shako is that of an unhappy
child. But it was part of the Victorian tradition to ship boys
to India. So fitted out with flannel, quinine, essence of
ginger and Jeremy's opium, Walter Landor was conveyed to
his ship by father and eldest brother. 'A sad trial', wrote
Dickens, 'thank God it is over. The dear boy bore it a great
deal better than we could have hoped.'

Walter Landor never set foot on English earth again.
The climate of India affected him adversely during his attachment to the East India Company and, after his exchange into
the Black Watch and his posting to a hill station, his health
broke down completely. Many rosy-faced English lads have
died in the far corners of the world and Walter joined their
company. Invalided home too late, death snatched him as he
was passing through Calcutta. He died there of a haemor-
rhage on the last day of 1863.

Chapter 23

SEPARATION

Unless we hoped and feared, life would have no meaning for us. Apart from such commotions of our inner selves there could be no living. BENEDETTO CROCE

TEN days after Walter Landor had sailed for the Indies his father was reading *A Christmas Carol* to enraptured audiences at Manchester and deriving immense pleasure therefrom. He was receiving overtures, too, from 'Manchester Magnates' begging him to produce a play again in their city. Most willingly did he agree to do so, and writing to Wilkie Collins said that he had arranged for *The Frozen Deep* to be acted in the Free Trade Hall on August 21 and 22. 'It is an *immense* place and we shall be obliged to have actresses; I am already trying to get the best who *have been* on the stage.' Two days earlier he had written to Mrs. Compton asking her co-operation. 'The place is out of the question for my girls. Their action could not be seen, their voices could not be heard'; but Mrs. Compton could not oblige, and so he applied to Wigan, manager of the Olympic Theatre, for names of substitutes and on his recommendation engaged Mrs. Ternan and her two daughters, Maria and Ellen, for the parts. One member at least of this theatrical family was already known to Dickens, for some months earlier he, who rarely missed seeing a new play, had watched Ellen Ternan act the part of Hippomenes in *Atalanta*,[1] a play by Talfourd. Going to Ellen Ternan's dressing-room before she went on the stage, he found her in tears at having 'to show so much leg'. Charmed by her modesty, Dickens thought her 'most attractive and a sweet little thing'. After 'Boz' had engaged the professional ladies to replace 'the Tavistock girls', he bustled up from Gad's Hill to give them 'a three-days drill in

[1] Haymarket, April 1857.

390

their parts' and now for the first time we become aware that a serious emotional disturbance may be brewing. Little, fair-haired Ellen Ternan, with her sympathetic blue eyes, took up such a worshipping attitude and seemed so pathetically anxious to interpret every line and gesture according to Dickens's wishes that she completely captivated him. The rehearsals took place at Tavistock House and the more its owner coached his team, the more his infatuation for Ellen grew. Both the Miss Ternans were charming and both ran in and out of the study, but only one sat on the arm of the manager's chair, sang duets with him at the schoolroom piano and seemed, to the family, to take possession of the house. *The Frozen Deep* had always to be followed by a farce so that the audience should not be sent away in tears. The farce chosen on this occasion was *Uncle John*. 'Uncle John' was an old gentleman who had educated a young girl and in the process had fallen in love with her. When she was eighteen he asked her to marry him, and the piece opens on their wedding morning with the arrival of Uncle John's niece and her husband. This couple somehow contrive to persuade the bride that she is really in love with her drawing-master and each to believe the other the prey of unrequited passion. After a few rehearsals Dickens's emotional equilibrium was upset. In the play Uncle John had to load his bride with 'wonderful presents—a pearl necklace and diamond earrings', and his impersonator found it irresistible to give his sweet little friend some real jewelry. Kate Dickens, who knew the plot and the words only too well, realised what must be going on when a bracelet ordered for Ellen was delivered to her by mistake. It annoyed her extremely, for her husband was not a boy and after twenty years of married life it was an insult to her to make love under her very roof to a girl of eighteen. At once she flared into a scene with Charles, who told her that it was within her power to show her confidence in him and her belief in the girl's innocence by calling on her mother. He did not at all want his daughters to think he was not behaving correctly, the daughters of course being of an age to notice things and draw their own conclusions. The second girl, Katey, was quite alive to the situation and tells[1] us that at the very commencement of this affair, as she passed her parents' bedroom, the door of which was ajar, she heard sobs, and on going in found her mother seated at the dressing-table putting on her bonnet. When she asked what the tears were about a stifled voice replied, 'Your father has asked me to go and see Ellen Ternan'. 'You shall not go,' said Katey, stamping her foot; but Mrs. Dickens did as she was asked, for her complyingness, where Charles was concerned, was boundless.

On August 20 Dickens, in 'inimitable' form, went up to Manchester with his troupe, where *The Frozen Deep* was played on August 21 and 22, followed as usual by *Uncle John*. Never had Dickens acted so well, never had he enjoyed himself so much. Wilkie Collins says 'he electrified the audiences', and well he might, for he had fallen violently in love and was a passionate youth again.

The part of the heroine, Clara Burnham, was not played by Ellen Ternan but by her sister Maria. And Dickens in a letter to Miss Coutts appears to be making an effort to put her off the scent of any scandal for he focusses all interest on Maria and does not so much as mention her sister. If his sub-editor, Wills, now Miss Coutts's secretary, has been gossiping to her, this letter should disarm criticism:

Perhaps Mr. Wills has not told you how much impressed I was at Manchester by the womanly tenderness of a very gentle and good little girl who acted Clara's part. She came to see the play beforehand at the Gallery of Illustration, and when we rehearsed it, she said, 'I am afraid, Mr. Dickens, I shall never be able to bear it: it affected me so much when I saw it, that I hope you will excuse my trembling this morning, for I am afraid of myself.' At night when she came out of the cave and Wardour recognised her I never saw anything like the distress and agitation of her face—a very good little pale face, with large black eyes:

[1] G. Storey, *Dickens and Daughter*, p. 96.

—it has a natural emotion in it which was quite a study of expression. But when she had to kneel over Wardour dying, and be taken leave of, the tears streamed out of her eyes into his mouth, down his beard, all over his rags— —down his arms as he held her by the hair. At the same time she sobbed as if she were breaking her heart, and was quite convulsed with grief. It was of no use for the compassionate Wardour to whisper, 'My dear child, it will be over in two minutes—there is nothing the matter—don't be so distressed!' She could only sob out, 'O! it's so sad, O! it's so sad,' and set Mr. Lemon (the softest-hearted of men) crying too. By the time the curtain fell we were all crying together, and then her mother and sister used to come and put her in a chair and comfort her, before taking her away to be dressed for the Farce. I told her on the last night that I was sure that she had one of the most genuine and feeling hearts in the world; and I don't think I ever saw anything more prettily simple and unaffected. Yet I remember her on the stage, a little child, and I daresay she was born in a country theatre. . . . Miss Maria Ternan, that is the young lady.[1]

It might be possible to put Miss Coutts off the scent, but it was less easy to delude Forster to whom on the same day he wrote:

You are not so tolerant as perhaps you might be of the wayward and unsettled feeling which is part (I suppose) of the tenure on which one holds an imaginative life, and which I have, as you ought to know well, often kept down by riding over it like a dragoon—but let that go by, I make no maudlin complaint. I am always deeply sensible of the wonderful exercise I have of life and its highest sensations and have said to myself for years, and have honestly and truly felt, this is the drawback to such a career and is not to be complained of. . . . I claim no immunity from blame— there is plenty of fault on my side in the way of a thousand uncertainties, caprices, and difficulties of disposition. The gist is that it is a mistake to marry too young and that the years are not making things easier . . . reasons have been

[1] 1877. II. N.L.

growing which make it all but hopeless that we should even try to struggle on. . . . It is too late to say put the curb on.[1]

The elation at Manchester was followed by a very bad slump in spirits. 'Partly from grim despair and subsidence from excitement and partly for the sake of *Household Words*', he invited Wilkie Collins to take a tour with him *anywhere*. 'I want to escape from myself, my misery is amazing.' To Stone he spoke of 'low pulse, low voice, low spirits, intense reaction'. Early in September the two friends went off to Carlisle, and climbing Carrock Fell, Collins sprained his foot and had to be transported 'Wardour-wise' to the hotel whence they moved to Allonby, 'a deserted, clean little place with fifty houses, five bathing machines, five young men and five young women'. The landlady of the Ship hotel recognised her illustrious guest at once; she had seen him years earlier at Greta Bridge, when, as a girl, she had been slipped into the coffee-room to have a look at him. This, on the whole, dull outing was chronicled for *Household Words* as *The Lazy Tour of Two Idle Apprentices*.[2] Doncaster was included in the schedule as 'the St. Leger with all its saturnalia' was being run. In spite of his annual trip to see the Derby run, racing was not at all in Dickens's line: every moment spent on the Doncaster course was hateful to him in spite of the fact that on being handed a card of the race he ticked off three successive winners. He came away certain that if a boy had a taste for betting nothing would cure him sooner than a visit to Doncaster 'to see the misery caused by losses on the turf'.

During the whole tour Dickens was restless and could concentrate on nothing. Why did he feel so desperately low? Had he perhaps missed something very important in life, a great friendship, a great romance, a great tragedy? What could it be that spurred him into such dissatisfaction with his lot? Was there some part of him undeveloped or was it merely that some men never find rest in this life?

[1] 1877-8. II. N.L.   [2] October 1857.

Could it be entirely Kate's fault that he felt like that? After all they had never really been in step. He had developed, but she had remained more or less what she had been in the beginning, amiable, complacent, and now, according to his ideas, subsiding into a kind of fatuity. Viewed objectively, she was a mediocre, kindly woman who did not fill the bill of celebrity's wife. How badly she contrasted with the women he had met in Paris! Could one want a more intelligent and sympathetic wife than Madame Scribe, who was older than Kate, or Madame Viardot, who was the same age? His thoughts then strayed on to masterful George Sand and muse-like Madame de Girardin. What a mistake it had been to marry a woman so limited in knowledge and sympathy as Kate, a woman who could contribute nothing to any discussion and viewed every subject with apathetic want of interest or a meaningless smile. As he reviewed the past he began to wonder whether she had ever suited him at all. It was the American tour that had first revealed to him her springlessness and lack of resource. Only the efforts of an extremely competent maid had dragged her through those months of travel. He had given her chances of education and experience of the world, but she had never even responded to the stimulus of housekeeping in a foreign country. What tears there had been at Genoa, what repinings in France! Her main interest was the nursery; it was natural enough that she should be absorbed in that way, but babies as the one bond and topic of conversation were liable to be boring. He had nothing to reproach himself with. He had been a good father and had done all that was possible for his earthly children, but he could not pretend to idealise them as he did his spiritual children, Oliver, Nell, Paul and the rest. Kate had sometimes complained of his friends and their off-hand manners, of John Forster in particular, who hardly noticed her at all. 'Fuz' had never thought her adequate or interesting, and how right he had been! 'She is amiable and comply-ing but nothing on earth would make her understand me.' It was something to be able to write frankly to Forster, though

the situation as he saw it was an irremediable one.   Here was
the world-famous Charles Dickens with his genius, his
compelling imagination, his very peculiar disposition, his
caprices, his impatience, his tempers, driven nearly demented
by one woman's fatuity, a fatuity that was magnified for him
by those relations of hers who were always in the house,
whose faces now appeared to him idiotic, and whose manners
now struck him as exasperating.   But in condemning them
he did not condemn his dear Georgy, who never lost her
charm or interest and now shone as the paragon of an entirely
worthless family.

In making these reflections he generated in himself a fund
of self-pity and refrained from dealing with the core of the
situation, his infatuation for Ellen Ternan.   The terror as
well as the beauty of love lies in the fact that it alters all values.
Men talk of a world well lost for love when it is love itself that
has caused their world to perish and appear as worthless as a
worn-out shoe.   Dickens's attitude to his own life changed
from the fatal moment at Manchester when he believed himself capable of loving a young girl in the same idealistic
whole-souled way that he had once adored Maria Beadnell.

The close companionship of Wilkie Collins and his levity
on sex-relationships combined with his own passion for Ellen
made Dickens feel as if he had renewed his youth, almost as
if he belonged to another generation.   Kate might look her
part of materfamilias; it was hard for him to believe himself
the father of ten children, when he felt more like their elder
brother than their parent.   What must he now do to readjust
his life?   Readjust it he simply must.

A letter[1] written to his wife's maid at this time shows how
his mind was working.   It embodied what in Victorian days
was a momentous decision—self-banishment from the large
double bed in which he had lain beside his wife for all the
years of their marriage.   Anne is instructed to have the
recessed communicating door between the dressing-room and
the bedroom closed by a carpenter who must fill the space

[1] 890.   II.   N.L.

with white deal shelves and enclose it with 'a light deal door, painted white'. He has ordered for his own use a small iron bedstead and the bedding to go with it. Anne is specially warned not to talk about these arrangements and is told 'the sooner it is done the better'.

Forster says that at this time he found Dickens impossible to deal with and 'inaccessible' to friendly advice, but he says nothing in his *Life* about the Ternan family and nothing about the Manchester performances. It is obvious that he wished to have the episode expunged, for it did 'Boz' no credit after twenty years of respectability to go off the rails with an actress. As far as Forster was concerned, Ellen Ternan did not exist and therefore could have had nothing to do with the separation. Thus, leaving out of his account the principal factor in the situation, he was obliged to own that there was nothing in the actual circumstances in which Mr. and Mrs. Dickens found themselves that would not have admitted of reasonable rearrangement. A middle course, to his regret, was not taken. Even so he consoled himself by assuring those principally concerned that no decent person could regard the separation contemplated save as 'a purely private family matter' which it would be most ungentlemanly to allude to. This opinion put heart into Dickens as it removed his fear that his position with the public would be 'aspersed' if scandal were permitted to attach to his name.

Despite spiritual, psychical and physical upheavals appearances were still kept up during the autumn of 1857 at Tavistock House. Dickens took the chair in November at the fourth Anniversary Dinner of the Warehousemen and Clerks Schools at the London Tavern. He spoke of schools he did not like, of his own school and master, 'by far the most ignorant man I have ever had the pleasure to know, one of the worst tempered men that ever lived. . . . I did not like the ladies' school with which my school danced on Wednesdays.' The Schools for which he is appealing are designed to educate 'Orphans and Necessitous Children'. A beginning had been made four years earlier with a rented house at New Cross.

Dickens urged his hearers to enlarge the scope of their activity.
In toasting the president, Lord John Russell, he said of him
that as with 'the seal of Solomon there was enclosed in a not
very large casket the soul of a giant'.

Miss Coutts was invited to attend the party given by Mr.
and Mrs. Dickens on December 1, 1857, to listen to the new
Christmas story for *Household Words*, about the behaviour of
white women during a pirate's raid at Silverstore, Belize, 'off
the Mosquito shore'.   It was said to have been suggested by
accounts of the Indian Mutiny.   Entitled *The Perils of Certain
English Prisoners*, the second of its three dull chapters was
written by Wilkie Collins.   There was nothing of the old
Christmas spirit about any of it and the party dispersed feeling
that a light had gone out.

Under the blight of impending change Christmas and
Twelfth Night were lived through by a diminished and rather
dejected family.   Henry Fielding, aged eight, had been
packed off to join his brothers at school at Boulogne, which
left Charley, the two girls and Edward Bulwer Lytton, aged
six, at home.   Charles Dickens continued to function
normally in the world's eye as editor, serial writer and chairman of charity banquets.   In February he spoke for the
Hospital for Sick Children.   Addressing 150 guests, he made
amusing allusions to the spoilt children of the well-to-do,
children who come down to dessert, children who won't go
to bed, children who kick and say they hate us.   It is not for
these he speaks, but for the children he has seen languishing
in damp, bare rooms, for the babies pining to death in egg-
boxes.   Why in the name of GOD must such things be?   The
old courtly house in Great Ormonde Street now converted
into a child's hospital already deals with 10,000 of such out-
patients a year.   The in-patients in their doll-like beds can
only number thirty and even these cannot be maintained
without further support.   It was exactly the kind of appeal
Dickens could drive home with his plea to those present to
think 'of the dear child you love, the dear child you have lost,
the dream-child you might have had'.   He melted the hearts

of his hearers and by so doing added £3000 to the funds of the hospital.

The letters written by Dickens this spring are concerned chiefly with plans and projects for 'readings'. It had become to him the most reassuring of exercises to play upon an audience in this way. Each reading not only gave him fresh zest, but endowed him with the power of riding, as in a life-boat, over the troubled waters of private life.

Under the placid round of family existence at Tavistock House a silent conflict was seething. There was Charles set on readjustment without publicity; Georgina willing to co-operate in securing this solution; and Kate the sport of she did not know what kind of forces. In the background the watching eyes of Mrs. Hogarth, her daughter Helen, and her sister Helen Thomson missed nothing of the changes and turns of the situation: their sympathies were all with Kate. How was it that Georgy did not seem to share them?

By degrees their suspicions of Georgy grew. Could she be acting the part of confidante to Charles? Was it she who was responsible for the proposals for readjustment in domestic affairs at Tavistock House? Was it she who, after the significant blocking of doors between bedroom and dressing-room, suggested further segregation? A letter written by Helen Thomson to her friend Mrs. Stark in Glasgow[1] makes it clear how disappointed the Hogarth contingent were with Georgina: 'We had thought her disinterested'. Someone had proposed to Kate that she should have her own suite of rooms quite apart from his, that she should act hostess at parties and make *actes de présence*, if necessary, at public functions. Another suggestion was that they might play Box and Cox between Tavistock House and Gad's Hill, yet another that she should settle abroad. These mortifying proposals in-volving her, as they would have done, in much pretence were all declined by Kate. If Charles felt like that about her, it would be better to be gone altogether or to die. The idea of separation from her children upset her terribly: her spirits

[1] Unpublished MS. (W. Dexter).

had never been high and now she spent hours together in tears.

Resenting these attempts at compromise, the Hogarth family intervened; rather than have poor Kate subjected to insulting offers they would prefer that she should be provided with a separate establishment. It was pitiful to see her in so low a condition. And so a legal separation was put through by Forster, who saw that the situation was intolerable to Dickens. Mark Lemon chose a solicitor for Kate and during the actual negotiations Mrs. Hogarth carried her daughter off to Brighton. On her return Kate became party to a settle-ment securing her £600 a year, and was installed in a small house in Gloucester Crescent on the edge of Camden Town. While this arrangement was being put through Charles suddenly became aware that certain 'scandalous rumours' anent Georgina were circulating within the family. These rumours maddened him, as well they might. He took prompt measures to scotch them, presenting the hostile Hogarths with a document and threatening, if they refused to sign, that Kate would be turned out of the house without a penny. The Hogarths stood out against his ultimatum for 'a fortnight of sleepless nights' and then put their names to the following declaration:

> It having been stated to us that in reference to the difficulties which have resulted in the separation of Mr. and Mrs. Charles Dickens, certain statements have been circu-lated that such differences are occasioned by circumstances deeply affecting the moral character of Mr. Dickens and compromising the reputation and good name of others, we solemnly declare that we now disbelieve such statements. We know that they are not believed by Mrs. Dickens and we pledge ourselves on all occasions to contradict them as entirely destitute of foundation.
>
> [Here follow the signatures of
> Mrs. Hogarth and Helen Hogarth.]

So far few people were in the secret, just the family, near friends and kind Miss Coutts, who tried in writing to effect a reconciliation and then offered a temporary home to Kate whom she knew well and liked. Charles wrote a long, rather hysterical letter to Miss Coutts and stated that things had gone too far to admit of compromise.

Georgy was at this crisis intensely useful to Dickens. She kept his house together. She had Mamey and Katey under her thumb and managed to persuade them by her own cheerfulness that there was nothing to be regretted in the banishment or, as she called it, the 'voluntary departure' of their mother. A more natural and happy arrangement could not be thought of. They must all be very loving together and take care of Papa. In a way Georgina covered the scandal of Ellen, for people soon began to talk about the invidious position of a sister-in-law being content to supplant her own sister at the head of Charles Dickens's house.

With the exception of Miss Coutts, Charles now treated any sympathiser with Kate as a 'disloyal' friend. Mark Lemon and his family came into this category and so did F. M. Evans of Bradbury and Evans. W. M. Rossetti, dining with a friend of Kate's, Rintoul, founder and editor of *The Spectator*, heard the separation canvassed and the verdict go dead against Dickens, but this was all in strict privacy. It may be said that the separation, owing to Kate's determination 'to resign herself to God's will', passed off well and so secretly that except to the family and a few intimate friends it might have remained a nine days' wonder. The Dickens façade remained unchanged: Charles moved on in his majestic way, responding with Thackeray for Literature at the Academy banquet (May 2) and speaking for the Artists' Benevolent Fund. Then, seized by a fit of terrifying exhibitionism, he decided to take the world into his confidence in a personal statement in *Household Words*. He was anxious that Mark Lemon should also print it in *Punch*. When Mark Lemon very sensibly refused, Charles cut him dead. He also drafted a second statement for the discretionary use of Arthur Smith, his sub-editor.

The first statement was printed on June 12, 1858, in

Household Words, on the front page, headed 'Personal'. In it he explained that owing to his long friendship with the public he feels he must take them into his confidence over a personal matter of a domestic and sacredly private character of which they are almost certain to have heard reports. He solemnly declares that all the lately whispered rumours 'are abominably false, and that whosoever repeats one of them after this denial, will lie as wilfully and as foully as it is possible for any false witness to lie before Heaven and earth.'

This statement, as Forster plainly told him, served but to draw attention to what, if treated with silence, might have slipped by almost without notice. To his friend's horror, Dickens consulted Delane about printing the 'personal statement' in the *Times* before publishing it in *Household Words*, but, to Forster's relief, this came to nothing. Worse, however, was to follow, for the second statement, drafted for Arthur Smith's confidential use, also found its way into print. In this document Dickens dwelt on the incompatibility of temperament that had always existed between himself and his wife, and stated that had it not been for Georgina the separation would have taken place earlier. Georgina has sacrificed her youth and life to his family. For some years Mrs. Dickens has been asking to go away and live apart. He has prevented her doing so. It is at Forster's suggestion that he has finally consented to reconstruct and rearrange his home. Mrs. Dickens has thankfully agreed to his terms. He hopes no one will put any misconstruction on the separation, which the children thoroughly understand and accept. He goes on to say that 'two wicked persons' (by whom he means Mrs. Hogarth and her daughter) have coupled with the separation the name of a young lady for whom he has a great attachment and regard. 'Upon my soul and honour, there is not on this earth a more virtuous and spotless creature. I know her to be innocent and pure and as good as my own dear daughters. Further, I am quite sure that Mrs. Dickens, having received this assurance from me, must now believe it, in the respect I know her to have for me, and in the perfect confidence I know her in her better moments to repose in my truthfulness.'

Handed to Arthur Smith for 'discretionary use', this letter somehow found its way into the *New York Tribune* and from that source was copied into several English newspapers.

If we examine the statements we find that they are a smoke-screen put up not only to cover Kate's disappearance but to defend Georgina's continued presence at Tavistock House. There is something about them that creates suspicion: it is almost as if an alibi had been faked. And, oddly enough, as we shall presently see, Dickens's statements were backed up by letters from Georgina to Maria Winter. Both Charles and Georgina felt the need of justifying themselves. Dickens desired to absolve himself from the accusation of ingratitude and cruelty, Georgina wished to set herself right with Charles's friends, and both of them followed Forster in hiding up the explosive charge, Ellen Ternan. Between them they invented a new set of circumstances, a new chronicle of married life, all of which falls to shreds when the letters written by Charles to Kate on his Italian tour of 1853 are considered. These intimate, warm-hearted letters, as we have already seen, show Dickens as a normal affectionate family man. They allude to common experiences in Italy nine years earlier, revive old jests, poke fun at his companions Egg and Collins, and towards the end of the eight weeks' tour reveal the most simple and unfeigned pleasure at getting home. To 'my dearest Catharine' he wrote, 'I shall be very happy to be at home myself and to embrace you, for of course I miss you very much'. The letters are far from perfunctory. He sends love to the children and 'last but not least to yourself, whom I hope so soon to see in a blooming state'. 'Looking forward to meeting you so soon, ever, my dearest, most affectionately C. D.'

There is nothing here to support the contention that the marriage had been acutely unhappy for years and years, and evidently Dickens felt this aspect of his case to be weak, for to strengthen it he made mysterious allusions to a 'mental disorder' which caused his wife to think 'she would be better away'. In fact she, who took the initiative in nothing, was credited with initiating the separation. It would have been better for Dickens's reputation as an honest man if he had admitted that he had fallen violently in love with a girl of eighteen and that the sensation of youth released in him made him regard his own children as 'brothers and sisters' and his own wife with physical disgust. After all, the senses know no constancy. Kate was certainly dull and she may have been a bore, but her husband with his mercurial temperament had really been lucky to be linked with anyone who asserted herself so little and was on the whole so amenable. Their marriage, like many Victorian marriages, had been of the kind indicated in the Church of England wedding service as 'for the procreation of children', of whom they had ten in fifteen years, to say nothing of four miscarriages. There is no record that Kate ever complained of her fate though she must often have had reason to do so, for her lively husband's attitude to pregnancy and childbirth was outwardly unsympathetic and often that of a low comedian. It is remarkable that she betrayed no jealousy of her sister Georgina, who usurped many of her privileges and replaced her as diner-out and hostess during many weeks of every year. In all but parent-hood Georgina played the part of an unofficial wife. 'Do you believe in a sister-in-law living in the house?' someone asked Kate Perugini in her old age. 'No, no, it is the greatest mistake!' she exclaimed. We must remind ourselves that Charles Dickens had never even at Furnival's Inn lived in a *solitude à deux*. There were but three rooms in their suite; but somehow they had squeezed Mary in. At Doughty Street they had made a home both for Mary Hogarth and Frederick Dickens, and after their return from America had adopted Georgina as a permanent member of the household; and so it went on till Tavistock House days when the Hogarth parents were often put up for months together. There is no question but that Charles had been a very good family man and had shouldered one responsibility after the other. Parents, brothers and his wife's relations, all had been helped, and all had proved unsatisfactory and all ungrateful. When he began to suspect that Kate was siding with her parents against Georgina, he lost his sense of propriety and in a blind rage threatened to drive her from the house.

At the time of the separation Kate was forty-three years old and Charles forty-six. They had been married for twenty-two years. When pressed out of her home Kate left behind her Edward Bulwer Lytton aged six, Henry Fielding aged eight, Sydney Smith aged ten, Alfred Tennyson aged twelve, Francis Jeffrey aged thirteen, two girls of eighteen and nineteen, and the oldest child of all, Charley, aged twenty. Walter Landor, aged seventeen had, as we have seen, been banished to India. It would have been an extraordinary step for any woman in Kate's position and of her indolent disposition to take voluntarily and that is why one must use the word 'pressed'. For some time an influence had been prising her slowly out of control till the tendrils that bound her to family life had relaxed so much that by a determined effort she could be easily dislodged. The family were, taking them all in all, rather characterless as well as very young, and made no stand against their father's decision. The predicament was puzzling to young minds, but it was drummed into them that 'their father's name was their best asset'. Though the little boys felt twinges of terrible loneliness, the family, as a whole, swallowed the fairy-tale they were told by kind Aunt Georgy and accepted their situation as inevitable, just as a little later on the Dickens sons were hypnotised into looking upon their early exile to India or the Antipodes as 'inevitable'. Georgina Hogarth could on occasion act with resolution and finality.

What are we to think of this survivor of the cataclysm that drove father, mother, aunt and sister from Dickens's house for ever, and to whom Kate, till dying of cancer twenty-one years later, never spoke again? Who but Georgina could have contrived the circumstances that levered the mother of her nephews and nieces out of the house of which she remained the permanent and apparently satisfied inmate? The part played by this attractive young woman appears equivocal. Was she pursuing some scheme of her own when making up to Maria Winter? Why did she write so affectionately to explain to her how the separation between her sister and her brother-in-law had come about? 'My dearest Maria' was told that no one was in any way to blame, that it was all quite natural, that Kate and Charles had agreed to live apart and would be happier like that. Poor Kate's incapacity for looking after children was no secret to anyone: they had always been thrown on others. 'My sister has often expressed a wish to go and live away', but Charles would never agree to it. Now by mutual consent and for *no other* reasons they have come to an arrangement to live apart. Georgina need hardly tell her 'dearest Maria' that where such a public man as Charles is concerned 'wonderful rumours and wicked slanders have been flying about'. Charles's friends must show their friendship by 'quietly silencing with the real solemn truth any foolish or wicked person who may repeat such lies and slanders'.

One asks oneself for what reason except that of pleasing Charles or of entering into sole possession of the home did Georgina become demonstratively affectionate to a woman whom she had a short while previously dismissed as almost a comic figure, 'a kind of good-natured woman, but fearfully silly'. How she and Charles had laughed together over Flora Finching when he was writing *Little Dorrit*! We should note the fact that once Georgina was firmly in control at Tavistock House, Mrs. Winter dropped as if through an oubliette out of her affections and correspondence.

For a long time Georgina had off and on acted as amanuensis to Charles. Nearly all *The Child's History of England* is in her handwriting, and she had always encouraged him in his self-absorption by saying, 'a man of genius ought not to be judged by the common herd of men'. For a long while she had made things difficult for Kate by always siding with Charles in any minor dispute. Georgina, it is evident, had a love of power and liked to control so celebrated a person as her brother-in-law and to make herself indispensable in his eyes. He praised her a great deal and thought that she took immense trouble over the children, who otherwise would have been neglected. According to Mrs. Hogarth, all that Georgina ever did for the children was to teach the little boys to read before they went to school: she had nothing to do with the girls; they had a competent governess. The curious method she adopted when editing a selection of Dickens's letters—that of cutting out sentences in praise of her sister— may indicate the jealousy that is part and parcel of possessive love.

By midsummer Kate was settled in Gloucester Crescent. Charley, by his father's wish, went to live with her, but Dickens was afraid lest Leech or anyone else should suppose he 'sided' with his mother. 'Between the children and me there is absolute confidence', he wrote, when forwarding him a copy of a note received from Charley in which he told his father, 'Don't suppose that I am actuated by any feeling of preference for my mother to you. God knows I love you dearly and it will be a hard day for me when I have to part from you and the girls.' Charley may have had a kindly nature, but he was determined to persevere with his courtship of Bessie Evans, the daughter of the man his father now looked on as his mortal enemy. It was perhaps as well that in future they would not be called on to live under the same roof. 'Dear Charley', wrote Kate, 'is so kind and gentle. I hope to resign myself to God's will and to lead a contented, if not a happy life . . . my position is a sad one. Time only can blunt the keen pain I feel at my heart.'

Chapter 24

READING FOR A LIVING

And if I laugh at any mortal thing
'Tis that I may not weep.

BYRON

DURING the negotiations recorded in the last chapter Dickens worked to organise a series of entertainments calculated to absorb his leisure for the rest of the year. Beginning with an advertisement in *Household Words* on April 2 of sixteen readings to be given at the St. Martin's Hall, he went on to plan a comprehensive tour in the provinces to include both Scotland and Ireland. Forster objected strongly to this rather cheap-jack way of earning a livelihood, but when remonstrated with, Dickens countered his objections by saying that everyone believed he took a fee, even when he was reading for charity. 'Let me read where I will,' he said impetuously, 'an effect is produced which seems to belong to nothing else.'

The condensation of excerpts from his own novels and stories so as to get the maximum dramatic effect took up a good deal of time. He contrived sixteen of these arrangements in all.[1]

A Christmas Carol	Mr. Chops the Dwarf
The Trial from Pickwick	The Poor Traveller
David Copperfield	Mrs. Gamp
The Cricket on the Hearth	Boots at the Holly Tree Inn
Nicholas Nickleby	The Barbox Brothers
Bob Sawyer's Party	The Boy at Mugby
The Chimes	Dr. Marigold
The Story of Little Dombey	Sikes and Nancy

The favourite among these for seventeen years was 'A Christmas Carol'. In these readings so certain were his impersonations that he could cut out much of the descriptive

[1] See *Charles Dickens as a Reader*. C. Kent, 1872.

matter in his books. For example, Scrooge, who is carefully delineated in the 'Carol', came to life in one sentence, 'Ah! but he was a tight-fisted hand at the grindstone was Scrooge', delivered in a grating, shrewd voice. The elision in the pathetic parts was ruthless, though a few of the poignant points were left in the life and death of Tiny Tim. The visit of Bob to the death-bed was cut out, but Dickens got all the greater effect from the mother's words over her mourning needlework, and over the father's promise to visit the grave. 'He broke down all at once. He couldn't help it. If he could have helped it, he and his child would have been further apart perhaps than they were.'

'Bob Sawyer's Party' is just another chapter from *Pickwick*. 'The Trial from Pickwick' has not been corrected or cut. Except for the compression at the opening of chapter thirty-four, Bardell *v.* Pickwick was read as originally written. 'David Copperfield', on the other hand, has been rearranged and greatly cut. It opens on the beach at Yarmouth and closes with the death of Steerforth. 'Nicholas Nickleby' is entirely concerned with the Yorkshire school, the meeting with Mr. Squeers, the journey north, life at Dotheboys Hall and the final departure.

The Cricket on the Hearth was too short and slight to be cut at all. In 'The Chimes' the introduction was omitted and the reading opened with the words, 'High up in the steeple of an old church, far above the town and far below the clouds dwelt the Chimes I tell of'. The whole of Will Fern's speech is omitted.

'The Poor Traveller' is the only Dickens story of which an army officer is the hero. Richard Doubledick, who has made a mess of life, walks to Chatham to enlist and get himself killed. Captain Taunton reforms him and turns him into a good sergeant-major. At Badajos, Taunton, supported by Ensign Doubledick, performs acts of great valour and receives a mortal wound. Doubledick registers the face of the Frenchman who kills Taunton and swears to have his revenge. Doubledick fights again at Quatre-Bras and Ligny and falls

half dead on the field of Waterloo. He is adopted by
Taunton's mother and stays with her at a house near Aix.
There, looking down from a gallery, he recognises the French
officer. The spirit of Taunton takes possession of him, the
man had merely done his duty as he had tried to do his.
That evening Doubledick touches the Frenchman's glass with
his own and secretly 'forgave him in the name of the Divine
Forgiver'.

Some of the readings are very poor indeed, for instance
'The Boy at Mugby' about a juvenile 'refreshmenter', 'The
Barbox Brothers' and 'Mr. Chops the Dwarf'. One of the
most popular readings was about the elopement of a boy of
eight with a girl of seven, 'Boots at the Holly Tree Inn'.
Provincial audiences found it very sweet and touching.
'Little Dombey' moved every listener to tears and so did
'Dr. Marigold', which at the time was considered 'one of the
most humorous revelations of imaginative literature'. Dr.
Marigold was a cheap-jack with a clever dog 'who had taught
himself to growl if anyone bid as low as sixpence'. In impersonating Pickleson, 'the giant with the little head and less
in it', Dickens spoke in a high falsetto. Tears gushed when
Dr. Marigold went through his accustomed patter on the
footboard with his poor little Sophy slowly dying on his
shoulder.

Something more than histrionic skill must have gone to the
fascination of audiences. The reader himself must have
radiated the magnetism that hypnotised these seated crowds
of people. His capacity for suggestion seems to have been
unlimited. Moncure Conway (who as a boy had run to see
him alight from a coach at Fredericksburg) said that it was
quite impossible to convey the idea of the readings, Dickens
being in himself a whole stock company with endless voices
and power of putting shapes across.

The texts of the readings were revised and re-revised; they
were scored, interwoven and cobwebbed with lines, often of
different colours. The script of 'Little Dombey', for
instance, was corrected and emended in red ink and in blue.

In 'Sikes and Nancy' there were a mass of stage directions to himself: 'action', 'cupboard action', 'murder coming' and so on.

The readings were a quicker way of making money than novel-writing, but they involved him in careful work and numberless rehearsals. For the actual performances Dickens put himself entirely into the hands of his manager, Arthur Smith, who relieved him of all worry; he merely had to turn up at the right time in the right place. After his London season had ended on July 22, he opened his provincial tour on August 2 at Clifton and closed it on Saturday, November 13, at Brighton. His programme included 'The Story of Little Dombey', 'The Poor Traveller', 'Boots at the Holly Tree Inn' and 'Mrs. Gamp'. There were eighty-seven readings given at forty-four different places. It was a great strain on the nerves, though he came back home every few days to rest and to keep an eye on *Household Words*. Cuthbert Bede went to hear him read the 'Carol' at Wolverhampton. He was introduced by his friend Arthur Smith to the reader, who told him what a contrast there was between the quiet, sympathetic audience of the Midland town and the frigidly genteel audiences of London who sometimes had almost stopped him from reading at all.

From one cause and another Dickens found himself more variable in mood and self-control than ever. There are few happy pictures of him at this time. One of them, a dinner at Forster's with Lord Chief Justice Cockburn as a guest, was broken in on by Landor 'who was fleeing from justice', in other words a law-suit at Bath. Dickens went out to console Landor who had been shown into a bedroom. It was thought that he might talk over with him the unpleasant crisis in which he was at the moment involved and which made it improper that he should meet the Chief Justice. Dickens came back into the room laughing; he said he had found Landor 'sitting on a bed, very jovial, and that the whole conversation was upon the characters of Catullus, Tibullus and other Latin poets'.

Among Dickens's younger cronies was Edmund Yates, the

bright but tactless journalist who at this time was contributing regular articles, at £3 a week, to *Town Talk*. His pen-sketches of celebrities, unsigned, had already featured Dickens. To use Yates's own words, 'it had given satisfaction and I felt I could not do better than follow on with a pen-portrait of his great rival'.[1]

Mr. Thackeray [he wrote] is forty-six years old, though from the silvery whiteness of his hair, he appears somewhat older. He is very tall, standing upwards of six feet two inches, and, as he walks erect, his height makes him a conspicuous figure in every assembly. . . . No one meeting him could fail to recognise in him a gentleman; his bearing is cold and uninviting, his style of conversation either openly cynical or affectedly goodnatured and benevolent; his bonhomie is forced, his wit biting, his pride easily touched. . . . His success with *Vanity Fair* culminated with his *Lectures on the Humourists of the Eighteenth Century*, which were attended by all the court and fashion of London. The pieces were extravagant, the lecturer's adulation for birth and position was extravagant, the success was extravagant. No one succeeds better than Mr. Thackeray in cutting his coat according to his cloth. Here he flattered the aristocracy, but when he crossed the Atlantic George Washington became the object of his worship, the 'Four Georges' the object of his bitterest attacks. . . . Our own opinion is that his success is on the wane. . . . There is a want of heart in all he writes. . . . It was with the publication of the third and fourth numbers of *Vanity Fair* that Mr. Thackeray began to dawn upon the reading public as a great genius. This great work which—perhaps with the exception of *The Newcomes*—is the most perfect dissection of the human heart, done with the cleverest and most unsparing hand, had been offered to and rejected by several of the first publishers of London. But the public saw and recognised its value; the great guns of literature, the *Quarterly* and the *Edinburgh*, boomed forth their praises.

Yates went on to speak of other novels and was so pleased with his article that he told Trollope all about it, and it seems

[1] Edmund Yates, *Recollections*.

that Trollope told Thackeray and so the mischief began. Thackeray naturally resented what he regarded as a personal attack by a young member of his club. He wrote an angry letter to Yates.

We meet at a club where, before you were born I believe, I and other gentlemen have been in the habit of talking without any idea that our conversation would supply paragraphs for professional vendors of 'Literary Talk', and I don't remember that out of that club I have ever exchanged six words with you. Allow me to inform you that the talk which you have heard there is not intended for newspaper remark and to beg—as I have the right to do —that you will refrain from printing comments on my private conversations; and that you will forgo discussions, however blundering, upon my private affairs; and that you will consider any question of my personal truth and sincerity as quite out of the province of your criticism.

Instead of apologising, Yates drafted a truculent reply which Dickens persuaded him not to send, it was 'too flippant and too violent'. He said that Thackeray in *The Yellowplush Papers* had held up Lardner and Lytton ('lisping Bulwig') to ridicule and that in *The Book of Snobs* he had given 'sketches of three at least of the members of the club and illustrated them with recognisable caricature drawings'. It was no better than a fresh attack. With Dickens's help he composed another letter, but even so did not apologise.

Thackeray on receiving it decided to report the incident to the committee of the Garrick, and by them Yates was called on to make ample apology or retire from membership. He declined to do either and appealed to put his case before a general meeting. At this meeting Dickens, Wilkie Collins and Samuel Lover spoke in his favour, but the decision went against him. He then started an action at law, and Dickens, who throughout had been his adviser, wrote to Thackeray asking whether he could appoint some third person to meet him and find an accommodation of 'this deplorable matter'. Thackeray forwarded this letter also to the committee. The committee did not accept the offer. When the legal proceedings owing to a technicality fell through, Yates left the Garrick Club, and Dickens, who walked out with him, resigned his place on the committee. Not very long after, in high dudgeon at the blackballing of a friend, Dickens resigned from the club himself.

The way Dickens championed Yates in this matter shows how much he was under the Collins influence and how in a way he liked to flout public opinion. He went out of his way to insult Evans for sympathising with Kate, writing to him that he could have no truck with anyone who had been false to him under the greatest wrong he has ever known. He also made secret plans to dissolve partnership with Bradbury and Evans in *Household Words*. Katey is a witness to his strange irascibility, part of which we must attribute to his uneasy conscience and all of which she put down to his infatuation for Ellen Ternan. His balance she thought had been completely upset. From a psychological point of view, 1858 was a thoroughly unsatisfactory year, for though 'Boz' felt young and free again and could make more money than ever before, he had lost his self-esteem and moral standing, requisites which neither wealth nor success could redeem. In Katey Perugini's words,

> More tragic and far-reaching in its effect was the association of Charles Dickens and Ellen Ternan and their resultant son than that of Nelson and Lady Hamilton and their daughter. My father was like a madman. He did not seem to care a damn what happened to any of us. Nothing could surpass the misery and unhappiness of our life.[1]

At some time in 1858 Ellen Ternan was living (possibly with her mother) at 2 Houghton Place, Ampthill Square, on the confines of Camden Town, and later on we find her set up in what Katey terms 'an establishment of her own at Peckham'. This establishment was Windsor Lodge, a house standing in a garden and facing country fields. Peckham,

[1] *Dickens and Daughter*, p. 94.

then a rural locality, was on the south side of the Thames and therefore almost equally accessible from Gad's Hill and from Wellington Street, Strand. Like the piano legs and mantelpieces of the Victorian era the tenancy of this house was well covered up. The Camberwell rate-book reveals that it was rented in 1867 by 'Frances Turnham' (Dickens was at the time in the United States) and from 1868 to 1870 by 'Charles Tringham'. Local gossip purveyed by a char-woman and a job-master spoke of Charles Tringham as an author engaged in writing a mystery story. Visited by Mr. and Mrs. Thomas Wright in 1935,[1] the then occupants of Holme Dene (alias Windsor Lodge) pointed out the sumach tree and the quince tree under the shadow of which Mr. Tringham had liked to sit. The brackets of the Venetian shutters were also shown, though the shutters had gone. They were said to be of the sliding pattern exactly like those installed at Gad's Hill Place.

Thomas Wright, who made a specialty of discoveries in the private lives of the eminent, wrote an article[2] concerning an interview he had sought with a friend of Mrs. Ternan and her girls—Canon Benham. The article was written on the assumption that the liaison was a short and temporary one, an opinion that he endorsed the following year. By 1938, however, he had nosed out the Peckham establishment which, if it proved nothing new, demonstrated that the liaison, far from being ephemeral, lasted twelve years. *Dickens and Daughter*, giving Katey Perugini's account of Ellen Ternan, had not appeared when Mr. Wright's autobiography was published. It is not to be supposed that with Ellen Ternan Charles Dickens entered into the ideal relationship he had all his life hankered for; nevertheless the association must have

---

[1] *Thomas Wright of Olney*, 1938.

[2] Thomas Wright, in the *Daily Express* of April 3, 1934, stated that Canon Benham had conversed with him about Ellen Ternan and said that she had 'disburdened her mind' to him. He repeats this in his *Life of Charles Dickens* (p. 356). Canon Benham was a friend of Mrs. Ternan and her family. In telling the story I have relied not on Mr. Wright but on the information supplied by Dickens's own daughter, Mrs. Perugini.

given him some pleasure as it was kept going till his death, and letters prove that the adaptable Georgina made a friend of the girl and welcomed her to Gad's Hill. There are notes in print from Dickens to his manservant, John, ordering him to convey delicacies to 'Miss Ellen' when poorly. 'Take Miss Ellen a little basket of fresh fruit, a jar of clotted cream from Tucker's and a chicken, a pair of pigeons or some nice little bird. Also on Wednesday and Friday morning, a little variety each day.' Such notes convince us of his solicitude and kindly affection for the girl who had thrown in her lot with his. Probably his letters to her would reveal his passion and warmth, but these are either lost or destroyed.

So much for the existence of 'the explosive charge' unacknowledged by Forster, but for which some less drastic and painful solution of the domestic dilemma might have been arrived at. The terms of the settlement made with Kate allowed her to have access to the children, but on the condition that they were not to be brought in contact with the Hogarths or Helen Thomson or the Evans family. How this worked out in practice it is hard to say, for the girls Mamey and Katey were so intimidated by their father's state of mind that they did not dare, during the first months of separation, to show any sympathy with their mother. Later on when things had settled down in their new groove it seems certain that the boys were allowed to go to Gloucester Crescent, always provided that there were no Hogarths or Evanses about.

Mamey, the eldest Dickens daughter, was entirely under Georgina's influence and never went to see her mother. Katey went occasionally; Charley, at the time a clerk in Baring's bank, lived, as we know, with her until by some arrangement of his father he was sent to China the following year. Kate Dickens was then alone except for the visits of the boys during their holidays.

For some time, indeed ever since the Manchester performance of *The Frozen Deep*, Dickens had been wondering

The Last Reading

March 15, 1870.

whether he could so steep himself in the French Revolution as to convey to his public what it actually felt like to be living through its terrors. All that he had gone through over the separation had unsteadied him and had made it almost impossible to settle down to work of the usual kind. It was imperative that he should get out of his own *milieu*. Making the resolution not to look at books dealing with any other subject, he began a course of reading, but from every book he waded through he turned with ever increasing admiration and amazement to Carlyle's *French Revolution*, 'which was aflame with the very essence of the conflagration'. He, too, would become an actor in these scenes and allow them to possess him utterly. Of his completed book he says, 'I have so far verified what is done and suffered in these pages, as that I have certainly done and suffered it all myself'. One of his projected titles for the book was 'Memory Carton' which gives the clue to the state of mind which he had induced in himself. His decision to write an historical novel was wise since it enabled him to regain an emotional balance that for some time had appeared highly precarious and which the recurrent excitement of readings did nothing to stabilise.

On the other hand, the direct appeal of the readings gave him immediate confidence in his public; there was no waiting for proofs, nor delay of publication, but the effort always involved a great outpouring of sensibility which was hurled back at him by displays of personal affection from his auditors. Till he had found the knack of managing his voice he would lose it before the end of the evening and altogether exhaust himself by impersonating character after character. He read to halls crammed to capacity, and always the hordes turned away insisted on their right to hear him on another occasion. Fresh readings had constantly to be planned to meet the immense demand. For these public appearances Dickens chose his clothes very carefully, always took a dresser to fix him up advantageously and always wore a buttonhole. In Ireland, ladies, sitting with their chins against the platform, would gather up the petals falling from his red geranium and

even beg the denuded stalk as souvenir. This was all gratifying enough to an actor's self-esteem, but occasionally a tactless
representative of 'the Emerald press' would administer a cold
douche by observing that 'though Mr. Dickens was only
forty-six, he already looked like an old man'.

In Belfast and Dublin he scored great successes and even in
Cork more than a thousand stalls were reserved in advance for
three readings. Exultant, he wrote to Wills, 'I made last
week a clear profit of £340 and have made in the month of
August a profit of one thousand guineas'. In England it was
the same story. 'Little Darlington covered itself with glory'
and at Durham he 'had a capital audience'. Walking from
Durham to Sunderland he felt as if he were making fancy
photographs of the Pit country. 'I couldn't help looking on
my mind, as I was doing it, as a sort of capitally prepared and
highly sensitised plate'. It was a great pleasure, he said, to
work with this mind, it 'took the impression so easily'.
Readings on the whole were a fatiguing enterprise, for he had
often to travel by night, especially at week-ends, when the
restrictions on Sunday travelling were severe. At York he
was pleased when a lady begged to touch 'the hand that
had filled her house with many friends'. Mamey and Katey
joined him at Newcastle and went the rounds, just as their
mother had done on all his theatrical tours except the last.
Their presence on a platform effectively disarmed criticism;
'the dear girls', said their father to Georgy, 'have really been
a great success'. Four readings at Edinburgh went off
brilliantly, although Dickens had been warned that there was
a certain coldness about the audiences there. He told Wills
that the triumph there was 'the greatest he had ever made.
The city was taken by storm and carried. "The Chimes"
shook it; "Little Dombey" blew it up. On the last two
nights the crowd was immense and the turn-away enormous.
Everywhere nothing was heard but praises, nowhere more
than at Blackwood's shop, where there certainly was no disposition to praise.' The girls, made much of, were enraptured
with Edinburgh. James Payn (later editor of *Chambers's*

Journal) went on an excursion to Hawthornden in company
with the whole family. A more delightful talker than
Dickens it had never been his lot to meet, for he eschewed all
commonplaces and never uttered a platitude. Hawthornden
was not open to the public the day they went there so it was
difficult to get access to the glen or to see the house. Payn,
expostulating with the custodian, explained how distinguished
was the visitor and how short his stay in Edinburgh, but
the man seemed never to have heard the name of Dickens.
In the end Payn had his way and they saw what they had
come to see. 'We laughed all the time', recorded Dickens.
The custodian's face, Payn tells us, registered extreme surprise when the great man handed him one of his usual lavish
tips.

After further triumphs at Manchester and Birmingham the
tour concluded at Brighton on November 13, and two days
later the conductor was back in his office getting to work on
the Christmas number of *Household Words*.

The Christmas number, however, was not his only concern
since his plans for eliminating Bradbury and Evans from
partnership in the magazine had by this time taken shape. He
would teach his 'enemies' a lesson they would not soon forget.
Before Christmas a writ was served, on his behalf by Forster,
on Bradbury and Evans which eventuated in the filing of a
bill in Chancery dissolving the partnership. By order of the
Court the right to use the name of the periodical *Household
Words* together with 'the printed stock and stereotyped plates
of the same' was put up to auction at Hodgson's on May 16,
1859. Dickens was the purchaser at £3350.[1] To Georgy he
wrote that he only had to pay down £500 in cash.[2] It was a
very severe blow to Bradbury and Evans as the author also
refused them any further novel contracts and returned to
Chapman and Hall, now a prosperous firm with premises
in Piccadilly. Acting throughout in a very disagreeable,
peremptory way, Dickens somehow managed to float a new
magazine, *All the Year Round*, of exactly the same format and

---

[1] E. Yates, *Recollections*.   [2] May 16, 1859.

make-up as *Household Words*, five weeks before the old contract expired. Strong objection to his procedure was raised by Bradbury and Evans and Dickens dealt with this in the last number of the expiring magazine. Like a cock flapping his wings, the conductor indulged in a good crow:

The first page of these Nineteen Volumes was devoted to a Preliminary Word from the writer by whom they were projected, under whose constant supervision they have been produced, and whose name has been (as his pen and himself have been) inseparable from the Publication ever since. The last page of the last of these Nineteen Volumes is closed by the same hand. He knew perfectly well, knowing his own rights and his means of attaining them, that it *could not be* but that this work must stop if he chose to stop it. He therefore announced many weeks ago that it would be discontinued on the day on which this final Number bears date. The Public have read a great deal to the contrary, and will have observed that it has not in the least affected the result.

It was war to the knife between Dickens and Bradbury and Evans, who now as a counterblast to *All the Year Round* launched a new magazine, *Once a Week*. 'What fools they are', commented Dickens, 'to try to make it look like *Household Words* and *All the Year Round*!'

The office of *Household Words* had been at 16 Wellington Street, Strand; the new office was at number 11 in the same street. Dickens carried Wills on with him and Wilkie Collins too, whose artist brother Charles now became a regular contributor and incidentally a person of some interest to Katey.

Determined to invigorate the new magazine, Wills was instructed by his employer to approach 'both the Trollopes', to secure a story from Mrs. Gaskell, and poems from young George Meredith, who had just taken Forster's place as literary adviser to Chapman and Hall. The said employer would write to George Eliot himself, and would get Mrs. Carlyle to speak to Ruffini about articles on the fighting in Italy (describing the battlefield of Magenta and the sack of Perugia) to be entitled 'A Track of War'. His blood being up, Dickens could spur himself as well as his contributors to action, managing to get the first instalment of *A Tale of Two Cities* ready for the first number of the new magazine. It was much shorter than most of Dickens's novels and was to be followed by *The Woman in White*. 'The Roving Englishman' would offer a new and, it was to be hoped, popular feature. It was written by Grenville Murray, vice-consul at Mytilene, who in one number presented so merciless a caricature of Sir Stratford Canning (as Sir Hector Stubble) that Canning's friends, fearful lest he might miss it, all sent him copies; the Foreign Office bag to Constantinople bulged with them. Charles Lever and Charles Reade also wrote for Dickens. Reade is described by Katey as 'perching his person upon a small circular-topped piano stool and singing comic songs in a tiny voice'. Charles Collins, so soon to become her husband, was 'Eye-witness'. Enough has been said about the inauguration of the new magazine to show that Dickens expended a great deal of energy upon it and made of it an immediate success. He could never afford to let up on his own writing, and Frith tells us that, when putting the finishing touches to his portrait of Dickens in Tavistock House, he noted his sitter pulling at his imperial and muttering to himself as he pored over a small portion of *A Tale of Two Cities*. A parcel of books lay on the table. Tapping one of them, Dickens said, 'That's a very good book by George Eliot, but unless I am mistaken George Eliot is a woman'. It was *Adam Bede*.

Meanwhile offers from New York for readings became more and more tempting, and by July 1859 Dickens thought he was far enough advanced with his new novel to venture on an American tour in September. He could perhaps, if he worked hard enough, finish the book before he sailed. His friend J. T. Fields was very insistent that he should start at once, but he delayed deciding to do so and the opportunity vanished with the looming up of the Civil War six months later.

In the autumn of 1859 Dickens began to wish to get rid of Tavistock House. The conventional Forster told him it would be very damaging to his reputation if he did not maintain an establishment in London for the benefit of the girls, but after considering the arguments for and against, he decided to complete the sale. Most of the furniture was transferred to Gad's Hill, but some was reserved to furnish a sitting-room and two bedrooms at the office of *All the Year Round* so that he or any of the family could stay in London when they wanted to. At Gad's Hill he could house plenty of furniture, for he had built additional bedrooms and turned the coach-house into living-rooms for sons and servants. The book-backs were carefully transferred to his country library, where they gave him the same pleasure as they had done when he first designed them for Tavistock House.

Dickens now took great pride in his Kentish freehold, for he felt it rounded off his career in a very satisfactory way. Cobham Woods and Park lay behind the house, the distant Thames in front, the Medway with Rochester and its old castle and cathedral to one side, 'the whole stupendous property' lying on the Dover Road. One of the first occasions on which he entertained there was on his daughter Katey's wedding day. Katey had become engaged to his new contributor, Charles Collins, a very tall young man with 'orange-coloured' hair framing a white face, who had belonged to the pre-Raphaelite brotherhood though never as a full member. His best painting, 'May in the Regent's Park', was exhibited at the Academy of 1852 when, in response to a suggestion by Ruskin, the walls blossomed with hawthorn and flowering shrubs. During the engagement he took Katey to sit to his friend John Millais for the girl in 'The Black Brunswicker'. Dickens viewed him leniently though he could not, knowing the strange nervous nature of the man, have thought him really a suitable husband for Katey; but Katey was proving less amenable to Georgy's management than Mamey and showed signs (to which she owned later) of wishing to escape control. Family life might run more smoothly without her. The wedding took place at Gad's Hill with Holman Hunt as best man. After the guests had gone

Mamey went up to her sister's bedroom, and on opening the door found her father on his knees with his face buried in Katey's wedding gown. She stood there quietly for a minute or two and then he, becoming aware of her presence, said in a broken voice, 'But for me Katey would not have left home'.[1]

For the Christmas number of *All the Year Round* (1859) Dickens produced the first of nine yearly stories, *The Haunted House*, written partly by himself and partly by Wilkie Collins. The idea of collaboration, which in itself was a very poor one since it appeared to stultify Dickens's genius, was originated by Collins at the time he became the adored young friend of the editor of *Household Words* and wanted to make himself indispensable to his patron. From time to time we find Dickens regretting that material good enough to go into a novel was being frittered away in these anonymous Christmas numbers, but he could never resist giving pleasure to his dear Wilkie, who was amiable enough to make himself responsible for the greater part of each story. For *The Haunted House* he wrote six out of the eight chapters. It must not be overlooked in discussing these Christmas numbers that they were very enriching, as they sold in large quantities, sometimes as many as 250,000 to 300,000 copies being printed.

As soon as Dickens had cut adrift from London he began to express his dislike of the place, a dislike that had been growing on him for years. He found the Thames 'most horribly stinky', it made him sick to cross Waterloo Bridge or London Bridge. Nobody seemed to know how to tackle the river and the 'cartloads of chloride of lime that are shot into the filthy stream' have no effect upon it.

> London is a vile place. . . . I have never taken kindly to it since I lived abroad. Whenever I come back from the country now and see that great heavy canopy lowering over the house-tops I wonder what on earth I do there except of obligation.

It was not till nine years later that a good road was built from Westminster Bridge to Waterloo Bridge. Trees were then

[1] G. Storey, *Dickens and Daughter*.

planted and a footway opened to the Temple. Because of these improvements the scour of the river deepened and quickened and soon a neat embankment rose from Westminster to Blackfriars. Dickens said it was the finest public work ever executed.

Great play is always made with Dickens's love of London but there is little evidence of that love in his books. London was, in boyhood and youth, his medium—the place in which he grew up, learnt about life and made a position for himself. It was the only medium he really knew and it was perfectly natural that he should make it the setting of his first work and that it should figure preponderatingly in his novels. Great as was his interest and his curiosity, love is not the word that expresses his attitude towards London. He sketched, however, incomparable vignettes of its streets and their denizens as well as of the spirit of its differing localities. But in considering Dickens's feelings about London we must never lose sight of the fact that as soon as he could possibly afford it (and that was at the age of twenty-seven) Charles Dickens moved his domicile out of authentic London into Regentsland, thus showing his personal preference for modern drainage, clean surroundings and green open spaces.

Dickens may now be considered as settled for life. It is to be hoped that he derived some happiness from his Ternan connection, but it seems plain that Ellen was an ornament or addition to an existence that would have been quite wretched without the support and companionship of Georgy. The girl, however, taught him something real about women and his later heroines benefited from her example. The characters of Lucie Manette, Estella and Bella Wilfer are supposed to be modelled on her, but probably it is the very charming Rosa Bud who best embodies her qualities. Anyway, the day of the long-suffering angel is done. She is now replaced by someone more complicated, more sensitive and more human. We might expect to find Georgy in one or other of the female characters in the novels, for she was her brother-in-law's constant mainstay. Little sentences in his letters show on what comfortable, confidential terms they were. She pays the house-bills with the money he provides; she finds papers in his private drawers; if he is unwell she goes to London to be with him, leaving Mamey in charge of the boys. They dine out together; 'Laura (Lady Olliffe) wants us to dine at the Mansion House. Shall we go? Perhaps it would be as well to take the opportunity . . . bring my dress suit and black trousers.' One could go on quoting indefinitely, but these few sentences suffice o show what an important part Georgy played in Dickens's life and how dependent he was on her.

Let us stand back for a moment and look at Charles Dickens in 1860. He is a world figure (aged forty-eight), financially prosperous and immensely successful. He has Britain at his feet: obviously he has gained the world: but has he somehow managed to abdicate the overlordship of his soul? To those who knew him intimately his life appeared to have changed in quality. The old equal friendships were a thing of the past, they had been replaced by intimacies with younger men, like Wilkie Collins, George Sala, Percy Fitzgerald, Edmund Yates. To some extent their relations to him were syco-phantic, for they were all definitely inferior in character and ability to the older men who had dropped away, and they all derived their livelihood from him. Dickens's very amuse-ments tended to be those of a younger man, though he was so conscious of being an older one in looks that he darkened his grizzling locks and beard with dye, as we may see in the photographs of 1858. Even if the stories of a French mistress are not true and the frequent journeys to Paris were under-taken for some other reason, it is clear that in slipping his marital moorings he had lost balance and sense of direction. With the new way of life went a passion for novelty. Illus-trations by 'Phiz', for instance, no longer appeared suitable for his stories; modern designs by very young Marcus Stone or Luke Fildes were preferred and took their place. He had fallen out of love with his old setting and he did not find it too easy to create a new one.

Prosperity enveloped him as with a garment. *All the Year Round* attracted to itself an ever vaster public. Dickens could get £1000 for a short story any day of the week. His family responsibilities have lessened. Charley is in the Far East, Sydney is at sea, Walter in India, Alfred in Australia, whither he is planning to send another boy to join him. Impetuous, warm-hearted Katey has left the shelter of his roof and has a house of her own. Mamey and Georgy cosset him and produce the comfortable home-like atmosphere on which he is so dependent. Mamey and Georgy never criticise his ways, they understand him perfectly. Georgy indeed complaisantly enough calls her sister's supplanter 'dearest Ellen', and invites her to Gad's Hill.[1] Easy-going as his circumstances were, he found himself plunged from time to time in profitless retrospection and a passionate wish to kill the past. How would it be to destroy the letters he had received during a lifetime? To biographers who might write asking to see his letters from Maclise or Leech he could then reply, 'Shocked by the misuse of the private letters of public men, which I constantly observed, I destroyed a very large and very rare mass of correspondence'. And this is what he really did. Old letters from Catharine, from 'Fuz', from Talfourd, from Ainsworth, from Miss Coutts, from Maclise, from all the people he had known and loved in his passage through life, were assembled in their packets. He would not untie them, he would not re-read them for he did not want to remember anything of the old days; these reminders of past joys must go. As the last packet was thrown on to the bonfire he exclaimed, 'Would to God every letter I had ever written was on that pile!' Henry Fielding and his brother Edward Bulwer Lytton, who had watched the proceedings, then roasted onions on the ashes. The ghosts of old friendships could no longer haunt Dickens, for had he not buried the dead past as his friend Longfellow said it ought to be buried? Nothing must exist for him henceforth but the living present, genius within and God o'erhead. Even the pet names he had given

[1] *Dickens and Daughter*, p. 128.

to his boys no longer reminded him of the grand figures after whom they had been called, those gods of his youth to whom he had paid domestic homage. 'Wally' did not bring Landor to mind nor 'Syd' Sydney Smith. As for 'Harry' and 'Ally', who could guess that they were called after Henry Fielding and Alfred Tennyson? And 'Frank', once the baby Francis Jeffrey, he had almost forgotten after whom he was named; and as for 'Plorn' he had long ceased to be Edward Bulwer Lytton. Blurred and smudged associations at best, and the irony of it all was that they none of them could write and that none of them cared about books! Must everything as in dreams fade phantom-like in time's desert? Was life really like that? Was the flame of human endeavour and human aspiration always extinguished, leaving behind no vestige of its heat or brilliance? Melancholy questions leading to melancholy conclusions.

Luckily Dickens had his routine work at the office to attend to and the obligation to grind out a series of papers, *The Uncommercial Traveller*, as stop-gaps for the magazine. He was worried at the effect Charles Lever's novel *A Day's Ride* was having on the circulation. It was obviously a dismal failure, must be cut short and immediately followed by a novel of his own. Luckily he knew what he wanted to write about. At last, with forty-eight years of life behind him, he was free to settle down to tell the story of Cooling and the marshes by the river. Wandering there he can recapture the mood of boyhood and weave the story he knows to have been waiting for him ever since the day he first saw the coffin-shaped stones covering the bodies of the thirteen little Comport children. The story was no trouble to invent, it was all lying there in his mind. He was 'Pip' every bit as much as he was Oliver, Paul and David. Recoiling sharply to the imaginations of childhood and the half-fearful dreams of hulks, gibbets and escaped criminals made him in a way happy; he had returned to the empyrean of reality, to creation; he could still know himself for the angelic lad, sweet and sensitive, who had lured the hearts of countless readers from their breasts. He could once again see the prison ships at Egypt Bay, 'the old battery at Cliffe', the old sexton who knew him as a boy. How wonderful to shake himself free of facts, of reference books and all the grim reading he had done for *Hard Times* and *The Tale of Two Cities* and let himself go with the kind of people he loved and understood, the Gargerys who were so like the Peggottys and the Toodles and the rest of the pure in heart. He knew that people liked crime entanglements in novels nowadays; the new novel must have its melodramatic framework. He had used the device in *Bleak House*, he would use it again. All 1860 and part of 1861 was devoted to this book, *Great Expectations*, and he felt as he had felt in writing *David Copperfield*. Sensible of this identity of mood, he re-read his earlier book, for he must make sure the new novel was not too like the old. Some people have called *Great Expectations* the better novel of the two and in certain respects of even rarer limpidity. It appeared in *All the Year Round* from December 1860 to August 1861 and while writing it he gave no public readings.

In November 1860, feeling the need of change and motion, he went with his dear Wilkie to Bideford and posted to Liskeard. It was not as productive as the old tour he had made when beginning to write *Martin Chuzzlewit*, but it restored his elasticity and eagerness to write. Clovelly delighted him enough to make him open his Christmas story, *A Message from the Sea*, with the description of a village 'built sheer up the face of a steep and lofty cliff'. Collins at this time was still working on *The Woman in White* which, like Bulwer Lytton's *Strange Story*, was nearing completion. Both were booked for *All the Year Round*. The circulation of the Christmas number for 1860 reached a quarter of a million copies. At last Dickens had found out how to give the public exactly what it wanted. He had been experimenting in magazine editorship for over twenty years and now he knew the measure that must be meted out to eager readers.

Chapter 25

LONDON AND GAD'S HILL

*The contagion of sympathy runs electrically through
society, searches high and low for congenial powers, and
suffers none to lurk unknown to the professor.*

DURING the spring of 1861 Dickens rented 3 Hanover
Terrace so that his girls might enjoy a London 'season'
while he gave six readings at the St. James's Hall to what he
termed 'model audiences'. The series enabled him to clear
£500. If money could satisfy him he was getting plenty of it,
for *Great Expectations* was 'doing gloriously'. He had a mind
at this time to introduce his third son, Francis Jeffrey (a
stammerer to whom all professions were closed), into the
office of *All the Year Round*, as he seemed to be 'the only
one of the family with natural literary taste and capacity'.
Two years later Francis Jeffrey, tried and found wanting, was
packed off to join the Bengal Mounted Police. Letters show
that, like some of the older generations of his family, he spent
more money than he received. Writing to Georgy, who it
appears paid her nephew the allowance of £3 a month allotted
to him by his father, Dickens says, 'Perhaps it would be a
damaging thing, suddenly to withhold from him money that
he expects. Therefore I would give him his month's three
pounds—with a caution. . . .'

The lesson taught him by salvaging his impecunious
brothers made Dickens fear a like disappointment in his own
children, especially if they remained in London. Members
of the estranged Hogarth family were inclined to attribute
the exodus of Charles's sons to the influence of their aunt
Georgina, whose affection for their father seemed to take a
more and more possessive turn. Dickens would sometimes
joke about the helplessness of his sons and say he thought he

ought to be presented 'with a smock frock, a pair of leathern breeches, and a pewter watch for having brought up the largest family ever known with the smallest disposition to do anything for themselves'.

Charley, who had returned from China as much in love with Bessie Evans as ever, now decided to get married. His attachment had been for some time past a source of mortification and annoyance to his father, who had rather hoped that the journey to the Far East might cause him to change his mind, but when he saw that Charley's heart was fixed, he showed himself paternal and kind to the young couple though he refused ever to darken their doors. 'I will never go to Mrs. Charley's house', he wrote to Georgy and of course he did not attend the wedding, the vendetta between himself and Evans being still operative.

When *Great Expectations* was completed, that is to say in the late summer 1861, Dickens, with Georgy and Mamey in attendance, went to stay at Knebworth for a week, ostensibly to discuss the future of the Guild of Literature and Art and to see how the houses at Stevenage were progressing. During this visit he walked with Mr. Arthur Helps, Lord Orford and 'the girls' to inspect the buildings. After doing so they all crossed the road to pay a visit of curiosity to the so-called 'Hertfordshire Hermit', James Lucas, who appears as Mr. Mopes in *Tom Tiddler's Ground*.[1] Lucas, though he had abjured washing and slept on cinders, was an educated man and the son of a West India merchant. He was intensely annoyed with Dickens for singling him out as subject of a story and gave vent to his feelings in the press. Rather unexpectedly he has a place in the *Dictionary of National Biography*.

The rest of the summer was spent at Gad's Hill preparing for an extended reading tour which was to include Norwich,

[1] See *The Queen*, December 21, 1861, showing the Committee of Concoction (Sala, Collins, Hollingshead and the editor): 'It was decided that the next number of *All the Year Round* should consist of seven chapters entitled *Tom Tiddler's Ground*'.

Ipswich, Colchester, Canterbury, Hastings, Brighton, New-castle, Edinburgh, Liverpool, Chester, Plymouth and Tor-quay. For this tour Dickens set himself to prepare new effects. Writing to Forster, he says:

> With great pains I have made a continuous narrative out of *Copperfield* that I think will reward the exertion it is likely to cost me. I have also done Nicholas Nickleby at the Yorkshire school, also the Bastille prisoner from *A Tale of Two Cities*.

By now he was treating each reading as if it were to be a play in which he was not only to act every part himself, but to learn every word by heart. It was a great blow to Dickens when his excellent manager, Arthur Smith, fell ill and had to give up working for him. His place was taken by one Head-land, who muddled the tour, the tickets and the bills in the most incompetent way, though even so he failed in choking off the audiences.

The series of readings had to be broken at Liverpool because of the death of the Prince Consort, and Dickens promised disappointed audiences to return later to compensate them for what they were missing. 'What Jackasses people are making of themselves over this death!' he exclaimed, unconsciously echoing the impatient sentiments of Macready on hearing of the mortal sickness of William IV. He was to some degree consoled for the interruption of his tour by the phenomenal popularity of his new Christmas story, *Tom Tiddler's Ground*, of which 300,000 copies were sold.

Soon after New Year it was considered correct for him to resume reading and in a hectic tour he visited Birmingham, Leamington, Cheltenham, Plymouth, Torquay, Exeter and Liverpool. In March and April he addressed himself to 'perfectly astonishing audiences' at the St. James's Hall. For the London series he established himself in a friend's house, 16 Hyde Park Gate, which he had exchanged for three months against Gad's Hill. He found it 'the nastiest little house in London'. 'I have hit upon nothing for a story', he wrote, 'again and again I have tried, but this odious little house has stifled and darkened my invention.' To celebrate John Forster's birthday (April 2) a dinner was given at the Star and Garter. After it Dickens, who was feeling wonderfully well, walked back to London with Lehmann.

During the spring he spoke at two public banquets, one of them in aid of the Artists' General Benevolent Institution[1] and the other the annual feast of the Newsvendors' Benevolent and Provident Institution.[2] At the first of these dinners he reminded those present that an artist is not a man who can make his livelihood out of buying and selling, that he is compelled to strike out of himself every spark of the fire which lighted, burned and, perhaps, consumed him. He must 'win the battle of life with his own hand, and with his own eyes . . . by his own unaided self'. It was a plain duty to help the artist, it was really part payment of the great debt which all sensible and civilised creatures owe to art, a way of expressing appreciation and a mark of respect. He added that artists of the highest rank were not slow or cold in supporting the Institution for which he was appealing.

Dickens told the Newsvendors (after giving a bird's-eye survey of the function of the modern newsman and the paper he is responsible for) that the newsman's profits were small, that he was subject to anxiety and much personal wear and tear. Indispensable to civilisation and freedom, he is looked for every day with pleasurable excitement. Society owes much to the newsman and it is only just that it should afford him assistance in times of sickness and indigence. No organisation could be more worthy of support.

In the summer he rested at Gad's Hill. F. D. Finlay, editor of the *Northern Whig*, stayed with him there in June. He was met by his host driving a jaunting car and found a pleasant little family party consisting of the Charles Collins, Mamey and Georgina. The food was excellent and elegantly served. Everyone seemed gay and they played croquet by day and vingt-et-un by night. Finlay was particularly taken with Georgina Hogarth, 'a really delightful person', easy in manner

[1] March 29, 1862.   [2] May 20, 1862.

and conversation and quite unassuming.

In July Georgy, to her brother-in-law's great distress, fell seriously ill and when she became better he decided to arrange for her to recuperate in Paris. Leaving strict injunctions with Mamey to bring her over as soon as he had found a suitable lodging, he crossed to France, visiting Hazebrouck and Dunkirk on his way to *la ville lumière*. In Paris Dickens rented 24 rue du Faubourg St. Honoré, and there they all three lived till close on Christmas. Wills came over from time to time to the Hôtel St. Honoré opposite, in order to put through the forthcoming issue of *All the Year Round*. On his November visit he brought with him a 'boxful' of flowers from Miss Burdett Coutts to be delivered by Dickens's hand to the Empress Eugénie. Dickens unscrewed the box, as 'if exhuming a dead body from a coffin'.

He reported 'Flowers a little crushed but corpses in very good preservation', screwed the box down again and started for Compiègne. At the station he hired the only omnibus and went 'to titivate', dressed in a delightful little bedroom trellised and creepered, then drove off again in the omnibus to the Palace. When the driver asked him whether he should go to the *cours d'honneur* Dickens replied '*Décidément*'! Arrived, he sent in a letter and card for the Duke of Atholl, and was shown to his rooms. His Grace in a dressing-gown poured tea for him, a servant brought in the box, the flowers were exhumed, and pronounced 'in wonderful preservation considering'. The Duke would deliver Miss Coutts's letter to the Duchesse de Bassano and get the Imperial gardener to touch up the bouquets. Presently the simple, elegant Duchess came in, had a chat about the flowers, then said good-bye. It was a fiasco from the undertaker's angle, for he would have liked to meet the Empress—but she was not even told that Mr. Dickens had called.

Somehow even his beloved Paris induced no cheerful mood. Wherever he went in the streets, the theatres, the restaurants, Dickens was haunted by the great figures of the past. Some of them were dead, one of the noblest was an exile. Sadly he wrote:

> Last time I was here, I went to the theatre with Scribe, and the last time but one, Victor Hugo had the most fantastic of apartments, and stood in the midst of it, a fine-featured, fiery-eyed, gallant fellow. Now Scribe is in Père la Chaise, the fantastic apartment in the Channel Islands, and Victor Hugo is an old photograph in the shops with a quenched eye and a stubbly beard and no likeness to anyone I ever saw.

Though there was no inspiration or exhilaration to be drawn from the life of Paris, Dickens at any rate could make arrangements with Sir Joseph Olliffe to read at the Embassy in aid of a British charity. Readings from old works were considered by some of his admirers an unsatisfacotry substitute for a fresh book, but it was essential for him to keep his name before the public somehow and he had no fresh book on the stocks. The title of a possible novel was hovering in his mind, *Our Mutual Friend*, but so far no story had gushed up from the hidden springs of creative life to give the words any meaning. Perhaps having to take 'the girls' about was preventing him from settling to work; when he returned to Paris in the New Year he would return alone and see whether solitude would not serve his turn better than company.

Christmas was spent at Gad's Hill with the boys, and Mamey, whose amiability sometimes makes the impression of imbecility, says, 'These "tides" were the happiest of all'. Her father, on the other hand, writes as if he were rather oppressed. 'The house is pervaded by boys.' 'Every boy has an incalculable power of reproducing himself in every part of the house at every moment.' 'They boil over the house. . . .' These are constantly recurring phrases. He hears their boots trampling about, their whistling, their shouts; he cannot write at all. He managed to see the holidays through without betraying irritability or displeasure, and it cheered him to know how well his Christmas story, *Somebody's Luggage*, was selling. Though not quite as popular as its predecessors, it had put a good deal of money into his pocket. *All the Year Round* might be said to be going better than ever. At the end of January he escaped to Paris. There he stayed at the Hôtel du Helder, and for some reason connected with his interest in the Revolution spent his birthday at Arras thinking on the 'amiable sea-green Robespierre'.

The readings presided over by Lord Cowley at the British Embassy were 'a brilliant success'. Two were given in January and 'never, never, never was anything like the enthusiasm'. Dickens was positively chased out of Paris by his admirers, but not before he had promised to return for two more readings. These also went off incredibly well.

Going a good deal to the play, Dickens lost his heart to Fechter as the lover both in the *Maître de Ravenswood* and in the *Dame aux Camélias*. He had already met Fechter in London when he was playing *Hamlet* and *Ruy Blas* and had tried to persuade him to engage Maria Ternan for his cast. Now for the first time he was swept off his feet by what he called this actor's 'unmistakeable genius'. The critics had done their best to crush him, but the critics, he thought, were entirely wrong-headed. 'By Heavens!' he exclaimed after watching him in the *Maître de Ravenswood*, 'the man who can do that can do anything.' The very manner in which, as lover, he pressed the hem of the lady's dress was 'something wonderful'. Then, too, Fechter's interpretation of *Ruy Blas*, *Hamlet* and *Othello* were to his English admirer simply perfection. Knowledgeable people thought Dickens mistaken in his estimate, as the man was really but a moderately good actor, and this general opinion was to be confirmed when he became lessee of the Lyceum Theatre in London in the summer of 1863 with Dickens as his financial backer. Dickens, however, for the time being was infatuated by him.

His dear Madame Viardot proved as fascinating as ever. In *Orphée*, indeed, Dickens found her 'unapproachably fine'. After being much moved by her performance, he ran into M. Viardot in the corridor, who took him, 'disfigured as he was by crying', to her dressing-room. Could she have been paid a more touching compliment? He managed to turn the tables on the great contralto a few days later when he read *The Cricket on the Hearth* aloud at the Ary Scheffers. It is Mr. Arthur Russell who tells how 'when the reading was over Madame Viardot was asked to sing, but could not do so as she was still choked by tears'.

Forster deals very shortly with the years between 1862 and 1867 and says that he relied much on the papers known as *The Uncommercial Traveller* to write on them at all. He was no longer in close touch with Dickens, and did not find his activities so interesting as of old. We know that he continued to disapprove of the readings.

'The girls' always looked forward to a 'season' in London, and the 'season' of 1863 was to some extent rendered romantic by the arrival of the sea-king's daughter, Princess Alexandra of Denmark, who made her first public appearance as Princess of Wales at the unveiling of the Memorial to Prince Albert in June. From Alfred Tennyson with his poem of welcome to the humblest citizen all were out to give their hearts to the lovely bride. As Bulwer Lytton said, 'The Princess seems to have bewitched the English world'.

The year 1863 was a year of deaths. Augustus Egg died in Algiers, Mrs. John Dickens in London, Mrs. George Hogarth also in London. Thackeray died suddenly, at the age of fifty-two, on Christmas Eve, and Walter Landor Dickens in India on the last day of the year, though the news of his death did not reach his father till February, by which time Francis Jeffrey was more than half-way to Bengal.

For the *Cornhill Magazine*, of which Thackeray was editor, Dickens was requested to write a valedictory article. A few weeks earlier Thackeray had come up suddenly to Dickens in the Athenaeum and had shaken him warmly by the hand, thus putting an end to the Yates feud which had kept them apart for five years. It was considered appropriate by contemporaries that one great novelist should write about another even though he might be no admirer of his work. Dickens said he had known Thackeray for twenty-eight years, ever since he had proposed to illustrate *Pickwick*, and that he had last seen him just before Christmas at the Athenaeum Club. He went on to tell how when Thackeray had stood for Oxford he had made a droll appeal to the speaker to come down and tell his constituents who he was, 'for he doubted whether more than two of the electors had ever heard of him and he thought there might be as many as six or eight who had heard of me'. He and Thackeray had of course had their differences of opinion. 'I thought that he too much feigned a want of earnestness and that he made a pretence of undervaluing his art, which was not good for the art that he held in trust.'

Dickens would not take on himself to discourse on Thackeray's works, but he had on the table before him all that he had written of his latest story. This was *Dennis Duval* 'which might have rivalled *Esmond*'. The condition of the little pages of manuscript where Death stopped his hand shows that he had carried them about, and often taken them out of his pocket here or there, for patient revision and interlineation. The last words he had corrected in print were, 'And my heart throbbed with an exquisite bliss'. Dickens reminded his readers that Thackeray was in his fifty-third year and that the mother who had blessed him in his first sleep also blessed him in his last. Great things were known of him in the way of warm affection, quiet endurance, unselfish thoughtfulness for others and generosity. These things may not be told. No one more genial, natural, cordial, fresh and honestly impulsive has been seen in these times. 'No one can be surer than I of the greatness and goodness of his heart.'

A great concourse of mourners stood round a grave at Kensal Green on December 30 of the year 1863. An observer says of Dickens on this occasion 'he had a look of bereavement on his face which was indescribable'. When all others had turned aside from the grave, he still stood there, as if rooted to the spot, watching with almost haggard eyes every spadeful of dust that was thrown upon it. Walking away with some friends, he began to talk, but presently his voice quavered a

little, and shaking hands all round rapidly, he went off alone.[1]
Even more 'woefully upsetting' to him was the death of his
crony John Leech which took place shortly afterwards.

For Christmas 1863 Dickens wrote part of *Mrs. Lirriper's
Lodgings* and cogitated over the novel for which he had the
name but not the story.   Two years had gone by without a
long book, but at last he found himself able to get the first
three numbers down on to paper.   He then went off with
Browning and Wilkie Collins 'to keep Shakespeare's birthday
in peace and quiet' at Stratford.   The first instalment of *Our
Mutual Friend* was issued on May 1 and thirty thousand copies
of it were at once sold.   On May 11 Dickens presided at the
Adelphi Theatre over a meeting called to found Shakespeare
schools in connection with the Royal Dramatic Academy.
He was anxious that a start should be made with forty foundation scholars, all to be children of actors, actresses or dramatic
writers.   The Provost of Eton was supporting the scheme
and he took occasion to say that he believed 'there is not in
England any institution so socially liberal as a public school'.

From February to June 1864 he rented 57 Gloucester Place
and indulged in a perfect orgy of dining out.   'The most
severe dinner-eating season I have ever known in London.
Every week I had sworn to go out no more and every week
I have perjured myself seven times.' Various diaries of the
moment record some of these outings, one a dinner with
Fechter in St. John's Wood to meet Bulwer Lytton, and
another with Chorley in Westbourne Terrace.   To many of
them he was accompanied by Georgina. Browning and
others were at Chorley's party and Sir George Grove noted
'Dickens was very amusing, but not in the least forced.   He
was full of a ship of Mormon emigrants which he had been
seeing, 1200 of the cleanest, best conducted, most excellent
people he ever saw.'   This excursion may be seen reflected
in an article entitled 'Bound for the Great Salt Lake' in *The
Uncommercial Traveller*.

In June Dickens fled to Belgium to recuperate from all the

[1] *Dickensian*, 1937, p. 131.

port, champagne and rich food. He complained of severe pain in the left foot and leg but did not call it gout though at times it almost incapacitated him. Ten days abroad worked wonders and on his return Dickens settled down at Gad's Hill to his novel, swearing he would 'stick to his last', and 'dine out never again till next year'. No readings were arranged while he applied himself to his creative work and, with the exception of visits to the office of *All the Year Round*, he remained absorbed in *Our Mutual Friend*.

During the summer Charles Collins's health gave cause for great anxiety; it had broken down in the spring and Katey had taken him to Wiesbaden, but the German doctors could not do much for him and she had now settled with him at Nice. His illness had been diagnosed as cancer and Dickens began to think that Katey would soon be left 'a young widow'; but Charles Collins survived his father-in-law.

In November we find Dickens writing to his manager, Wills, alluding to his generous present of a brougham, a 'token of your ever generous friendship and appreciation'. The carriage will be to him 'a memorial of happy intercourse and perfect confidence that have never had a break and that surely never can have any break now but one'. In return he proposed Wills for the Garrick Club, getting Wilkie Collins to second him. It was very mortifying to them both that their candidate should be blackballed and because of it both resigned membership.

Dickens liked receiving large presents and was delighted when the ninety-two sections of Fechter's gift of a Swiss chalet began to arrive at Higham station. There was a discussion where it should be erected; the garden was too small to hold it, and as it was intended for quiet work it had to be sited at some distance from the house. Finally it was put up on the other side of the Dover Road to be approached by a flight of steps leading to a tunnel, like the Pope passage at Twickenham.

In the early part of 1865 Dickens was in Paris again for a brief holiday, after which he worked 'like a dragon' on *Our*

Mutual Friend. His swollen feet, treated with 'poppy fomentations', prevented him from taking exercise so he allowed his thoughts to dwell on the American war, and told Fanny Kemble that he 'was a southern sympathiser to the extent of not believing in the northern love of the black man nor that the northern horror of slavery had much to do with the war'.

For May and June the Dickens party was in London, this time at 16 Somers Place. The usual round of public engagements was fulfilled, the usual mill of private dinners. There were family concerns, too, to occupy his mind, for Alfred Tennyson d'Orsay was to be sent out of the country. For two years the boy had been working in a 'China house in the city', no doubt the house to which his brother Charley had gone to work after his return from the East and which now had failed. Writing to Henry Layard, Dickens informed him that his young son was sailing for Melbourne on May 29. 'At his own desire Alfred Tennyson,' he said, 'will seek his fortune.' He had obtained a few introductions for him, and possibly Layard may furnish others, perhaps one to the Governor?

Again Dickens crossed to France, this time with Ellen Ternan, and on their way back both were involved in the Staplehurst accident, when eight coaches toppled into the river and a number of people were killed and injured. Ellen was not hurt, neither was Dickens, who set to work with the flask strapped like field-glasses to his person to pour brandy down the throats of persons suffering from shock, concussion and broken limbs. Some of them died immediately. Dickens did not understand it at all and noted with sad surprise that 'Mr. Dickenson was the first person the brandy saved'. He worked hard in extricating the victims and later was presented with plate by the railway company for his services on the occasion. In a postscript to *Our Mutual Friend* Dickens says that Mr. and Mrs. Boffin were also involved in the accident but suffered no permanent injury.

In July he went to Knebworth for the formal inauguration

of the houses built by the Guild of Literature and Art. Owing to the provisions of the Act constituting the Guild it had not been possible to implement any of its intentions for seven years. Only now, in the year 1865, were the three Guild houses, built on land given by Lord Lytton, ready for occupation. It had always been part of the scheme to provide artists and authors with quarters where they could confederate themselves into a society for the diffusion of light and culture; at least this was Dickens's idea, but it worked out quite differently. The houses were located on the road near Stevenage and a party was given to celebrate the founding of a new Arcadia. Every artist and author of eminence was bidden to the feast and 'the county' was invited to meet them. They did not mix, and Charles Collins heard 'the county' commenting on the party and saying that they had been asked to meet 'a dem'd funny set of people'. At the luncheon that followed the throwing open of the houses, both Dickens and Bulwer Lytton, as co-founders of the Guild, were announced to speak.

During the morning Percy Fitzgerald had a talk with John Forster, who made the unpleasant impression on him of 'being impregnably mailed in self-complacency'. He was also carried off by Dickens to be introduced to the master of Knebworth. They found him lying on a divan smoking a chibouk. He mumbled a few words of greeting, seemed but dimly conscious of their presence, and had a far-away look in his eyes. By luncheon-time he had revived enough to make an eloquent speech, and, when all but the house guests had left, became brilliant, talkative and droll, discussing with Dickens his own novel, *Strange Story*, with great animation.

In thanking Bulwer Lytton at the luncheon for the toast he had proposed in his honour, Dickens explained that 'the three houses built in the Gothic style' had been erected out of Guild funds on land donated by the master of Knebworth. They had surveyed these satisfactory buildings and were now enjoying the hospitality of their originator. He would like to make it clear that the ladies and gentlemen, whom we shall invite to occupy the houses we have built will never be placed under any social disadvantage. They will be invited to occupy them as artists, receiving them as a mark of the high respect in which they are held by their fellow workers. As artists I hope they will often exercise their calling within those walls for the general advantage; and they will always claim on equal terms, the hospitality of their generous neighbour. . . . Health, long life, and prosperity to our distinguished host. Ladies and gentlemen, you know very well that when the health, life and beauty now overflowing these halls shall have fled, crowds of people will come to see the house where he lived and wrote. . . . This is the home of a very great man whose connection with Hertfordshire every other county in England will envy for many long years to come.

It is sad to have to record that the well-intentioned efforts of the promoters of the Guild failed completely in persuading authors or artists to come and live rent free in the houses at Stevenage designed for their comfort. No one of them would consent to do so on any terms. Those approached pointed out that the times of the trains would make it impossible for them to reach their proposed residences after the theatre. Others went so far as to ask what they were to be paid for 'being buried alive' at Stevenage. To the unprejudiced person visiting them to-day the houses seem entirely without point. Three miles from Knebworth, its hospitality could not be frequently enjoyed: facing a dusty high road, they were just too far from the station to be convenient to anyone. R. H. Horne called them 'those doleful cottages standing in a field'. To authors and artists the whole scheme was tainted with the idea of patronage, and, though paved with blameless intention, the road to Stevenage appeared to them the road to extinction.

Chapter 26

AMERICA AGAIN

An educated American is one of the most endearing and generous of friends.　　　CHARLES DICKENS

ON finishing *Our Mutual Friend* in September 1865, Dickens light-heartedly polished off a Christmas story, *Dr. Marigold's Prescriptions*, and then devoted his attention exclusively to preparing new readings, making no attempt to write another novel until his return from America in April 1868. Among the scenes dramatised at this time was the murder of Nancy by Bill Sikes from *Oliver Twist*. Dickens experimented with this presentation until he could say, 'I have got something so horrible out of it that I am afraid to try it in public.' It curdled the blood of his family to hear 'the awful noises' he made in rehearsing his effects in the garden at Gad's Hill, and it awed them to see his exhaustion afterwards, 'as if it took all the breath out of his body'. The murder reading was not brought into his repertory for three years.

On St. Valentine's Day 1866 Dickens took the chair at the annual dinner of the Dramatic, Equestrian and Musical Fund at Willis's Rooms. To his delight ladies were present at the table, and he laid 'the utmost devotion sanctioned by St. Valentine at their feet'. He spoke of the professional brotherhood that honoured the claims of kindred 'in the dingiest and dirtiest concert room, in the least lucid theatre, in the raggedest circus-tent ever stained by weather'. He could say from experience that there is no class or profession that so well helps the other. In toasting the ladies he gave the name of the distinguished actress Mrs. Stirling, who responded on behalf of her sex. Soon after this date Dickens felt himself to be very unwell. The doctor said he was suffering from 'irritability of the heart', but the observable symptoms were great pain and lameness of one leg and the word 'erysipelas' was whispered. It appears that his heart was not contracting properly and he was dosed with iron, quinine and digitalis. To take his mind off his fast-ageing body, he chose this moment to accept a contract offered by Chappell to read for thirty nights in England, Ireland, Scotland or Paris. Chappell guaranteed all expenses incurred by the reader, his servant and his 'gasman', and proposed to pay him £500 at the start, £500 half-way through and £500 at the finish. The organisation of the tour was to be Chappell's business and no responsibility of any kind was to be thrown on Dickens. He merely had to decide the composition and order of his programmes and to turn up at the time and place arranged for.

As *Dr. Marigold's Prescriptions* had sold over a quarter of a million copies, its author decided to introduce it into his repertory. Unable to judge of its effects without an audience, he summoned friends to the furnished house he was at the moment renting in Southwick Place (6), to hear him read the sketch aloud. He was practically word-perfect for he had rehearsed it to himself 'considerably over two hundred times'. Robert Browning received a note inviting him for '6.30 sharp' on Monday March 18 to listen to 'Dr. Marigold'. John Forster had suggested that the poet might be interested. Collins, Fechter, Chappell and Dolby were also invited and were so warm in their praises that 'Dr. Marigold' was adopted forthwith as a reading.

Dickens chose Wills to companion him on his tour and Chappell's business manager, Dolby, joined them in the railway carriage. To begin with Dickens seemed a little suspicious of Dolby, perhaps not without reason, for in the end he turned out to be 'the chiel amang them taking notes'. At the opening reading at St. James's Hall on April 10 the cheapjack 'Dr. Marigold' was welcomed by an enthusiastic audience. To Carlyle, who was present, the reader appeared to act better than Macready and 'to make a whole tragic, comic, heroic *theatre* visible, performing under one hat, and keeping us laughing—in a sorry way some of us thought—the whole night'. 'Dr. Marigold' was next repeated in the St. George's

Hall, Liverpool, where the listeners were noticeably slower at the uptake than in London. Something of a scrimmage over seats was going on when the reader, at the advertised hour, took his place on the platform. In so doing he lost the effect of a majestic, spot-lighted entry. It was a lesson to him never again to enter a hall until told by his manager that all was ready for his appearance.

The setting contrived by Dickens for his readings is described by Dolby, whose business it was to convey the properties about. At the back of the platform was a large screen or framework covered with canvas, over which a maroon-coloured cloth was tightly stretched: in the centre stood the reading-desk, rather spindly in effect, with a projecting ledge on the left for gloves and handkerchief, and on the right for water-bottle and glass. Further forward were two upright rods (secured by copper-wire guys) supporting the gas apparatus. Reflectors were arranged so that 'the reader's face and figure were fully and equally distinct to the vision of the audience'. After the readings Dickens would often say that he felt as if he had been slowly cooked.

The first strangeness with Dolby soon wore off and Dickens became quite friendly and affectionate with him. Beside 'Dr. Marigold', the readings included 'David Copperfield', the 'Trial from Pickwick' and 'Little Dombey'. Shuttling about from place to place proved very tiring and more than a little tiresome, but all inconveniences were forgotten the moment Dickens found himself standing at his desk facing an audience. He then felt fresh, confident and master of the scene. He would read in Liverpool one night, Manchester the next, then Liverpool again, followed by Edinburgh, Glasgow, London, Aberdeen, then Glasgow and Edinburgh again, and once more fulfil an assignment in Manchester. When not in bed wrestling with acute catarrh or on a platform, Dickens spent his time wholly in a railway carriage. Dolby noticed that whenever an express gathered speed his companion would writhe with the nervousness induced by the Staplehurst smash. The tour ended as it had begun, with

'Dr. Marigold' at the St. James's Hall.

Though, in a sense, it had been a triumph and had once more demonstrated how great was his power of attracting audiences, Dickens ended the round 'tired and depressed'. Chappell, having made a handsome profit, begged him to carry out a second tour of fifty nights. The reader raised his price to seventy pounds a reading instead of fifty, and after some bargaining agreed to perform for forty-two nights for £2500, beginning on January 15, 1867.

This contract at least gave him the chance of a six months' rest which was really essential, for during the tour he had had to tonic himself up with oysters and champagne and had slept badly after readings. In May he had suffered from streaming colds and even fainting attacks, all indicative of the strain he was putting on his nervous system, his liver and his heart, but he still had great resistance and as usual the resumption of routine life at home helped him back to health.

In the odd evenings between readings he spoke during the spring of 1866 at three public dinners. He also dined out privately, though not so frequently as of old. One evening at the Forsters he met Mrs. Carlyle. It was the day after her husband had delivered his inaugural address as Lord Rector of Edinburgh University. She came into the room flourishing a telegram from Professor Tyndall announcing the great success of the speech. Her good spirits made her unusually expansive, and 'the radiance of her enjoyment was upon her all night'. She gave Dickens the subject for a novel taken from her own observation in her own street: it was to be about the house opposite. She was positive that from the blinds, the curtains, the callers, the vehicles that drew up at the door, the life within might be deduced and a romance constructed. As the party broke up before she had finished her story she laughingly promised Dickens to continue it at their next meeting. But there never was to be another meeting, for, three weeks later, Mrs. Carlyle died suddenly after picking up a pet dog which had been run over in Hyde Park. Taking the injured dog in her arms she got back into her brougham to drive home. The coachman presently sensed that something was wrong and looked into the carriage. Mrs. Carlyle sat there dead with the dog on her knees. No one who knew Mrs. Carlyle could fail to miss her desperately when she died. There was a richness and solidity about her intellectual gifts, her knowledge of books and her capacity for friendship, a 'beyond and beyond quality which is so rare and so irreplaceable'. She occupied a most special niche in Dickens's pantheon, and when he heard of her death he said, 'None of the writing women came near her at all'.

In the early autumn of 1866 Dickens busied himself as usual with his Christmas story for *All the Year Round*. It was entitled 'Mugby Junction'. He read one of the chapters, 'The Boy at Mugby', to Mary Boyle, Mamey, Katey and Georgy, and they all shook with laughter till the tears flowed. Encouraged by this demonstration, he combined this sketch and another chapter, 'The Barbox Brothers', into a reading for his Christmas party at Gad's Hill in 1866, a party which included Henry Layard and was so large as to overflow into the Falstaff Inn. Local M.P.s and officers from Chatham were invited to be present and Dickens even had his desk sent down from London for the occasion. The reading was not a success; at least it did not seem to amuse the audience as much as he had hoped it might. The girls' facile laughter had misled him sadly over his effects. He repeated the reading at his opening meeting on January 15 at the St. James's Hall, but there also it had no success. When Liverpool and Birmingham condemned it, it was thrown out of repertory. The grind of the readings, even though they were mapped out in every detail, was intense. 'Nearly every week we were in London for a reading at the St. James's Hall and on the following morning set off for some provincial town.'

Dickens took every chance that offered of air and exercise. He walked, for example, from Preston to Blackburn, passing on his way Hoghton Tower, a curious old ruin with a farmhouse attached. This place went to the making of *George Silverman's Explanation*, a £1000 tale written for American publication. 'I feel as if I had read something (by somebody else) which I shall never get out of my head', wrote Dickens to Wills when composing it. This story has been examined in the light of Freudian psychology. The clergyman hero has been interpreted as being the victim of an abnormal rift between idealistic love and physical desire, he can only mate with a woman he does not idealise. This want of harmonisation is put down to his upbringing. He has been reared in a slum, longed to be loved, always disapproved of, but always his childish ego has found itself adorable, important and beyond criticism. Viewed objectively, it is a tiresome story, though viewed subjectively it may be, as its elucidator supposes, a clue to Dickens's own psychology.

The matter that preoccupied Dickens most during 1866 was the prospect of the American tour he had been urged to undertake by J. T. Fields. There was not much time in which to think about it, for the presidential election was due in 1868, and the very latest date for which he could get a good contract was November 1867. As Dolby was going to America on business, he instructed him to spy out the land and report whether it was really worth while to undertake so exhausting an enterprise. Dolby must certainly try to have a heart-to-heart talk with Fields. He would give him an introduction and he could also deliver into his own hand a Christmas story, *Holiday Romance*, written for Fields's *Children's Magazine*.

Dolby sailed on August 3 and was back by September 29 with promises of rewards so large that Dickens was persuaded that it would be well worth his while to make the American tour. Forster put all the pressure he could on his friend to hold him back, but something about the glittering returns dangled in front of his eyes fascinated Dickens and made him determined to set out, though he knew perfectly well that he was going to hate every moment of exile and feel ill all the time. He at once commissioned Dolby to return to America by an October boat to organise details of the tour.

It was J. T. Fields who was really responsible for tempting him in this way by offering to guarantee £10,000 and bank the money in England in advance. Talking it over with Wills at the office, Dickens said, 'My worldly circumstances are very good. I don't want money. . . . Still, at the age of fifty-five or fifty-six, the idea of making a very great addition to one's capital in half a year is immense.' Wills, like Forster, did his best to prevent his accepting any American offer, but he brushed his objections aside and despite all persuasion booked passages for himself and his two men in the 'Cuba' for November 9.

Dolby meanwhile, as Dickens's forerunner, was being made a great fuss of in Boston. He had been met at the wharf by Fields, Ticknor and James Osgood, who introduced him to Oliver Wendell Holmes. Emerson took him round the halls and public rooms in which readings might take place. Dolby finally decided on Tremont Temple which held 2000 people, had a sloping floor and excellent acoustics. He then visited Longfellow at Nantucket and went on, escorted by Osgood, to New York. There he saw Horace Greeley of the *New York Tribune*, William Cullen Bryant, editor and proprietor of the *Evening Post*, and J. Gordon Bennett of the *New York Herald*, a very powerful trio of press magnates. All showed great eagerness over the Dickens readings and all guaranteed that no echoes of past unpopularity should mar the warmness of a universal welcome. After booking the Steinway Hall, New York, Dolby took rooms for Dickens at the quiet Westminster Hotel. Forster continued to object very strongly to the whole enterprise but his friend put on an adamantine expression and would listen to nothing.

People who knew Dickens best were most apprehensive about the second American tour, for not only was his health undependable, but no one really knew what attitude the ordinary American was going to take up towards him. Twenty-five years had passed since the burning of *Martin Chuzzlewit* in New York; there really had been time to forget, for a new generation had grown up on the novels.   Even so Dickens, in spite of Dolby's assurances, was a little nervous about American public opinion.   The press had been pretty plain-spoken in old days and maybe still cherished a grudge against him.   When a New York paper stated that 'even in England he is less well known than here', it reassured him somewhat, as did the words that followed, 'millions treasure every word he has written and tens of thousands would make a large sacrifice to see and hear the man who has made so many hours happy'.

Many friends wrote him letters of farewell and arranged send-off dinners for him.   Frith, dining with Wilkie Collins (November 1) to meet him, says, 'We were none of us in evening dress and Dickens wore one of the large black cravats not yet gone out of fashion and a wonderful pin large in size, strange in form'.   A touch of the old Inimitable flashed up as everyone fixed their eyes on his scarf-pin.   Smiling, he said, 'I hope you all like my pin; it is uncommon, I think. I hope there is no such pin as this in America.   I have invested in it for the whole and sole purpose of pleasing my friends over the water.'   Next evening he attended a banquet at the Freemasons' Tavern with Lord Lytton in the chair.

> Happy is the man [said Lord Lytton] who makes clear his title deeds to the royalty of genius while he yet lives to enjoy the gratitude and reverence of those he has subjected to his sway. . . .   Seldom has that kind of royalty been quietly conceded to any man of genius until his tomb becomes his throne and yet there is not one of us now present who thinks it strange that it is granted without a murmur to the guest whom we receive to-night.

Such vials of eulogy were poured on Dickens's head on this occasion that he almost collapsed with emotion.   He took the opportunity when rising to reply to affirm his faith in the American people.   'I know full well, whatever little motes my beamy eyes may have descried in theirs, that they are a kind, large-hearted, generous and great people.   In that faith I am going to see them again: in that faith I shall, please

God, return from them in the spring; in that same faith to live and die.' Quoting in lieu of further thanks a short sentence of his own, he ended on Tiny Tim's note, 'God bless us every one'.

On Friday November 8 a royal saloon conveyed Charles Dickens to Liverpool. Equipped with his high reading-desk, his books, his 'sun-pictures' of himself and Gad's Hill (inside and out) and attended by his faithful John and his gasman, he embarked on the 'Cuba' on November 9. Ten days later he stepped ashore at Boston and drove to reserved rooms in the Parker House which had been filled with flowers and books by Mrs. J. T. Fields. There he held a colloquy with Dolby who told him that the first reading had been fixed for December 2. This meant that he would have to kick his heels for ten days, a rather annoying proceeding when one wanted to spend as little time in America as possible. There were to be eighty-four readings in all, but for various reasons, the impending presidential election being one of them, they were in the end cut to seventy-six. The chief difficulty Dolby had to contend with was the unprecedented demand for tickets. For thirteen hours he had sat at his desk in Ticknor and Fields's book-store selling tickets and taking $12,000. He had thought to defeat speculators by refusing to sell more than six tickets to any applicant, but was euchred when they sent fifty buyers at a time to join the queue. The result was that the undergraduates of Harvard could not buy a single ticket and private people who by queuing up for hours had secured seats were immediately approached to sell them at an enhanced price. Dolby was dubbed 'pudding-headed' by the press and abused for the way he was muddling the readings, but he stuck to his job and in the end things went smoothly.

While tickets were being sold Dickens was greatly in demand as a guest. He dined with Longfellow at 'the awful hour of 2.30 P.M.' and sat on till 8 P.M. thinking 'of nothing but the beautiful Mrs. Longfellow burning to death'. He renewed acquaintance with Emerson and Oliver Wendell Holmes and met Agassiz. His old friends Felton, Washing-

ton Irving and Prescott were dead, but Henry Dexter, the
sculptor, visited him, and Putnam, his secretary of twenty-five
years earlier, was delighted to welcome him and talk of former
adventures.   Putnam was now grey-haired and without front
teeth, but he did not look so venerable as Longfellow whose
hair was as snowy as his beard.   People had changed, Boston
itself had altered and grown.   Hot and cold baths had come
in, and the comfort of the hotel was great.

Dickens was billed to read for four nights in succession,
that is Monday to Thursday inclusive, for three weeks, first
in Boston and then in New York and later in other cities.
To open with, he read the 'Carol' and the 'Trial from Pickwick' and on the following night 'Copperfield' and 'Bob
Sawyer'.   Writing home, the reader said, 'The success here
COULD NOT be greater . . . I was as cool as though I were
reading at Chatham'; and to Mamey he betrays a spark of his
old inimitability in 'your respected parent is immensely popular
in Boston society'.   His 'dear Meery's' buttonhole turns up
on his dressing-table every evening which gives him the
homely feeling of being loved for his own sake.   The money
takings were really exciting.   He was able to remit £3000
in gold at $7 to the pound on December 15 and a month later
consigned another £10,000 to London.

In New York he read four times in the week of December 9
and four in the week of December 16.   The city was plastered
with orange bills, a colour he was said to favour.   Two tons
of paper had been ordered to advertise readings that did not
require advertising at all, for every meeting was sold out as
soon as announced.   In order to cosset himself and rehearse
his effects Dickens henceforth refused all social engagements.
To take the air and to convey him to his appointments he
hired a brougham and, when the snow fell, a sleigh.   In this
he drove 'furred up to the moustache, with furs on the coach-
boy and on the driver, with an immense white, red and yellow
striped rug for a covering, you would suppose me to be of
Hungarian or Polish nationality'.   Suffering a good deal from
what he called 'American catarrh', brought on chiefly in heated

trains, he spent his days on a sofa and his evenings on a platform.   Some people thought he resembled the Emperor Louis
Napoleon, others were reminded of the Emperor of China
and others again thought that he looked the typical American
gentleman.

In New York he lodged at the quiet hotel discovered for
him by Dolby: it really was as quiet as Mivart's in Brook
Street and he could get in and out unobserved by a private
door.   The waiters were French and this gave him the pleasant
illusion of living in Paris.   The Westminster was to his thinking 'a faultless hotel'.   In New York his success was greater
even than in Boston; the people seemed quicker at the uptake
and certainly were more demonstrative.

When the eight readings at New York were over Dickens
returned to Boston for two or more readings and, as he had
parted with Dolby, who had gone on to Philadelphia, he
accepted the hospitality of Mrs. Fields.   His rooms in her
house were festooned with holly and moss, looking glasses
and picture frames included.   It all produced such a homely
impression that he was deeply affected, and when a sea-captain
arrived to present him with a sprig of English mistletoe he
could not restrain his tears.   After reading in Boston on
December 23 and 24, though suffering from a heavy cold, he
took the train for New York on Christmas Day.   As the cold
became worse he felt less and less inclined to face an audience,
but somehow forced himself to do so.   It surprised him to
see that at almost every theatre a version of one or other of
his novels was being played.   'I can't get down Broadway
for my own portrait.'   It seems that Dolby had not organised
the tour with any foresight, for he again had to trek back to
Boston for readings on January 3, 4, 6 and 7.   On January 8
he was back in New York, but four days later went to Philadelphia where George W. Childs, owner of the *Public Ledger*,
met him at the station and showed him every civility.   The
treatment he now received was in strong contrast to his former
visit.   After reading twice at Philadelphia he was told he really
must go to Chicago and that if he didn't the people there

would have fits. 'Well, I had rather they had fits than I did,' was his retort. From Philadelphia he went back again to New York. On January 17, 18, 19, 20 he was advertised to read in Brooklyn at the church of Mrs. Stowe's brother Mr. Beecher. This unnecessary double crossing caused him immense fatigue and occurred over and over again during the tour.

Dickens had a very good reason for not wanting to go to Chicago. His brother Augustus ('Moses') had already been there and the newspapers blazoned the news that he had gone away leaving a wife behind him 'in deep poverty'. Having made this discovery, the reporters featured her as 'starving' and inquired why a man who was taking tens of thousands of dollars out of the country could not spare a dime for his own kith and kin. Once again Dickens felt obliged to defend himself by making a personal statement. He explained that the only legal Mrs. Augustus Dickens was living in England and that for many years he had helped to support her.

At Baltimore there was feasting on canvas-back duck, terrapin and blue oysters, a reading in 'a charming little theatre', and then a move to Washington where he put up at a quiet German establishment kept by one Wheleker, who owned the best restaurant in the city and had a reputation equal to Vérey in London. He provided Mr. Dickens with a suite of rooms, a French waiter and perfect cooking. At Washington, however, Dickens did not feel at all well and found it difficult to adapt himself to what he called 'its congress of climates'. Breaking his rule never to accept hospitality, he dined with his old friend Charles Sumner to meet the Secretary for War, Mr. Stanton. Mr. Stanton had served with Abraham Lincoln in the same capacity during the Civil War and at that time had never gone to bed without reading something from *Pickwick*, with the result that he could repeat, if he were started with the first lines, whole chapters from memory. Mr. Dickens capped this anecdote by saying that he had been sent Russian copies of his books from the Crimea. They had been found, sometimes stained with blood, in the enemy's camp.

They went on to talk of President Lincoln and the manner

of his death, and Mr. Stanton told the story of the last cabinet meeting over which the President had presided. He himself was late, and, as he appeared, Lincoln broke off what he was saying with, 'Let us proceed to business, gentlemen'. Instead of lolling in his chair, as his custom was, the President sat upright and still. As he left the meeting Stanton said to the Attorney-General, 'What an extraordinary change in Mr. Lincoln!' And the Attorney-General replied, 'We all saw it before you came in. While we were waiting for you, the President, with his chin well down, said, "Gentlemen, something very extraordinary is going to happen, and that very soon". "Something good, sir, I hope," interposed the Attorney-General, whereupon the President said very gravely, "I don't know; I don't know. But it will happen, and shortly, too!" All present were impressed by his manner and the Attorney-General asked him straight, "Have you received any information, sir, not yet disclosed to us?" "No," answered the President, "but I have had a dream. And I have now had the same dream three times. Once on the night preceding the Battle of Bull Run. Once on the night preceding" such another (naming a battle also not favourable to the North). His chin sank to his breast again and he seemed to be reflecting deeply. "Might one ask the nature of this dream, sir?" said the Attorney-General. "Well," replied the President without lifting his head or changing his attitude, "I am on a great broad rolling river— and I am in a boat—and I drift—and I drift——!—but this is not business!" ' Suddenly raising his face and looking round the table as Mr. Stanton entered he said, 'Let us proceed to business, gentlemen'. Mr. Stanton and the Attorney-General agreed, as they walked away together, that it would be curious to notice whether anything untoward ensued; they would both watch coming events. Mr. Lincoln was shot that night.

On his birthday, February 7, Dickens had an interview with President Andrew Johnson. He was due to read that

evening and in the afternoon Sumner found him lying
poulticed and voiceless in his bedroom. It did not seem
possible that he could face an audience, much less use his
throat. And yet that very evening he looked debonair as he
entered the hall and, though he had been croaking harshly
all day, his voice rang strong and clear. At his command was
always a reservoir of nervous force that could be drawn on in
an emergency. It had got about that it was his birthday and
'exquisite flowers in baskets and bouquets' arrived at his rooms
as well as presents of gold and silver pins, studs and links.
The platform was like a bower; the audience, however, being
official, was cold in the extreme. The President, chief
members of the Cabinet, Judges of the Supreme Court and
the members of the Diplomatic Corps, as well as naval and
military authorities in full uniform, were all there, but there
was practically no applause, only some 'feeble clapping'.

When we know what Dickens's regimen was during this
tour, it is almost a miracle that he survived the experience.
He took a tumbler of new cream with two tablespoonfuls of
rum before rising: at twelve he had a sherry-cobbler and a
biscuit: at three a pint of champagne. Just before the reading he slipped down an egg beaten up in sherry, and in the
interval between items on the programme sipped strong beef
tea. For supper he was given soup, wine, and often, before
turning in, a dose of laudanum. Between stimulants and
sedatives he managed to fulfil his obligations, but it was at a
considerable cost, and even he must have realised that he was
shortening his life.

From Wheleker's hotel window Dickens could see the
Treasury buildings and was intrigued by the bevy of ladies
who issued from them daily. It was a very great surprise
to him to learn that all the clerks in the Treasury were ladies
(for copying and official work) and that this innovation had
come in during the war and had been found most satisfactory.

Dickens left Washington on February 9 for Baltimore
while Dolby went on ahead to arrange further readings at
Hartford, Providence, Worcester and other cities. By

February 22 they were both at Parker House once more.
A new threat imperilled the readings, for when the rumour
got about that President Johnson was to be impeached, the
sale of tickets at once began to drop. Visits to Albany,
Buffalo, Syracuse, Rochester and Springfield convinced Dolby
that the tour should be wound up without delay. Dickens
insisted on a short holiday at Niagara Falls and then returned
to Boston, giving a farewell reading on April 8.

At this leave-taking the reading-stand was wreathed with
flowers and palm leaves. Delighted as always by attentions
of this sort, Dickens said, 'Before allowing Dr. Marigold to
tell his story in his own peculiar way, I kiss the fair hands
unknown which have so beautifully decorated my table this
evening'. Responding with a sob in his voice to the applause
that roared up at the conclusion of this reading from a standing audience, he addressed himself 'to the great public heart'
laid bare before him, bidding it a loving good-bye. After
going through all this he made 'burnt brandy punch' at Mrs.
Fields's house, 'sang songs and made everyone laugh tremendously'.

The press of America gave him a dinner on April 18 at
Delmonico's in New York at which he kept everyone waiting
for an hour. Rumours flew round the room. Some said he
had erysipelas in the foot and could not get a boot on; others
that Dolby had been to every shop in New York to get a
gout stocking, but that as New Yorkers never had gout he
had failed to do so; others that an English gentleman had at
last been found ready to surrender his gout stocking for the
evening, so as to enable Dickens to meet the pressmen. At
last he entered on the arm of Horace Greeley. Once again
the strains of 'God save the Queen' sounded in his ears as
he hobbled in, and his thoughts went back to the scene of
twenty-five years earlier when an alert, agile young man had
stepped lightly to the same tune into a Boston banquet. The
tours had had few points of resemblance but this certainly
was one.

There were two hundred guests at this dinner and the

speakers included Charles Eliot Norton. Dickens, taking his cue from Greeley, reminded those present of the link between himself and them. He too had worked for the press and attributed his success in authorship to the severe training of newspaper work. After complimenting America on the growth and changes evident in her cities and on the remarkable increase in the graces and amenities of life, he went on to stress the essential unity, in spite of points of difference, of the two great nations, America and England, and declared that the notion that an American should be regarded as a foreigner in England was to his thinking incongruous and absurd. He concluded with these words:

> Finally, gentlemen, and I say this subject to your correction, I do believe that from the great majority of honest minds on both sides, there cannot be absent the conviction that it would be better for this globe to be riven by an earthquake, fired by a comet, overrun by an iceberg, and abandoned to the arctic fox and bear, than that it should present the spectacle of these two great nations, each of which has, in its own way and hour, striven so hard and so successfully for freedom, ever again being arrayed one against the other. Gentlemen, I cannot thank your president enough or you enough for your kind reception of my health, and of my poor remarks, but believe me, I do thank you with the utmost fervour of which my soul is capable.

At the final New York reading he took his leave saying:

> I shall never recall you as a mere public audience, but rather as a host of personal friends, and ever with the greatest gratitude, tenderness and consideration. God bless you and God bless the land in which I leave you.

Then using Peggotty's words, as if in eternal farewell, he said, 'My future life lies over the seas'. Two days later he boarded the 'Russia'. Among the friends who waved him farewell from the tender was bearded and benevolent-looking Anthony Trollope.

Chapter 27

THE LAST YEARS

If we judge from history, of what is the book of glory composed? Are not its leaves dead men's skins: its letters stamped in human blood: its illuminations tears and broken hearts?

ON seeing Dickens fresh from his voyage, his doctor exclaimed, 'Good Lord! seven years younger!' But then his patient was tanned by sea air, and in such good spirits at getting safely home that he gave a carefree impression to everyone. He seemed to take new delight in Gad's Hill, in the singing of the birds, the welcome of the dogs and the ringing of the church bells. Having the true Victorian predilection for glass and gilding, he brightened up the chalet by installing in it five mirrors. These gave him great pleasure 'as they reflected and refracted in all kinds of ways the leaves quivering at the windows, the fields of waving corn, and the sail-dotted river'. High up among the trees he sat at his writing-table, birds and butterflies flying in and out, green branches swaying all about him and shadows of clouds passing across his manuscript.

Another source of pleasure was the success of Wilkie Collins's drama *No Thoroughfare*, adapted from his last Christmas story. It had a complicated plot based on a confusion of identity between foundlings and culminated in a fight in an Alpine pass. It was drawing full houses at the Adelphi with 'Fechter playing the part of Obenreizer to perfection'. The play certainly had good things in it, though to Dickens's thinking it dragged a bit in places. However, it was considered good enough to be produced in Paris, and as Fechter was going over to see how it went in French, he decided to accompany him. The friends crossed the Channel (May 30) in time for the first night, from which in the end they stayed away. Nervous and depressed, Dickens sat at an adjacent café with Fechter (whose face was the colour of lead) and waited till Didier, the translator, came over between the acts to report that all was going well. Next night they felt bold enough to attend the performance and then returned to London to give a first-hand account of their experience to the company at the Adelphi.

Owing to Wills having had an accident, Dickens found himself at this time entirely responsible for the production of *All the Year Round*. Wilkie Collins's story, *The Moonstone*, had been accepted as a serial, but its construction Dickens found was really very wearisome, and running through it was a 'vein of obstinate self-conceit that makes enemies of all readers'. In June he was already beginning to worry about the Christmas number: 'I cannot raise the ghost of an idea for it,' he wrote to his manager. 'I am in a positive state of despair. I have invented so many of these Christmas numbers and they are so profoundly unsatisfactory after all. . . . I can see nothing with my mind's eye which could do otherwise than reproduce the old string of stories in the old inappropriate bungling way.' In the end he gave up the idea of producing a Christmas number at all. His example had been too widely imitated and he was 'tired of being swamped by other people'. There had been nine of these Christmas stories all written in collaboration with Wilkie Collins. In most of them Dickens was responsible for less than half the script. For instance in *Somebody's Luggage* he wrote four out of ten chapters; in *Mrs. Lirriper's Lodgings*, two out of seven chapters; in *Dr. Marigold's Prescriptions*, three out of eight chapters; in *No Thoroughfare*, which is divided into an overture and four acts, only the overture and the fourth act are by Dickens. No one at the time of publication knew who had written what as contributions to *All the Year Round* were anonymous.

Gad's Hill was the scene of much hospitality this summer. Longfellow and his daughter came for a week-end and so did the Charles Eliot Nortons. Very special arrangements were made to drive them about in a chaise with four horses and two red-jacketed postilions in accordance with the tradition of the old Dover Road. Sir James Emerson Tennent, the admired friend to whom he had dedicated *Our Mutual Friend*, was also favoured by this attention. Gone were the days when Dickens drove his own guests about the country. Ever since the Staplehurst accident he had not dared to drive himself on the roads nor did he get on a horse 'for fear of a momentary seizure'. This he confided to de Cerjat.

Plans were maturing in his brain at this time for shipping Edward Bulwer Lytton overseas to join Alfred Tennyson in Australia. In a way it is the most peculiar of the evictions, and the most cold-blooded, for Plorn had been Dickens's idol as a child. The allusions to him in letters are more numerous and tender than the allusions to any of the other children, and yet, when the time came, his expatriation was planned and carried out as 'all for the best' despite the protest of the victim. As the day drew near for Plorn's departure Dickens wrote, 'He seemed to me to become once more my youngest and favourite little child'.

Mrs. Dickens appeared momentarily out of the shadows in which her life was then lived with a few words of sadness: 'I miss you most sadly, my darling Plorn. Please God you and dearest Alfred will be happy.' These words suggest that the relations between the boys and their mother had been maintained and it is possible that they were the secret cause of their Aunt Georgina's resolve to get the young nephews out of the country, for, as far as she was concerned, her sister no longer existed. Handing him a New Testament, Dickens impressed on Edward Bulwer Lytton the truth and beauty of the Christian religion and 'the wholesome practice of private prayer' which he himself 'had never abandoned', and in a letter written to be studied on board ship, Dickens enjoined on his young son that

this life is half-made up of partings and these pains must be borne. It is my comfort and my sincere conviction that

you are going to try the life for which you are best fitted.
. . . What you have always wanted until now has been a
steady, constant purpose. I therefore exhort you to persevere in a thorough determination to do whatever you have
to do as well as you can do it. I was not so old as you
are now when I first had to win my food, and I have never
slackened at it since.

Plorn cried in the railway carriage and was supposed to
have brightened visibly when Aunt Georgina's farewell gift
of cigars was handed to him. Six months later Dickens
received a report from the Mr. Rusden to whom Plorn had
been consigned. It was evidently not too satisfactory, for
Dickens wrote in reply: 'Plorn is a queer wayward fellow.
I am heartily sorry he should have disappointed you. . . . I
still hope he may take to colonial life.'

In September the most independent and successful member
of the family, Henry Fielding, went up to Cambridge, where
his father allowed him £250 a year, supplied him with wine
and warned him he must contract no single debt. Dickens
had had enough of family debts to sicken him. There were
his parents, his brothers, his brother-in-law and now his own
Charley who had just been declared a bankrupt. It was
more than enough for one lifetime.

You know [he wrote to Henry Fielding] how hard I
work for what I get, and I think you know that I never
had money help from any human creature after I was a
child. You know that you are one of many heavy charges
on me, and that I trust to your so exercising your abilities
and improving the advantages of your past expensive
education, as soon to diminish this charge. . . .

The third tour of readings (arranged for before the journey
to America) opened at the St. James's Hall on October 5, 1868.
Visits to Manchester and Liverpool followed. The arrangement with Chappell had been for a hundred readings at £8000,
but the prospect of a general election caused some modifica-
tion in the original programme as it was considered wiser to
suspend all readings in November. This gave Dickens a

breathing-space in which to try out his murder scene from *Oliver Twist*. He thought it would produce a 'petrifying' effect and he must leave it to Chappell to decide whether to sanction it as part of the regular programme or not. It was arranged that a private rehearsal of the reading should be given before fifty critics, artists and literary men at the St. James's Hall on Saturday evening, November 14. They assembled in response to an invitation to a 'Private Trial of the Murder in *Oliver Twist*'.

Before going on the stage, Dickens said to Charles Kent, 'I want you to watch this particularly, for I am very doubtful about it myself'. He then flung himself into impersonating Fagin, Morris Bolter, Bill Sikes and Nancy. Fagin, the Jew, was complete with high shoulders, contracted chest, bird-like claws, and penthouse eyebrows working almost like antennae. Morris Bolter appeared as a long-limbed, clownish, sneaking varlet, and then Sikes was before them, a burly ruffian with a voice of Stentor delivering appalling blows with passion. Lastly, Nancy exquisitely pathetic from the scene of suppressed emotion on London Bridge to her last gasping shrieks of 'Bill!—dear Bill!' There was more in this reading than histrionic skill: there was the growing power to hypnotise a number of people simultaneously.

Forster was dead against the proposal; the subject seemed to him altogether outside the province of a reading. Mrs. Keeley, the famous actress, who was present at the experiment, was eagerly asked by Dickens, 'What do you say? Do it or not?' whereupon she replied, 'Why, of course do it. Having got such an effect as that, of course it must be done. But', looking straight at him with her black eyes and speaking in her famous deep voice, she added, 'the public have been look- ing for a sensation these last fifty years or so, and by heaven they have got it!' On the night of the reading the ladies' doctor, Priestley, buttonholed Dickens and said, 'You may rely upon it that if only one woman cries out when you murder the girl, there will be a contagion of hysteria all over the place'. These comments made Dickens very apprehen-

sive of the result of a public performance. For the trial
reading fifty persons were assembled all of whom could be
relied on not to scream, or so he believed.

Dickens had arranged new effects and a surprise for this
occasion. Beside the usual back-screen, he had two side-
screens of the same maroon colour and beyond them were
curtains to shut in the stage. The setting gave more value
to desk and reader. When the reading was over, the bright
gas reflectors were turned by Dickens's order away from
himself on to the guests. Though the ladies in their coloured
dresses looked like 'a great bed of flowers and diamonds',
their faces were pale and horror-stricken. No one could
question the success of the experiment in mass-hypnotism.
Next moment curtains and screens were whisked away and a
supper-table, beautifully lighted, was revealed with a staff of
men ready to open oysters and bottles of champagne. How
fortunate it was that smiles could be so rapidly restored by a
glass of wine! How fortunate that he, Charles Dickens, had
thought to order it!

Next morning came a note from his old friend, the Reverend
William Harness, telling him that the reading was 'a most
amazing and terrific thing'. He added, 'I am bound to tell
you that I had an almost irresistible impulse upon me to
scream and that if anyone had cried out I should have followed'.
The murder of Nancy by Sikes was now put into repertory
and its first public performance advertised for January 5, 1869.

Just before Christmas he gave a reading at the St. James's
Hall of *A Christmas Carol*. Mamey and Georgy were commissioned to give the desk a festive look by entwining holly
round its front legs and in and out of the fringe that ran along
its top. A little bunch of holly should also be affixed to
each corner.

Christmas was spent quietly at Gad's Hill, and a few days
after the first public reading of the Sikes murder had proved
its drawing power Dickens set out for Ireland. 'Miss
Hogarth', he wrote to Dolby, 'so clearly wants a change that
I think I will take her to Ireland along with the caravan as

she is a good sailor. She is highly delighted.'

The Irish readings were to take place at Dublin and Belfast. Police had to control the crowds round the Rotunda, which were specially large on the 'murder' night. Two hundred extra seats had to be squeezed in, and the performance was described in the press as 'a masterpiece of reading by the greatest reader and greatest writer of his age'. The Ulster Hall, Belfast, was rather sparsely filled by a not very demonstrative audience, an audience Dickens found it difficult to get in tune with.

After a short stay in London came a tour of the west country. For Macready's sake a reading was given at Cheltenham. Macready was old and ill, and, when fetched from his stall by Dolby to come and see Dickens in his dressing-room, could only gasp a vague compliment, 'It comes to two Macbeths!' His speech then trailed off into irrelevancies; he was but a wraith of his former self. From Cheltenham Dickens went for a week-end to Dolby's house at Ross and actually walked from Ross to Monmouth, eleven miles at the smart pace of four miles an hour. Dolby then took him on to Clifton where the Sikes and Nancy scene caused a 'contagion of fainting'. Bath and Torquay followed. Bath Dickens described as 'a mouldy old roosting place that comes out mouldily as a let. . . .' 'I hate the sight,' he added, 'of the bygone old Assembly Rooms and the Bath chairs trundling the dowagers about the streets.' It made him think of his first visit to St. James's Square eighteen years earlier, when he had gone laughing down the street with 'Fuz' after a merry dinner with Landor. 'Landor's ghost goes along the silent streets before me. . . . The whole place looks like a cemetery which the dead have succeeded in rising and taking. Having built streets of their old gravestones they wander about scantily trying to look alive—a dead failure.'

It was a relief to get to Torquay with its signs of spring and its plate-glass windows through which he commanded both sea and sunshine. Sea and sunshine were no longer of much avail to him for he had tired himself to death and his feet were badly swollen. Sir Henry Thompson suddenly forbade all further readings. Engagements in London and Scotland had to be cancelled; but after one week's rest Dickens jumped up from his bed and insisted on taking to the road again. All the time his 'atrocious novelty' was getting more and more of a hold on him. Out of four readings he would repeat the murder three times, pleading in excuse to Dolby, who saw how deleterious were its effects, that it had become 'a kind of hobby'.

At Glasgow there was an enormous cram for 'the novelty', and at Edinburgh Ballantyne, having a seat behind the screen, was nearly frightened off it by the screeches. Dickens was pleased as he came off the platform to see that every vestige of colour had left Ballantyne's face and that 'he sat staring over a glass of champagne in the wildest way'. And so the *tour de force* was repeated until April 10, when a banquet was given in Dickens's honour in the St. George's Hall, Liverpool. It was presided over by Lord Dufferin, and Lord Houghton, Anthony Trollope, G. A. Sala and Mark Lemon (reconciled over Thackeray's grave) were among those present. The toast of Her Majesty's Ministers was proposed by Mr. Philip Rathbone and replied to by Lord Dufferin, who gave the health of Charles Dickens whom Lord Houghton, in a speech on the Houses of Parliament, accused of not properly appreciating the House of Lords. Dickens met this charge by speaking handsomely of Lords Brougham, Lytton, Russell and Cockburn, none of them hereditary peers, and then went on to show his horror of patronage by saying:

When I first took literature as my profession in England I entirely resolved . . . that whether I succeeded or whether I failed literature should be my sole profession. It appeared to me that it was not so well understood in England as it was in other countries that literature was a dignified profession by which a man might stand or fall. I made a compact with myself that in my person literature should stand by itself, of itself, and for itself.

A turn of giddiness overtook him at Blackpool, and at

Chester he felt deadness of the left side. It was obviously impossible to go on with the tour so Dolby took him back to Gad's Hill with twenty-five readings undelivered. To compensate Chappell for their loss, he promised, if any way possible, to make good the deficiency at some future date.

Dickens ever since Mary Hogarth's death had been deeply interested in dreams. Over a quiet cigar he would from time to time talk over his experiences with George Lewes.[1] Sometimes one could dispel a recurring dream by recounting it, sometimes the same dream would return in moments of crisis, but there were other stranger dreams that seemed to embody a kind of prevision. For instance after a particularly stimulating reading he dreamt that he was in a room in which everybody was dressed in scarlet, and that he stumbled up against a lady standing with her back to him. As he apologised she turned her head saying, 'My name is Napier'. The face was unknown to him. Two days later he read again and before he went on the stage a friend came into his waiting-room accompanied by an unknown lady in a scarlet opera-cloak— 'This lady', said his friend, 'is very desirous of being introduced to you.' 'Not Miss Napier?' jokingly inquired Dickens. 'Yes, Miss Napier,' replied his friend.

In May Dickens entertained Mr. and Mrs. James T. Fields of Boston, both in London and at Gad's Hill. American tradition has it that Mrs. Fields had lost her heart to him and doted on every word that fell from his lips as well as every word that fell from his pen, and he certainly was very fond of her. The Fields were shown Windsor and Richmond and then were taken to the east end of London to see the beer taverns of the German sugar bakers in the Ratcliffe Highway, and the less agreeable opium dens in the same locality. This was a favourite excursion to which De la Rue, Yates and other friends were treated. Dolby, who used to make the rounds with him, said that Dickens on these outings looked

[1] *Fraser's Magazine*, XXI.

the picture of health and was in very high spirits.

In June he was well enough to enjoy spending a night with Lord and Lady Russell at Pembroke Lodge in Richmond Park. He found his host in 'wonderful preservation, brighter and more completely armed at all points than I have seen him these twenty years'. How they agreed, having both read Mrs. Beecher Stowe's book on Lady Byron, that the whole edition should be made a bonfire of! Young Lord Ribblesdale, who was staying with his stepfather, committed his impression of Charles Dickens to paper. Dickens, he says,

was extremely smartly dressed—over-dressed I should say. In the day-time he wore a pair of striped trousers—stripes were the vogue—of broad black and blue, a frock-coat open to a low double-breasted waistcoat, with a general effect of gold chains, charms and eye-glasses; a splendid black satin scarf of amplitude and lustre secured by a fine pin. . . . His evening clothes were extremely well-cut, the shirt frilled with bright, perhaps diamond studs.

At dinner he ate and drank very little. Champagne did not circulate at Pembroke Lodge, nor was it the fashion of those days to have whisky and sodas, but there was port and madeira and we sat for some time over the wine. Mr. Dickens drank madeira sparingly. I remember noticing that with the warmth of the room and food a vein in the centre of his forehead became very prominent.

A few weeks later Dickens attended a dinner (at the Crystal Palace) of Oxford and Harvard boat-racing crews and complimented a young Harvard man, Richard Dana, as having written the best sea book in the English language. In September he went to Birmingham (the city to which, ever since the doge-like giving of the ring sixteen years earlier, he had felt himself indefinably wedded) to address the Birmingham and Midland Institution at the opening of its winter session. No man, he told his hearers, can improve himself without in some degree improving other men. In Birmingham at least it was realised that the more cultivated the employee the better for the employer, and the more cultivated the employer the better for the employee. Of the two thousand five hundred members of the Institute he was glad to know that half were weekly wage-earners, and that many of them were women. The penny evening classes (on arithmetic, chemistry, music) and the library, lecture hall, laboratory and art department would all encourage the artisan to think, and to rise superior to

> Those twin gaolers of the daring heart,
> Low birth and iron fortune.

Dickens expressed the hope that the Institution would conceive of its place of assemblage as high ground from which the human soul may aspire to be wiser and better. Above all things its members must never patronise or be patronised, 'for the bestowal and receipt of patronage has been a curse to England'. Warning his hearers against what Sydney Smith had called 'the foppery of universality', he urged them to have the courage to be ignorant of a number of things so as to avoid the calamity of being ignorant of everything.

> The one safe, serviceable, certain, remunerative, attainable quality in every study and in every pursuit is the quality of attention. My own invention or imagination such as it is . . . would never have served me as it has, but for the habit of commonplace, humble, patient, daily, toiling, drudging attention. . . . Like certain plants which the poorest peasant may grow in the poorest soil, it can be cultivated by anyone and it is certain in its own good season to bring forth flowers and fruit.

Shortly after Christmas Dickens had to return once more to Birmingham to deliver prizes at the Institute. Feeling very ill he made a short speech, and only struggled through the occasion with difficulty. It was with intense relief that he resumed his seat at his writing-table in the chalet at Gad's Hill.

On two and sometimes three nights a week Dickens transferred himself to Windsor Lodge to enjoy the company of Ellen Ternan. In a facsimile letter reproduced by Thomas

Wright in his autobiography Canon Benham writes of Dickens: 'I have one curious relic, the pen with which he wrote part of the last number of *Edwin Drood*. It was given me by the lady concerning whom he quarrelled with his wife.' This pen was treasured by the Canon and shown by him to Wright at 32 Finsbury Square.

He was careful to arrange that the new book he was engaged on should come out in the old way in illustrated monthly numbers. Charles Collins was to design the cover and Luke Fildes, by John Millais' advice, the plates. The terms offered satisfied the writer: he was to get £7500 for the copyright, and half profits after 25,000 copies had been sold. He was also to receive, from an American firm, £1000 for advance sheets. Writing he now found 'a severe labour' and we may note that the manuscript of this book is very carefully written, revised, corrected and remodelled. As usual, the title presented difficulties, but these were solved round the dinner-table at which, after much discussion, a toast was drunk to *The Mystery of Edwin Drood*.

The first number appeared on April 1. It was to Forster's surprise as good as, if not better than, anything his friend had ever written. The opening chapter delighted him and he pronounced the story 'a clincher!' Only twenty-three chapters in all were written, but these chapters have given rise to more discussion than all the other novels put together. The first scene is laid in the opium den in the east end of London to which the author had taken Mrs. J. T. Fields and other friends. In this squalid place, John Jasper, the choirmaster of Cloisterham (black-haired, pale-faced, and so un-English in type as to suggest the Eurasian), in waking from a narcotised vision, rites to reconcile white elephants, nautch girls, dark faces and flashing scimitars with the emerging walls of a cathedral tower. In a remarkable paragraph Dickens dislocates humdrum life and presently introduces us to a Cloisterham (Rochester) outwardly staid, yet vibrating to the impact of mysterious evil. Against the pious background of cathedral routine are thrown, as by some magic lantern, shapes and omens of sinister significance.   The very rooks that wheel about the tower are omen-ful, so is the tapping of the stone-mason Durdles in the crypt.   The actions and words of Jasper suggest abnormality, the Landless link with Ceylon conveys a sense of far horizons.   It is all as different as it can be from the Pickwick-Wardle Rochester with which Dickens's writing life opened.   Cloisterham is now a dead and mouldering place fostering human corruption.   And, strangest of all for Dickens, the family festival of Christmas is denatured by crime.   The taste for horrifying an audience had projected itself into the plot of *Edwin Drood*.

Edwin Drood is a student-engineer working in London who frequently comes to stay with his uncle, John Jasper, at Cloisterham.   Since childhood in the East, he has been betrothed to another orphan, Rosa Bud, their dead parents having arranged the match.   Rosa is being educated at Miss Twinkleton's Academy at Cloisterham and Jasper, who gives her music lessons, is violently in love with her.   It riles him to hear Edwin say casually:

> My dead and gone father and Pussy's dead and gone father must needs marry us by anticipation.   Why—the Devil, I was going to say—if it had been respectful to their memory—couldn't they leave us alone! . . . *Your* life is not laid down to scale, and lined and dotted out for you like a surveyor's plan.   *You* have no uncomfortable suspicion that you are forced upon anybody. . . . *You* can choose for yourself.   Life for *you* is a plum with the bloom on.

On hearing these words Jasper is strangely affected, sweat-drops appear on his forehead as he grips the arms of his chair, and a film comes over his eyes.   Murmuring that he has taken opium for a pain, he presently adds banteringly, 'There is said to be a skeleton in every house; but you thought there was none in mine, dear Ned'.   It transpires that he hates his post, and that the musical services considered so beautiful by the cathedral congregation seem to him 'quite devilish'.   Edwin, when he leaves, remarks cheerfully that in less than a year he and Pussy will be married and go off to the East. Jasper looks at him quizzically and says:

'You won't be warned then?'
'No, Jack.'
'You can't be warned then?'
'No, Jack, not by you. Besides I don't really consider myself in danger.'

Thus is the mystery set. But what has Jasper in his mind?

Attached to the cathedral is the stone-mason, Durdles, a firmly established, grim character who pokes his way about the earthy damps of the crypt, sometimes opening with his pick an abbot's coffin and seeing for a fleeting moment the phantasm of a church dignitary that on the instant dissolves into powder. Scooting through the close, never far from Durdles, is a hideous small boy shrieking, whistling and shying stones who answers to the name of 'Deputy'. In pompous Mr. Sapsea, the auctioneer of Cloisterham, we have a figure of the Chadband type who consults Durdles about his wife's tomb. Jasper, present at this consultation, watches Mr. Sapsea hand over the key of a vault to Durdles. Jasper makes up to Durdles for his own mysterious purposes so that he may familiarise himself with the interior of the cathedral by moonlight.

Next on the scene are Neville Landless and his sister Helena hailing from Ceylon. They are dark, gipsy-looking, and half shy, half defiant in manner. Twin-like understanding exists between them. By the arrangement of their guardian, Mr. Honeythunder, they become resident in Cloisterham, Neville reading with minor-canon Crisparkle and Helena boarding with Miss Twinkleton. Neville shocks the minor-canon by alluding to his stepfather as a cruel brute whom he would 'like to have killed', adding that his sister had run away from him several times 'dressed as a boy and showing the daring of a man'.

Neville Landless and Edwin Drood do not hit it off, latent jealousy over Rosa being the cause. One evening as they walk and argue, Jasper intervenes and asks them in for a drink. After one glass their speech becomes thick and indistinct and they quarrel openly. Drood sneers at Neville, 'You are no judge of white men!'—an allusion to his dark skin. Neville dashes the dregs of his drink over him, but is prevented by Jasper from throwing the glass too. He then flings out of the house, whereupon Jasper goes round to Crisparkle's gasping, 'We have had an awful scene with him . . . murderous! he might have laid my dear boy dead at my feet'.

A more soothing note is sounded by Mr. Grewgious of Staple Inn, guardian to Rosa Bud, who comes to Cloisterham to discuss the girl's future. He impresses on her that two young people cannot be bound by the will of others, but must act according to their own free will and conviction. On his way home he calls in at the cathedral to tell Jasper that he has informed Miss Bud that a betrothal by deceased parents cannot be considered binding on the parties concerned. Jasper's lips go white and he asks, 'Why?' 'My duty,' replies Mr. Grewgious, adding, 'God bless them both!' as he leaves. 'God save them both!' cries Jasper. 'I said bless them,' repeats Mr. Grewgious. 'I said save them,' returns Jasper. 'Is there any difference?' Again we ask ourselves, What is in Jasper's mind?

Meanwhile minor-canon Crisparkle (living with his china-shepherdess mother in the close) is deeply puzzled by Landless who tells him that he is in love with Rosa Bud and hates and despises Edwin Drood. He tells the strange young man that his love is 'outrageously misplaced'; as Miss Bud is to be married shortly, Neville really must compose his differences with Drood. He then goes to talk things over with the choirmaster whom he finds lying down. Jasper calls out, 'What is the matter? who did it?' and then mumbles something about 'dreaming at a great rate'. The clergyman explains that he wants to effect a reconciliation between Neville and Edwin, whereupon Jasper reads him a passage from a diary of his own about the 'demoniacal passion of this Neville

Landless, his strength in his fury and his savage rage for the destruction of his object'. Can the canon answer for the young man's behaviour which bodes no good to his dear Ned. The canon says 'Yes,' so a dinner of reconciliation is arranged for Christmas Eve.

While this has been going on at Cloisterham Edwin is being interviewed in London by Mr. Grewgious who impresses on him too that two young people cannot be bound by the will of others. He hands him a family ring wherewith to plight his troth. If there is no marriage he must return the ring. Edwin puts it into his pocket and goes to Cloisterham to see Rosa. They mutually agree to break their engagement, but how announce this decision to Jack? Rosa thinks they may leave it to Mr. Grewgious. Edwin concurs, and confesses to Rosa that he is secretly afraid of Jasper. He does not tell her of the ring in his pocket and the author warns the reader that because of this 'a chain was forged and riveted to the foundations of heaven and earth and gifted with invincible force to hold and to drag'.

On the first day of the week in which Christmas Eve is the last Jasper visits the crypt by moonlight calling for Durdles on his way. Durdles warns him not to stumble into a mound near the gate. It is quicklime, 'quick enough to eat your boots . . . quick enough to eat your bones'. Jasper plies Durdles with drink and after they have explored the tower the stone-mason falls in a stupor on the floor of the crypt, leaving Jasper free to make any use he pleases of the great keys he carries.

Neville Landless prepares to take a walking tour at Christmas and buys a knapsack and a heavy walking-stick. He takes the stick with him when he goes to say good-bye to his sister before dining with Jasper. It is Christmas Eve. Jasper sings divinely at vespers and is congratulated by Crisparkle, but maybe his throat is delicate, for it is wrapped with a black scarf. Quite unexpectedly Opium Sal turns up in Cloisterham and, accosting Edwin, asks him for money. Noticing a funny look in her eyes he asks, 'Do you eat opium?' 'I smokes it,' she replies. He gives her money and she asks, 'What's your Christian name?' 'Edwin,' he answers. 'You may be thankful your name ain't Ned . . . it's a bad name . . . a threatened name,' murmurs Opium Sal as she moves off.

We hear nothing of the dinner of reconciliation, but early Christmas morning Jasper hurries round half dressed and half demented to Crisparkle's house to inquire where his nephew is. Crisparkle has no idea and Jasper says, 'He went down to the river last night with Mr. Neville. . . .' 'Where is Mr. Neville?' Mr. Neville has already started on his walking tour. The young man is pursued, overtaken and brought back to Cloisterham under suspicion of having murdered Edwin Drood. He declares that he walked with Edwin from the river to Jasper's house where he had left him. Next day the river is dragged. Crisparkle in diving recovers a shirt-pin and finds a gold watch caught in the weir. As there is no proof that Drood is dead Neville goes to work in London, where Helena joins him. Rosa Bud takes refuge with her guardian, for Jasper has told her he loves her and will pursue her to death. A stranger appears in Cloisterham whose business it seems is to watch Jasper. His thick white hair, large head, feminine hands and black eyebrows are suggestive of disguise.

Jasper re-visits the opium den in London. Opium Sal hears him mumbling of something he has done over and over again. She suspects him of having murdered Drood and goes ahead of him to Cloisterham to watch him on his return. Next morning after matins Opium Sal tells Datchery that she knows Jasper 'better far than all the Reverend Parsons put together know him'. It is at this point that death stopped the writer's hand.

If this were an ordinary murder story we should think the number of clues offered absurd. There is almost nothing for us to find out. We are aware that Jasper wraps a scarf round neck or arm, aware that Mrs. Sapsea's tomb is accessible and that quicklime can be had for the shovelling. We know that Crisparkle goes diving in the coldest weather and it is only natural that if a gold watch has been thrown into the weir he should retrieve it. Every clue indicates Jasper as the murderer. Furthermore we know from Luke Fildes, the illustrator, that Drood was to be strangled by Jasper's black scarf, and we have it from Forster that the victim was to be identified by a gold ring which the quicklime could not destroy. We know that Drood had a gold ring in his pocket. If Dickens had lived to complete the story we should probably find that the root of the antagonisms between the characters lay in their Eastern past, and it is fairly clear that Jasper will be convicted on the evidence of the only creature who could have watched his actions on Christmas night— the ragamuffin Deputy. Some of the people who have contrived endings for *The Mystery of Edwin Drood* have puzzled out who Datchery could be. William Archer and Andrew Lang thought he was Drood himself; Mr. Cumings Walter suggests that as Helena Landless and Datchery are never on the scene together Datchery must be Helena in disguise. We see into the minds of all the characters in this book except Jasper's. No inkling as to what he thinks or why he reacts in the strange way he does is given, and just because of this we are tempted to construct theories as to his motives. One theory gathers importance as the mystery is discussed: it is that Jasper was secretly a Thug striving to commit a ritual murder. Dickens, who had published *The Moonstone* in *All the Year Round*, found Wilkie Collins's method of telling this story extremely tiresome. He was sure he could do something better in the way of a murder mystery himself. He had read his contributor, Meadows Taylor's book, *The Confessions of a Thug*, and he had read *Le Juif errant* by his friend Sue in which a Thug figured. It might be possible to create a character so far from normal that he acted in certain stages of consciousness as if he were a Thug, while at other times he practised a kind of animal magnetism by means of which he could suggest thoughts and actions to persons in his *entourage*. According to Meadows Taylor the essence of Thug practice was to sacrifice a human life to Kali, Goddess of Destruction. The sacrifice, however, was unacceptable to the goddess unless carried out in a prescribed way. The victim must be a traveller and a guest. The Thug, after entertaining his victim and speaking fair with him, slings a white silver-weighted scarf round his neck from behind and squeezes the life out of him. The body must be stripped and buried in a secret place prepared for its reception. In this novel we find broad hints of thuggery in Jasper's scarf, in his blandishment and entertaining of Edwin and in his interest in Mrs. Sapsea's vault, but the body though divested of watch and tie-pin is not stripped. The murder has not, it seems, been carried out by an initiated Thug but by a man dreaming of becoming a Thug. On the whole it is not a very satisfactory solution of the mystery to say that Jasper on one plane of consciousness is a Eurasian organist who because of his passion for Rosa Bud kills one rival and hunts down the other, and on another plane of consciousness is an amateur Thug endeavouring to carry out a ritual sacrifice to Kali. What then was Dickens up to in constructing this story, every sentence of which is loaded with meaning, every word of which is significant? He has never written in this precise, intensely careful way before. What does it all mean? The mystery cannot lie in the identity of the killer, but in the character and mentality of Jasper himself. The book leaves an earthy taste in the mouth, the earthy damp of a mouldering, silent city so abounding in monastic graves that its children 'grow small salads in the dust of abbots and abbesses'. All its life is of the past. Even the pawnbroker has taken in no pledges this long while and offers, vainly, an unredeemed stock for sale.

Laying aside the problems raised by the story, we find that the book is distinguished by writing of a superb kind that rivets the attention and must embody the last impressions of Rochester Dickens ever received:

Not only is the day waning, but the year. The low sun is fiery and yet cold behind the monastery ruin, and the

Virginian creeper on the Cathedral wall has showered half its deep red leaves down on the pavement. There has been rain this afternoon, and a wintry shudder goes among the little pools on the cracked uneven flag-stones and through the giant elm-trees as they shed a gust of tears.

The disintegrating quality of the minster is steadily imposed on us:

> . . . a city of another and bygone time is Cloisterham, with its hoarse Cathedral-bell, its hoarse rooks hovering about the Cathedral tower, its hoarser and less distinct rooks in the stalls far beneath. Fragments of old wall, saint's chapel, chapter-house, convent and monastery, have got incongruously or obstructively built into many of its houses and gardens, much as kindred jumbled notions have become incorporated in many of its citizens' minds.

In those last months of his life, when Dickens was wandering in and out of the precincts and down by the tidal river, he was obsessed by the death-diffusing character of the minster, and contrasted it with the ever-renewed life of the waters by which he walked. Listen to the reflections of Mr. Grewgious as he enters the cathedral, saying, 'It's like looking down the throat of Old Time!'

> Old Time heaved a mouldy sigh from tomb and arch and vault; and gloomy shadows began to deepen in corners; and damps began to rise from green patches of stone; and jewels, cast upon the pavement of the nave from stained glass by the declining sun began to perish. Within the grill-gate of the chancel, up the steps surmounted loomingly by the fast-darkening organ, white robes could be dimly seen, and one feeble voice, rising and falling in a cracked monotonous mutter, could at intervals be faintly heard. In the free outer air, the river, the green pastures and the brown arable lands, the teeming hills and dales, were reddened by the sunset: while the distant little windows in windmills and farm homesteads, shone, patches of bright beaten gold. In the Cathedral, all became gray, murky and sepulchral, and the cracked monotonous mutter went on like a dying voice, until the organ and the choir burst

forth, and drowned it in a sea of music. Then, the sea fell, and the dying voice made another feeble effort, and then the sea rose high, and beat its life out, and lashed the roof, and surged among the arches, and pierced the heights of the great tower; and then the sea was dry and all was still.

Can one doubt from this masterly, sensitive presentation that it is Dickens himself who wanders at evensong among the columns and the tombs and Dickens himself who walks beside the river with its seaweed fringe of which

an unusual quantity had come in with the last tide, and this, and the confusion of the water, and the restless dipping and flapping of the noisy gulls, and an angry light out seaward beyond the brown-sailed barges that were turning black, foreshadowed a stormy night. In his mind he was contrasting the wild and noisy sea with the quiet harbour of Minor Canon Corner. . . .

Is it any wonder that Longfellow thought *Edwin Drood* was 'a most beautiful work, if not the most beautiful of all'?

They are so intense, so personal, so vivid, the impressions made by these last walks whether they be taken in winter or on a summer day 'in silent streets with the sunblinds barely flapping in the south wind'. The dead hand was on Cloisterham as it was on other survivals from the past—the Law Courts and the Houses of Parliament. It was 'a city with all changes behind it and no more to come'. What was to happen to a country that sacrificed so universally to outworn tradition? It was easy to see what Progress thought of it all as the express trains tore screaming through Cloisterham.

We do not know what Forster thought, for his one remark on *The Mystery of Edwin Drood* is that it seemed to him 'quite free from the social criticism which grew more biting as Dickens had grown older'. Did not Forster perceive that the book contained the most biting criticism of all, of a civilisation rotting with worship of a dead past?

For the first time in January 1870 Dickens tried to combine readings with writing. Perhaps he knew how short a time he had in which to do either. Twelve readings had been promised to Chappell, the first of which was due to take place on January 11 and the last on March 15. For this series he rented 5 Hyde Park Place, the house of Mr. Milner Gibson. By special request of his theatrical friends he gave a morning reading (3 P.M.) of 'Sikes and Nancy'. His performance astonished the actors and actresses present and made his own pulse jump from 72 to 112: it took ten minutes on a sofa for him to get his breathing normal again. The audiences at the St. James's Hall were immense and sometimes they rose and cheered in a body as he entered as well as when he left. It was on March 15, 1870, that he read for the last time. Radiant pendants glittered over the heads of the two thousand persons who had assembled to listen. His last words were, 'From these garish lights I vanish now for evermore with a heartfelt, grateful, respectful and affectionate farewell'. Tears rolled down his cheeks as he left the platform with the dragging step of a mourner. The prolonged thunder of applause penetrated to the green-room and lured him back for an instant to kiss his hand to the audience. On this occasion Mamey said 'he had never looked handsomer', but Charley noticed that he had mispronounced some of his words, saying Pickswick or Pickwicks for Pickwick.

But ten days before this farewell reading Dickens had written to the Clerk of the Privy Council to accept the Queen's gracious offer of a baronetcy. On account of 'the divine William and Falstaff', he wished to be styled Sir Charles Dickens of Gad's Hill.[1]

Owing to the impending honour or to Mamey's social ambitions, fashionable, rather unsuitable things began to happen to her poor father; for instance, he was presented to the Prince of Wales at a levee by Lord de Grey and, a few days later, Mamey was in her turn presented to the Queen by Countess Russell. These formalities over, both father

[1] 765. III. N.L.

R

and daughter were eligible to be summoned to a Court ball, an empty compliment except to Mamey, who had taken to hunting in the home counties and canvassing in the Conservative interest.

One day Dickens showed some photographs of the American Civil War to Arthur Helps, who was much interested. Helps described the sun-pictures of battle-scenes to the Queen, who at once expressed an impatient desire to see them too. Dickens, on being approached by Helps, said he would be proud and happy to wait on her as might suit her pleasure and so at long last these two great Victorians met face to face. The talk went on for one and a half hours and Her Majesty kept Dickens standing the whole time.   It was not permissible for any man to sit in the presence of his sovereign, and the Queen, wishing to honour her guest, remained standing too, but unlike Dickens she was not suffering from painful, swollen feet.   She asked Mr. Dickens's opinion on 'the servant question', and wondered whether he could account for the fact 'that we have no good servants in England as in the olden times'.   She also touched on the cost of living. At the close of the interview Dickens was handed an inscribed copy of her *Journal of Life in the Highlands* in return for which she hoped to receive a complete set of Mr. Dickens's works if possible that very afternoon.   Mr. Dickens pleaded to be allowed to have a special set bound for her in red and gold.   To this request the Queen graciously gave her assent.

The Academy dinner in May was presided over by Sir Francis Grant.   Dickens had to reply for Literature and in his speech was careful to include women, 'who even in their present oppressed condition can attain to quite as great distinction as men'.   Paying a tribute to his dear Daniel Maclise, now dead, he looked at his picture, 'The Earls of Desmond and Ormond', hanging on the wall behind the President's chair and spoke of this artist's 'prodigious fertility of mind'.   Gentle, modest, frank, large-hearted, he could say that 'no one ever went to his rest leaving a golden memory more pure from dross or having devoted himself with a truer chivalry to the art-goddess whom he worshipped'. These were the last words Dickens ever spoke in public.

Life still interested him acutely even though friends were falling by the wayside. He had new friends, but none like the old. Dickens missed Maclise and Lemon terribly. Of course it was interesting to breakfast with Mr. Gladstone and dine with Lord Stanhope, interesting too to meet Mr. Disraeli again, whom he had not seen since Gore House days, and whom he still regretted had given up literature for politics, but the old convivial gatherings with equals were gone for ever. He now had to make do with celebrities.

The last London dinner-party attended by Dickens was given by Lord Houghton in honour of the Prince of Wales and the King of the Belgians. To Mary Boyle, who saw him just before he left his house, Dickens said he would dearly like to send an excuse but that he had promised not to fail his host. When he got to Lord Houghton's he could not mount the stairs so awaited the royal guests till they came down to the dining-room. Even at Hyde Park Place he was subjected to a whirl of entertainments. Both Mamey and Georgy loved parties and it amused them immensely to arrange receptions and concerts to which people of distinction flocked. One evening Santley sang and Joachim and Hallé played, and afterwards supper on a lavish scale was partaken of. Lady Freake, a new friend, asked the help of her host in producing three little plays in which his 'girls' had promised to act. The scenery was at that very moment being painted by Millais. Dickens was reminded by this request of happier days at Tavistock House and, as the theatre still excited him as nothing else did, he agreed to help. On the morning of the day of production, Dickens was seen at the office by Dolby, who thought he looked noticeably ill. He said he was about to sign his will, but mortally stricken as he knew himself to be, he kept his engagement with Lady Freake. It was not so long since he had confessed to Charles Kent, editor of the *Sun*, that his most cherished day-dream all through life had been to run a great theatre, a noble company

—all absolutely under his command, even to the editing and altering of every play produced.

The day after the theatricals he travelled to Gad's Hill and before taking up his pen in the chalet had a prowl round the house. The newly built conservatory blazed with geraniums: the windows of both drawing-room and dining-room looked into it; the mirrors hung on their walls reflected splashes of colour. What an eminently successful 'improvement' it was and how pleasantly it contrasted with 'the green mansions' across the road!

Dickens worked on *Edwin Drood* all the day of his seizure, sitting up at his desk in the chalet. At dinner that night, Georgy, his only companion, suddenly realised that he was looking desperately ill. A few minutes later he had a stroke from which he never regained consciousness. Mamey and Katey were summoned from London, and next day Katey was sent back there to break the news to her mother. She returned in company with Ellen Ternan. Millais, who had seen so much of Dickens over the Freake plays, came down too and made a pencilled sketch of the bandaged head in which Katey saw 'a likeness to Tennyson'. Mary Boyle also came and sat outside in a hired fly till Charley came into the porch and led her to the syringa-scented study in which lay the body of her adored friend. She was enfolded by Georgina in a warm embrace and then went sadly back to London.

Dickens had expressed a wish to be buried near Gad's Hill in great simplicity, but the Archdeacon of Rochester offered to furnish a grave inside the cathedral. Local arrangements of every kind, however, were upset by an article in the *Times* (inspired, it is believed, by Lord Houghton) demanding burial at Westminster Abbey. John Forster called on Dean Stanley to explain that there could be no question of a public funeral, for his friend had left instructions that he was to be buried in a strictly private way, and that no public announcement as to the time or place of interment should be made. The mourning coaches must be limited to three, and the horses must be plainly harnessed, without trappings or plumes; moreover, 'no scarf, cloak, black bow, long hatband, or any other revolting absurdity' was to be displayed on the occasion.

At 9 A.M. on the Tuesday after his death three carriages drove into Dean's Yard behind a hearse. Twelve mourners dismounted and walked into the Abbey to stand beside a grave in the Poets' Corner while the committal sentences were spoken. No choristers were present, but when the short service ended, the organ played a Dead March. By order of the Dean the grave was not to be filled in for two days. When reporters came to inquire the hour of the funeral cere-mony, they were told it was over. As soon as it became generally known that the coffin could still be seen, an ever-swelling stream of mourners flowed through the transept. At dusk on Waterloo day the Abbey was closed to the public, but Lord Houghton received word from Dean Stanley that the grave of Charles Dickens would not be closed till near midnight. With a lantern to light his steps, Lord Houghton walked to the Poets' Corner to look at the plain oak coffin that cased the body of the genius he had known from boy-hood up. Bagehot was certainly right, 'no other Englishman had attained such a hold on the vast populace'.

Lord Shaftesbury's reflections were more romantic. As he looked back over the years, he saw as in a vision a young champion of the disinherited slashing at the same social evils he had spent his own life in combating. 'He was set, I doubt not, to rouse attention to many evils and many woes. God gave him a general retainer against all suffering and oppression.'

INDEX